Natural History Knowledge, Tamil Coast and the Atlantic within Reach:

Circulation and Construction, 1639-1857

Natural History Knowledge, Tamil Coast and the Atlantic within Reach:

Circulation and Construction, 1639-1857

S. Jeyaseela Stephen

KALPAZ

First Published, 2019

Published by

Kalpaz Publications
C-30, Satyawati Nagar,
Delhi – 110052
Ph.: 011-47034999, 9811692060
www.kalpazpublications.com
E-mail: kalpaz@hotmail.com

Printed at: G. Print Process, Delhi

Cataloging in Publication Data—DK
Courtesy: D.K. Agencies (P) Ltd. <docinfo@dkagencies.com>

Stephen, S. Jeyaseela, author.
Natural history knowledge, Tamil coast and the Atlantic within reach : circulation and construction, 1639-1857 / S. Jeyaseela Stephen.
pages cm
Includes bibliographical references.
ISBN 9789353240608

1. Animals—India—Tamil Nadu—History. 2. Natural history—India—Tamil Nadu. 3. Coastal animals—India—Tamil Nadu—History. I. Title.

LCC QL309.S74 2019 | DDC 591.95482 23

Contents

List of Illustrations

Acknowledgements

Between Berlin where this work started and Pondicherry where it is coming to a close, I have been blessed with an extraordinary community of friends and colleagues who had been involved in this research work. I owe an enormous debt of gratitude to all those who encouraged, inspired and helped me through the process of writing this book. A full list of debts accrued during these years would stretch a very long list. Hence I wish to acknowledge the support of those people and institutions chiefly did the most to make this book what it is today. The germ of the idea for this book had taken root and blossomed with the earlier research project on the history of science which consisted of four parts. I had completed the first three parts of the work i.e., (a) botany and chemistry, (b) medicine, (c) earth and space sciences which resulted in a publication titled '*A Meeting of the Minds: European and Tamil Encounters in Modern Sciences*, 1507-1857', Primus, New Delhi, 2016. The section dealing with zoology took much time to nurture and nourish its growth since a lot of primary sources and illustrations that were collected had to be analyzed and studied in detail since my mind was nearly as blank as possible for the study. I had the good fortune of discussing ideas, problems, and shorter and longer pieces of text with a number of friends and colleagues. Completing both the project and the book, with the beginning and the end had been a kind of journey. So many of those I have encountered along the way have helped in ways they often did not realize. Dr. Kampchen helped me in cultivating the German language skills I never dreamt I would come to rely upon so heavily. Field trips to Germany had been helped through the grants made by the University of Greifswald and the University of Kiel. My profound thanks are due to Prof. Dr. Martin Krieger so essential for carrying out the work.

A large part of the enjoyment of writing this book lies in meeting people from around the world who shared a common interest, and in learning from them what is often the knowledge or skills acquired during a lifetime of devoted research or practice. First, last and at all stages in between comes my well wishers who have had to put up with the apparently endless business of a book on natural history coming about. Some kept a tutelary watch on this work throughout and making countless suggestions and corrections to the materials I drafted. Translating the documents from Latin and German took a lot of time. I am profoundly grateful to all those in the various archives, museums and libraries in Europe who helped and so often dug up books as fragile and sometimes as smelly as could be. A selected number of libraries, museums and art galleries were kind enough to waive permission fees for materials and images held in their trust. The extent to which I have depended on all these scholars will be evident to any reader of this book.

The primary sources used here are diverse in nature and I am grateful to the authorities of Archiv der Franckeschen Stiftungen, Halle; Museum fur Naturkunde der Humboldt-Universitat zu Berlin; Staatliche Museer zu Berlin; Nationalmuseet, Copenhagen, Zoological Museum, University of Copenhagen; Muséum Nationale de L'Histoire Naturelle, Paris; Archives Academie des Sciences, Paris; Bibliothèque Nationale de France; Bibliothèque Sainte Genevieve, Chantilly, Paris; British Library, London; British Museum, London; Natural History Museum, London; Royal Society, London; Bodleian Library, University of Oxford; Biblioteca Casanatense, Roma: Archivum Romanum Societatis Iesu, Roma; Instituto Arquivo Nacionais/Torre do Tombo, Lisboã; Bibliotheca Nacional de Lisboã; Biblioteca da Ajuda, Lisboã; Nationaal Archief, Den Haag; National Archives of Mauritius; Library of the University of California, Los Angeles; Linda Hall Library of Science, Engineering and Technology, University of Missouri, Kansa City; Cornell University Library and the Library of Zeno Payne Metcalf. I also received help and support in India from Tamilnadu State Archives, Chennai; Library of Madras Literary Society, Chennai; Madurai Province Jesuit Archives, Shenbaganur; Saraswati Mahal Library, Thanjavur; Historical Archives of Goa, Panaji; The Asiatic Society, Kolkata and the Zoological Survey of India and so I thank for their best help. I extend my thanks to shri. Amit Garg, Gyan Books, New Delhi for undertaking the publication. I hope this book would be welcomed by the readers.

S. Jeyaseela Stephen

Abbreviations

AASP	:	Archives, Académie des Sciences, Paris
AFSt	:	Archiv der Franckeschen Stiftungen, Halle
ARE	:	Annual Report on Epigraphy
ARSI	:	Archivum Romanum Societatis Iesu, Roma
BA	:	Biblioteca da Ajuda, Lisboã
BL	:	British Library, London
BM	:	British Museum, London
BNL	:	Bibliotheca Nacional de Lisboã
BNFP	:	Bibliothèque Nationale de France, Paris
BORP	:	Board of Revenue Proceedings
CSV	:	Coleção São Vicente
DCB	:	Diary and Consultation Book
DRI	:	Documentos Remetidos da India
EFI	:	English Factories in India
EI	:	Epigraphia Indica
EICR	:	The East India Company Records
GM	:	Generale Missiven
HAG	:	Historical Archives of Goa, Panaji
HB	:	Hallesche Berichten
IANTT	:	Instituto Arquivo Nacionais/ Torre do Tombo, Lisboã
IOL-NHD	:	Natural History Drawings of the India Office Collections
IPS	:	Inscriptions of Pudukottai State
MB	:	Modi Bundles

MDR	:	Monçoes do Reino
MJLS	:	Madras Journal of Literature and Science
MNB	:	Museum fur Naturkunde Berlin
MNHNP	:	Muséum Nationale d'Histoire Naturelle, Paris
MPJA	:	Madurai Province Jesuit Archives, Shenbaganur
NA	:	Nationaal Archief, Den Haag
NHB	:	Neuere Hallesche Berichte
NHML	:	Natural History Museum, London
NMC	:	Nationalmuseet, Copenhagen
OIOC	:	Oriental and India Office Collection
RFG	:	Records of Fort St. George
RSL	:	Royal Society, London
SGR	:	Surgeon General's Records
SII	:	South Indian Inscriptions
SMB	:	Staatliche Museer Zu Berlin
SMLT	:	Saraswati Mahal Library, Thanjavur
TAS	:	Travancore Archaeological Series
TCR	:	Tirunelveli Collectorate Records
TDR	:	Tanjore District Records
TNSA	:	Tamilnadu State Archives, Chennai
VOC	:	Verenigde Oost-Indische Compagnie
ZMUC	:	Zoological Museum, University of Copenhagen

1

Introduction: The Fauna of the Tamil World before the Advent of the Europeans

This book presents the study of animals an exercise in human history and nature. Wild animals were domesticated and tamed by humans. Animals have often been influenced in their behavior by the proximity of humans and by changes in human behavior. The humans have also adapted sufficiently to animals and such adaptations have varied between places and periods in history. The mutual adaptations seemed to imply the learning processes at both sides of the frontier between humans and animals too.

The Sangam Literature and the Fauna of Ancient Tamil Country

It is a fact that the weather and climate of a region determined the nature and the daily lives of the people. The fauna of Tamil country is of no exception and it has been varied and plenty being tropical. The five natural geographical regions mentioned in the sangam Tamil literature like the *kurinchi*, *mullai*, *marutham*, *neithal* and *paalai* have been attributed with various kinds of birds. The *mayil* and *kizhli* (peacock and parrot) were said to be the natives of *kurunchi*. The *kaatukozhi* and *vettai paravai* (wild fowl and partridge) belonged to the *mullai*. The *vandaalam*, *maganril*, *kambul* and *kurugu*, (the stork and the swan) had been special to the *marutham*. The *kadal kaakka* (sea crow) was the natives of *neithal*. The *puraa, parundhu* and *garudan* (pigeon, kite, vulture and the falcon) belonged to the *paalai*.[1]

Similarly the five natural geographical regions have also been attributed with various kinds of animals. The *puli*, *karadi* and *yaanai* (tiger, bear and elephant) were the natives of *kurunchi*. The *muyal* and *maan* (hare and the deer) belonged to the *mullai*. The *yerudhu* and *neernaay* (buffalo and otter) had been special to the *marutham*. The *surrah* fish (shark) had been the native of *neithal*. The *sennaay* (wild dog) belonged to the *paalai*.[2]

Tamils have noted carefully the genus and species of the fauna with the different usage and kinds of words. There were three types of crocodiles mentioned such as (a) *idangar* (b) *muthalai* and (c) *karaam*. Ayingurunuru mentions that the female crocodile ate its babies.[3] Crocodiles were said to have reared in the ditches of forts. Thiruvalluvar had mentioned that the crocodile had high strength and power only in water.[4]

The shells and conches found on the seashore of the Tamil coast are mentioned in Maduraikanchi.[5] *Vazhalai*, *panilam*, *valampuri* and *idampuri* were the various types of shells recorded in Tamil literary sources.[6] The *sippi* (oyster) which yielded pearls had been also referred to in Puranaanuru and Nattrinai.[7] *Nandu* (crab) is mentioned in Aganaanuru and there were two types while one lived on the land and the other on sea.[8]

Many kinds of doves are known to Tamils. *Maada puraa* (the blue rock pigeon) was mentioned in Aganaanuru and Perumpaannatrupadai.[9] *Saambal puraa* (the little brown dove) was mentioned in Aganaanuru and Pathitrupaththu.[10] The *pachchai puraa* (the imperial green pigeon) is mentioned in Ayingurunuru.[11] *Bogil* a kind of dove was also mentioned in Aganaanuru.[12] A Tamil poem of the third/fourth century AD records the presence of white storks.[13]

*Udumbu (*the large land-monitor) is mentioned in Tamil literary works.[14] Nattrinai mentions that people ate *udumbu* after hunting.[15] *Oonthi* or *Oonaan* (chameleon) is mentioned in Nattrinai and Kurunthogai.[16] There were two types of *aamai* found while one was on the land (tortoise) and the other was at sea (turtle) referred to in Puranaanuru and Nattrinai.[17] *Thavalai* (frog), *therai* (toad) and *nunal* (a type of frog) had been also mentioned in Kurunthogai, Nattrinai and Ayingurunuru.[18]

Paambu/aravam (snake/serpent) is mentioned with its varieties.[19] *Arasara* called the blue *naagm* or *raja naagam* (krait) had been stated that if it bites an elephant would die. *Malaipaambu* (mountain snake) is mentioned in Malaipadukadaam.[20] *Suruttaipaambu* (coiled snake) was fond of eating lizards. *Kadal paambu* (sea snake) is also mentioned in Aganaanuru.[21] Tamil literary sources report that snakes normally went out in search of food in the night.

Several proverbs were cast by Tamils who carefully noted the behavior of animals. There is a reference to the frogs with the adage that 'the frog's worst enemy is its own mouth'. Another proverb notes that 'the tiger will not eat grass even if it is hungry'.

The Use of Animals and Birds as Royal Emblem by the Rulers

The rulers of Tamil country in the ancient and medieval period had chosen a particular animal or bird as their royal crest or emblem. Tiger had been the crest of the dynasty of the Chola kings of the sangam period and it is found mention in the literary works. The copper plate grants of Anbil and Tiruvalangadu of the medieval Chola rulers bear the figure of the tiger.[22] Thus the tiger emblem had adorned the official documents of the Chola state used for the purpose of administration to give them authenticity. Many of the coins of the Cholas also contain the figure of tiger.

The Pandya rulers of the sangam age used the figure of fish as their royal emblem. It continued to be used even in the medieval times for we find the inscription of Jatavaraman Sundara Pandya I of the thirteenth century found in Ranganathaswami temple at Srirangam where it has been shown flanked by two fish, one on either side of the inscription.[23] The same inscription states that the fish was the emblem of the king's banner.[24] The Dalvaipuram copper plates do contain the figure of the two carps.

The Pallava rulers used the figure of bull as their official symbol. Raja Simha Pallava (700–28) is described as he who has the bull on his flag.[25] The bull symbol also appears on the obverse of many of the coins of the Pallava rulers. Some of the copper plate grants have lion crest and these had been specially issued by the Pallava kings after their victories in the battle fields to mark the donations made.[26]

Inscriptions of Ravivarman Kulasekhara who ruled in the early part of the fourteenth century from places like Srirangam, Kanchipuram and Tiruvadi mention that the king had the *garuda* (vulture) bird emblem on his banner.[27] Thus all the rulers of Tamil country had adopted some animals and birds as their emblems.

Royal Gifts of Animals and Birds from Tamil Coast to China and South East Asia

Wang Mang of Han dynasty (25-221 AD) in China desired to maintain very cordial relations with the rulers of South India. As a result he sent envoys to Tamil coast and they brought the gift of a rhinoceros (*Dicerorhinus*) to China. Ban Gu the famous literate in the Han dynasty who composed the work titled 'On the West Capital' had confirmed saying that the emperor's court in China kept so many animals received from the outside world including the rhinoceros that came from South India.[28] Narasimha Varman III (AD 844-66) the Pallava king had sent ambassadorial missions with gifts of beautiful talking parrots and leopard to the Chinese court.[29] There were several exchange of envoys by Maaravarman Kulasekhara Pandya (AD 1268-1318) and the Chinese emperor between 1283 and 1291.[30] At that time the Pandya envoys in 1287 presented tributes which reportedly included a strange animal to the emperor of China. In the year 1289 two zebras were presented to the Chinese emperor. In 1291 the Pandya king had again sent envoys and at that time two cows, one buffalo and one small tiger were brought to China.[31] In 1297 the emperor of China in return gifted a tiger-shaped insignia made of two precious stones to the Pandya Ruler.[32] Overseas trade between China and Tamil coast was carried only via Java. A Chinese source of the thirteenth century mentions various types of merchandise exchanged and handled at the ports of Srivijaya which included turtles.[33]

The Elephant and the Horse in the Royal Army of the Tamil Kingdoms

Elephants were captured and tamed on behalf of the king for religious and ceremonial purposes and also for use in the war. We find mention of the wounded elephants during elephant-hunting.[34] Puranaanuru, the Tamil poetry of the sangam age contains references to domesticated elephants that were used in the armies. It describes that the elephants stood in the middle of a large army like the navy in the ocean.[35] Aganaanuru describes the elephants as the highest form of gifts and the generosity of the Tamil rulers. Riding on elephants were also royal prerogative jealously guarded by the kings.

The sangam literary works provide accounts of the role played by elephants in the battles. The practice of using the trained elephants in wars was part of the royal entourage. Some of the Pallava rulers were noted for their knowledge of *gaja sastra* (the science of elephants).[36] Elephants formed a large section of the armies of the Pallavas. The strength and brute force of the elephant corps of the Chola army are described in Anbil and Tiruvalangadu copper plates.[37] Elephants were also used by the Chola rulers in medieval Tamil country. The head of an army generally went into battle mounted on an elephant. *Chau-ju-ka*, the Chinese account in AD 1178 mentions that the Chola government owned 60,000 war elephants and every animal was with seven or eight feet high.[38] Plenty of elephants were maintained in the capital city of Thanjavur. We find mention of *aanai atkal theru* (street of the mahouts or elephant trainers) and *aanaikaduvaar theru* (street of the servants who supplied food to the elephantry) located in *purambadi* of the city.[39]

Horses were not the native animals of Tamil country. Pattinapaalai refers to import of horses in the ancient period but the places of export had not been mentioned.[40] Horses were used by the Tamil rulers because there was a cavalry wing in the royal army. The Maduraikanchi states that horses were specially selected for their swiftness of movement.[41] An inscription refers to Rajasimha Pallava as one who is fond of horses.[42] The medieval Chola rulers used horses in the army and we find mention of Vichcaatha mutharayan a horse soldier in the army (*kudirai sevagar padai*) in an inscription of 1009 during the rule of Raja Raja I.[43] The Karandhai plates record that even when he was a boy Rajendra Chola I (1012-1044) was well trained in horse riding.[44] Horses were counted by Hindus among the most noble of beasts while donkeys were considered impure animals. Mules were owned by washer-men and untouchables who transported defiling substances. Horses were central to many forms of warfare, whether for cavalry mounted infantry, flied artillery or the baggage train. Horses were mainly imported from Pegu.[45]

The Arabs and the Muslim Tamil traders came to control a modest flow of horses to South India in the medieval period. Horse was an engine of war and a symbol of nobility. Horses were closely associated with royal courts in the beginning mainly sought for pomp ceremonial purposes and later deployment in warfare. The Pandya rulers of Tamil Country began to use increasingly horses in war and so there arose a demand for Persian horses for import. The Arabs and the Persian merchants imported horses and met the requirements of the military of the Pandyas. *Chetti* merchants in that medieval period had come to be known as *kudirai chettis* (chetti horse dealers).[46] The Tamil speaking merchants obtained special expertise and developed skill in loading and unloading the horses from ships. They also had servants who knew to care the animals in the long distance voyages. Kayal was an important port where many horses landed from Persia and Arabia and they were sold to the medieval Pandya rulers. The milk white Persian horses that came by sea routes had been described by Marco Polo (1254-1324) the Venetian.[47] Wassaf had mentioned that the climate of Tamil country was very favourable for breeding horses. But the Tamils did not know how to maintain or train horses. As a result these animals became unfit necessitating fresh import of horses as often as possible from Arabia.[48]

The demand for horses in South India continued and the Nayaka rulers under the Vijayanagara empire encouraged the trade in horses. Fernão Nuniz the Portuguese traveller reported that the officials of the king of Vijayanagar were asked to pay the full price of a horse even if a dealer whose horse died on the way brought only the tail of that horse.[49] Krishna Devaraya the king (1509-1529), himself had declared thus: 'Make the merchant of distant foreign countries who import elephants and good horses attach to yourself by providing them with gifts and decent dwellings in the city, by affording them daily audiences, presents and allowing decent profits. Then the animals will never go into the hands of your enemies'.[50] Portuguese accounts and contemporary travelogues record that the king of Vijayanagar had 20,000 horses.[51]

Animals and Birds in the Hindu Religious Context

Cosmology came to be explained and related to theology by the spiritualists and so we find God and nature linked and described in Tamil literary sources like *Paripaadal.* Thirunaavukkarasar the Saiva poet too had linked the nature and God. Cobra the most dread of the snakes has been highly respected and worshipped by Tamil Hindus and normally left unharmed by the public who considered it to be sacred. The serpent carving at Mahabalipuram during the age of the Pallavas is important to note. There are also animals like the elephants and lions carved in stones at Mahabalipuram that had been noticed by John Goldingham in 1798.[52] The Hindus had also worshipped the birds such as eagle. Several birds and animals also found depicted abundantly in the art and architecture of the temples. The elephant was held in high esteem and the deity pillaiyar had been the elephant faced. The parrot has been associated with manmathan, the muthevi with donkey, subramaniyar with peacock and the various avataras of Vishnu such as the first incarnation with fish, the second with tortoise, the third with boar and the fourth with lion and etc. These animals and birds have been ascribed to as vehicles of Hindu deities that had been pointed out by Pierre Sonnerat the French traveller in Pondicherry during 1775-80.[53]

Jean de Mandeville the medieval traveller pointed out the cow as holy animal and idol of the Hindus being the most patient and the profitable animal. Friar Odoric of Pordenonewho visited South India in AD 1330 had also reported the same.[54] Giovanni Borghesi the Italian who was Pondicherry in 1701 and Benjamin Schultze (1689-1760) the Protestant missionary in Tranquebar in 1726-30 had also confirmed and they explained how the natives had worshipped the cow.[55]

Role of Animals in the Everyday Life Situation of the People

The land near the villages in Tamil country were thrown open for common pasture, the grazing right being ascribed to each man by restrictions and regulations settled by the village community as a whole. To do justice to each of its members, a tax was levied on the herders as grazing fee.[56] The people who took care of the livestock were called *idaiyars*. The community paid a professional tax called *idaipattam* to the Pallava kings. Later we find the tax called *idiayar vari* (a tax on the idaiyar community) paid to the Chola state.[57]

According to Tamil inscriptions livestock such as sheep and ram were gifted to temples.[58] It became a common practice to grant these milch animals and they were gifted mostly to burn *nanthaa vizhlakku* (lamps). The people called *manradis* looked after the *semmariaadu* (sheep) and *vellaadu* (goat) which were donated to temples by the devotees and measured out the ghee to the lamps set by them. The *manradis* in AD 962 had taken care of the sheep donated and also gifted them to the temples.[59]

An inscription records the presentation of two perpetual lamps to a temple and for the sake of its maintenance, a supply of 120 sheep had been fixed. These sheep were given to some shepherds under the trusteeship of the members of the village assembly of Thiraimur and the priests of the temple.[60] Records neatly mention that 25 sheep donated fetched one *aalakku* ghee daily as interest.[61] Another record mentions that one *ulakku* ghee was collected as interest per day from 50 sheep or 50 rams.[62] But the number of sheep supply had been increased over a period of time. We find mention that 28 sheep were required to be gifted for one *aalakku* of ghee daily in AD 1116 against the earlier supply of 25 sheep.[63]

According to records the village assembly had engaged itself in protecting the animals. At Tirunamallur the gift of 100 undying and under-aged big sheep was granted to the village assembly on condition that a stipulated quantity of ghee was to be supplied for burning lamps in the local temple. It did not mean that the donors were to replace the dead or aged animals. It was the duty of the donee to maintain the total number of animals at any cost. In fact the usage of the phrase such as under-aged and undying indicated that those sheep died or ceased to supply milk had to be replaced by others that were born in the mean time.[64]

Inscriptions record numerous instances of the gift of cows, she-buffaloes and bulls to temples in the medieval period. The village assemblies and others had made the grants.[65] The number of cows fixed to be supplied for burning a lamp in the temple is interesting to note. We find 25 cows were gifted for one *ulakku* ghee supply per day.[66] This practice became a standard one for long and we also notice that 13 cows were gifted for two *aalakku* of ghee supply daily.[67] Cows granted to maintain lamps were received by the *manradis* who were expected to provide the prescribed measure of ghee.

Raja Raja Chola I (985-1016) reassigned the large grant of livestock granted to the temples. It required that the shepherds received gold and the cows were to be exchanged for ewes in the local market place. They were to negotiate these exchanges at the prevailing rates of market exchange. The local cash standard for ewes as reported in an inscription was three ewes per *kasu* of gold, although ewes of less quality appear to have been purchased at the rate of four ewes per *kasu*. In better exchanges one cow was sold for two ewes, one she-buffalo was sold for six ewes and one heifer for one ewe as did one calf.[68] The prices were determined by the milk output of each of the animals as one she-buffalo's output was equal to that of three cows or six ewes.[69] Cattle were normally sold in the fairs and markets. Uththiramerur had a cattle market as mentioned in an inscription.[70]

The writings of Hamsadeva a Jain poet in the thirteenth century on the animals and birds are well known. Religions in India that were rooted in nature and its forces had concepts of creation and role of man. Hinduism and Buddhism had considered that man essentially is a part of nature and nature has to be treated as such. Hamsadeva had mentioned 21 groups of animals and 15 groups of birds. These were chiefly from the village of Mandaka. He stated in detail the animal and bird varieties, colours, time of full passion, delivery time, temper, main food and utmost of age. Among the qualities he stated three types such as superior, middle and inferior while the temper and nature of all animals and birds he said four types such as cruel and hot temper, bad and mean, dull nature and calm temper. Some details of animals like the elephant that lived for 100 years are unbelievable.[71]

We find thus people in the past during the ancient and medieval times had paid some attention to understand the animals. The entrenched idea of the human as a unique kind of being had nourished a presumption that Homo sapiens should be the proper object of historical studies neglecting the animal studies and its linkages with men. Hence it had also for long dominated the trend in historical writings. Language had been the key marker of humanity's difference from other species because the animals had codes, calls or songs. Humans had in fact a mode of communication of a wholly other order. Animals were also conventionally read as objects of fable, allegory or metaphor. However, in the early modern age after the advent of the Europeans to Tamil coast there had been a change and we find a focus on the fauna, flora and the study of natural objects linking the long separated field of the humans from the animals. This had been an important exercise in order to understand the nature and the agency of animals in human cultures around the world. In the course of time the aesthetic engagement of art had developed with a view to illustrate natural history more with drawings, paintings and collection of specimens and descriptions. Therefore this book aims to engage in the study of fauna conducted by the Europeans enabling natural history in the making of global science.

The Organization of this Book

The introduction sets the stage for the work's substantive chapters, laying important groundwork in the process. It deals with the scientific sense that was present among the Tamils and traces the details that had been known through Tamil literary works. It is important to know of the past so that it would be found useful and necessary to compare the ideas of the Tamils in the earlier centuries with that of the European discoveries of the early modern age. The chapter therefore presents a window into the complex connections between the history of natural science locally in Tamil country in South India and before the commencement of global networks. It traces the fauna of ancient Tamil country as found in the Sangam literature, how the rulers adopted birds and animals as royal emblems, how the royal gifts of animals and birds were transported between Tamil coast, China and South East Asia in the ancient and medieval period, the use of elephant and horse in the royal army of the kingdom of the Tamil rulers, demand for horses developed in the medieval period necessitating the importing of the animal from Persia and Arabia into Tamil country. It explains how animals and birds came to be widely depicted in the Hindu religious contexts and situates the everyday life of the Tamils with the use of animals.

Chapter two thereafter delves deep into the period of Portuguese contacts with India and how elephant and rhinoceros came to be exported to Portugal and how the two animals became a celebrity in Lisbon and Rome. The chapter also traces how the drawings of the animals sent from India to Europe came to be printed in Europe in the sixteenth century, how the trade and transport of animal products and animals developed between Tamil coast and South East Asia in the early modern age. The study assigns priority to animal trade by the merchants particularly horse imports developed in Tamil country after the advent of the Europeans and how importing elephants and trade came to be developed in Tamil country in the early modern age. While situating the scenario thus the chapter explains how the study of fauna also got developed in Europe and later resulted in the growth and development of the study of natural history by the Europeans on the Tamil coast.

Chapter three explores the study of various animals by the Europeans in Tamil country. Louis Le Comte the French Jesuit in 1690 and Giovannio Borghesi the Italian physician in Pondicherry in 1703 had described various strange animals they found. We find that the details passed on to Europe had appeared in print. The long-tailed squirrel was known to John Ray and Johann Friedrich Gmelin in Europe. Nikolaus Dal the missionary in Tranquebar wrote on wild fox during 1733 and 1736. Again the wild fox, jackal and fox had caught the attention of Johann Philipp Fabricius in Madras and he wrote about them in 1756. A wild cat was sent in 1759 by Robert Clive from Madras to the Duke of Cumberland in London and we find its description. The European missionaries wrote on the types of dogs and the native treatment given to mad dog-bites. Johann Christian Wiedebrock and Johann Balthasar Kohlhoff the missionaries in Tranquebar wrote on the hound in 1763. A report was prepared on *udumbu* by Johann Christian Wiedebrock in Tranquebar during 1765. Christian Pohle another missionary in Tranquebar wrote on mongoose in 1784. Christoph Samuel John in Tranquebar made a study of rats and peruchaali and he communicated the details to Prof. J.R. Forster in Germany in 1793. He also mentioned the types of monkey in one of his letters sent to Halle in 1795. The serious study of zoology made by the Europeans on the Tamil coast had an impact on Serfoji II, the ruler of Thanjavur and so he began to collect animals for his menagerie between 1805 and 1827. Further he commissioned artists and they prepared an album containing the drawings and paintings of animals describing in detail. T.C. Jerdon and Walter Elliot developed interest in the study of mammals of Tamil country and we find the description of lemur, hog, bear and the tiger during 1845 and 1848. Jerdon continued his studies and wrote on marten, wild goat, wild ox, jackal and the squirrel. He pointed out three types of monkey, four types of cat, five types of mongoose, and described udumbu. T.C. Jerdon studied also the micro-mammalia and he found two types of chameleon found in the Nilgiris and one type at Madras, besides two types of mouse, five types of bat and five types of shrew in Tamil country. Thus the study and the collection of animals had been renowned in its time for the quality of its holdings and Tamil coast emerged as a centre for advanced studies in animal science. It spearheaded the use of such collections as a pedagogical tool, and it was central to the teaching of animal science in Europe too. The animals sent from the Tamil coast had a prominent position in the collection. The connoisseurs in Europe analyzed the data on various animals sent from Tamil coast and the knowledge was made open to the public through printing in Europe in various languages. Gifts of animals came to function as a currency in an economy of scientific donations and it was distributed and got redistributed in return for or in the expectation of financial and political support for conducting further studies.

Chapter four explores the anatomical studies of reptiles and animals undertaken by the Europeans in Paris, London and Madras. It exposes how a tortoise from the land sent from Pondicherry to France in 1674 was dissected in Paris and the results of the anatomical description had been communicated in French through a publication in Paris in 1686 and later its translation in English appeared in print in London in 1688. Further an elephant was dissected by Dr. A. Suply the French surgeon at Fort St. George in Madras in 1715 and this report both in French and English found way to London for dissemination of comparative anatomical knowledge to the world. Thus the study of animal anatomy that gained momentum in the early modern age had been described.

Chapter five traces the study of insects and reptiles by the Europeans in Tamil Country between 1690 and 1853. Louis Le Comte wrote on the glow worms he found in Pondicherry in 1690. Martin Lister wrote on the long worm in Madras and its bite from which the Englishman suffered in 1695-97. Samuel Brown the English Company doctor described the treatment to poisonous insect bites in Madras in 1700. Johann Gerard Koenig in Tranquebar noticed thirteen types of insects during 1770 and 1777 and five types of insects in Madras during 1778 and 1785. Further, six uncommonly rare and scarce insects were reported from the Coromandel Coast to Johann Christian Fabricius the zoologist in Denmark. A study of hover flies and stilt-legged flies had been conducted by C.S. John in Tranquebar and the details were communicated to Denmark and Norway during 1780 and 1805. The English in Madras imported cochineal insect from South America and conducted experiments in dyeing at Saidapettai between 1786 and 1812.

With regard to reptiles the missionaries in Tranquebar had noticed a centipede in 1718 and found four types of scorpions during 1763 and 1765. The details of the study of scorpions and the beetle and its bites by Christoph Samuel John in Tranquebar were communicated to Professor J.R. Forster in Germany in 1793. Leeches were noticed by the French in Pondicherry and they exported to Mauritius and Paris during 1833 and 1848. Seven types of lizards were found in Tamil country were made known in 1853 by Walter Elliot and T.C. Jerdon in Madras. Thus the chapter shows how the non-textual objects of knowledge were felt important and the missionaries had sent the information on the curious insects and reptiles from the Tamil coast to Europe. These were very diverse and represent the kingdom of nature (animal) and were primarily destined for natural history collection in Europe and further study.

The sixth chapter explores the study of avifauna and the process of collecting, understanding, transforming and fusing knowledge of birds that were shaped by the Europeans on the Tamil coast from time to time. It highlights the role of Edward Buckley in Madras and the first record of bird watching during 1701 and 1710, the list of 27 birds found by him in the region of Fort St George, Madras and the drawings prepared and sent to London. Further it traces the study of nightingale and other birds reported by Christoph Theodosius Walther in Tranquebar (1726-33), swans, ducks, kingfisher and other birds noticed by Christian Friedrich Pressier in Tranquebar in 1729, birds found in Pondicherry, Gingee and Tamil Country known to the Europeans (1756-1789) and storks, cranes and other birds observed by Christoph Samuel John in Tranquebar (1781-1793). Carl Linnaeus in Europe had introduced the system of binomials to the study of birds in 1735 and this had an impact in India too and as a result the study of birds was undertaken by Pierre Poivre and Pierre Sonnerat in the French settlement of Pondicherry and by Thomas Caverhill Jerdon in Madras, Nilgiris and Nellore, had the zoological naming of the birds. The study lists 38 birds reported by Jerdon from the Tamil region and the methods and means adopted for the study of birds by Jerdon, preparing the drawings of birds by Jerdon and the role of Krishna Raju the native artist of Nellore in litho printing besides the Firm of Reeve Brothers in London and the assistance sought for printing by Jerdon. Finally the chapter also traces the native response to the European study of birds and how Serfoji II the Raja of Thanjavur developed interest and began his collection of birds in Thanjavur besides preparing an album of the drawings and paintings of birds in 1812 and providing the detailed description. Thus the chapter focuses upon how the Tamil coast emerged as a node in the circulation of knowledge in the global network and as a part of the circulation process, new scientific knowledge on birds developed and how it was constructed in a contingent local fusion of knowledge negotiated between multiple actors such as locals as well as between interested far-away individuals in Europe.

Chapter seven examines the types of snakes and the treatment for snakebites observed by the Europeans on the Tamil coast during 1701 and 1853. Johann Christian Wiedebrock and Johann Balthasar Kohlhoff in Tranquebar made a study of some snakes in 1764 and it was followed by a detailed study of 22 snakes by Christoph Samuel John in Tranquebar between 1785 and 1792. The details were communicated by C.S. John from Tranquebar to Prof. Johann Reinhold Forster in Germany. Christian Pohle in Tranquebar also studied some snakes in 1793. Wilhelm Friedrich Gericke in Tranquebar made his observation on the treatment for snakebites in 1767. Pierre Sonnerat in Karaikal noticed the treatment for snakebites during 1775 and 1780. William Petrie in Madras expressed his opinion on the identification of snake in Madras in 1787. The description of sea snake was provided by Walter Elliot in Mylapore in 1840. A detailed study of 15 snakes found in Madras and Nilgiris was undertaken by T.C. Jerdon during 1853.

However, Christian Friedrich Schwartz made his observation on the native medicine used for snakebites in Thanjavur in 1788. William Boag expressed his opinion on the Tamil medicine for snakebites in 1809. The treatment to snakebites was reported by William Mackenzie in Madras in 1820. Thus the native Tamil medicine and local cultural elements were sought to be introduced to Europe paving way into Western medicine and greatly opened up a creative potential for an inter-cultural assimilation and synthesis. Thus the Western medical-zoology came to be developed and there came up a respectful dialogue, based upon a shared medical understanding. The chapter also explains how natural history is perceived to be a socially negotiated, produced and situated knowledge which was created and utilized to various ends by both indigenous people and Europeans in the often asymmetrical power relation of the colonial encounter. At the same time, the circulation of medical-zoology knowledge has to be seen as a central part of this process of constructing scientific knowledge and, consequently, the nature of this process and the various agents who facilitated and embodied the negotiation in the intercultural encounter came to the centre stage. In this connection the study of ophiology and toxicology has been situated because the religious instruction in the mission had coupled with the interest in non-religious, 'curious' and scientific information about Tamil country necessitating such a development.

Chapter eight assigns importance to the study fish and aqua-fauna conducted by the Europeans in Tamil country between 1779 and 1853. Johann Gerard Koenig in Madras had begun his study of fish in 1779 and he carried out the work till 1785. A detailed study of fish and its varieties in Tranquebar was commenced by Christoph Samuel John in Tranquebar in 1779 and it continued for long till the year 1801. Johann Gottfried Klein in Tranquebar also joined in the same mission in 1789. Later Johann Peter Rottler in Tranquebar in 1791 had continued in the venture. These three missionaries had extensive contacts with Marcus Elieser Bloch in Germany who launched an exploration into the study of fish collection from 1786 to 1795. Patrick Russell in Madras conducted his private study on fish varieties between 1788 and 1805. Thereafter we find the native response by Serfoji II, the Raja of Thanjvaur who made his collection of fish from Adirampattinam during 1805 and 1821. Further Thomas Caverhill Jerdon the English company official in Madras investigated into the fish types found from the rivers of Cauvery and Bhavani, the fresh water fish varieties from the tanks and ponds of the Carnatic region, the fish types found at Coimbatore, Salem and Erode, the fish varieties in the coastal cities of Tranquebar, Pondicherry and Madras between 1837 and 1849. Jerdon began to report the Tamil names of fish for the information of the Europeans and he also pointed out the rare and new varieties of fish unknown to the audience in Europe.

Further, pearl fishing on the Tamil coast stimulated the study of sea animals and marine fauna by the Europeans. Johann Gerard Koenig conducted a study of shells in Tranquebar during 1770-71 followed up by Christoph Samuel John who did extensive collection and study of various types of shells and conches at Rameswaram and Tuticorin during 1779 and 1797. With the flow of new information to Copenhagen, Johann Christian Fabricius in Denmark conducted a detailed study of mud crabs, crayfish and lobsters from Tranquebar and he published the details for the purpose of attracting the wider audience. The study of creatures living in water interested some Europeans in Tamil country. T.C. Jerdon the assistant surgeon of the English East India Company conducted a study of crocodile found in the Vellore fort. He also studied the tortoise and turtle found in Madras in 1853. Six types of frogs noticed by T.C. Jerdon and Walter Elliot in Nilgiris and the Carnatic region were reported in 1853. It is clear that the missionaries and the East India Company servants and officials had functioned as nodes in a system of circulation of aqua-fauna knowledge on a global scale. The accumulated, edited and redistributed knowledge about fish types of the Tamil coast were transmitted all over Europe. The kinds of information going to Europe from the Tamil coast was from the mission station feeding the Europe with the stream of raw data flow. But still, the driving force of the circulation had hand in Europe about to know the riches and wonders of the Tamil seas and the ocean. The curiosity and circulated knowledge was aimed to gain support for the researchers and to maintain the missionaries in Tamil country who functioned and helped a wide network of readers among the common people, academics, enlightened reformers, the nobility and royalty in Europe.

Chapter nine on conclusion sums up and what emerges is the image of the study of natural science that had been functioning as nodes in a long-distance network which accumulated, edited and redistributed and non-textual knowledge about Tamil coast with the aim of furthering the social and political agendas on the eve of the crown rule in India. The accumulation of knowledge for redistribution was equally important. The same goes for the calculation as a process of restructuring the science objects into new forms. Finally the collected knowledge and redistributed appeared in printed journals across Europe and it was done with the aim of gaining sponsors and maintaining support throughout the world.

Seen together, the chapters offer a striking picture intellectually as well as visually of the complex world associated with the representation of animals in the early modern age. Hence I hope that readers will benefit through reading into the central role played by animals in the early modern natural philosophy in Euro-Tamil relations.

Notes

1. A. Thirumalai Muthusamy, *Sanga Ilakkiyathil Vilangugazhlum Paravaigazhlum*, Chennai, 1959, p. 7.
2. *Ibid.*
3. *Kurinchi paatu* (of Kapilar), ed. M. S. Purnalingam Pillai, Madras reprint, 1994, 256-57; *Puranaanuru*, ed. U.V. Swaminatha Aiyar, Madras, 1971, 37, P. L. Samy, *Sanga Noolgazhlil Sila Uyirinangal*, Chennai, 1993, p. 11; P.L. Samy, *Sanga Ilakkiyathil Vilangina Vizhlakkam*, Tirunelveli, 1970.
4. *Thirukural* (Parimelazhagar Urai), ed. M. Virasamy Pillai, Madras, 1849, kural no. 495.
5. P. L. Samy, *Sanga Noolgazhlil Sila Uyirinangal*, pp. 11-2.
6. *Nattrinai*, ed. A. Narayana Samy Aiyar, South India Saiva Siddhanta Pathippu Kazhagam, Tirunelveli, 1976, 172, 331, 25; *Maduraikanchi*, ed. U.V. Swaminatha Aiyar, in *Pathupaatu*, Madras, 1974, 330, 261; *Nedunalvaadai*, ed. U.V. Swaminatha Aiyar, in *Pathupaatu*, Madras, 1974, line 142.
7. *Puranaanuru*, 53, Nattrinai, 87.
8. *Aganaanuru*, eds. N. M. Venkatasamy Nattar and R. Venkatachalam Pillai, 3rd edn., South India Saiva Siddhanta Pathippu Kazhagam, Madras, 1957, 350, 20. It is known that there were two types of crabs while one lived on the land and the other at sea.
9. *Aganaanuru*, 307.
10. *Aganaanuru*, 271; *Pathirtupathu*, ed. Avvai Durai Samy Pillai, 2nd edn., South India Saiva Siddhanta Pathippu Kazhagam, Tirunelveli, 1955, 4: 43.
11. *Ayingurunuru*, ed. U.V. Swaminatha Aiyar, 6th edn., Madras, 1980, 325.
12. *Aganaanuru*, 129.
13. R. Guha, ed., *Nature's Spokesman: M. Krishnan and Indian Wildlife*, 1st edn., New Delhi, 2000. The text runs thus. 'O stork, O stork, O red-legged stork, with coral-red beak, sharp tapered like the split tuber of the sprouting palmyra, should you and your spouse turn northward from sojourning at the southern waters of Kanyakumari'.
14. *Malaipadukadaaam* (of Perumkausiganar), in *Pathupaatu*, Tamil University, Thanjavur, 1985, 507-508; *Nattrinai*, 24, 29; *Puranaanuru*, 152, 325, 326, 333.
15. *Nattirani*, 59.
16. *Nattrinai*, 92, 186, *Kurunthogai*, ed. U.V. Swaminatha Aiyar, 4th edn., South India Saiva Siddhanta Pathippu Kazhagam, Tirunelveli, 1978, 140.
17. *Puranaanuru*, 379, 389; *Nattrinai*, 280.
18. *Kurunthogai*, 148; *Nattrinai*, 347; *Ayingurunuru*, 468, 494.
19. *Puranaanuru*, 309, 329, 382; *Nattrinai*, 75.
20. *Malaipadukadaam*, 261.
21. *Aganaanuru*, 340.
22. *Epigraphia Indica*, vol. I to XXXII, Calcutta/ Delhi, 1892-1978 (hereafter EI), vol. XV, no. 5; *South Indian Inscriptions*, Publications of the Archaeological Survey of India, vol. I to XXVI, New Delhi, 1890-1990 (hereafter SII), vol. III, no. 205.

23. EI, vol. III, no. 2, p. 8.
24. *Ibid.* vol. XXVII, p. 14.
25. SII, vol. I, no. 29, verse 1, p. 23.
26. C. Minakshi, *The Historical Sculptures of the Vaikuntha Perumal Temple Kanci*, Memoirs of the Archaeological Society of India, New Delhi, 1940, p. 54.
27. EI, vol. IV, no.18, p. 149; EI, vol. IV no. 17, p. 147; EI, vol. VIII, no. 2, p. 8.
28. Wei Luling, 'The Silk Road Linking Chennai and China', *Contributions of Tamils to the Composite Culture of Asia, Part II*, Chennai, 2014, pp. 173-198, see p. 190.
29. Haraprasad Ray, *South India during the 15th Century: Studies in Sino-Indian Relations*, UGC Report, Jawaharlal Nehru University, 1996, pp. 18-9; See also, Haraprasad Ray, *Trade and Diplomacy between India and China: A Study of Bengal during the 15th Century,* Delhi, 1993.
30. S. Jeyaseela Stephen, *Expanding Portuguese Empire and the Tamil Economy, Sixteenth-Eighteenth Centuries*, Delhi, 2009, p. 47.
31. W. W. Rockhill, 'Note on the Relation and Trade of China with the Eastern Archipelago and the Coast of the Indian Ocean During the Fourteenth Century', in *Toungpao*, vol. 16, 1914, pp. 419-47; vol. 17, 1915, pp. 61-159.
32. *Ibid.*
33. F. Hirth and W. W. Rockhill, *Chau-ju-Kua: His Work on the Chinese and Arab Trade in the Twelfth and Thirteenth Centuries Entitled Chu-Fan-chi*, St. Petersburg, 1912, p. 61.
34. Thomas R. Trautmann, *Elephants and Kings: An Environmental History*, Ranikhet, 2015, pp. 202-7.
35. *Puranaanuru*, verse 13.
36. SII, vol. I, no. 25, pp. 14-8.
37. EI, vol. XV, no. 5; SII, vol. III, no. 205.
38. F. Hirth and W.W. Rockhill, Chau-Ju-Ka, p. 96; K.A. Nilakanta Sastri, *Foreign Notices of South India*, Madras, 1939, p. 144.
39. S. Jeyaseela Stephen, 'Thanjavur: The Making of a Medieval Metropolis', in Yogesh Sharma and Pius Malekandathil, eds., *Cities in Medieval India*, Primus, 2014, pp. 209-239, see p. 215.
40. *Pattinapaalai*, ed., U. V. Swaminatha Aiyar, in *Pathupaatu*, Madras 1918, 185.
41. *Maduraikanchi*, II, 48-52.
42. SII, vol. I, no. 25, p. 16.
43. *Annual Report on Epigraphy* (including Indian and South Indian Epigraphy from 1881 to 1922, 1923-1945, 1950 to 1990) New Delhi/ Madras, 1887–1955 (hereafter ARE), 48 of 1897; SII, vol. V, no. 1411.
44. K. G. Krishnan, *Karandhai Tamil Sangam Plates of Rajendra Cola I*, New Delhi, 1984, verse 42, p. 72.
45. K. A. Nilakanta Sastri, *Colas*, Madras, 1984, p. 607.
46. ARE, 322 of 1958-59; 556 of 1904. See also, Chellian, *Perumparanattru Padai: Six Long Poems from Sangam Tamil*, n.d., p. 78.

47. Yule, ed., *The Travels of Marco Polo,* London, 1938, Book I, pp. 83-4.
48. K. A. Nilakanta Sastri, *The Pandyan Kingdom*, Madras, 1972, pp. 169-71.
49. Vasundhara Filliozat, *The Vijayanagar Empire as Seen by Domingos Paes and Fernao Nuniz*, New Delhi, 1977, pp. 87-8.
50. A. Rangasvami Saraswathi, 'Political Maxims of the Emperor Poet Krishnadevaraya', *Journal of Indian History*, 6, 1925, pp. 60-72.
51. João de Barros, *Decada da Asia: dos Feitos, que os Portuguezes Fizeram no Descubrimento, ae Conquista dos Mares e Terras do Oriente*, Lisboã, 1973, decada I part I, p. 210. Ludovico di Varthema, *The Itinerary of Ludovico di Varthema of Bologna from 1502 to 1508*, London, 1928, p. 51.
52. John Goldingham, 'Some Account of the Sculptures of Mahabaliporum Usually Called the Seven Pagodas, *Asiatick Researches*, vol. V, Calcutta, MDCCXCVIII, pp. 69-80, see, pp.71, 73.
53. Pierre Sonnerat, *Voyages aux Indes Orientales et a la Chine*, Paris, MDCCLXXXII, pp. 156-185.
54. Jean de Mandeville, *Mandeville's Travels*, ed., C. M. Seymour, Oxford, Clarendon, 1967, see chapter XVIII.
55. Giovanni Borghesi, *Lettera Scritta da Pondischeri a 10 di febbraio 1704 dal dottore Giovanni Borghesi medico della missione sepedita alla China dalla santita di N.S. Papa Clemente XI nella quale si contengono, oltre a un pieno raconto del viaggio da Roma fino alle coste dell' Indie oriental, Anatomische, Botanische, naturali e d' altri generi e trasportata del Manuscritto Latin in Lingua Toscana di Gio Mario de' Crescembeni custode d'Arcadia, e Accademico Affrordita*, Roma, 1705, p. 221; C. S. Mohanavelu, *German Tamilology: German Contributions to Tamil Language, Literature and Culture during the Period 1706-1945*, Saiva Siddhanta Pathippu Kazhagam, Madras, 1993, p. 168.
56. ARE, 391 of 1921.
57. Noboru Karashima, *South Indian History and Society: Studies from Inscriptions, AD 850-1800*, Delhi, 1984, p. 113; K.R. Srinivasa Aiyar, *Inscriptions in the Pudukottai State,* Pudukottai, 1929 (hereafter IPS), no. 364, 366, 486; ARE, 383 of 1939-40.
58. ARE, 626 of 1916, 632 of 1916.
59. ARE, 266 of 1938-39.
60. SII, vol. III, no. 72.
61. SII, vol. XIV, no. 185, no.188.
62. SII, vol. XIV, no. 158, 166, 210; ARE, 626 of 1916, 632 of 1916.
63. SII, vol. V, no. 744; ARE 713 of 1916.
64. EI, vol. VII, p. 137, EI, vol. VII, p. 137.
65. *Travancore Archaeological Series*, IX vols, Trivandrum, 1910-41, (hereafter TAS), vol. IV, part I, no. 127; SII, vol. XIV, no. 16; ARE, 626 of 1916, 632 of 1916.
66. SII, vol. XIV, no. 184.
67. SII, vol. XIV, no. 189.

68. SII, vol. II, no. 95; George W. Spencer, 'Temple Money Lending and Livestock Redistribution in Early Tanjore', *Indian Economic and Social History Review*, vol. V, no. 3, 1968, pp. 277-293, see, p. 284, Kenneth R. Hall, *Trade and Statecraft in the Age of the Colas*, Delhi, 1980, pp. 117-8.
69. George W. Spencer, Temple Money Lending, p. 281
70. ARE, 74 of 1898; SII, vol. VI, no. 359.
71. Hamsadeva, *Mriga-Pakshi–Sastra*, trs., M. Sundaracharya, P. N. Press, Kalahasti, 1927, p. 134.

2

Animal Commodities and Europeans: The Trade and Traffic, 1510-1857

In medieval Europe, the interest in the history and geography of the world outside developed. As a result many persons aimed to travel to the East via the land route. In search of direct sea route to India, Vasco da Gama left Lisbon and his ships reached Calicut on 20 May 1498, by circling Africa via the Cape of Good Hope. This inaugurated in opening maritime connection of the Atlantic with India. Portuguese thereafter set up a vast commercial network by establishing fortresses and trading-stations on coastal India.

The Elephants and Rhinoceros Exported from India to Portugal: The Two Celebrity Animals in Lisbon and Rome

In the course of trade in pepper and spices in Malabar the Portuguese found exotic animals and birds. Some live animals such as the elephant had become an important one for they had never seen before in Europe. Alvaro Velho's narrative of Vasco da Gama's first trip to India had noted the ways of fighting of elephants, as well as several traditional methods used to capture them in the wild.[1] An elephant was sent for the first time from Cannanore to Lisbon in 1510.[2] Two elephants were transported in 1512 from Cochin to Lisbon in the ships that sailed.[3] One elephant was sent in 1513 to Lisbon.[4] In 1515 three elephants were sent in the ships that sailed from Cochin to Lisbon.[5] These elephants on arrival in Portugal were stabled along with other animals in the palace of king Dom Manuel I (r.1495-1521) in his palace at Estãos and in his palace at Ribeira in Lisbon. It is reported in the chronicle of Damião de Gois that Dom Manuel was the first

Christian king of Europe to receive elephants from India, of which he had five altogether (four males and a female). When riding through the city of Lisbon, a Persian horse with a Persian hunter carried a lynx sent by the king of Ormuz and these elephants went behind and before His Majesty came.[6]

Gaspar Correia the Portuguese chronicler in his *Lendas da India* in 1512 provides the first European descriptions of an Indian rhinoceros. He said that it is a gentle beast but low and long-bodied. It had the skin, hands and feet of an elephant and a long head and eyes close to the snout like a pig. Above the nostrils, it had a short, thick horn which was finer at the tip. It ate grass, straw and cooked rice.[7] Two Indian rhinoceroses were also later sent to Portugal.[8] Albrecht Durer (1471-1528) describes on 1 May 1513 what he knew about the animal that a live animal rhinoceros brought from India to the great and powerful king Dom Manuel I of Portugal in Lisbon. It had the colour of a speckled tortoise, and it was covered with thick scales. It was like an elephant in size, but lower on its legs and almost invulnerable. It had a sharp strong horn on its nose which it sharpened on stones. The stupid animal had been the deadly enemy of the elephant which was very frightened of it as, when they met, it ran with its head down between its front legs and gores the stomach of the elephant and throttled it, and the elephant cannot defend it off. Because the animal was so well armed, there was nothing the elephant could do to it. It is also said that the rhinoceros was fast, lively and cunning.[9] Sultan Muzaffar II, the ruler of Gujarat presented a rhinoceros as a gift to Affonso de Albuquerque the Governor of Portuguese India who sent it to king Dom Manuel I in Lisbon where it arrived on 20 May 1515.[10] Later the same year the animal was shipped from Marseilles as a gift from the king for Pope Leo X, but unfortunately the ship sank and the rhinoceros had drowned.

Dom Manuel the king of Portugal sent a mission in 1514 to Pope Leo X, in which exotic animals from India played a prominent role. These included a trained cheetah, an Indian fowl, dogs, parrots and parakeets, and a young elephant named Hanno.[11] The elephant together with his trainer received great attention from the Pope.[12] It is worth noting that an elephant had already figured in Ludovico di Varthema's book on India, the travelogue first got published in Rome as early as in 1510.

The elephant (Hanno, corruption of *Aana* meaning elephant in Malayalam) was in Vatican the papal city, particularly in public festivals before its death on 8 June 1516. The Pope commissioned Raphael to make a drawing of the animal to perpetuate the memory of the creature. A pen and ink drawing of Hanno after a Raphael drawing (which no longer survives) has been found at the Kupferstichkabinett in Staatliche Museer zu Berlin. Though the authorship is unknown, and the copy presents obvious similarities and closer to Raphael's original.

Dom Manuel the king of Portugal sent another embassy to Pope Leo X in 1516 with an Indian rhinoceros. The king himself described it thus, something so new and never before seen in these parts and almost never found in printed books. The rhinoceros gift did not arrive at its destination alive because of a shipwreck near Genoa. The letter of king Manuel to Miguel da Silva, his ambassador in Rome dated 11 August 1516 confirms the loss of everything that was being transported in the ship. It has been stated that the great displeasure felt had been that His Holiness did not see an animal that was such a great novelty.[13]

The Indian Animal Drawings and the Development of Printing in Europe

Portuguese in Malabar sent in the course of time many animal products such as elephant tusks, rhinoceros horns, bezoar stones, musk, animal skins and bird feathers to Lisbon.[14] These products brought by the Portuguese were highly prized due to their rarity and decorative value. Duarte Barbosa a clerk employed in the Portuguese trading factory of Cannanore between 1511 and 1516 makes reference to serpents, elephants, as well as to some of the valuable products made from other animals such as musk, bezoar stones and pearls.[15] Tome Pires, a royal apothecary sent to India in 1511 by King Dom Manuel I describes the hooded rattlesnake. He says that that the *cobras de capello* are small and black, as thick as thumb and three or four spans long. They had fangs, and the loose skin on their heads made a kind of covering called a hood (*capello*) when they raised them. If these snakes bit, the people killed them at once.[16] A manuscript presents some representations of exotic animals such as the elephant, various kinds of birds, and two hooded rattlesnakes as well as an illustration of a snake with two heads.[17] It was perhaps commissioned by a Portuguese noble made by an Indian artist, or by a Portuguese artist then living in Goa.[18]

An elephant's illustration was done by the Portuguese artist and architect Francisco de Holanda in 1539-40 when he visited Rome to study the antiquities in a tour sponsored by king João III of Portugal (the son of king Dom Manuel). He made a pen drawing of the elephant Hanno. Although Holanda was a renowned artist, the elephant's proportions are misrepresented in his drawing. It is available in Biblioteca San Lorenzo de el escorial, Spain. It should be noted that this was a sketch of the traveller.[19]

Giulio Romano and Giovanni da Udine have also made drawings of elephant, either from life or on the basis of Raphael's drawings. An Indian elephant offered by king John III of Portugal to Archduke Maximilian II of Austria in 1563 seems to have been influential in the depiction of this animal in the Netherlands.[20]

Dom Sebastião the king of Portugal in 1577 was very fond of the female rhinoceros living in his menagerie in 1577. Hence he commissioned Pero Andrade Caminha the artist for a drawing. The illustration is found at the end of a manuscript titled 'A summary of the kings of Portugal with a brief accompanying description'. It states that this is an illustration of a female rhinoceros which is not as fast as the male and has longer ears. She is very docile and languid. She eats whatever she is given, straw, barley, wheat and other vegetables. She is the size of a large bull. They say she is expert at curing lepers, that a black man who had taken care of her was cured by her breath and that her blood is used in medicine. His Majesty the king holds her in such high esteem that he ordered an illustration of her.[21] The two depicted horns indicate that the rhinoceros was not from India but Africa. Thus the advent of the Portuguese in India began with the study of animals and natural history in the first age of globalization.

An elephant noticed by Cristovão da Costa who was in India from 1568-71 had appeared for the first time in print in his work titled 'Treatise on drugs and medicines from Eastern India with their plants' published in Spain in 1578.[22] Two illustrations of an Indian elephant had been presented while one represents an elephant leaning against the trunk of a coconut palm and the other represented an elephant prepared for war, with a model castle on his back. Cristovão da Costa asserts that the drawings were based on first-hand observation.[23] Johann Theodor de Bry reused the observations of Jan Huyghan van Linschoten's India Orientais (volume four, 1601 and volume five, 1603) and he issued a volume on animals, only those which were regarded as strange and unknown to Europeans. It featured notably elephants, crocodiles, chameleons and leopards from existing zoological accounts. Indeed one later engraving issued after 1612 shows a variety of animals from North India in a general depiction.[24]

Horse Trade and the Europeans on Tamil Coast

Portuguese merchants like Pedro Alvarez de Mesquita and Diogo de Lisboã who were stationed at Kanyakumari took the horses in their ships to the East Coast ports of Kayal and Punnaikayal. Further some *casados* (married settlers) in Cochin also took horses to the Tamil coast because of the profit derived from horse trade.[25] Owing to the great demand for horses the Portuguese Viceroy encouraged the Portuguese to purchase the horses directly from Arabia. These imported horses were sold to the various *nayaks* although its main sales were at the city of Vijayanagara where the emperor very much needed the swift moving horses for his army. The rulers depended on the horses to carry on their warfare. Horses brought by the Portuguese to Cochin were purchased by native merchants and taken to Tamil country owing to its proximity. According to one record, as many as forty horses were purchased at Cochin for resale at Kanyakumari.[26] António Fernandes, a native of the Malabar Coast had his horse trading establishment at Kanyakumari.[27]

So lucrative was the trade in horses that Ruy Gonsalves de Caminha took the profession of a horse dealer before he took up the post of the Portuguese Comptroller of Finance in 1547.[28] The horses that were brought from West Asia to the ports of the Western Coast of India were however allowed to be taken for resale only after paying taxes.[29] Some of the Portuguese merchants who lived in Kanyakumari were constantly on the lookout for information about the arrival of horses from Arabia at Cannanore and Chaul so that they could go and buy them for resale in the Tamil region.[30]

The Portuguese are reported to have sold horses to the *nayak* of Kanyakumari region as early as on 11 October 1512.[31] When they were planning to gain a foothold in the Pearl Fishery Coast then centred at Kilakkarai, the opportunity to sell horses to the *nayak* of Paramakudi who was in dire need of it for his army came in handy.[32] The Portuguese in the Pearl Fishery Coast requested the Portuguese Viceroy of India to arrange for the supply of horses which came from Ormuz to the ports of Goa, Chaul and Cannanore. The Viceroy in turn took special efforts to supply the requisite number of horses as per the demands placed by the Captain of the Fishery Coast in order to supply Tumbichi Nayaka of Paramakudi. Later evidences suggest that some Portuguese private merchants also began to participate in this lucrative horse trade with the *nayak* of Paramakudi.[33] João da Cruz, a horse trader in his letter written to Dom João III, asked the king of Portugal for the exclusive privilege of selling horses in the *nayakdom* of (Chembeche Naque) Thumbichi Nayaka.[34] Some clever Portuguese merchants could even win over the patronage of the local ruler who allowed them to carry on their horse trade in the Kilakkarai region.

The king of Portugal had appointed Cosme de Paiva in 1542 as Captain of the Fishery Coast who took temporary residence at Tuticorin to protect the *paravas* against attacks from pirates.[35] He also took interest in developing the horse trade with Maravarman Sundara Pandya (1531-1555), the Pandya ruler of Tirunelveli. During 1544 he sold horses for personal gain and took little care of the paravas.[36] There were several brokers and agents in Chaul who supplied horses to the Tamil coast.[37] However the horse trade with the Pandya ruler declined in the second half of the sixteenth century.

The Portuguese who traded with the ports of Thirumalairayanpattinam and Nagore on the Coromandel Coast had obtained the permission of Sevvappa (1535-1563), the nayaka of Thanjavur to settle down at Nagapattinam. In return, they agreed to bring horses to Nagapattinam from the ports of the Western coast which received its supply from West Asia. It may be recalled that some Portuguese who specialized in horse trade with the Coromandel stayed at Kanyakumari and purchased horses that came from West Asia soon after they received news about it.[38] Some of the *casados* in Kochi also participated in the export of horses to Nagapattinam.[39] As the *nayak* of Thanjavur was desperately in need of horses he used to send his men asking for horses from the Portuguese at Nagapattinam.[40] Portuguese sources record that some of these horses became sick due to unfavourable climate even before they could be offered for sale at Nagapattinam. Hence a Portuguese *casado* of Nagapattinam by name Marcos was appointed by the Portuguese Captain of the Coromandel Coast to treat the sick horses. He was paid four *pardaus* for rendering this special service.[41]

Horses of South Asian and South East Asian origin from various regions in due course of time came to be traded and they were sent to the Tamil Coast. It is evident that horses that were of four years to eight years had been felt as good and suitable for trade. Yellow, white, grey and black horses are mentioned. Horses were also used for mundane work and used in communications. The prices of horses fluctuated rapidly in response to demand and supply factors that were very difficult to predict. Horse trade was monitored by government and the shipping of live horses required considerable amount of working capital, needed much care and attention on board ship. Returns were substantial but risks were high. It may be said that horse trade was not traditional as opined by scholars in fact it must be said as modern at that point of time.

The import of horses and the ship arrivals from time to time have been found in the records particularly from Manila to Madras during 1686 and 1697. Horses came from Aceh in Indonesia and the trade had flourished during 1686 and 1727. Trade in ponies had also been found mention from Pegu to the Tamil coast between 1686 and 1717. Ships sailed with horses from Syriam and Pegu to Madras have been reported during 1700 and 1740.[42] As a result, there were several ships of the merchants of various places being mentioned in records such as Madras merchants, Cuddalore merchants, Kunimedu merchants, Pegu merchants. However the trading and the ownership must be either of partnership or collective. A new group of traders had emerged and we find Borneo merchants, Julfa merchants, (Armenians of New Julfa) Tonkin (Vietnamese) merchants, Mindanao (Philippines) recorded in the documents. Such traders were never found mention in the earlier pre-European period of horse trading with the Tamil ports. Triangular shipping that developed had contributed to the growth of the port of Madras that became a mid-point in Asian trade. Traders of the Tamil Coast had imported large number of horses from Pegu, Syriam, Aceh and Manila which were grey and white colour. The ships of the *chettis* of Kunimedu, Cuddalore and Madras had brought a minimum of fifteen, twenty four, forty and forty five and a maximum of 123 horses. It shows that the ships were of very large size. The Sultans of Kedah and Aceh, the kings of Arakan and Thailand who owned large sailing vessels sent their royal ships with animals to Madras, Cuddalore, Porto Novo and Pondicherry and in return took large quantities of cloth. Sheikh Mohammed *marakkayar* and Miran *marakkayar* of Pondicherry, Nalla Bukku *marakkayar* of Porto Novo owned many ships and they sailed to Banten, Aceh, Kedah and Tennaserim with the sailing permits from various European companies and traded in horses.[43]

The *chettis* began importing horses from Myanmar in the seventeenth century. Syriam was the major port in the kingdom of Pegu. It was situated on the estuary of a river about 50 miles upstream from Pegu, the capital city. In 1690, horses were brought to the Tamil coast from Pegu by the native traders who exported textiles. Some of the *chettis* who had settled in Myanmar had strong commercial relations with the rulers and nobility. Horses were mainly imported from Pegu but these were inferior in breed.[44] The sale of textiles facilitated the purchase of horses which were procured every year in view of the demand in the markets of the Tamil country. Horses were also imported from Manila, Persia and Arabia, and their prices had been mentioned. According to sources there were two types of horses from West Asia. The Persian horse was of grey colour and it was the costliest one and in 1717 one horse was sold for 150 *pagodas*. The Arabian horse was sold for 130 *pagodas* and the white Arabian horse was sold for100 *pagodas*.[45]

In 1734, a ship of the king of Aceh sailing to Porto Novo was seized, and the French in Pondicherry took away the forty-four horses on board.[46] The ships that arrived in Pondicherry on 30 December 1740 from Aceh, brought 250 horses that were purchased in Manila.[47] Again, 123 horses first came from Aceh to Manila, and then the ships brought the animals to Pondicherry on 8 January 1740.[48] On 11 April 1740, a ship from Manila brought nineteen horses to Pondicherry.[49] Horses were used by the Europeans as gifts to be sent to rulers for obtaining privileges. Ships also sailed from Pegu to Pondicherry and on 8 January 1741, mention is made of four horses which were imported.[50] Further, forty-two horses were brought from Aceh to Pondicherry on 9 April 1742.[51] It is also mentioned that on 5 January

1743, horses were brought in a ship from Aceh, but the number is not specified in the record.[52] On 16 April 1753, twenty-four Aceh horses were brought in a ship from Manila to Pondicherry. Monsieur Delarche at that time purchased a horse for 610 rupees, and another one for 303 rupees.[53] In 1755, a big horse was sold in Pondicherry for around 700 rupees. The selling price of a horse, thus, ranged between 600 to 700 rupees.[54] Horses brought in big ships were transferred into boats to reach the seashore in Pondicherry.[55] In January 1756, forty horses for the French East India Company, and fifteen horses for the officials of the Company arrived in the ships that reached Pondicherry from Aceh.[56] Leading natives like Ramachandra Aiyan and Vasudeva Pandit, employed in the sea-customs office in Pondicherry rode on horseback inside the town as they were given the privilege.[57] Thus, horses were also used by the natives. Horse-drawn carriages and sedan-chairs were used by Europeans in Pondicherrry.[58] Horses of various breeds, from Manila, Pegu, Aceh, Turkey and Arabia, were found in Pondicherry.[59] In one instance, Ananda Ranga pillai did not participate in the auction for the Manila horses because of the soaring prices of horses.[60] He owned several horse stables, and this indicates that he was engaged in horse trade in Pondicherry.[61] Ranga Pillai had been also engaged in animal trade as he hailed from the *idaiyar* caste, where men were skilled in looking after animals. He appointed Ramayya Pillai to look after the business.[62] The First Carnatic War (1744-48), the Second Carnatic War (1749-54) and other wars had necessitated import of horses for the army. Mohammed Ali, the Nawab of Arcot purchased elephants at Tirupati that came via overland route from Rajasthan in north India since 1761. Antoine de Letang the captain of cavalry in Pondicherry collected the details on the practices of maintaining the horses from the best authors and founded upon experiments made during a residence of ten years in Tamil country wrote a book and it was printed in Pondicherry in 1795.[63] It is also interesting to note that *Aswasastra* (the science of horses) was also compiled in Marathi by Salihotra during the rule of Serfoji II (1777-1832) the ruler of Thanjavur.[64] It may be said that the illustration of the winged horse portrayed in the work is mythological and may not be scientifically acceptable.

Elephants Imported to Tamil Country and Trade in the Early Modern Age

Before the advent of the heavy artillery rendering assistance in the military we find elephants alone remained extremely useful as working animals. Portuguese on the Tamil coast developed keen interest in the supply of elephants from Myanmar and Sri Lanka to the nayak of Gingee. They also supplied elephants of Sri Lanka to the nayaks of Thanjavur and Madurai. The importance of elephants as symbols of status and power had very much developed by the rulers in Tamil country. Although the *marakkayars* were the traditional traders of rice and textiles with Sri Lanka, they turned to import elephants from Sri Lanka as there was heavy demand in south India. Many elephants were imported by the *marakkayar* merchants from Sri Lanka to Nagapattinam.[65] Some of the *marakkayars* had specialized in the transportation of elephants and we find a merchant by name Chilay Marakkayar who provided his ship for carrying elephants to Goa as requested by the Portuguese Viceroy.[66] The elephants of Sri Lanka could be tamed easily and therefore were esteemed highly by Achyutappa nayak (1563-1580), the ruler of Thanjavur and the other rulers who needed them for their army. The best and the most thoroughly trained elephants were priced between 1000 and 1500 *cruzados*.[67] Sometimes the Portuguese also presented these elephants as gifts to the rulers and in one such case we find that as many as three elephants were presented to the *nayak* of Thanjavur.[68]

Portuguese in Nagapattinam held sway over the seas and therefore insisted on traders to obtain sailing permits from the Portuguese Captain for carrying on navigation.[69] Some merchants like Khawaja Marakkayar of Nagapattinam trading collected these *cartazes* from the Portuguese after paying the stipulated amount.[70] There were instances of ships at Nagapattinam being attacked and confiscated by the Portuguese on account of the negligence in observing all the conditions stipulated in the *cartaz* issued by the Portuguese Captain at Nagapattinam. It was insisted that owners of the ships should collect these *cartazes* from Nagapattinam to reach the port of call and the same vessel should, on its return journey, pay a stipulated amount of tax for the import of commodities at the Portuguese customs house at Nagapattinam. Although a *cartaz* was issued at a nominal rate of one *tanga* per *cartaz*, Coromandel merchants were prohibited from carrying certain commodities as they were declared as items of royal monopoly by the Portuguese. Raghunatha nayak (1580-1630), the ruler of Thanjavur who was annoyed at the way the Portuguese acted in issuing *cartazes*, captured a Portuguese ship at Nagapattinam on 27 January 1625.[71] The *nayak* intervened in the matter and demanded as to why *cartaz* was not given to a ship in December 1624 which planned to take merchandise leaving the port of Nagapattinam.

In fact it is evident from some records that the nayak of Thanjavur was more interested in the purchase of elephants than the *nayaks* of Gingee and Madurai. The reasons for evincing interest in elephants by the *nayak* of Thanjavur are not explicitly stated in the documents. António Vaz Pereira, the Portuguese Captain at Nagapattinam made special arrangements to sell all the elephants that were brought from Sri Lanka to Nagapattinam by the Portuguese to the *nayak* of Thanjavur in 1607 knowing his requirement.[72]

In 1614, Jeronimo de Azevedo (1612-1617), the Portuguese Viceroy of Goa wrote in his letter that the *nayak* of Thanjavur alone enjoyed the exclusive right to buy all the elephants from the Portuguese.[73]

Venkatapatidevaraya II (1586-1614), the titular Vijayanagara emperor however was not at all interested to buy elephants. The *nayak* of Thanjavur always wanted the elephants to be delivered at Thanjavur and only then payment was made for the elephants. The then ruler of Kandy who did not realize the importance of animal trade, allowed the Portuguese to engage in commerce and elephants were sent from several ports of Sri Lanka for eventual delivery to the *nayak* of Thanjavur. This elephant trade continued up to 1620.[74]

Some of the Coromandel sea-going vessels sailed from Sri Lanka and they carried fourteen to fifteen elephants. These *naus* (cargo ships) were exceedingly strong.[75] The prow of the *naus* were built in such a way as to facilitate their movement in narrow channels and transport elephants safely from Sri Lanka to the Tamil Coast. Six elephants were brought to Nagapattinam in 1622 and they were sold for a total amount of 3990 xerafins.[76] The *nayak* of Thanjavur is reported to have asked for more elephants from Sri Lanka on 18 February 1630. This was agreed to by the Portuguese in order to ask for help from the *nayak* in their attempt to capture Pulicat, the chief settlement of the Dutch in Coromandel.[77]

The import of elephants had come from Arakan in Myanmar to the Tamil coast and it flourished well. The king of Arakan had large fleet of ships and he pursued trade very vigorously with the Tamil Coast. The port of Mrauk-U, (Mrohaung) the capital of Arakan (since AD 1434) was a great trading centre. On 14 April 1626 the ship of Thiruthundamma the king of Arakan (1622-1638) arrived at Pulicat. It brought a total of thirteen elephants. Out of these it is mentioned that eight belonged to the king and three elephants were that of the *kotwal* of the king of Arakan and two elephants belonged to the *havildar* of Pulicat. It is mentioned that this voyage took thirty three days.[78] Another ship belonging to the *kotwal* of Arakan had reached Pulicat in 1626.[79] On 17 April 1626 two ships of the king Arakan arrived at Pulicat. It had brought nineteen elephants.[80] All these ships returned by carrying many bales of textiles of the Tamil coast. Two ships of Thiruthundamma the King of Arakan carried elephants to Pulicat on 14 April 1627.[81] The ships of the King of Arakan sailed to Pulicat with fourteen elephants consigned to Chinnana *chetti* to be sold on the king's account.[82] Elephants were continuously shipped every year from Arakan, Tennaserim and Melaka where they were found in abundance.[83] In Madras Kelavi *chetti*, the trader owned a ship and it sailed regularly and brought elephants from Arakan and Pegu.[84] Elephant trade between Arakan and the Tamil Coast did not flourish under the rule of Sandathuhamma (1652-1684). Around 1685 the ruler of Ava conquered Pegu and there had been political problems but later trade in elephants developed. Residents of Madras like Francis had brought regularly elephants from Arakan and exported via Pegu.[85]

The rulers of Tamil country had an insatiable demand for elephants and it was one of the strands that connected the Coromandel Coast with South East Asia. The trade in horses was mainly in the hands of the *chettis* and the *marakkayars* of the Tamil coast who sailed to South East Asia and they met the demand of the rulers. These native merchants brought elephants from Arakan, Kedah, Aceh, Perak, Tennserim with a minimum of fourteen in a ship and a maximum of twenty four elephants which had been mentioned. It therefore goes beyond doubt that these native ships had high tonnage and capacity. Elephants were the principal export from Aceh between 1640 and 1663, averaging thirty per year. In the year 1651 alone, over one hundred animals had been exported from Tenasserim in Thailand.[86] The trade had flourished the trend had continued till 1746 as found in later records. The Nawab of Arcot received elephants from Kedah.[87]

The Dutch East India Company came to participate in elephant trade from Sri Lanka to Tamil coast. It branded the elephant with the VOC logo before sale. It was a lucrative item of revenue for the Dutch. The sale of elephants during 1675-79 and 1697 had been reported in Dutch sources. The Dutch Governor of Sri Lanka held elephants in a public auction where all the buyers had a chance to make a bid. Such auctions had been conducted at the markets in Jaffna, Mannar, Galle and Matara. Of these, the largest sale was in Jaffna and the next was in Galle. The merchants of the Tamil coast went to purchase the elephants from the sale.[88] The profit in elephant trade by the Dutch during 1646 and 1650 was 18,652 *reals* of 48 *stuivers* by selling 22 elephants. It had been reported that the income would have been much higher, had the captured 24 wild elephants not died at the stable which happened during the period of taming and training. It is evident that the total income of the Dutch from the sale of elephants was 72% between 1667 and 1670.[89]

Hendrick Becker the Dutch Governor of Sri Lanka had stated the three ways of obtaining the elephants by the Dutch East India Company in 1716. These include (a) annual tribute (b) presents and (c) on payment for those in excess of the tribute by the elephant hunters.[90] The sale of elephants during the first half of the eighteenth century by the Dutch in Sri Lanka had yielded an average profit of 100,000 guilders per year. An average number of 80 to 100 elephants were shipped annually. However, after 1740, there had been a period of rapid decline in the elephant trade of the Dutch in Sri Lanka and the reasons are varied in nature. The Anglo-French war and the Carnatic wars of the mid-eighteenth century was said to be a hindrance to the elephant trade as it prevented the merchants from sailing for export and import of elephants. Further, the practice of the *vanniyars* in Sri Lanka not paying the tribute on time was important. Again the lack of tamed elephants to control the wild elephants had severely affected the elephant trade of the Dutch company. As a result, the Dutch trade in elephants declined during 1740 and 1757 dropping to annual average sale of fifteen elephants.[91] In the mid-end of eighteenth century the elephant export trade from Sri Lanka, Myanmar and Thailand to Tamil coast was dead. In 1740 the Dutch had exported elephants from Coromandel to Jakarta because the animal had been scarce in Sumatra. Thus elephants were also no longer needed to the same extent as earlier in Tamil country.

Trade in elephants by the French had been developed and the fact that twenty-one elephants were carried in a ship in 1688 to Pondicherry speaks of its volume.[92] The trade in textiles provided the funds for the purchase of elephants that were imported to Pondicherry. Elephants from Kedah and Perak were imported to Pondicherry. It is stated that elephants were available in plenty and were sold at cheaper rates than anywhere in Asia.[93] Alexander Hamilton mentioned that the export of elephants to Coromandel was the most sought after part of trade in 1693.[94] Among the rulers, the King of Thailand was a monopolist in trade. He owned a number of ships and traded in elephants.[95] King Narai (1656–88), the ruler of Thailand, had great admiration for the trade of the *marakkayars*. It was at this time, that Tamil Muslims also held high offices in the island of Ujang Selang (Phuket). One of the *marakkayars* in 1670 became the Governor of the region of Ujang Selang.[96] The native Thai tin miners resisted this appointment, and there was a rebellion against the *marakkkayar* in which he was killed.[97] The ships of the officers of the king of Thailand sailed to Pondicherry with 2 elephants (besides 150 chests of copper) belonging to the king.[98] In 1688, the king of Thailand also welcomed the trade conducted by the *marakkayars* with Tennaserim. Elephants (besides huge quantities of tin) were imported.[99] The trade of Tennaserim with Pondicherry was substantial in terms of the supply of elephants and elephant tusks. In 1695, king Phetracha of Thailand exported elephants for sale on the Coromandel Coast. In the same year, Prince Sorasak sent a ship laden with twenty elephants.[100] In 1697, the king had a new ship and exported elephants.[101] He also sent two ships exclusively from Mergui to trade with the Coromandel Coast in textiles. One, thus, finds that ships of the king of Thailand continued to visit the ports of

Coromandel as late as 1702.[102] King Phetracha and Prince Sorasak sent several ships with elephants to Coromandel mainly to obtain large cargoes of textiles.[103] The ship of the king of Thailand named Lakshmana Prasad, which sailed from Tennaserim, brought thirteen elephants to Pondicherry on 29 April 1745. Similarly, the ship Nanak owned by the king brought 13 elephants on 29 April 1745.[104] Elephant dealers like Eramma Nayakakar and Suga Singh in Pondicherry are mentioned in the record of 6 October 1746.[105] In 1703, Daud Khan, the Nawab of Arcot wrote a letter to the French in Pondicherry in which he expressed his unhappiness over the seizure of a ship that brought elephants. He insisted on the return of the ship Mira Madut immediately to its owner named Claomica *marakkayar*, a resident of Porto Novo. He also mentioned that he had planned to send textiles to Kedah for sale and in return wanted to purchase elephants.[106] The Nawab also used his ports for elephant trade, and in 1711, 19 elephants were imported to Santhome of Mylapore for 7,600 *pagoda*s. In 1712, 12 elephants were imported for 3,000 *pagodas*.[107] The ship of the king of Kedah reached Porto Novo and it brought eleven elephants in 1739.[108]

Europeans on the Tamil coast have mentioned that a large trunk was always esteemed a great beauty in an elephant. They were not so particular, and sometimes preferred a female elephant for hunting and riding on, when she had been known to have remarkably good paces, and to be of a mild and tracts able disposition. According to Europeans, an elephant was said to be perfect, when his ears were large and rounded, not ragged or indented at the margin; his eyes of a dark hazel colour, free from specks, the roof of his mouth, and his tongue, without dark or black spots of any considerable size; his trunk large, and his tail long, with a tuft of hair reaching nearly to the ground. There must be five nails on each of his fore feet, and four on each of the hind ones, making eighteen in all; his head well set on, and carried rather high. The arch or curve of his back rose gradually from the shoulder to the middle, and thence descending to the insertion of the tail; and all his joints firm and strong.[109]

The English East India Company officials in Madras have recorded that the elephants from kingdom of Pegu were of a superior breed. On the Malabar Coast, elephants of Travancore were taken as far north as the territories of Mysore for sale but these elephants were much inferior to the Sri Lanka elephants. It is also affirmed in 1822 that elephants in Malabar were inferior and also of small size. The Nawab of Arcot had complained in 1823 about the elephants he received as part of an annual tribute from the queen of Travancore. He said that the elephants were not fit for riding. In reply the queen had asked the English East India Company to forward three elephants to the Nawab and to apologize for the inferior quality of the elephants gifted. She explained that this inadequacy arose from the small size of the Travancore elephants, and not from any want of attention on the part of Her Highness to the due performance of her obligations to the Nawab her most respected ally and protector.[110]

Most of the European accounts respecting the Asiatic elephant had been given by many gentlemen who resided many years on the Tamil coast. It has been said that elephants of Africa were said to be smaller than the Asiatic, yet credibly informed in 1799, by the ivory-dealers in London, that the largest tusks generally came from Africa, and they were of a better texture, and less liable to turn yellow, than the Indian ivory. This probably was owing to the tusks having lain longer in Africa, before they were imported, than those brought from Asia.[111]

Elephants continued to be shipped by the English from Sri Lanka to Tamil country. They were sent mainly to the port of Cuddalore on the Coromandel Coast and they were transported via land route to reach Mysore. In 1800 an agreement was reached with the British government of Sri Lanka for the supply of elephants.[112] The agent for the supply of elephants from Sri Lanka mentioned that the elephant with the height of twelve feet would be sound for service. But there were elephants found only with five cubits and upwards in height. Therefore he was of the opinion that none under that height should be purchased at any time for the use of the English East India Company. He said that elephants of twelve feet size would answer well as working elephants whether male or female. He added that the two lots received in September and October in 1802 although the best, in point of size, were in such wretched order, that two of them had died in the voyage in the ships on the way to Cuddalore, while two elephants died on the road way transporting to Mysore, and two had also died after arrival in Mysore.[113] Thus he expressed his concern and the difficulties in the purchase and transport of elephants.

Barclay the English captain in-charge of the elephants in 1800 had mentioned that the elephants in the royal menagerie of Tipu Sultan at Mysore had always received ghee and curd along with their rice. Owing to escalation of prices in maintaining the elephants, if these articles were struck away from the diet by the English East India Company he said that the elephants would certainly suffer very much, perhaps be rendered quite unserviceable.[114] Barclay also mentioned that the elephants in Bengal did not require the ghee and curd for food. Further he added that two drivers per elephant were required in Mysore while the elephants in Bengal required only one driver.[115]

The British military auditor-general in India had recorded that an elephant from Sri Lanka fetched 2,000 rupees each, but an elephant of Bengal could be procured for 750 rupees. He therefore recommended that the supply of elephants from Sri Lanka to be discontinued since adequate elephants could be easily procured at cheap rates from Bengal.[116]

Elephants from the forests of Tamil country were also hunted and brought for taming. It is interesting to learn that in 1822 an illustrated treatise on *Gaja sastra* (the science of elephants) was compiled in Marathi by Balakappiyamuni one of the scholar poets of Serfoji II the ruler of Thanjavur.[117] It deals with the capture, maintenance, breeding, training and treatment of the elephant.

Elephants from Madurai and Coimbatore found in Tamil country had been suggested for purchase in large numbers in 1825. The reason was that the elephants from Madurai had already been introduced in the army of the English Company. Those elephants in Coimbatore which were often found as a threat to cultivation could be tamed and used. The English company in a large measure had faced with the task of destroying those elephants that ravaged the villages in Coimbatore. In 1822, the collector of Coimbatore sent a map of the region to the board of revenue and reported that out of the total 8,000 square miles area of the district, 3,700 miles area were subjected to the ravages of the elephants. The English company decided at that time to employ a group of 7000 to 8000 peons as in the past to keep wild elephants in check and to protect cultivation. However, later in 1824 the proposal was modified when the collector requested to send some hunters from Chittagong to Coimbatore to train a few chosen inhabitants in the modes of entrapment used in Bengal.[118] The collector of Madurai at that time had given the needed information and advice to the collector of Coimbatore as to how to trap elephants that were a threat to cultivation.[119] It is mentioned that at the foot of Nilgiri hills near Seermoogay there remained a settlement where wild elephants in the past had been caught. The details had been printed with plates in the Madras Journal of Literature and Science in 1857.[120] Thus we find knowledge about various types of elephants and places from where they hailed from had crossed over in numerous ways.

Europeans on the Tamil coast during their animal trade and commercial expansion were not innocent gatherers of information but they constructed and circulated the knowledge from local to global. It is significant therefore to understand how the Coromandel region or the Tamil coast was represented in and by Europe in the various centuries between 1500 and 1857 for a better and fuller understanding of the regional specificities and their nuances and complexities of fauna knowledge networks. How the European curiosity had helped in making of a body of animal science knowledge from the Tamil coast and it systematically developed is equally important. How Tamils and Tamil coast came to be understood by Europe through natural history has been therefore primarily investigated in the following chapters. The perspectives of book had been concerned with the European understanding and presentation of their own scientific endeavors ad intra, i.e., in Tamil country, and ad extra, i.e., for their European supporters and future scientists in the field of natural history.

Notes

1. J. M. Garcia, *As Viagens dos Descobrimentos*, Lisboã, 1983, pp. 219-20.
2. Raymundo António Bulhão Pato and António da Silva Rego, ed., *Cartas de Affonso de Albuquerque*, 7 vols, Lisboã, 1884–1935, tome VI, p. 412.
3. *Ibid.*, tome VII, p. 12.
4. *Ibid*, p. 104.
5. *Ibid.*, tome VI, p. 206.
6. I. V. Barbosa, *Apontamentos para a Historia das Coleccoes de Zoologia em Portugal*, Lisbon, 1885, p. 5; D. de Gois, *Cronia do Felicýssimo Rei D. Manuel, 1566-1567*, Coimbra, 1926, p. 198.
7. A. F. da Costa, *Les deambulations du rhinoceros de Modofar*, Lisbon, 1937, p. 46; G. Correia, *The Three Voyages of Vasco da Gama and his Viceroyalty from the Lendas da India: Translated from the Portuguese with Notes and an Introduction by H. Stanley*, London, 1869.
8. Donald F. Lach, *Asia in the Making of Europe*, 2 vols., Chicago, 1970, vol. I, p. 120.
9. John Rowlands,*The Age of Dürer and Holbein: German Drawings, 1400–1550*, London, 1988. The rhinoceros woodcut by Durer is at the British Museum in London.
10. Giulia Bartrum,*German Renaissance Prints, 1490–1550*, London, 1995, pp. 49–50, no. 35.
11. Silvio A. Bedini, *The Pope's Elephant*, Manchester, 1997.
12. D. F. Lach, Asia in the Making of Europe, pp. 135–44.
13. A. F. da Costa, Les deambulations du rhinoceros, pp. 46-7.
14. N. Vassalo e Silva, 'Preciosidades e Maravilhas entre Goa e Lisboã', in *Exotica: Os Descobrimentos e as Camaras de Maravilhas do Renascimento*, eds., H. Trnnek and N. Vassallo Silva, Lisboã, 2001, pp. 27-37.
15. Duarte Barbosa, *The Book of Duarte Barbosa: An Account of the Countries Bordering on the Indian Ocean and their Inhabitants, Translated from the Portuguese Text by M. L. Dames*, London, 1918-1921, vol. I, p. 198.
16. Tome Pires, *The Suma Oriental of Tome Pires*, edited and translated by A. Cortesão, London, 1944, vol. I, p. 172.
17. L. Matos, *Imagens do Oriente no seculo XVI: Reproduçao do Codice Portugues da Biblioteca Casatanense*, Lisboã, 1985.

18. Pedro Dias, *Historia da Arte Portuguesa no Mundo, 1415-1822: Espaço Indýco*, Lisboã, 1998, p. 21; L. Matos, Imagens do Oriente no seculo XVI, p. 24.
19. D. F. Lach, Asia in the Making of Europe, p. 142.
20. *Ibid.*, p. 133, pp. 150-158.
21. I. C. Almeida and R. A. Lino, *O Rinoceronte: Pegadas na Torre*, Lisboã, 1992, p. 47; P.A. Caminha, *Sumario dos Reis de Portugal*, Belem, 1992.
22. Cristoval Acosta, *Tractado de las drogas, y medicinais de las Indias Orientales, consus Plantas debuxadas albuio por Cristobal Acosta medico y cirurjana que las vio ocularmente*, Burgos, 1578.
23. P. M. Jones, 'Image, Word, and Medicine in the Middle Ages', in *Visualizing Medieval Medicine and Natural History, 1200-1550*, eds., J. A. Givens, K. M. Reeds and A. Touwaide, London, 2006, pp. 25-50.
24. D. F. Lach, Asia in the Making of Europe, pp. 135–58.
25. Elaine Sanceau, *Coleção de São Lourenço*, Lisboã, 1973-83, vol. II, p. 335, 364 and 372; S. Jeyaseela Stephen, 'The Nayaks of Tamil Country and the Portuguese trade in war Animals' in Pius Malekandathil and T. Jamal Mohammed, eds., *The Portuguese, the Indian Ocean and European Bridgeheads, 1500-1800*, Tellicherry, 2001, pp. 212-22.
26. Armando Cortesao and Luis de Albuquerque, *Obras Completas de Dom João de Castro* (hereafter *Obras Completas*), Coimbra, 1976, vol. III, p. 215.
27. Coleção São Lourenço, vol. II, p. 300, 335 and 368.
28. Coleção São Lourenço, vol. II, p. 85.
29. Gaspar Correa, *Lendas da India*, 4 vols, rpt., Porto, 1975, tomo II, pp. 65-66.
30. Obras Completas, vol. II, p.100; vol. IV, p. 50.
31. Letter of Affonso de Albuquerque written from Cannanore, *Cartas de Affonso de Albuquerque,* vol. I, pp. 88-89.
32. Diogo de Lisboã was selling horses in 1524. Instituto Arquivo Nacionais/ Torre do Tombo (hereafter IANTT), Lisboa, MSS, Corpo Cronologico (hereafter CC), IIa-114- 4.
33. IANTT, *Chancelaria de D. João III, Priveligios*, Livro 1, fl.97v. Privileges for the sale of horses were given to Andre Luis at Vedalai on 1 February 1538. Orders were also issued from Lisbon in this regard again on 2 August 1552.
34. Letter of Joao da Cruz to the king of Portugal dated 20 December 1553. See Georg Schurhammer, 'Iniqitembrane and Bete Perumal: Chera and Pandya kings in South India', *Journal of the Bombay Historical Society*, vol. III, 1930, pp. 1-40.
35. IANTT, *Chancelaria de D.João III*, Livro 21, fl.39.
36. Letter of Francis Xavier to Mansillhas, 5 September 1544 written from Alandalai, see Hugues Dider, *Correspondance 1535-1552: Lettres et Documents*, Paris, 1987, pp.132-33; see also Georg Schurhammer, 'Iniqitriberim and Bete Perumal: Chera and Pandya Kings in Southern India, 1544', in *Orientalia*, Rome, 1977, p. 263.
37. Biblioteca da Ajuda (hereafter BA) Lisboã, *Livro das Merces que fez Dom João de Castro*, MSS Codice 51-8-46, fl.92v.

38. Armando Cortesão & Luís de Albuquerque, Obras Completas, vol. III, 100; vol. IV, 50.
39. Letter from António Fernandes to Viceroy of Goa dated 2 August 1546 and the letter of Manoel Lobato to Viceroy dated, 25 August 1547, See Coleção São Lourenço, vol. II, pp. 335 and 364-372.
40. Samuel Purchas, *His Pilgrims,* 10 vols., Glasgow, 1905, vol. II, pp. 227-28.
41. IANTT, CC, Part IIa-117-156.
42. S. Jeyaseela Stephen, 'Shipping and Trade in Elephants and Horses of Asia: The Commercial Topography of the Tamil Merchants and Rulers, 1626-1765 AD', G. John Samuel, ed. *Contributions of Tamils to the Composite Culture of Asia, Part II*, Chennai, 2014, pp. 199-231.
43. *Ibid.*, pp. 211-8.
44. Records of Fort St. George, *Diary and Consultation Book* (hereafter DCB), 1672-1746, 1749-1757, C.M. Schmidt, J.J. Cotton, A.V. Venakatarama Ayyar, B.S. Baliga et al, eds., 90 vols, Published by Madras Superintendent, Government Press, Madras, 1910-1953, see DCB 1690, p. 21; DCB 1692, p. 1.
45. DCB 1717, pp. 11, 181.
46. Frederick Price, H. Dodwell and V. Rangachari, (eds.,) *The Private Diary of Ananda Ranga Pillai, Dubash to Joseph François Dupleix, Knight of the Order of St. Michael, and Governor of Pondicherry: A Record of Matters Political, Historical, Social, and Personal, from 1736 to 1761*, vol. I, 1904; vol. II, 1907; vol. III, 1914; vol. IV, 1916; vol. V, 1917; vol. VI, 1918; vol. VII, 1919; vol. VIII, 1922; vol. IX, 1924; vol. X, 1925; vol. XI, 1927; vol. XII, 1928, Madras, Delhi, rpt, 1980, (hereafter ARP Diary), vol. I, pp. 183–4.
47. *Ibid.*, vol. III, p. 184.
48. *Pratiyegamana Ananda Ranga Pillai Avargalin Sostha Ligitha Dinapadi Sethi Kurippu*, vol. I, (1736-1746) Pondicherry, 1948; vol. II, (1746-1746) Pondicherry, 1949; vol. III, (1746-1747) Pondicherry, 1950; vol. IV, (1747-1748) Pondicherry, 1951; vol. V, (1748) Pondicherry, 1954; vol. VI, (1748-50) Pondicherry, 1956; vol. VII, (1751-52) Pondicherry, 1963, vol. VIII, pt I, (1751-52) Pondicherry, 1986; Pt II, (1752-53) Pondicherry, 1988 (hereafter Pratiyegamana Ananda Ranga Pillai), vol. I, p. 80.
49. *Ibid.*, vol. I, p. 87.
50. *Ibid.*, vol. I, p. 108.
51. ARP Diary, vol. X, pp. 2–3.
52. *Ibid.*, vol. I, p. 208.
53. M. Gobalakitchenne, *Ananda Ranga Pillai Vrintha Naatkurippu, Srimukha Aandu, 1753-54*, Chennai, 2008, p. 8.
54. Pratiyegamana Ananda Ranga Pilliai, vol. IX, p. 79.
55. ARP Diary, vol. II, p. 242.
56. Alfred Martineau, *Dupleix et L'Inde Française*, Paris, 1923–7, vol. II, p. 154.
57. ARP Diary, vol. I, p. 369.
58. *Ibid.*, pp. 279–80.
59. *Ibid.*, vol. II, p. 178.

60. *Ibid.*, vol. I, pp. 325–6.
61. *Ibid.*, vol. II, p. 73.
62. *Ibid.*, vol. III, p. 430; vol. II, p. 73.
63. British Library (hereafter BL), London, Shelf mark 7293.bb.25, *The practice of farriery calculated for the East Indies collected from the best authors and founded upon experiments made during a residence of ten years in this country, by Antoine de Letang, captain of cavalry Pondicherry, printed for the author*, 1795. See also, *The Practice of Farriery Calculated for the East Indies*, Madras, 1839.
64. Savithri Preetha Nair, *Raja Serfoji II: Science, Medicine and Enlightenment in Tanjore*, New Delhi, 2012, p. 80.
65. Duarte Barbosa, vol. II, p. 113.
66. K.S. Mathew, *Indo-Portuguese Trade and the Fuggers of Germany,* New Delhi, 1997, p. 211.
67. Duarte Barbosa, vol. II, p.117.
68. Historical Archives of Goa (hereafter HAG), Panaji, *Assentos do Conselho da Fazenda,* codex 116, p. 9. As per this record two elephants were given to the nayak of Madurai.
69. IANTT, *Coleçao São Vicente* (hereafter CSV), MSS vol. X, fl.128.
70. Pissurlencar Panduranga, *Assentos do Conselho do Estado,* vols. I-V, Goa, 1972. This practice of taking Portuguese cartaz for the ships which began in 1502 continued to be in vogue at Nagapattinam during the early years of the seventeenth century.
71. Pieris, 'The Portuguese in Ceylon', *Journal of the Royal Asiatic Society of Ceylon Branch,* Vol, XXVII, p.102.
72. Bulhão Pato, *Documentos Remetidos da India,* vols. I-V, Lisboa, 1880-1935, vol. III, pp. 55-56.
73. IANTT, MSS, *Documentos Remetidos da India* (hereafter DRI), Livro 27, fl.116.
74. Tikri Abeysinghe, *A study of Portuguese Regimentos on Sri Lanka at the Goa Archives,* Colombo, n.d, p. 9.
75. Duarte Barbosa, vol. II, p.113.
76. Bibliotheca Nacional de Lisboa (hereafter BNL), Codice 11410, fls. 95-103[v].
77. HAG, MSS *Monçoes do Reino* (hereafter MDR), Livro 13B, 5-6/3-2, fl. 30[v].
78. Om Prakash, *The Dutch Factories in India: A Collection of Dutch East India Company Documents Pertaining to India,* vol. I, 1617-1623, Delhi, 1984; vol. II, Delhi, 2007, See, vol. II, p. 247.
79. Nationaal Archief (hereafter NA), Den Haag, MSS VOC 1095, fl. 30v, See the Pulicat Dagregister (1626-1628) entry dated 23 April 1626.
80. NA, VOC, 1095, fls. 28-47.
81. NA, VOC 1095, fl. 38, See the Pulicat Dagregister entry dated 14 April 1627.
82. J.A. Van der Chijs, et al., *Dagregister Gehouden int Casteel Batavia vant Passerende daer te Plaatse als Over Geheel Nederlandts-India, 1628–1682*, 31 vols., The Hague- Batavia, 1887–1928 (hereafter Dagregister), 1641, see 20 May 1641, p. 322.
83. DCB 1690, p. 21.

84. DCB 1703, p. 15.
85. DCB 1703, p. 20.
86. Anthony Reid, 'Humans and Forests in Pre-Colonial Southeast Asia', *Environment and History*, vol. 1, no. 1, 1995, pp. 105-7.
87. S. Jeyaseela Stephen, Shipping and Trade in Elephants and Horses, pp. 202-11.
88. Sophia Pieters, *Memoir of Rycklof van Goens, Junior, Governor of Ceylon, 1675-1679 to his Successor Laurens Pyl Late Commandeur, Jaffnapatnam*, Colombo, 1910, pp. 4-5; S. Anthonisz, *Diary of Occurrences during the Tour of Gerrit de Herre, Governor of Ceylon from Colombo to Jaffna July 9, to September 3, 1697*, Colombo, 1914, p. 16.
89. E. Reimers, *Memoir of Joan Maetsuyker President and Commander-in-Chief Delivered to his Successor Jacob van Kittensteyn on the 27 February 1650*, Colombo, 1927, pp. 14-15.
90. S. Anthonisz, *Memoir of Hendrick Becker Governor and Director of Ceylon for his Successor Issac Augustyn Rumpf 1716*, Colombo, 1914, p. 14.
91. Sophia Pieters, *Memoir of Van Imhoff 1740*, Colombo, 1911, p. 78; S. Arasaratnam, *Memoir of Julius Stein van Gollensee Governor of Ceylon 1743-1751 for his successor Gerrit Joan vreeland 28th February 1751*, Colombo, 1974, p. 27; E. Reimers, *Memoir of Joan Gideon Loten, Governor of Ceylon Delivered to his Successor Jan Schreuder on 28 February 1757*, Colombo, 1935, p. 37.
92. Lotika Varadarajan, *India in the Seventeenth Century: Memoirs of Francois Martin*, Delhi, 1980 (hereafter Memoirs), vol. II, part I, pp. 1126–7.
93. Thomas Bowrey, *A Geographical Account of the Countries Around the Bay of Bengal, 1669–1679*, ed. Sir Richard Temple, Cambridge, 1905, p. 273.
94. Alexander Hamilton, *A New Account of the East Indies*, London, 1930, vol. II, p. 71; RFG, DCB, see 1693, p. 59.
95. NA, MSS VOC 1269, fol. 468; Tapan Raychaudhuri, *Jan Company in Coromandel, 1605–1690: A Study in the Interrelations of European Commerce and Traditional Economies*, The Hague, 1962, pp. 63–4.
96. W. Ph. Coolhas, ed., *Generale Missiven van de Gouverneurs-Generaal en Raden Aan Heren XVII der Verenigde Oostindische Compagnie*, 9 vols., 'S Gravenhage, 1960–84, see vol. IV, p. 283; See also Thomas Bowrey, A Geographical Account, p. 257.
97. GM, vol. IV, 13 February 1679.
98. RFG, DCB 1692, p. 1.
99. Tapan Raychaudhri, Jan Company in Coromandel, p. 121.
100. NA, VOC 1596, fol. 54, see the letter of van Sen to Governor-General dated 8 December 1697.
101. S. Jeyaseela Stephen, 'Maritime Trade between the Tamil Coast in South India and Thailand', *Proceedings of the Sixth International Conference on Thai Studies*, vol. 7, Chinag Mai University, 1996, pp. 209–18.
102. NA, VOC 1676, fols. 73–4, 76–7; VOC 1596, fol. 54.
103. *Ibid.*, VOC 154, fol. 1087v–88; VOC 1580, fols. 32–3, 54–5; VOC 1596, fol. 54; VOC 1676, fols.73–7, 92–5.

104. Pratiyegamana Ananda Ranga Pillai, vol. I, p. 206.
105. ARP Diary, vol. I, p. 36.
106. *Ibid.*, vol. II, p. 10.
107. RFG, *Public Consultations, 1672–1750*, 36 vols., Madras, 1910–38 (hereafter *PC*), see 26 November 1733.
108. NA, VOC 2505, fol. 1534.
109. John Corse and Joseph Banks, 'Observations on the Different Species of Asiatic Elephants, and Their Mode of Dentition by John Corse, Esq. Communicated by the Right Hon. Sir Joseph Banks', *Philosophical Transactions of the Royal Society of London*, vol. 89 (1799), pp. 205-236.
110. BL, The Board of Control, Board's Collection, 1796–1858, The East India Company Records (hereafter EICR), EICR, F/4/946, File 26558, p. 7, see the letter of Lieutenant Colonel D. Newall the British resident in Travancore to Mr. Wood the Chief Secretary dated 9 April 1822.
111. John Corse and Joseph Banks, Observations on the Different Species of Asiatic Elephants, pp. 205-236.
112. Letter of Frederick North, the Governor of Ceylon to Right Honourable Lord Clive dated 12 June 1800, in EICR, F/4/95, File 1933, p. 109; Letter of the collector of Janapatam to Major Robert Turing dated 15 August 1800, in EICR, F/4/95, File 1933, p. 117; Letter of the military board dated 14 February 1803, in EICR, F/4/154 File 2690, p. 33.
113. Letter of H. Mackay, the agent of public cattle dated 1 February 1803, in EICR, F/4/154, File 2690, p. 34.
114. R. Barclay, in-charge of public elephants in Mysore to Captain John Macleane, the secretary of the military board, extracted from a letter from the military board dated 23 May 1800, in EICR, F/4/95, File 1933, p. 86.
115. *Ibid.*, pp. 86-88.
116. Minutes of the military auditor-general, in EICR, F/4/154, File 2690, p. 43.
117. K. S. Subrahmanya Sastri, ed., *Gaja Sastra of Paalakaapya Muni*, Tanjore, 1958.
118. Letter of J. Sullivan Esqr the collector of Coimbatore to the president and members of the board of revenue dated 2 March 1824, in EICR, F/4/862, File 22786, p. 106.
119. Letter of R. Peter, the collector of Madurai in an extract of the board of revenue dated 17 March 1825, in EICR, F/4/862, File 22786, p. 176.
120. 'Description of the method adopted in the Coimbatore district for catching wild elephants by Captain D. Hamilton, Assistant Conservator of Forests', *Madras Journal of Literature and Science* (MJLS), New Series, no.5, October – December 1857, pp. 58-60.

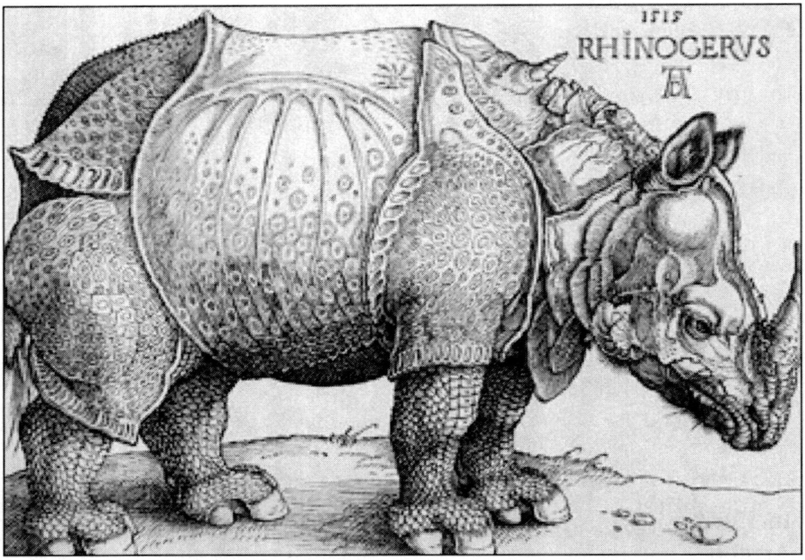

2.1. Rhinoceros woodcut by Albrecht Durer, 1515

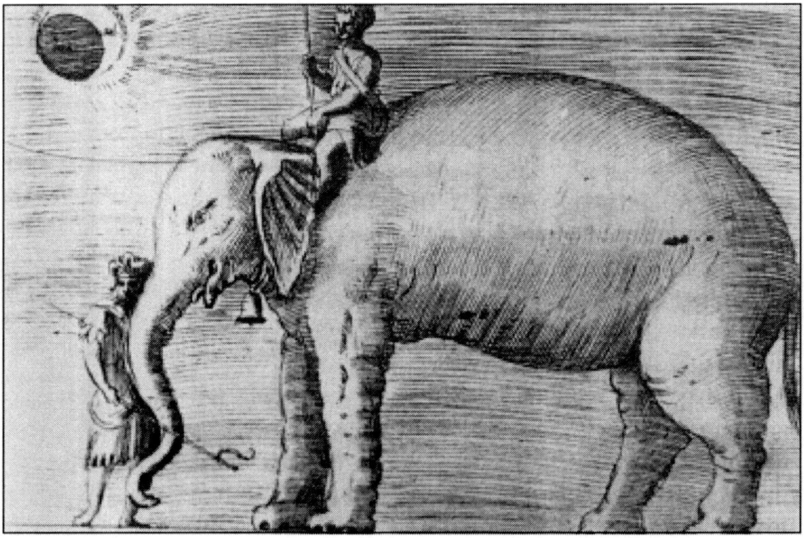

2.2. The elephant from Cochin presented to Pope Leo X by Dom Manuel I, the -King of Portugal, pen drawing by Francisco de Holanda, 1539-40

3

The Amazing Animals of Tamil Coast and Zoology, 1639-1857

In Europe the animal world was known through the writings of Aristotle (384-322 BC) of Greece. He had classified according to their way of living, actions, habits and body parts. He also divided the animals into two as invertebrates and vertebrates. He observed insects, fish, birds and whales and the insect orders like Coleoptera, Diptera were created by him. His classical work *De Generatione Animalium* is concerned with the generation of animals. It describes the reproduction and development of many kinds of animals. In his writings *De Historia Animalium*, he provided an account of the development of the hen's egg. He compared reproductive methods of different animals and provided a classification. He concluded by observing the development of hen's egg that the development always proceeded from simple formless beginning to the complex organization of the adult. One of his earliest works saw the light of printing titled '*De Animalibus*' in Venice in 1476 (just after 20 years Johann Gutenberg invented printing with movable type). This new translation of the book from Greek into Latin was done by Theodore Gaza (AD 1400-1475).[1] The natural historians of Northern Europe saw many discrepancies and errors in Aristotle's works. They realized that Aristotle had only been aware of animals in the Mediterranean area. The travels to the New World and India had opened the scholars' eyes to the fact there were many more animals than were ever anticipated by the ancients in Europe and they demonstrated that new research agenda was the need of the hour and immediately required to be carried out.

Conrad Gessner (1515-1565) the Swiss published *Historiae Animalium* in 1551 and it is one of the first modern works that appeared on zoology.

This beautiful work which is highly illustrated with hand-colored woodcuts drawn from personal observations was published in Zurich. It had built a bridge between ancient, medieval, and modern science. Gessner chronicles data from old sources, such as the Old Testament, Aristotle and medieval bestiaries, and added his own observations, creating a new, comprehensive description of the animals. Following Aristotle's classification the first volume dealt with viviparous quadrupeds; the second volume with oviparous quadrupeds; the third with birds; and the fourth with aquatic animals. The animals were ordered alphabetically in each volume. The collection of the woodcuts grouped more systematically was issued as the *Icones animalium* (1553 and 1560) and the *Icones avium* (1550 and 1560). The fifth volume on serpents was published posthumously in 1587.[2] Ulisses Aldrovandi an Italian published (1522-1605) his works on natural history in 1599 and 1602 and it was a landmark.[3] Thus the sixteenth century saw the publication of illustrated printed books on the topics of animals and anatomy and these were significant in the scholarly and scientific study of nature. Further Jan Jonston (1603-1675) the Polish physician and naturalist published *Historia Naturalis* in seven volumes between 1650 and 1653. These included birds, fish and cetaceans, four-footed animals, insects, serpents and dragons.[4] All fauna in this encyclopaedic work had been divided into two categories of the sanguineous and the exsanguineous. Further these categories were divided into subcategories, the criteria of classification being mainly of ecological character—the habitat of a given animal and the food. Jonston's classification had surpassed the earlier classifications proposed by Aristotle, Conrad Gessner and Ulisses Aldrovandi.

In Europe a few individuals at that time regarded nature as a subject worthy of inquiry. The first museum of natural history was set up in Italy in 1550 with a massive influx of New World objects into Europe. There was transition that took place between the humanistic view of the world, and the scientific one. With the new and rare collections of Europe around the world, the items came to be roughly divided into three categories such as *naturalia, artificialia* and *scientifica* in the studies. The love of the marvelous and monstrous had been mixed the animal and the vegetable, and also the animal and the human. The items in the collection in Europe for both their scientific and aesthetic value had often been not clearly distinguished between useful objects and artistic ones. Though collections were a way of ordering the world the systems in use were largely visual and personal. Systems of scientific order were still in the formation around the turn of the seventeenth century.

Tamil coast in the age of expanding European commerce emerged as a site of natural history. The Europeans developed abiding interest in the marvels of nature. The curiosity about nature's best-kept secrets attracted them to engage in the study of the rare fauna of Tamil coast. Natural history encompassed collecting, describing and classifying the animals. The Europeans learnt that Tamils had many domestic animals for their own purposes and the people considered cow as a sacred animal. The Portuguese on the Tamil coast slaughtered oxen and cows for meat. The selling of oxen for the purpose of slaughter by the natives to Portuguese was prohibited in 1684 by the *nayak* ruler of Thanjavur. We find complaints lodged and registered against the Christians of Nagapattinam and Tharangambadi who indulged in the sale of animals for slaughter to the Portuguese.[5] The French in Pondicherry in February 1689 ordered the purchase of buffaloes in large numbers to be slaughtered for meat and salted for the requirements of their ships and crews. The Maratha ruler of Gingee who heard it therefore issued a strong disapproval related to cow and buffalo slaughter in Pondicherry. François Martin the agent of the French East India Company therefore found it expedient not to antagonize the regional authority.[6]

Nayaka rulers of Tamil country collected taxes on cattle. The revenue terms such as *nall erudhu*, *nar pasu* and *nar kidaa* suggest and imply the collection of taxes on good ox/bullock, good cow and good sheep and it increased the income to the state. The rates of taxation were not uniform throughout but varied from locality to locality. The *nayak* of Srimushnam levied and collected annually one-fourth *panam* per *pasu* (cow), half *panam* per *yerumai* (buffalo) and a quarter *panam* on eight *kidaa* (sheep) in the early sixteenth century. During the times of drought on the Tamil coast in 1540 ten large chickens were sold for a *panam* and in 1560 four chickens alone fetched a *panam*. The Portuguese had noted the escalation of prices in their records.[7] Europeans were in need of meat for the use of the crew in the ships on voyages. We find mention of Jean-Baptiste Tavernier who visited Santhome of Mylapore in August 1652 that the Portuguese Governor was kind enough to supply hams, ox and fish which were needed by the crew.[8] Abbe Carre the traveller also recorded that on his sailing from Madras to Surat when the ship stopped at Goa in December 1673 there came several boats filled with pigs, oxen, sheep and fowls and these got a ready sale from the ships.[9] Europeans needed mainly animals like sheep, goat, cow, buffalo and fowls for they ate meat.

Slaughtering the animals for meat provided forum for selling the skins. It is mentioned that buffalo and goat-skins were available in plenty at Santhome of Mylapore and the Portuguese exported it to Thailand. It was also exported to Japan by the Dutch East India Company since there was a good market for leather. The Dutch in Pulicat had obtained the buffalo and goat skins in the Mylapore area and exported 1511 pieces in the year 1635 alone. The native merchants had conducted extensive trade in goat-skins and exported on a large scale to Thailand. The Dutch who aimed to prevent the trade had not been very successful at all.[10] Tortoise shells, deer skins and tiger skins were also available for export on the Coromandel Coast. The servants of the Dutch East India Company exported 8882 tortoise shells from Devanampattinam to Jakarta in the year 1636. The Dutch in Pulicat in 1643 exported 30,000 to 40,000 pieces of goat-skins which they obtained from Santhome of Mylapore and exported to Japan.[11] The native merchants continued to export goat-skins to Thailand which also found way finally to Japan as late as 1654.[12]

Transporting Lesser Civet-Cats from Kedah to Pondicherry, 1639-40

Native merchants evinced interest in obtaining exotic animals. Kesava *chetti* the merchant and revenue-farmer of the port of Pondicherry conducted trade with South East Asia along with his son Lakshmana *chetti*.[13] He owned two ships and these vessels had sailed in 1639 to Kedah and Aceh. The ship from Kedah returned to Pondicherry in March 1640 laden with 17 lesser civet-cats (called *punugu punai* in Tamil, *Viverra malaccensis*) which were highly valued in Tamil country (besides two elephants and one horse).[14] On 25 March 1640 a large ship of the Sultan of Kedah also arrived Pondicherry with 25 lesser civet-cats (besides five elephants).[15] Thus civet-cat the small and slender carnivorous mammal had been in demand and so transported from South East Asia to Tamil coast. It is important and necessary to explain why civet-cats had been imported. Civet, a scented glandular secretion extracted from the anal glands was one of the most expensive materials utilized by apothecaries and perfumers in Tamil country. It had been also used to scent linen, pomades and handkerchiefs in addition to its wider use as a principal ingredient in perfumes. It had been normally mixed with floral scents like violet besides used as an ingredient in scented confectionary.

In Europe, civet was in high demand and the price quoted was high. We come to know that for 40 shillings (two pounds) an ounce the smallest quantities of civet were measured in miniscule grains at two pence a grain. The apothecary manuals list the number of grains required to manufacture individual concoctions by giving an indication of the relative expense of the treatment. Civet had been applied as a balsam and tincture. It was used by apothecaries and physicians as an aphrodisiac in treatment for sexual and hysteric disorders.[16] English records mention that it was used in the treatment for erectile dysfunction with 25 grains of civet (four shillings) for a single dose in England.[17] Civet taken in the form of ten grains (two shillings) in a refreshing balsam aided women who had debilitated themselves greatly in curing vices and diseases.[18] Thus the hot, moist, and anodyne qualities of civet made it a good Galenic humorial treatment for reviving the spirits, warming the stomach, relieving cholic in infants, guarding against pestilential disease and preventing suffocation of the womb.

Strange Animals Mentioned by Louis Le Comte from Pondicherry, 1690

Louis Le Comte (1655-1728) the French Jesuit reached China on 7 February 1688. He travelled via Pondicherry and returned to France in 1691. During his stay in the French settlement he noticed several strange animals which were new to him. He had given a wonderful account of a chameleon. The description was later printed in Paris in 1696. It had evinced much interest in France at that time. According to Louis Le Comte the chameleon was a kind of lizard and its size had been between eight and ten inches in length. There were many of them commonly found on the Coromandel Coast. The Jesuits in Pondicherry had bred them at their residence for experimental purpose. Le Comte said that the chameleons did not live upon air alone, as some naturalists had written, for they ate and that too very greedily. It is true indeed, that being of a very cold and moist temper, they could pass several days without aliment, but at the long run, if they were given no food they dwindle away by degrees, and at last died for hunger. Upon the whole, everything was very odd in the chameleon, had been that its eyes, head, belly, were exceedingly big. It had four parts, as a lizard. Yet had been so very slow in all its motions, that crawled rather than going; and it was the nature which had not bestowed upon it a tongue of a particular contexture, it could never catch the animals, in which does consist its nourishment. This tongue was round, thick, and at least a foot in length, it darted this tongue seven or eight inches out of its mouth with a marvelous flight. Now the substance of it was so viscous, that it detained flies, grasshoppers, and other such like insects, if it touched them but never so lightly with its tip. Its body was covered all over with a very fine skin, but was of a changeable colour, according to the various passions that agitate it. In joy, it was of an emerald green mixed with orange, etched with little grey and black strokes. Choler makes it dusky and livid; fear pale, and of a faded yellow; by times, all these colours and many more were confounded together, and at times there was composed such a pretty medly of shade and light, that nature does not afford a finer variety of shadowing, nor our finest pictures more lively, sweet, and proportional drawing.[19]

The Jesuits in Pondicherry had also exhibited two more little known animals in Europe to Louis Le Comte. One was called *Chien marron* (Tamil name untraceable) that took after the dog, wolf, and fox almost equally. It was of an indifferent bigness, the hair was grey and reddish. It had short tapered ears, the snout sharp, the leg high, a long tail, a body slender and well shaped. It did not bark like dogs, but cried just as infants did. In a word, it was naturally voracious, and when hunger pinched the animal, it entered into houses in the night, and fell upon people. The next animal was the mongoose (*keeripillai* in Tamil) which, as to its exterior shape, came very near the mammal weezel, except only that its body was longer and bigger, the legs shorter, the snout slenderer, the eye quicker, and somewhat less wild. This animal really was very familiar, and there was no dog that played and fawned more prettily with a man than this creature. Nevertheless it became angry and not to be trusted when it ate, always snarling at that time, and fell furiously upon those who would be troubling it. It loved eggs of the hens more than anything; but because its chaps were not wide enough to seize on them. It strived to break them by throwing them aloft, or by rolling them an hundred ways upon the ground. But if there chance to be a stone in its way, it lied upon it with its face downward, and striding with its hinder legs, it took the egg in its fore legs, and thrusted it with all its might under its belly till it was broken against the stone. It did not only hunt rats and mice, but serpents, of whom it was a mortal enemy, which it took by the head so cunningly, that it received no hurt by it. It was at no less enmity with chameleons, which at the very fight of it were seized with so mortal a fear, that they became immediately as flat as a flounder, and fell down half dead; whereas at the approach of a cat, or dog, or some other more terrible animal, they swell, were enraged, and betook themselves either to their own defence or to assault them.[20]

Rare Animals Mentioned by Giovannio Borghesi from Pondicherry, 1703

Giovannio Borghesi the Italian physician arrived in Pondicherry on 6 November 1703 and remained till February 1704. He had mentioned that there were many types of new animals found in Pondicherry which were not seen in Europe. He stated Asian palm civet (*mara naay* in Tamil) which was similar to the family of wolf. According to him it was a new animal and a second type of dog but different. The picture of *mara naay* drawn by Borghesi had been printed in a publication from Rome in 1705.[21]

Borghesi also mentioned that he had come across another animal a curious one which was so small but could kill an elephant of the large size. He stated that this animal resembled somewhat like a large lizard, except the head and tail, which were alike as to shape, being both pointed. This is the Indian pangolin called *udumbu* in Tamil (*Varanus bengalensis*). Borghesi also said that he had seen another curious animal (the two banded monitor) which moved in a straight line. Hence he had drawn the pictures in both style and these pictures appeared in print in Rome in 1705.[22]

Alangu the Indian Pangolin (*Manis crassicaudata*) and the Two-banded Monitor Known to the Dutch in Holland, 1703-4

The above mentioned two animals noticed by Borghesi had also come to the knowledge of the Dutch in Holland and we find additional details interestingly. An announcement was made to all gentlemen, merchants and inhabitants of the city of Amsterdam that there was the coming of the ships returning from the East Indies, and an East Indiaman who on the island of Ceylon in the year 1702 had caught a certain animal, with four feet, and its body covered with very thick scales. It was in Tamil language named *Allegoe* (*Alangu*), in Portuguese *Bitje de Bengonje*, and in Dutch the *Nigomsen Duyvel*. After it had been kept alive by him for eight days without food or drink, he had the animal in question killed, since it was only inclined to be evil. When it had been put in irons chained to its body, the aforesaid animal during the night had dug through the stone floor and caused damage to the foundations of a substantial building. The animal could control with its tail, the biggest elephants (which were numerous on the island of Ceylon), wrung them round the tusk and clenches so steadfastly, that the elephant with its immense strength could not shake it off, until the elephant walked into the water, where it would automatically loosen itself, since it could not endure water. The animal ate nothing but ants, which in the woods were abundant, using its tongue, as long as half a (Dutch) ell, spreading it wide on the ground. When the ants swarmed over it, drew it in slowly; what else it ate was unknown. Its meat was similar to pork, fit for human consumption in its entirety quite palatable, and was medicinal. Many natives had been killed by such a Nigoms' Devil, not by its bite, for it possessed no teeth. When the natives had caught the beast and carried it over their shoulders, it put his tail round the neck, and wrung it so tightly, that one could not free oneself, and was squeezed to death, just like some snakes, called wringers which were found, could strangle. If there was more to tell about this beast or its strength, it was not known, but the account given had been declared to be nothing but the truth, and so the animal had been exhibited in Amsterdam and to the people of all over Europe.[23]

Further, it has been reported that there was another lower living animal, the two-banded monitor, brought in the ship sailing to Holland from Ceylon and it was called *Campergoo* in Tamil. It was with four feet, belonging to the same genus as crocodiles or caimen, which was why the Indians, like the aforesaid crocodiles, worshipped them as their idols, but they do not do any harm. The crocodiles seem to be Indian gavlals (*Gavialls gangeticus*, Gmelin, 1789), as this gavlal was dedicated to the god Vishnu and therefore considered sacred. True, the spiny tail of the animal seems crocodilian, roundish head and the forked tongue point to a Varanus only. The Velten album helps us out to know that this was the awesome two-banded monitor (*Varanus salvator*, Laurent, 1768) whose habitat was water (just like the Indian gavial), which might reach a total length of almost 3 metres (9 feet). The species was known to be easily tamed in captivity, which was in keeping with the above statement that it was harmless; this could be said of the gavial, which belonged to the crocodile family.[24]

The Long-Tailed Squirrel Known to John Ray and Johann Friedrich Gmelin in Europe

The Protestant missionaries in Tranquebar in 1714 desired to know the different types of living creatures as known to the Tamils. Hence they enquired the details from the natives and received a favourable reply. It has been said that according to Tamils there lived 8,400,000 kinds of creatures in this world and they were different from one another and these were divided according to their genus and species. There were 1,100,000 kinds of creeping worms, 3,000,000 kinds of four-footed animals ranging from elephants to ants and 900,000 types of fish both in the rivers and seas.[25] Though the number of animals had been exceedingly fanciful there was an urgent need felt by them for an in depth investigation of the fauna of the Tamil coast.

John Ray (1627-1705) in 1701 and Johann Friedrich Gmelin (1748-1804) in 1789 in Europe came to know of the long tailed squirrel species (*anil* in Tamil, *Sciurus macrourtts*) which was found in Tamil country and Sri Lanka. They got the news from the servants of the East India Companies who returned to Europe. It had been reported that the squirrel was different and it was about three times the size of the European squirrel. The ears were tufted with black hairs and the end of the nose was pink-coloured. The cheeks, legs, and belly, were of a dull yellow and between the ears was a yellow spot. The crown of the head, and the back, were black and from each ear was a bifurcated line of the same color, pointing down the cheeks. The upper part of the feet was covered with black hairs and the lower part naked and red. The tail was nearly twice the length of the body, and it had been of a light am-color, and extremely bushy. The part next the body quite surrounded with hairs and on the remainder the hairs were separated, and lied flat.[26] However Malabar squirrel (*Ratufa indica*) later noticed and illustrated in colour by E. Barton in 1804-05 widely came to be known the British audience.[27]

The Wild Fox Noticed by Nikolaus Dal in Tranquebar, 1733-36

Nikolaus Dal (1690-1747) the Protestant missionary in Tranquebar wrote on *kaatu kuzhla nari* (wild fox) in his report on 17 February 1736. He mentioned that three years ago (in 1733) in Poraiyar a village situated in the environs of Tranquebar a wild fox had taken away the five years old baby whom the mother had placed in a cradle near the door of her house and went inside for eating. The fox had taken away the child and the mother was at loss to know what happened to her child. On the next morning she found the traces of blood and the bones of her child, which the animal had killed and eaten. Some of the bones were found hidden in the earth and she found some flesh in a thrown away vessel.[28] The missionary pointed out how dreadful the wild foxes were and doing harm to the people in the area.

The Wild Fox, Jackal and Fox Described by Johann Philipp Fabricius in Madras, 1756

Johann Philipp Fabricius the Protestant missionary arrived at Tranquebar in 1740 but two years later he entered into the service of the English East India Company as a missionary and moved over to Madras in 1743. He wrote in 1756 on wild fox. He said that he heard from the locals that a carpenter who went alone on a journey from Nagapattinam to some place was suddenly surrounded by a crowd of wild foxes. The carpenter though was brave enough to attack and kill some wild foxes by his axe, he could not escape because the other wild foxes had attacked and they tore him into pieces. The people of the locality on the next morning had found the bones of the carpenter. It evident thus that wild animals attacked people during the road travel which was not safe always but were dangerous. Fabricius also wrote on *nari* (jackal, *Canis aureus*) and *kuzhla nari* (fox). He stated that jackals and foxes were normally found in plenty around the area of Madras. During the nights they made a great noise around the walls of the town.[29]

The Wild Cat Sent by Robert Clive from Madras to the Duke of Cumberland in London and its Description, 1759-60

James Parsons in London at the request of the Reverend Dr Littleton, the Dean of Exeter, went to observe the wild cat called *verugu* in Tamil (*Felis chaus*) kept in 1760 in the tower of London sent by Robert Clive in Madras to His Royal Highness the Duke of Cumberland. He said that in order to find what class of animals the wild cat belonged to he made the drawing, and placed it before the Royal Society of London for its inspection. James Parsons said that he had endeavoured to make it as accurate as possible in all its proportion; yet he was afraid that he had made the ears a small matter too long. There was a figure of the wild cat in the London Magazine for December 1759, which had no resemblance at all to it, except in the ears, which the engraver, who drew it, had made to turn forwards, contrary to nature. However, the following description would James Parsons believed, would be the proper account of it.[30]

He stated that the wild cat was something taller than the largest sized cat being about fifteen inches high at the shoulders; slender and light, though strong. The head was small in proportion to the rest and the neck slender. It had nothing fierce in its aspect, but was mild, and very tame. It was exactly of a fawn-colour having its ears black on their outsides, and lined with white hairs, and some white round the root of each ear; it was also white under the throat and belly, and a little so on the backs of its limbs. Its eyes were small, and its head like that of a cat, but somewhat slenderer; its legs were gentle and straight, with the paws of a cat, had the power of dilating and contracting its toes, which were armed with strong nails, in the same manner as a cat or tiger did; and its actions were like those of a cat. James Parsons sat and watched its motions, and saw licking its foot, and rubbed it over its face several times, exactly like a cat; and was told by the man who showed it to him, that, if it was offended, it hissed. James Parsons had examined its teeth, and found them in the same number and manner with those of a cat. And as to its food, they gave raw mutton every day; and when it was sick which it often was, they gave it a live fowl, or rabbit, which it seized eagerly, and lied upon it without motion, for a considerable time, to suck the blood, and this proved a certain cure. The figure of the animal showed it to have also a tail like that of a cat.

James Parsons added that none of the natural historians had any account of this animal, that he had seen, except the learned Dr Walter Charleton (in his *Exercitationes de Differentiis et Nominibus animalium*) who had a bad figure of it engraved at the expense of Dr John Lawson, his contemporary at the royal college of the physicians, as it appeared in an inscription at the bottom of the plate, wherein the head was, contrary to truth, very large and strong in appearance, the tail like that of a fox, and the whole as strong as a mastiff dog; the name given it in the plate was the same with this, but differently spelled, thus *Siyah-ghush*. He had very justly ranked it among the cats, and had given such an account of the animal, as well deserved the notice of the Royal Society of London, of which James Parsons had made the following extract.

Among the wild cats, which varied according to the difference of climate, manner of living, and the like, none was more worthy of notice than that which had been kept in the park of king Charles II. It was sent to the king by an English gentleman, who was the governor of Surat, and the animal was called, among other names, in the Persian language, *Siyah-ghush*, referring to black-ear, also known all along the Coromandel Coast. It was about the size of a fox, but like a cat in its form; and had the cunning and cruelty of a leopard, with the limbs of a cat, but longer and stronger; having so much strength, that James Parsons saw it kill a hound that came in its way, in a moment. The legs were thick with hair, and its nails concealed under them, which were never extended but upon seizing its prey, which was common to lions, panthers, and domestic cats. But what seems peculiar to this animal was, that, having jumped upon his prey, he lied upon it unmoved, holding his bite, as if he was dead, whether for joy, or in order to drink the blood of the creature. The people in India had them bred up tame, because of their dexterity in catching birds, hares, rabbits, and such like; and such was their craft and fierceness, that they would seize even a fox; but their keepers would not suffer them to attack anything above their strength, and therefore they only set them at cranes, geese, ducks, pheasants, partridges, peacocks, and such-like game, which they seized by many kinds of deceit, to the great pleasure of the spectators; and caught those timid animals, the hare, rabbit, fawn, goat, etc., by swift running, and sometimes by craft. When they were sick (from over-gorging their stomach they often were) their keepers steeped a piece of tender meat in human urine, and fed them with it, and being bruised or tired by over-hunting, they gave them some mummy, wrapped up in their meat, and a warm place to rest in till they recovered. It is said that this wild cat, followed the lion at a distance, in order to feed on what he left of the animals he destroyed. James Parsons said that he was inclined to rank the wild cat among the cats; and joined with Carl Linnaeus, who, in his *Ordo Secundo* had a fifth species of *Felis*, which agreed well with the principal characters of the wild cat.[31] Thus we come to know that strange animals like wild cat had come to be transported by the English from Madras to London.

The Types of Dogs and the Native Treatment to Mad Dog-bites Noticed by the European Missionaries, 1756-1792

Europeans have noticed the *naay* (dog), *kaaval naay* (mastiff) and *vettai naay* (hound) in Tamil country. It is reported that Tirumalai Nayak who shifted his capital from Madurai to Tiruchirapalli found the dogs as a menace for barking at all times in the city. Hence he ordered in 1666 the slaughter of all the dogs in Tiruchirapalli owing to the heavy disturbance in the night.[32] This gave occasion for the people to say that even dogs could not live peacefully under his rule.

Treatment to mad dog-bites had been observed by the missionaries in Tamil Country. Jean-Baptiste du Choiseul, the Jesuit apothecary in the dispensary of Pondicherry, studied Tamil medicine on poisonous bites. He wrote a treatise in French entitled 'New, Sure, Short and Easy Method of Treating Persons Affected by Rabies' which was published in Paris in 1756.[33] Thus, we see that the French on the Tamil coast had learnt about the native medicines for treating poisonous bites, and took steps to preserve the medical heritage of the Tamils and also disseminated the knowledge to France.

Christoph Samuel John the Protestant missionary in Tranquebar wrote to the missionaries in Halle vide his letter dated 6 May 1792 mentioning the medical prescription against the bite of a mad dog that consisted of five local ingredients which he considered a rare medical formula. He said that a paste made of the five ingredients was fed to a dying chronic rabies patient. It saved the patient from death.[34]

Description of Tree-Cat by Johann Christian Wiedebrock and Johann Balthasar Kohlhoff in Tranquebar, 1763

Johann Christian Wiedebrock and Johann Balthasar Kohlhoff the two missionaries in Tranquebar wrote about a special kind of an animal the common tree-cat (*Paradoxurus musanga*, known as toddy-cat of the Europeans in Madras). They literally translated from Tamil name of the animal *mara naai* and called it a tree-dog and further mentioned also as *Baum Hund* in German in their report dated 29 July 1763. They neatly mentioned that the animal was medium size of a dog but looked more like a cat. The mouth was long and in black-brown colour. It had two black stripes on its back. The ears were small and pointed. In its feet it had claws with which it climbed the tree like a cat. It climbed the coconuts trees and ate the coconuts and it also drank the juice from the toddy pots, which were tied in the coconut trees to collect juice. When it tried to do it, the animal pushed the pots which fell down and broke. The missionaries in their report also provided information on the native profession of the toddy extraction from the palmyra trees. They said that the toddy extractors tied up the earthen pots beneath the pods of these trees and by certain indigenous technical process, made the juice of the palm into toddy liquor. The toddy collected was sold to the native village men who drank it. These tree-cats climbed such tall palm trees to eat away the palm fruits and destroyed these toddy pots and thus spilled the toddy causing immense loss to the toddy extractors.[35]

A Report on Udumbu by Johann Christian Wiedebrock in Tranquebar, 1765-1770

Johann Christian Wiedebrock in his missionary report dated 15 October 1765 wrote about *udumbu* in Tamil (*Varanus bengalensis*). He said that the animal was a special kind found in Tranquebar known as *iguana* and also called *Alangu* by the Tamils. In Poraiyar a village situated in the environs of Tranquebar this rare and strange animal was seen on the wall of the house of an oil merchant. The people had killed it with great difficulty. When the people had beaten the animal, it curved and caused sparks of fire. It could not be killed till an iron rod was pierced into its stomach. The strangest thing was that it had such a power that it could kill even an elephant. It curved around the elephant and pressed the trunk in such a way that the elephant died. Wiedebrock mentioned that *udumbu* lived in deep valleys and it was very rare to be seen. Even several of the oldest people in Tranquebar reported that they had never seen it.[36]

Johann Christian Wiedebrock stated that *udumbu* resembled somewhat like a large lizard, except the head and tail, which were alike as to shape, being both pointed, the former was not unlike a mole's. The whole length was one German ell and five eighths long, and its breadth half an ell. The tail was half an ell long, and its broadest part was a span wide. The fore-feet were a quarter of an ell long, the hind-feet a little longer. The snout was an eighth of an ell long, and the extremity of it a thumb in thickness. The whole body, excepting under the belly (where it was smooth for about the length and breadth of a man's hand) and under the feet was covered with hard, strong, sharp, and bright scales, shaped like a muscle-shell, the largest of which were of the length and breadth of three fingers. Under its scale there came out two or three hairs like hog's bristles. On its fore-claws were five strong long nails, on the hind-claws but four. When pursued, it rolled itself so together, that nothing but the back and tail were to be seen.

It is gleaned from the description of the animal that there were two known species in Europe by 1770. Of these one of them was covered with hair, the other with scales. The first was called *Myrmecophaga* and the other was known *Manis*. Linnaeus in his 12th edition of *Systema Naturae* had mentioned. The first type of the animal had five toes (*Manis pentadactyla*) the other four (*Manis tetradadlyla*). Between these two sorts, the present *udumbu* was then placed, having from the first the fore-feet and from the latter the hind-feet. This animal belonged therefore to the family of ant-catchers, which had no teeth, but had a long and round tongue, with which they caught the ants. Whether the tail of this animal was eaten as asserted by Mr Dame had not been able to be confirmed and found out at that time.[37]

Christian Pohle and his Notices on Mongoose in Tranquebar, 1784

Christian Pohle the missionary of Tranquebar in his report dated 16 November 1784 wrote about mongoose (*keeripillai* in Tamil) which he observed. He said that he had often heard about the mongoose and sometimes saw a wild one outside. He stated that he had purchased a tamed one and it was a small animal with four legs, a little bit bigger than a squirrel. Its head was like a fox and with grey, black and white hairs and a long tail. During day-time it caught rats, mice, birds, frogs, and snakes. It was also said that mongoose was a dangerous animal for it was fond of chicken. The missionary said that he fed his mongoose with raw meat and sweet milk. It was also fond of sugar-candy. This mongoose also made small holes into the earth and ate worms.[38]

Christian Pohle also added that he had made an experiment to know whether the mongoose could eat a snake. At first it pretended as if it wanted to play with the snake but then it caught the snake with the neck and shook it very fast so that the snake could not bite. The hair of the mongoose became erect and it growled. All tameness had gone away. It was said by people in Tranquebar that the mongoose attacked big poisonous snakes. In case if the snake had bitten it ate a special grass as anti-poison and attacked the snake again. This grass, it was said by people, that it remained a secret. If this special grass had been known to people it could be used to heal the snakebites.[39]

Christoph Samuel John and His Study on Rats and Peruchaali Communicated from Tranquebar to Prof. J.R. Forster in Germany, 1793

Christoph Samuel John wrote his observations on the rats and *peruchalli* to Professor J.R. Forster in Germany. In his letter he said that the ordinary rats in Tranquebar were not different from the European ones and they did great damage in the fields, gardens and paddy granaries. The cats here associate more with the rats by eating meat and they did not catch them. Many of the house-dogs were better in catching the rats. The rat-catchers (called *irulars* in Tamil) had special skills and so they caught them in a large number. Such a rat-catcher was rented always for days and nights in Tamil country. The rat-catcher sat with a small lamp in front of the hole, which he enlarged so that he can put a hollow bamboo stick into that hole. He then put a small stick with *karuvaadu* (a piece of dry fish) as the bait in the hollow of the bamboo stick and he waited till the stick moved and caught the rat. Within a day a rat-catcher had caught 160 rats in the storeroom of missionaries from which the catcher prepared himself a nice meal with some rats and he sold the rest of the rats to others. It is said that among the rats there were also some dangerous ones and their bites had terrible consequences.[40] C.S. John said that he was shocked to see that after a rat-bite a Christian had suffered from painful breathing trouble for several months and finally he died. The missionary said that he had not personally seen this type of dangerous rats. He added that in the region extending from Chidambaram to Pulicat there were terrible big rats which were of enormous size three to four times bigger than the ordinary ones. They caused a lot of damage and they were called *peruchaali* in Tamil.[41]

Types of Monkey Mentioned by Christoph Samuel John in Tranquebar, 1795

C. S, John had mentioned the different kinds of *kurangu* (monkey) in 1795. He described that baboon was a kind of monkey and it had extremely small brown eyes compared to its relatives, a long face. The fingers and nails were like those of the human beings, and it consumed coconuts and local fruits.[42] The missionary also said that there was another type called *karu mandhi* (black monkey-The Indian hooded leaf monkey, *Semnopithecus Trachypithecus*) which was different from the other monkeys.[43]

Collecting Animals by Serfoji II in Thanjavur, 1805-1827: The European Impact

Serfoji II the ruler of Thanjavur (1777-1832) took interest in the purchase of animals. Ashton the English company official procured fine specimens of dogs for the Raja. Dogs were also procured from Ettappa Nayak the *paalayakaarar* of Ettayapuram.[44] In 1805 Serfoji had an English dog of a good breed.[45] Elephants and monkeys were brought from Sri Lanka to Thanjavur.[46] Nagoji Sahoji the *havildar* of Thanjavur was sent to Madras so that he could purchase the animals like the foreign fox and Chinese hen that had then arrived in the European ships.[47]

A beautiful leopard (*siruththai puli* in Tamil, *Acionyx jubata*) was given as present by William Blackburn the British resident.[48] One young leopard was given by Fyfe another British resident.[49] C.S John the missionary in Tranquebar sent a large Cockatoo and a fine feathered Lury. He also gave the animal drawings done excellently by Kiruba Samuthiram the Tamil painter employed by him.[50] Vijaya Raghunatha Thondaiman the ruler of Pudukottai (1789-1807) presented Serfoji a sambar deer (*kalaimaan* in Tamil, *Cervus unicolor*).[51] Wild animals like tigers, leopards and bears were captured from the forests of Thanjavur. Tigers were a major attraction in the royal menagerie.[52] C.S. John in his diary had mentioned that a captured antelope was found in the palace mangerie.[53] Thus the palace menagerie in Thanjavur was filled with rare birds and animals.

Horses were bought by Serfoji from distant places like Male.[54] August Frederick Cammerer (1767-1837) the Protestant missionary in Tranquebar in 1811 sold his horse of Aceh to Serfoji for 25 *pagodas*.[55] Benjamin Torin the English Resident of Thanjavur purchased a horse for Serfoji from Europe a very beautiful one.[56] Narasinga Rao in 1820 had purchased horses and camels from North India for Serfoji.[57] A foreign horse was purchased in 1827 from Dr Nalig for a huge sum of 3000 *pagodas*.[58] The English Governor in Madras sold one fine horse from Europe and another from Arabia a very superior and rare variety for a sum of 3000 *pagodas* to Serfoji.[59]

Album Containing the Drawings and Paintings of Animals and the Artists Employed by Serfoji in Thanjavur

An artist (*moochy*) of Serfoji II is mentioned by Christian Pohle the missionary of Tranquebar in his letter to Halle in 1802. There had been also mention of another artist Kuppan Siddhar who had illustrated the animals and insects and he was employed by the king till his death in 1810.[60]

Serfoji's album contains fine drawings of spiders and frogs.[61] The green frog in the album was well described and it had been stated that it served as medicine. The witch craftsmen had very much used it. The album has drawings of crustaceans like crabs and tiger prawns, squids, jelly fish and sea worms.[62] There were also many kinds of shells and one shell has been described as of great curiosity.[63] The drawings were finally gifted to Benjamin Torin the English resident of Thanjavur who had presented them to the English East India Company in 1807.[64]

The Description of the Animals in the Album

Tiger had been illustrated and well described in the album. It is written that tiger had more strength than all the animals and its nature without provocation was fierceness and cruel. No mercy was to be expected from this animal which in its indiscriminate fury tore into pieces every animal that it met with. The tiger in Mysore or on the west part of the country was nine feet long from his snout to the tail and five and a half feet height. But the tiger drawn in this picture was got in the eastern part of the country. Its size was eight feet long from snout to the tail and four feet in height and it had been brought when it was young and continually confined in a strongest wooden cage.[65] C.S. John the missionary of Tranquebar who saw the tiger in the palace had also described in his letter sent to Germany.[66] of all the animal descriptions the lengthiest had been that of the royal tiger. The animal caught the deer the young kind of this animal would severe very soon to chase but old one would take up two years to practice for hunting. The male and the female of this kind were exact in hunting.[67]

It has been stated that the animal called *Siyah-ghush* had two colours both white and red. It seemed an elegant rough and short hairs the size of which was little bigger than a fox. But very fierce this animal was as well as a bird called bauze and horse of Kutch country were qualified to serve for many examples in the history of Muslims. This name of *Siyah-ghush* had derived by that elongated ears with hairs. This animal's food was the flesh of the sheep, birds and milk. The Nawab of Arcot was fond of rearing this animal.[68]

Kaatu Yerumai in Tamil (*Gavaeus Gaurus*, wild ox) had been described and it is said that the animal was from the forest of Putticandoo in Thanjavur kingdom. This beast was naturally wild and they are very cautious to keep themselves away from men. They never live long after they were taken from their forest. The drawing made of the animal was from the forest upon the sea not far from Vedaranyam. It was young and not fully grown and brought from the forest. The fleshy ball grown over the skull or between its horns was ½ feet in height and height of the animal was five feet and the length was six feet.[69]

Thomas Caverhill Jerdon and Walter Elliot in Madras: The Study on Lemur, Hog, Bear and the Tiger Described, 1845-48

Thomas Caverhill Jerdon (1811-1872) the assistant surgeon of the Madras establishment of the English East India Company and Walter Elliot in Madras evinced interest in the study of mammals found in Tamil country. They wrote the details for the audience in London. It is mentioned that the lemur (called *Thevangu* in Tamil) had been of a grayish rufescent colour above and beneath, but paler; a white triangular spot on the forehead extending down the nose fur was short, dense and soft; ears, thin, rounded. The length of one lemur was about eight inches, arm five inches; leg five inches. Jerdon said that this curious little animal was found in the forests but difficult to find owing to its small size and nocturnal habits. It had generally escaped the observation of the European travellers. Lemur that had been very abundant in the forests was brought alive in large numbers to the market in Madras. It is said that their eyes had been highly esteemed remedy for certain diseases of the eyes among the Tamil doctors. Jerdon said that he had purchased and kept several lemurs very safely which made their escape one night from his house in Fort St. George in 1845. He found them later along the windows, balcony and roofs in some of the public offices in the neighbourhood.[70]

It is reported that *kaatu panri* in Tamil (*Erinaceus micropus*, the south Indian hedge-hog) had its ears moderately large; form somewhat elongated; tail very short, concealed; muzzle rather sharp; feet and limbs very small;

head and ears nude, sooty colour; belly very thinly clad with yellowish hairs; spines ringed dark-brown and whitish, or whitish with a broad brown subterminal ring, tipped white. This hedge-hog was found at Madras and Nilgiris. Many years ago Jerdon had procured one live *kaatu panri* at Tiruchirapalli which he gave to Walter Elliot. The reason was to make Elliot believe that this specimen was the supposed *Erinaceus cottaris* sent earlier from Madras and kept in the India Museum established in London in 1801. Jerdon could never succeed to get another specimen from the Carnatic. He later managed to obtain a hedge-dog from the Nilgiris.[71]

Karadi in Tamil (*Ursus labiatus*, the Indian black bear) was said to be black, hair very long and shaggy; muzzle and tip of feet dirty white or yellowish; a white crescentic, or V shaped mark was found on the breast. This animal was found common from Cape Comorin to the Ganges, chiefly in the hills and jungles. The bear never had more than four incisors in the upper jaw.[72]

Puli in Tamil (*Felis tigris,* the tiger) was mentioned with bright fawn-colour, more or less tinged with rufous, and with dark stripes. The peculiarly striped skin of the tiger at once distinguished it from every other feline animal, and equally so does the intensity of the bright rufous ground hue, so exquisitely set off with white about the head. Again unless the lion, no other cat approached it in the massive proportions of the fore paw, as compared with the hind. Some of both sexes were made more heavily than others, with a greater development of the fold of skin along the belly, which added to their apparent bulk. The stripes of the tiger too varied much in different individuals, and occasionally were almost throughout double. The animal was found common from Cape Comorin to the Himalayas ascending the hills occasionally to an elevation of 6,000 or 7,000 feet. It was found in all forests and jungles occasionally visiting the more open and cultivated areas and harbouring in thickets especially in brushwood on river-banks.[73]

Marten, Wild Goat and the Wild Ox Noticed by Colonel Walter Campbell and T.C. Jerdon

The Indian marten (*Martes flavigula*) had its whole upper parts, with the body from the breast, and limbs, glossy blackish-brown, the chin and lower lip white; throat and breast yellow, more or less deep, and inclining to orange yellow, or yellowish-brown in some. The body was at times dirty brownish or chestnut brown, or mixed brown with gray, and the middle of the back was sometimes paler than the rest, or the same tint as the sides of the body. In some, the top of the head was pale brown, but it was edged by a dark peripheral line; and in others, there were one or more irregular dark spots between the forelimbs; soles nude. The length of the head and body was about twenty inches; tail about twelve inches with the hair. This marten was found on the Nilgiri hills. It was also very destructive to poultry.[74]

The Nilgiris wild goat (*Hemitragus hylocrius*) especially the adult male animal was of dark sepia-brown, with a pale reddish-brown saddle, more or less marked, and paler brown on the sides and beneath; legs somewhat grizzled with white, dark brown in front and paler at posterior. The head was dark, grizzled with yellowish-brown, and the eye was surrounded by a pale fawn-coloured spot. Horns short, much curved, nearly in contact at the base, gradually diverging; strongly keeled internally, round externally, with numerous close rings. There was a large callous spot on the knees surrounded by a fringe of hair, and the male had a short stiff mane on the neck and withers. The hair was short, thick, and coarse. Colonel W. Campbell the English company official stated that it was called the Chamois by the hunters of Madras. It was also called Ibex by the hunters in Madras. The animal had been largely found on the Nilgiris and neighbouring hills, extending south along the Western Ghats up to Cape Comorin.[75] Mr Gray the English company official gave a specific name and it precipice goat and it was the Tamil word for rock. Jerdon in an occasion saw about twenty wild goats in a flock but generally they move about not more than six or seven in a company. With the large herds there was almost always one very large old male, conspicuous by his nearly black colour. If alarmed or followed, the wild goats rush rapidly downhill, and were lost to sight among the inequalities of the ground, or go straight down to the hilly country at the foot of the slopes. Now and then they took shelter in woods, through which they would freely pass. The wild goats are very wary animals. They were so much hunted within the limited extent of the Nilgiris. The wild goats were also found in the highlands of Madurai and the neighbouring Palani hills. Jerdon mentioned that he long ago heard of the Nilgiri Ibex that had been killed near Dindigul and Madurai.[76]

Wild ox (*Kaatu Yerumai* in Tamil, *Gavaeus Gaurus*), the bison of hunters in Madras had the horns pale greenish with black tips, curving outwards, upwards, and slightly backwards, and finally inwards. The general colour was dark chestnut brown or coffee-brown; legs from the knee downwards white. Colonel Walter Campbell stated that Madras hunters called this animal a wild bull, and not a bison, for which he rebuked them.[77] Jerdon had always heard it called the bison, but in reality the name wild bull would be much more correctly applied to it. It was found in the Palani and Dindigul hills, the Sendamangalam range and the Shervaroy hills. The animal was particularly fond of the *avari kodi* when in blossom; that they would invade and destroy the fields of it in open day light in despite of any resistance the villagers could offer. In other respects the *kaatu yerumai* was a very inoffensive animal, rarely attacking any one it encountered, except in the case of a single bull driven from the herd.[78]

Description of the Jackal and the Squirrel by T.C. Jerdon

Nari in Tamil (the jackal, *Canis aureus*) had the fur of a dusky yellowish or rufous gray, the hairs being mottled black, gray, and brown, with the under fur brownish-yellow; lower parts yellowish-gray; tail reddish-brown, ending in a darkish tuft; more or less rufous on the muzzle and limbs; tail moderately hairy. The length from head to body, was around twenty-eight to thirty inches; the tail was ten or eleven inches and the height was about sixteen or seventeen inches. It was a very useful scavenger, clearing away all garbage and carrion from the neighbourhood of large towns, but occasionally committing depredations among poultry and other domestic animals. Sickly sheep and goats usually fall a prey to jackal and a wounded antelope was pretty certain to be tracked and hunted to death.[79]

The Malabar squirrel (*Sciurus malabaricus*) had ears, nape, back of neck, the back and sides of the body, bright maroon-chestnut; the posterior part of the back, rump, and upper portion of all the limbs, and the tail, black; forehead and interocular regions brownish; muzzle and cheeks rufous; neck, breast, and lower parts dingy-yellow; feet rufous in front, yellow internally; ears small, rounded, very hairy. The length from head to body was sixteen to eighteen inches; tail was with the hair twenty to twenty-one inches. The animal was found mainly on the slopes of the Nilgiris.[80]

The Three Types of Monkeys Reported

The Madras langur (*Presbytis primaus*) had been ashy, gray colour with a pale reddish or chocolate tint overlying the whole back and head; sides of the head, chin, throat, and beneath, pale yellowish, hands and feet, whitish, face, palms and fingers, and soles of the feet and toes, black; a high compressed vertical crest of hairs on the top of the head; hairs long and straight, not wavy, tail of the colour of the darker portion of the back, ending in a whitish tuft. Jerdon had seen this monkey on the Eastern Ghats near Nellore, and Tiruchirapalli. It was found both in forests and large groves. It was often domesticated at Madras and several other places.[81]

Karungalai or *kaar* in Tamil (*Presbytis jubatus*, the Nilgiris langur) had been of a dark glossy black colour throughout, except the head and nape, which were reddish-brown, the hair very long; in old individuals, a grayish patch was found on the rump. The length of the animal from head to body was twenty-six inches; tail thirty inches; but larger individuals were seen, though did not attain the size of Entellus. This handsome monkey was found on the Nilgiris and Anaimalai hills. The animal was shy and wary, and did not affect the neighbourhood of man. It was, or used to be, very abundant in the dense woods of the Nilgiris, and when they were beaten for game, these black monkeys would make their way rapidly and with loud cries rushed to the lowest part of the area and thence to some neighbouring woods at a lower level. The fur of the monkey was fine and glossy, and it was much prized.[82]

The Madras monkey was of a dusky olive-brown colour, paler and albescent on the belly, and somewhat ashy on the outer sides of the limbs; hairs on the crown of the head, radiated; tail, dusky-brown above, whitish beneath. The length of the animal from head to body was twenty inches and the tail fifteen inches. This monkey was found all over and it lived in towns and carried off fruits and grains from the shops of the dealers with the greatest coolness.[83]

The Four Types of Cats Described

The rusty-spotted cat (*Felis rubiginosa*) was greenish-gray, with a faint rufous tinge; beneath and inside of limbs white; a white superciliary streak, extended on the side of the nose; two dark face-streaks; top of head and nape with four narrow dark-brown stripes, becoming interrupted posterior, and passing into a series of rusty-coloured spots on the back and sides, somewhat longitudinal on the back, but roundish on the sides; tail short, more rufous than the body, and uniform in colour, or very indistinctly spotted, the tip not dark; the lower surface and inside of the limbs with large dark-brown spots; feet rufous-gray above, black on the soles; ears small; whiskers long, white; fur short and very soft. The length of the animal from head to body was sixteen to eighteen inches. Jerdon had only procured the rusty-spotted cats in the vicinity of Nellore and Madras. He said that Belanger the French East India Company official had purchased a rusty-spotted cat in Pondicherry. This very pretty little cat frequented grass in the dry beds of tanks, brushwood, and occasionally drains in the open country and near villages. Jerdon had a kitten of the animal brought to him when it was very young in 1846, and it became quite tame, and was the delight and admiration of all who saw it. Its activity was quite marvellous and it was very playful and elegant in its motions. When it was about eight months old, Jerdon introduced it into a room where there was a small fawn of the Gazelle, and the little creature flew at it the moment it saw it, seized it by the nape, and was with difficulty taken off. Jerdon lost it shortly after this. It would occasionally find its way to the rafters of bungalows and hunt for squirrels. Walter Elliot had seen several undoubted hybrids between this and the domestic cat. Jerdon who had also observed had confirmed the same opinion.[84]

Punugu punai in Tamil (*Viverra malaccensis*, the lesser civet-cat) was tawny gray or grayish-brown, with several longitudinal lines or streaks on the back and croup; the side spotted more or less in rows; some transverse bands on the sides of the neck, and also a few indistinct lines; abdomen without spots; head darker, with a black stripe from the ear to the shoulder; tail long, with eight or nine complete dark rings. The length of the animal from head to body was twenty-two or twenty-three inches; tail was sixteen or seventeen inches. This civet-cat was found all over India, from the foot of the Himalayas to Cape Comorin. It lived in holes in the ground or in banks, occasionally under rocks, or in dense thickets, now and then taking shelter in drains and out-houses. Mr. Hodgson the English Company official said that these animals dwelt in forests or detached woods and copses, whence they wandered freely into the open country by day (occasionally at least) as well as by night. They were solitary and single wanderers, even the pair being seldom seen together, and they feed promiscuously upon small animals, eggs of birds, frogs, insects besides some fruits or roots. Jerdon had several perfectly tamed civet-cats that caught rats and squirrels at times, as also sparrows and other birds. The civet was extracted by the Tamils from those animals kept in confinement.[85]

The lesser leopard-cat (*Felis Jerdoni*) had the size of the full-grown animal much smaller, than that of Felis rubiginosa; and the ground hue of the upper parts had been gray, untinged with fulvous. Jerdon first detected an adult male and a kitten of this species in the English Company Museum at Madras, and learnt later that there was an adult specimen also in the India Museum in London.[86]

The common tree-cat (*Paradoxurus musanga*, known as toddy-cat of the Europeans in Madras) had its general colour brownish-black, with some dingy yellowish stripes on each side, more or less distinct, and sometimes not noticeable; a white spot above and below each eye, and the forehead with a whitish band in some; a black line from the top of the head down the centre of the nose was generally observable. In many tree-cats the ground colour appeared to be fulvous with black pencilling, or mixed fulvous and black; the longitudinal stripes then show dark; limbs always dark-brown. Some appear almost black throughout, and the young were said to be nearly all black. Others appear fulvous-gray washed with black, the face black, and the tail very dark; and yet some others appear to have the sides spotted. Many of these variations were owing to the state of abrasion of the fur, which was yellowish at the base and blackish at the tip. One tree-cat was described as pale grayish-brown with longer black hairs intermixed, and most prevalent on the back of head, neck, and along the back; three black bands on the loins; head brownish, with a gray mark above and below the eyes; tail with the terminal fifth yellowish-white. Jerdon had several skins with the terminal portion of the tail yellowish-white, and one or two tree-cats with the whole posterior parts of the same hue. Some tree-cats had the abdomen marked with elongated white spots, and some occur with the tail spirally twisted, so that the extremity had the lower surface uppermost. Tree-cat was very abundant in the Carnatic, where it was popularly called the toddy-cat, in consequence of its supposed fondness for the juice of the palm. It lived much on trees, especially on the palmyra and coconut palms, and was often found to have taken up its residence in the thick thatched roofs of the houses of the natives. It was also occasionally found in dry drains, outhouses, and other places of shelter. The animal was quite nocturnal, issuing forth at dark, and living by preference on animal food, rats, lizards, small birds, poultry, and eggs; but it also freely partook of vegetable food, fruit, and insects. In confinement it would eat plantains, boiled rice, bread, milk and ghee. Jerdon had often known them taken in traps baited with a pigeon or a chicken. In Tamil country it was very often tamed, and became quite domestic, and even affectionate in its manners. Once Jerdon saw, many years ago, at Tiruchirapalli a tree-cat went about quite at large, and late every night used to work itself under the pillow of its owner, rolled itself up into a ball, with its tail coiled round its body, and slept till a late hour of the day. It hunted for rats, shrews, and house lizards. The activity of the tree-cats in climbing was very great, and they used to ascend and descend the house at one of the corners of the building in a most surprising manner.[87]

The Five Types of Mongoose Recorded

The Madras mongoose (*Herpestes griseus*) had tawny yellowish-gray colour, the hairs ringed with rufous and yellowish, the general result being an iron-gray tinge, with less of the yellow tint. The muzzle was concolorous with the body, as was the tail, which was not tipped with black, and was nearly equal in length to the body. The average length, of the animal from head to body was about sixteen to seventeen inches and tail was fourteen inches. Jerdon had witnessed many contests between a mongoose and cobra, and though the mongoose had in general succeeded in killing the serpent, it often declined the combat, or undertook it somewhat unwillingly. In none of the combats that Jerdon had seen had the mongoose suffered, but his belief was that it generally escaped being bitten by its extreme watchfulness and activity; or if bitten at all, had been so very superficially; and that perhaps the very thick skin of the animal might have had a certain degree of insusceptibility to poison.[88]

The long-tailed mongoose (*Herpestes monticolus*) had colours somewhat more yellow in its general tone, tail longer, tipped with maroon and black, and more hairy feet with dark reddish-brown; muzzle not dark, slightly tinged with reddish. Larger than griseus, the tail was nearly equal in length to the head and body. The length of a long-tailed mongoose was twenty inches; tail with hair was nineteen inches. This fine species differed conspicuously from griseus in its longer and dark-tipped tall, which also distinguished it from malaccensis. Jerdon had only procured this mongoose from Nellore where it inhabited forests among the hills.[89]

The ruddy mongoose (*Herpestes Smithii*) had the general colour ferruginous-brown, in some inclining to grizzled maronne-red, brighter where it joined the blackish limbs and black tip of the tail was muzzle dark; face rusty-red; head and legs redder than the other parts; feet black; the hairs were ringed black and white, and had a dark reddish tip. It approximated malaccensis in the character of the fur and also in size. The length of one ruddy mongoose from head to body was thirteen to fifteen inches and the tail was twelve to thirteen inches. This mongoose had been taken in the jungle near Madras and its surroundings. Jerdon had also procured it from the forest at the foot of the Nilgiris.[90]

The Nilgiri brown mongoose (*Herpestes fuscus*) had the general colour brown, the hair being ringed black and yellow, and tawny at the base; throat dusky-yellowish; tail nearly equalled in length to head and body. The length of one brown mongoose from head to body was eighteen inches and the tail with the hair was seventeen inches. Jerdon had procured this mongoose from the dense woods near Ootacamund, and had not seen it in any other localities of Tamil country. Jerdon sent this brown mongoose after its death to the Museum of the Asiatic Society of Calcutta founded by Nathaniel Wallich (1786-1854) in 1814.[91]

The stripe-necked mongoose (*Herpestes vitticollis*) was of a grizzled gray colour, more or less tinged with rusty reddish, especially on the hinder part of the body and tail; a dark stripe appeared from the ear to the shoulder; tail was rufous-black at the tip. The length of one stripe-necked mongoose (killed during hunting) in Nilgiris was twenty-one inches from the head to body and the tail with the hair was fifteen inches. Jerdon had himself killed it in the Nilgiris.[92]

The Description of Udumbu

According to T.C. Jerdon *udumbu* (the Indian Pangolin) had the tail shorter than the body, very broad at the base, with sixteen or seventeen scales in each longitudinal line; sixteen scales on the dorsal series in ten or eleven rows; middle nail of the fore-feet much stronger than the others. Scales thick, striated at the base, pale yellowish-brown or horny clay-colour; the lower side of the head, body, and feet nude, brownish-white; nose fleshy; soles of the hind-feet blackish; auricles indistinct. The length of one *udumbu* from head to body was twenty six inches and its tail was eighteen inches. This common pangolin, or scaly ant-eater, was found throughout India. It was strictly nocturnal, and feeds almost exclusively on ants, especially the white ants (termites). Its gait in walking was very peculiar, the back arched, the fore-feet with their anterior surface bent over and brought into contact with the ground, on which it progressed very slowly.[93]

The Different Types of Chameleons Found in Nilgiris and Madras

Chameleon (*Colotes versicola*) was called *oonaan* or *pachchondhi* by the Tamils. *Chamaeleo pumilus* had its head tuberculated; dorsal crest continued over the tail. Some large circular scales had mingled with the small and unequal granulose ones. Jerdon possessed a specimen of this small chameleon in spirit, which was said to have been taken at Coonoor on the Nilgiris. The length was five and a half inches, of which the tail had been two.[94]

Jerdon had procured *Gymnodactylus indicus* the small Gecko species, on the top of Dodabetta, the highest mountain of the group in Nilgiris. It was found concealing itself under stones in the day time. Its colours when fresh were a mottled brown, or greenish-brown, with a row of orange-yellowish spots along the back edged darker, and a line of similarly coloured spots on each side. The lips were also of the same tint besides the lower portion of the tail. Jerdon sent this specimen in the ship that sailed from Madras to London.[95]

Jerdon had no hesitation in considering *Chamaeleo zeylonicus* distinct from the African one, as well on account of the slight but permanent structural distinctions (the abdominal ridge being in the African one composed of very short and closely set spines), as the difference of locality, and the great difference in the change of colour of the two. In the Indian one, the only change produced was from one shade of green to another. In a state of quiescence, it was usually very pale green, sometimes dark blackish green; but when excited it was mottled very prettily with dark transverse blotches on a pale ground. Jerdon never saw any pure yellow or red colour in any state. It was found in all the forest districts and it was mainly used in medicine by some of the native doctors, and many generally be procured them in the market in Madras. The length of one chameleon was ten inches, of which the tail was more than half.[96]

The Two Types of Mouse Described

Micro-mammalia such as bats, shrews, rats and mice in Tamil country had been studied in detail by T.C. Jerdon. He had also provided the details of the various types found along with descriptions. The Nilgiri tree-mouse (*Mus nilagiricus*) had the colour bright chestnut-brown above and beneath the bright fawn yellow, with a distinct line of demarcation between the two colours. The head was rather elongated; ears long, oval; tail was somewhat hairy. Jerdon on several occasions had found this tree-mouse in woods on the summit of the Nilgiris near Ootacamund. The first he observed was brought into his house by a cat. Jerdon afterwards found the nest, a mass of leaves and grass, on shrubs and low trees, from four to six feet from the ground level, and in one occasion it was occupied by at least eight or ten full-grown mice.[97]

The large-footed mouse (*Mus crassipes*) was like *Mus homourus*, but it was with its tail rather longer than the head and body. The feet were particularly large, and the tail well furnished with coarse short setae. Jerdon had obtained two specimens of a mouse in a house in the Nilgiris which certainly differed both from *Mus urbanus* and *Mus homourus*. It was larger, and found with large head, ears and feet.[98]

The Five Types of Bat Described Jerdon and Walter Elliot

The long-tailed leaf-bat (*Rhinopoma Hardwickii*) had been thick, truncated, and surrounded by a small leaf; tragus, oblong, bi-acuminate; forehead concave, with a fossa or channel down the centre; fur, soft and very fine; dull brown throughout; face, rump, and part of the abdominal region, naked. It frequented old ruins, caves, clefts in rocks. In 1848 many leaf-bats were captured in Madras by Walter Elliot and Jerdon in a house for three successive nights. This bat was not of common occurrence there in general. They had been blown there by the strong westerly winds which had then set in from the rocky hills to the westward of Madras.[99]

The fulvous fox-bat (*Pteropus leschenaultia*) was of a fulvous ashy or dull light ashy-brown colour, paler beneath, the hairs whitish at the base; membranes, dark brown; fur, short and downy. The length of the fox-bat from head to body was five to five and a half inches inches and the breadth had been eighteen inches. Of another fox-bat the size length was six inches and breadth was twenty inches. Jerdon procured this species in Madras and Tiruchirapalli and knew nothing of its habits. It was stated that fox-bats were found in Pondicherry and they were sold. One specimen of the fox-bat from the Coromandel Coast was stated to have had the fur browner, a white collar with the hairs on the sides of the neck longer and directed forwards.[100]

The Indian horse-bat (*Hipposideros speoris*) had the ears large, erect, acuminate, rounded at the base, emarginated on the outer margin; facial membrane complicated; muzzle and short; interfemoral membrane was narrow, square, and enclosed the tail, while the half of the last joint was free; body, short, thick, of variable colour. Sometimes it had light mouse colour, paler beneath; at times, fulvous-brown; at other times, bright rufo-ferruginous or golden fulvous. Jerdon had procured the horse-bat at Madras and Nellore.[101]

The long-armed bat (*Taphozous longimanus*) had the ears oval, with many distinct folds, naked except at the base; tragus, securiform; fur, thick, close, fuscous-black or dark fuscous-brown above; beneath paler, except on the throat, the hairs being conspicuously tipped with grey; the upper hairs all white at their base; face, nude; and the membranes dark brownish-black. This long-armed bat was found very common at Madras. It frequented dark out-houses, cellars, stabling and old temples.[102]

The Coromandel bat (*Scotophilus coromandelianus*) had the ears rather large, broad; tragus lunate or slightly curved forwards, and obtuse and rounded at the tip; a minute praemolar above, situated laterally internally, not visible from without; two lower praemolars; two pair of upper incisors about equal in size; fur short; above colour was dingy fulvous-brown, beneath grayish fulvous; in some dark-brown was found both above and below. This minute bat usually concealed itself in the roofs of dwelling houses, in the holes of the thatch and under the tiles.[103]

The Five Types of Shrew Described

The common musk shrew (*Sorex caerulescens*, called musk-rat of the Europeans) was of uniform bluish-ash or pale gray colour, very slightly tinged with ferruginous, mostly on the hinder parts; naked parts flesh-coloured. The length from head to body was six to seven and a half inches and the tail was with three and a half inches or nearly four. This common musk-rat frequented houses at night, and hunting all round the rooms for cockroaches or other insects, occasionally uttering a sharp, shrill cry. It would not, however, refuse meat, for it was sometimes taken in rat-traps baited with meat.[104]

The rufescent shrew (*Sorex serpentarius*) was dusky-slate colour above, with rufescent tips to the fur; beneath, paler, with a faint rufous tinge about the breast; ears, moderately large; limbs, small; tail, slender; teeth, small. This musk-rat had been found more common at Tirunelveli.[105]

The Nilgiris wood shrew (*Sorex niger*) was of blackish-brown, with a rufescent shade on the upper parts; abdomen, dusky-grayish; tail, equal in length to the body, gradually tapering to a point; snout, much attenuated. It was tolerably common on the Nilgiri hills, frequenting the woods and gardens at Ootacamund, and dead specimens were also often found on the roads. Jerdon had seen a wood shrew that had turned out from the hollow of an old tree. It had a very faint musky odour.[106]

The Nilgiris pigmy shrew (*Sorex perroteti*) had its back deep blackish-brown; belly, pale; limbs and feet, brown; palms clad with hairs; ears large, conspicuous. This minute shrew was first noticed by George Samuel Perrottet (1793-1870) the French naturalist at Nilgiris. Jerdon took this species for himself so as to locate and find the same species in Madras. He opined that possibly other minute shrews were found in South India.[107]

The Madras tree shrew (*Tupaia elliotti/Anathana ellioti*) had the colour above pale rufescent or reddish-brown, the hairs being grizzled red and brown; chin, throat, breast, and lower parts yellowish-white; which was continued in a narrow line along the underside of the tail and nails nearly equal. This interesting tree shrew was noticed by Walter Elliott who procured it from the hills located west of Madras.[108]

To conclude it may be said that besides domesticated animals the Europeans on the Tamil coast found wild animals which were strange. They studied these new animals which they had not met with in Europe. They examined the structure, physiology and the biological characteristics of the animals. This type of work ranged all types of animals. It is interesting to note that the Europeans had purchased and kept animals in their houses for the purpose of study. They also received the news about animals from the natives of the Tamil coast. They purchased animals from the market for their study. They also went out for hunting in the jungles, used rifle, musket and telescope and obtained animals for examination and not a single tropical zoological specimen seemed to have escaped their watchful eyes. The Europeans had exported many strange animals in the ships that sailed from the ports of the Tamil Coast for these animals were rare. Some of the animals after death were well preserved and they sent them to the India Museum in London and Museum of the Asiatic Society of Calcutta for posterity. The idea of animal husbandry by the English East India Company in Madras gradually developed. Farming and animal husbandry got attention since these were found to be the two main economic activities in Tamil country. The Government of Madras focused its attention on *Amrit Mahal* the cattle breeding establishment in Mysore and it was finally taken over by government of Madras in 1813 for research on pack animals for the army.

Notes

1. Stefano Perfetti, *Aristotle's Zoology and its Renaissance Commentators, 1521-1601*, Leuven, Leuven University Press, 2000.
2. Laurent Pinon, 'Conrad Gessner and the Historical Depth of Renaissance Natural History', in *Historia: Empiricism and Erudition in Early Modern Europe*, eds., Gianna Pomata and Nancy Siraisi, Cambridge Massachusetts and London, 2005, pp. 241-67.
3. Ulysse Aldrouando, *Ornithologiae hoc est de Avibus Historiae Libri XII*, Bologna, 1599; Ulysse Aldrouando, *De Animalibus Insectis Libri Septem, cum Singulorum Iconibus as Vivum Expressis*, Bologna, 1602.
4. J. Jonston, *Historiae naturalis,* Libri I – VII , Lesnae – Frankofurti, 1650-1653. These include Theatrum universale de Avibus, Historiae naturalis de Avibus, Historiae naturalis de Exsanguinis aquaticis, Historiae naturalis de Piscibus et Cetis, Historiae naturalis de Quadrupedibus, Historiae naturalis de insectis, Historiae naturalis de Serpentibus, and Historiae naturalis de Insectis, Serpentibus et Draconibus.
5. S. Jeyaseela Stephen, ed., *Letters of the Portuguese Jesuits from Tamil Countryside, 1666-1688*, Pondicherry, 2001, pp. 291-2.
6. Alfred Martineau, ed., *Memoires de François Martin: Fondateur de Pondichéry, 1665-1694*, 3 vols., Paris, 1932-4, vol. III, p. 28.
7. S. Jeyaseela Stephen, *The Coromandel Coast and its Hinterland: Economy, Society and Political System, 1500-1600*, Delhi, 1997, p. 190.
8. Jean-Baptiste Tavernier, *Travels in India by Jean-Baptiste Tavernier*, ed., Ball, repr. Delhi, 2000, vol. I, p. 215.
9. Abbe Carre, *Voyages des Indes Orientales*, Paris, 1906, vol. III, p. 714.
10. Nationaal Archief (hereafter NA), Den Haag, MSS VOC 856, fl. 486, 13 August 1635; VOC 857, fl. 81, 13 February 1636; VOC 861, fl. 118, 28 February 1639; VOC 1124, fl. 668, 19 June 1635; VOC 1123, fl. 200v, 9 May 1638.
11. J.A. Van der Chijs, et al., *Dagregister Gehouden int Casteel Batavia vant Passerende daer te Plaatse als Over Geheel Nederlandts-India, 1628–1682*, 31 vols., The Hague- Batavia, 1887–1928 (hereafter Dagregister), 1636, p. 262.
12. Tapan Raychaudhuri, *Jan Company in Coromandel, 1605–1690: A Study in the Interrelations of European Commerce and Traditional Economies*, The Hague, 1962, p. 177.
13. NA, VOC, 1130, fol. 978; N. Macleod, *De Oost-Indische Compagnie als Zeemogenheid in Azie*, Rijswijk, 1927, vol. II, pp. 13–15, 170–1.
14. NA, VOC 1130, fl. 978.
15. NA, VOC 1133, fls. 435-6.
16. William Salmon and Royal College of Physicians, *Pharmacopœia Londinensis: Or the New London Dispensatory*, London, Nicholson, 1702.
17. John Marten, *A Treatment of the Venereal Disease*, London, 1711.
18. *The Ladies Dispensatory or Every Woman her own Physician*, London, 1740.
19. Louis Le Comte, *Nouveau Mémoires Sur L'état Présent De La Chine*, Paris, tome II, 1696, pp. 506-512. The text runs thus: Le caméléon est encore une autre espèce de lézard de huit à dix pouces de long, qui a servi de matière à nos

observations. On en voit à la côte de Coromandel, & nous en nourrissions en notre maison de Pontichéry; car ils ne vivent pas seulement d'air, comme quelques naturalistes l'ont écrit : ils mangent & même avec avidité. Il est vrai qu'étant d'un tempérament froid & humide, ils peuvent passer plusieurs jours sans nourriture; mais enfin, si on ne leur en donne point du tout, on les voit peu à peu languir, & ensuite mourir de faim. Au reste, tout est singulier dans le caméléon: ses yeux, sa tête, son ventre sont extrêmement gros; & quoiqu'il ait quatre pattes comme le lézard, il est d'une si grande lenteur en tous ses mouvements, qu'il se traîne plutôt qu'il ne marche, & si la nature ne lui avait donné une langue d'une conformation particulière, jamais il n'attraperait les animaux qui sont sa nourriture ordinaire. Cette langue est ronde, épaisse, & longue au moins d'un pied. Il la darde à sept ou huit pouces hors de la bouche avec une adresse merveilleuse: & la substance en est si visqueuse, qu'elle arrête les mouches, les sauterelles & autres semblables insectes pour peu qu'elles les touche de sa pointe. Tout son corps est couvert d'une peau très fine, mais de couleur changeante, selon les différentes passions qui l'agitent. Dans la joie il est d'un vert d'émeraude, mêlé d'oranger & haché de petites bandes grises & noires. La colère le rend obscur & livide; la crainte, pâle & d'un jaune effacé. Quelquefois toutes ces couleurs & plusieurs autres se confondent ensemble; & il se fait alors un si beau mélange d'ombre & de lumière, qu'on ne voit point dans la nature de plus belles nuances; ni dans nos tableaux, des peintures plus vives, plus douces, & mieux assorties. On me fit voir à Pontichéry deux autres espèces d'animaux peu connus dans l'Europe. L'un se nomme chien-marron, qui tient presque également du chien, du loup, & du renard: il est de grandeur médiocre, d'un poil gris & roux. Il a les oreilles courtes & pointues, le museau affilé, les jambes hautes, la queue longue, le corps grêle & déchargé. Il n'aboie point comme le chien, mais il crie à la manière des enfants; au reste, il est très vorace de son naturel, & quand la faim le presse, il entre la nuit dans les maisons & se jette souvent sur les personnes. La seconde espèce est la mangouze, qui pour la forme extérieure, approche assez de la belette, si ce n'est qu'elle a le corps plus gros & plus long, les jambes plus courtes, le museau plus délié, l'œil plus vif, & je ne sais quoi, de moins sauvage. Cet animal est en effet extrêmement familier, & il n'y a point de chien qui joue & qui badine plus agréablement avec les hommes. Cependant il est colère & traître quand il mange; grondant alors presque toujours, & se jetant avec fureur sur ceux qui se mettent en devoir de le troubler. Il aime surtout les œufs de poules, mais comme il n'a pas la gueule assez fendue pour les saisir, il tâche de les rompre en les jetant en l'air, ou en les roulant sur la terre de cent manières différentes. Que si pour lors il trouve une pierre auprès de lui, il lui tourne incontinent le dos, & élargissant les jambes de derrière, il prend l'œuf avec celles de devant & le pousse de toute sa force par dessus le ventre, jusqu'à ce qu'il se soit cassé contre la pierre. Il chasse non seulement aux rats & aux souris, mais encore aux serpents, dont il est le mortel ennemi, & qu'il prend sur la tête fort adroitement, sans en recevoir aucune blessure. Il n'est pas moins contraire aux caméléons, qui, à sa seule vue sont saisis d'une si grande frayeur, qu'ils deviennent tout d'un coup plats comme une feuille, & tombent ordinairement à demi-morts; au lieu qu'aux approches d'un chat d'un chien, ou de quelque autre animal encore plus à craindre, ils s'enflent, se mettent en colère, & prennent le parti de se défendre ou de les attaquer.

20. *Memoirs and Observations: Topographical, physical, mathematical, mechanical, natural and ecclesiastical made in a late journey through the empire of China and published in several letters, by Louis Le Comte, Translated from the Paris edition and illustrated with figures*, London, 1697, pp. 513-514.
21. Giovanni Borghesi, *Lettera Scritta da Pondischeri a 10 di febbraio 1704 dal dottore Giovanni Borghesi medico della missione sepedita alla China dalla santita di N.S. Papa Clemente XI nella quale si contengono, oltre a un pieno raconto del viaggio da Roma fino alle coste dell'Indie oriental, Anatomische, Botanische, naturali e d' altri generi e trasportata del Manuscritto Latin in Lingua Toscana di Gio Mario de' Crescembeni custode d'Arcadia, e Accademico Affrordita*, Roma, 1705, pp. 198-9.
22. *Ibid.*, p. 206.
23. F. F. J. M. Pieters, 'The menagerie of 'the white elephant' in Amsterdam: with some notes on other 17th and 18th century menageries in The Netherlands' eds., H. V. Lothar Dittrich, D. V. Engelhardt & A. RiekeMüller, *Die Kulturgeschichte des Zoos*, Berlin, 2002, pp. 47-66, see, p. 56.
24. *Ibid.*, p. 57.
25. Daniel Jeyaraj and Richard Fox Young, *Hindu–Christian Epistolary Self–Discourses: 'Malabarian Correspondence' between German Pietist Missionaries and South Indian Hindus (1712–1714)*, Harrassowitz Verlag, Wiesbaden, 2013, p. 282.
26. Thomas Pennant, *Indian Zoology*, Second edition, London, MDCCXC, p. 31.
27. Mildred Archer, 'Indian Paintings for British Naturalists', *Geographical Magazine*, 28(5) 1955, pp. 220-30; see also, Mildred Archer, 'India and Natural History: The Role of the East India Company, 1785-1858', *History Today*, 9 (2), 1959, pp. 736-743, see p. 739.
28. Gotthilf August Francke, ed., *Der Königl. Dänischen Missionarien aus Ost-Indien eingesandter ausführlichen Berichten, Von dem Werck ihrs Ams unter den Heyden, angerichteten Schulen und Gemeinen, ereigneten Hindernissen und schweren Umstanden; Beschaffenheit des Malabarischen Heydenthums, gepflogenen brieflicher Correspondentz und mundlchen Unterredungen mit selbigen heyden*, Teil 1–9, (Continuationen 1–108) Waiserihaus, Halle, 1710–1772 (hereafter Hallesche Berichten = HB), see, 59th Continuation des Berichts der Königliche – Dänischen Missionarien in Ost Indien, 1742, p. 840.
29. HB, 85th Continuation des Berichts der Königliche – Dänischen Missionarien in Ost Indien, 1756, p. 1641.
30. General Clive and James Parsons, 'Some Account of the Animal Sent from the East Indies, by General Clive, to His Royal Highness the Duke of Cumberland, Which is now in the Tower of London: In a Letter from James Parsons, M. D. F. R. S. to the Rev. Thomas Birch, D. D. Secretary to the Royal Society', *Philosophical Transactions*, vol. 51 (1759-1760), pp. 648-652. The paper was read on 27 March 1760.
31. *Ibid.*
32. Archivum Romanum Societatis Iesu, Roma, MSS Goa 54(a), Annual letter of Andres Freyre to Giovanni Paolo Oliva written from Kandalur dated 14 July 1667, in S. Jeyaseela Stephen, Letters of the Portuguese Jesuits, p. 4.

33. Claude du Choiseul, *Nouvelle methode sure, courte et facile pour le traitement de personnes attaques par de la rage*, Paris, 1756. Louis Pasteur the French biologist and chemist later became interested in rabies, and discovered the vaccine for rabies. Pasteur pronounced the foundations of experimental methods in microbiology, highlighted the role of microbes in the propagation of diseases and invented pasteurization. Louis Pasteur also introduced the vaccination for immunity to cholera. He had succeeded in growing the organism thought to cause fowl cholera in culture, and had shown chickens injected with the cultured bacterium developed cholera. Pasteur administered the first vaccine (in 1885) to a human patient, a young boy who had been bitten repeatedly by a rabid dog. Though Pasteur proved that vaccination worked, he was not aware of the mechanism involved.
34. Archiv der Franckeschen Stiftungen (hereafter AFSt), Halle, AFSt/M2 B1: 5d; AFSt/M2 B2, Berichte aus Zoologie und Botanik.
35. HB, 100th Continuation des Berichts der Königliche – Dänischen Missionarien in Ost Indien, 1766, pp. 408-9.
36. HB, 104th Continuation des Berichts der Königliche – Dänischen Missionarien in Ost Indien, 1768, p. 907.
37. 'An Account of a New Species of the Manis, or Scaly Lizard, extracted from the German Relations of the Danish Royal Missionaries in the East Indies, of the year 1765, published at Halle in Saxony, by Dr. Hampe, F. R. S', *Philosophical Transactions: Giving some account of the present undertakings, Studies, and Labours of the ingenious, in many considerable parts of the world*, vol. LX, 1770. London, MDCCLXXI, pp. 36-38. The paper was read on 6 October 1770.
38. Georg Christian Knapp et al., eds., *Neuere Geschichte der Evangelischen Missions-Anstalten zu Bekehrung der Heiden in Ostindien aus den eigenhändigen Aufsätzen und Briefen der Missionarien erausgegeben*, Waisenhaus, Teil 1–8 (Stück 1–95), Waiserihaus, Halle, 1770–8/95, 1848 (hereafter NHB), 1786, pp. 815-6.
39. *Ibid.*
40. NHB, 1793, p. 658.
41. *Ibid.*
42. AFSt/M2 E27:18, Tagebuch von Christoph Samuel John, 12 December 1803 - 31 December 1804, See also, NHB, 6 Bd., 63, s.260.
43. C. S. John, 'Beschreibung einiger Affen aus im nordlichen Bengalen, vom missionaries John zu Trankenbar', *Neue Scriften Gesellschaft Naturforschender Freunde zu Berlin*, 1: 211-218, see pp. 215-216; See also, J.B. Fischer, *Synopsis Mammalium Cotta*, Stuttgart, 1829.
44. Saraswati Mahal Library, Thanjavur (hereafter SMLT), *Modi Bundles* (hereafter MB), 123C/17-9; see also, P. Subramanian, Venkataramaiyaa and Vivekananda Gopal, *Thanjai Maraattiyar Modi Aavana Thamizhaakamum Kurippuraiyum* (Modi Records of the Mahratta Rulers of Tanjore in Tamil Translation), 3 vols, Tamil University, Tanjore, 1989 (hereafter MDT), vol. I, part III, p.140.
45. Tamilnadu State Archives (hereafter TNSA), Chennai, *Tanjore District Records* (hereafter TDR), vol. 3483, p. 299, 13 June 1805.

46. SMLT, MB, 31C/11; MDT, vol. I, part VIII, p. 350; MDT, vol. I, part VIII, p. 400.
47. SMLT, MB, 140C/6; MDT, vol. I, part II, p. 193.
48. TNSA, TDR, vol. 3429, pp. 245-6, 21 November 1821.
49. TNSA, TDR, vol. 4438 (2), p. 421, 5 December 1831.
50. TNSA, TDR, vol. 3487A, p. 47, 18 February 1806.
51. TNSA, TDR, vol. 3419, pp. 42-3, 10 April 1806.
52. TNSA, TDR, vol. 3452, p. 97, 24 June 1800.
53. AFSt/M2 E27:18, Tagebuch von Christoph Samuel John, 12 December 1803 - 31 December 1804, See also, NHB, 6 Bd., 63, s.259.
54. SMLT, MB, 140C/12-7; MDT, vol.1, part II, p. 185.
55. TNSA, TDR, vol. 3503, p. 131, 24 May 1811.
56. TNSA, TDR, vol. 3535, p. 65, 31 January 1819.
57. SMLT, MB, 31C/11; MDT, vol. I, part III, p. 350; MDT, vol. I, part VIII, p. 400.
58. SMLT, MB, 76/5; MDT, vol. I, part V, p. 215.
59. TNSA, TDR, vol. 3539, 2 April 1820.
60. TNSA, TDR, vol. 4429B, p. 200, 8 April 1821.
61. BL, London, *Natural History Drawings of the India Office Collections* (hereafter IOL, NHD), 7/1095; IOL, NHD 7/1112.
62. BL, IOL, NHD 7/1096-97; IOL, NHD 7/1094; IOL,NHD 7/1100; IOL,NHD 7/1101; IOL,NHD 7/1102-1103 and 1115.
63. BL, IOL, NHD 7/1104-1114; IOL, NHD 7/1111.
64. BL, IOL, NHD 7/1001-25.
65. SMLT, MB, 169C/5-6; MDT, vol. I, part II, p. 78.
66. AFSt/M2 E27:18, Tagebuch von Christoph Samuel John, 12 December 1803 - 31 December 1804, See also, NHB, 6 Bd., 63, s.250-60.
67. BL, IOL, NHD 7/1036.
68. BL, IOL, NHD 7/1034.
69. BL, IOL, NHD 7/1039.
70. Thomas Caverhill Jerdon, *The Mammals of India, Natural History of all the Animals Known to Inhabit Continental India*, London, 1874, pp. 15-6.
71. *Ibid.*, p. 63.
72. *Ibid.*, pp. 72-4.
73. *Ibid.*, pp. 92-7.
74. *Ibid.*, pp. 82-3.
75. Colonel Walter Campbell, *My Indian Journal*, Edinburgh, MDCCCLXIV, pp. 368-371.
76. Thomas Caverhill Jerdon, The Mammals of India, pp. 288-90.
77. Colonel Walter Campbell, My Indian Journal, pp. 100-101.
78. Thomas Caverhill Jerdon, The Mammals of India, pp. 302-3.
79. *Ibid.*, pp. 142-4.
80. *Ibid.*, p. 166.

81. *Ibid.*, p. 7.
82. *Ibid.*, p. 9.
83. *Ibid.*, pp. 12-3.
84. *Ibid.*, pp. 108-9.
85. *Ibid.*, pp. 122-3.
86. *Ibid.*, p. 107.
87. *Ibid.*, pp. 125-7.
88. *Ibid.*, pp. 132-4.
89. *Ibid.*, p. 135.
90. *Ibid.*, pp. 135-6.
91. *Ibid.*, pp. 136-7.
92. *Ibid.*, p. 137.
93. *Ibid.*, pp. 314-6.
94. T. C. Jerdon, 'Catalogue of Reptiles Inhabiting Peninsular India', *Journal of the Asiatic Society of Bengal*, vol. XXII, 1853, pp. 462-479, p. 466.
95. *Ibid.*, pp. 468-9.
96. *Ibid.*, p. 466.
97. T. C. Jerdon, The Mammals of India, p. 203.
98. *Ibid.*, pp. 204-5.
99. *Ibid.*, pp. 29-30.
100. *Ibid.*, pp. 19-20.
101. *Ibid.*, pp. 27-8.
102. *Ibid.*, p. 31.
103. *Ibid.*, p. 35.
104. *Ibid.*, pp. 53-4.
105. *Ibid.*, p. 55.
106. *Ibid.*, p. 56.
107. *Ibid.*, p. 58.
108. *Ibid.*, p. 64.

3.1. Asian palm civet noticed by Giovannio Borghesi in Pondicherry, 1703

3.2. A bison noticed by Colonel Walter Campbell

3.3. The long tailed squirrel found in Tamil country

3.4. A wild cat sent by Robert Clive from Madras to London, 1759

3.5. Ibex of the Nilgiris noticed by Colonel Walter Campbell

3.6. The Madras tree shrew found by George Robert Waterhouse

3.7. The king of Thanjavur riding on an elephant.

3.8. A tiger hunt on elephants.

3.9. The two-banded monitor noticed by Giovannio Borghesi in Pondicherry, 1703.

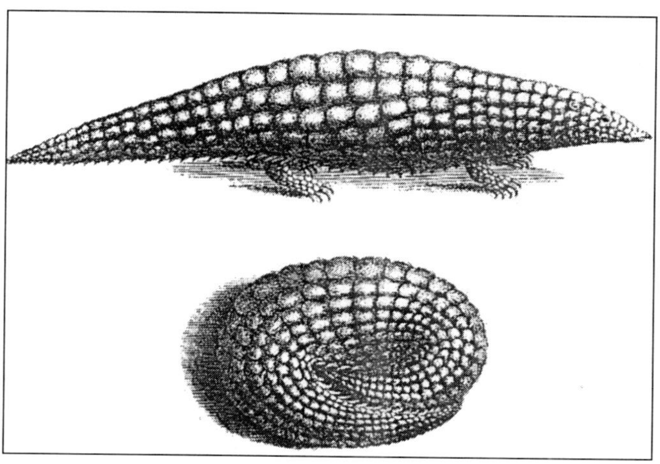

3.10. The Indian Pangolin from Tranquebar, 1768.

3.11. A chameleon sent from Tranquebar in 1741 by Johann Ernst Grundler preserved in spirit at Halle in Germany

4

Strange and Wonderful: The Study of Animal Anatomy and the Surgeons in Paris, London and Madras, 1675-1715

Berengario da Carpi (1460-1530) and Andreas Vesalius (1514-1564) the anatomists in Europe dissected live animals in the sixteenth century, but this did not become a method until the seventeenth century. The work of Galen (AD 130-210) the Greek physician 'On Anatomical Procedures' was translated from Greek into Latin by Johann Winter von Andernach (1505–74) the professor in Paris. The dissection of living and dead animals continued to contribute to the ongoing debates on living function as well as debates on the structure and function of nature as a whole, and on the proper methods to attain knowledge. Gaspare Aselli (1581–1626) made his discovery of the so-called lacteal veins which later proved to be crucial to a new theory of digestion and blood formation brought about by the circulation. William Harvey (1578-1657) announced his discovery of the circulation of the blood in 1628 through his *De motu cordis*, and his innovation was the key to experimental use of animals, especially live animals. With Harvey's work, dissection of live animals moved beyond demonstration to become a quintessentially experimental act that revealed new knowledge.

The Paris Academy of Sciences was founded by Jean-Baptiste Colbert in 1666 and its members pursued two intersecting animal projects, dissection of exotic animals and dissection of living and dead domestic animals the latter coupled with the dissection of human cadavers. These projects emerged as a new experimental comparative anatomy that valued animals both as models for humans and as legitimate objects of knowledge. The Aristotelian idea that animals could be classified into broad groups based on particular characteristics then came to be challenged. Claude Perrault (1613-88) a trained doctor who had obtained his doctorate in 1642 established a medical practice and as a member of the medical faculty at the University of Paris, he lectured on physiology and pathology. He was accepted into the Academy of Sciences in Paris in 1666 where he conducted investigations. He later died in 1688 having contracted an infection while performing a dissection on a camel. Claude Perrault and his colleagues in Paris, by contrast to Aristotle's idea, claimed to look at animals as individuals and as entire organisms rather than as members of a group. Particular parts enhanced their singularity rather than aiding in classification. Perrault claimed that classification was impossible in the then current state of knowledge, and humans remained a distant referent. In his reports of animal anatomy, Perrault felt much obliged to respond to ancient sources. In detailing his autopsy of a lion, he mentioned that the claws do not have cases as Pliny claimed but are retractable just as Plutarch and Solinus observed.[1] Perrault had paid much attention to anatomy than to classification. He carefully described the internal structure of each specimen. He refused to attempt a classification of the animals. He noted that as more animals of the same species were made available, their descriptions had been rewritten because it is important to know as much as possible the difference and the similarities that one often encounters in animals of the same species.

Dissecting a Tortoise Sent from Pondicherry to Paris by Joseph-Guichard Duverney, 1675

The French East India Company officials in Pondicherry on the Coromandel Coast had sent a male tortoise from the land to Louis XIV the King of France and it found way to the royal menagerie. Joseph-Guichard Durverney (1648-1700) professor of anatomy at the King's garden in Paris appointed in 1682 had conducted the dissection of this reptile in November 1675 after its death. He and Claude Perrault had jointly authored the anatomical description of the tortoise in 1676.[2]

The report mentioned that the tortoise was four foot long from the extremity of the mouth to the end of the tail, and fourteen inches thick. The shell contained three foot in length and two in breadth. How great so ever this tortoise was, it came not near those of which Elian and Pliny do speak, which was fifteen cubits, and every one of which was sufficient to cover a large cabin where several persons might lodge: But the tortoise from Pondicherry was a land tortoise and those that Pliny and Elian do make mention of were sea-turtles, where animals do generally grow much larger than those of the same species which do live upon land. Elian declares that land tortoises are not ordinarily greater than the large cods turned up by the plow when the land if light. The large sea-turtles which they do take near the Antilles according to the relations we had thereof, are not above as big again as the one from Pondicherry.[3]

The shell and all the rest of the tortoise was of the same colour, viz of a very dark gray. The upper part was composed of several pieces of a different figure though the most part were pentagonal. All these pieces were fixed and joined unto a bone which like a skull, enclosed the intrails of the animal having one aperture before, to let out the head, shoulders and fore-legs and another opposite through which came out the hinder-legs and thighs. This bone on which the scales were fastened, was a line and half in the thinnest place and near an inch and half in some places. It is generally double, there being upon the back and another under the belly, which, like two breast–plates or bucklers, are joined by the sides, and the tied together by strong and hard ligaments, but which do nevertheless grant liberty for any motion.[4]

At the great aperture before, there was at the top of a raised border, to grant more liberty to the neck and head for lifting themselves upwards. And this inflexion of the neck is of great use to the tortoise. For it serves them to turn again where they are upon their back. And their industry upon this account is very admirable. We have observed in a living tortoise that being turned upon his back, and not being able to make use of his paws for the turning himself, because that they could bend only towards the belly, it could help itself only by its neck and head, which it turned sometimes on one side, and sometimes on the other, by pushing against the ground to rock itself as in a cradle, to find out the side, towards which the inequality of the ground might more easily permit it to roll its shell, for when it had found it, it made all its endeavours on that side.

The three great pieces of the shell were upon the back forwards; they had each in their middle a round bunch standing up three or four lines, and an inch and half broad. The lower part of the belly was a little hollow. Authors have taken notice this cavity is peculiar to males. Upon the back there was a wound, occasioned by some blow that it had received when it was taken. This wound which pierced only the shell and part of the bone which sustained it, without penetrating on the inside, was not healed within more than a year which she lived, after her being taken.

All that proceeded out of the shells viz., the head, shoulders, forelegs, tail, buttocks and hind-legs, were all covered with a loose skin, folded in great winkle, and besides that grained like Spanish leather. This skin did not enter under the shell. To cover the parts which are there enclosed, but it was fastened about the edge of each of the two apertures: The skin of sea-turtle is covered all along the legs with little scales like fish.[5]

It had been mentioned that Albertas opined that great tortoises had a shell over their head in form of a buckler. The head of this tortoise from Pondicherry was only covered with a skin, which was much thinner than that of the other parts. It was seven inches in length and five in breadth and did in some measure resemble the head of a serpent. The lower jaw was near as thick as the upper. There were no apertures for the ears. The nostrils were opened at the end of the mouth by two little round holes, after an uncouth manner. The eyes were small and frightful. But we have observed nothing in respect of the tortoise, which may make us to comprehend why Gillius and Gesner, translated the words which Elim makes use of to express the deformity of the tortoise, have rendered it Crispissima aspect, instead of *Aspecta admodum torvo*: For the Greek signifies both, and the interpretation of the translators of Elian has nothing of the sense, as the other, which agree with the description of Pacuvius who says that the tortoise is truci aspect. The eye had no upper eye-lid, being shut only by the means of the lower, which is listed up to the eye-brow. Pliny reports that this is common to all oviparous quadrupeds.[6]

Towards the extremity of the jaw-bones, at the place of the lips, the skin was hard as a horn, and keen as in other tortoises; but these lips were jagged like a saw, and it wanted not on the inside two rows of real teeth, although Pliny affirms that tortoises have neither teeth nor tongue.

On each of the fore-paws it had five toes, or rather five bails, for the toes were not distinguished otherwise than by the nails. These paws had at the end but one round mass, from whence the nails grew out. The hinder-legs had only four. Both the fore and hind-legs were very short. The fore ones contained but nine inches in length, from the top of the shoulder to the end of the nails and hinder-legs eleven, from the knee to the end of the nails, the nails were long, being an inch and half, they were rounded away both above and below, their cut making an oval figure; they were blunt and worn away. Their colour was partly-coloured of black and white in different places, and without any order. We have observed that sea-turtles have claws much sharper, because that they do not wear them in swimming, as land tortoises do in crawling. We have found some that had only four nails on the fore-feet even as on those behind. Albertus tells us that there are always five on each foot. We have remarked that though the tortoise goes slowly, yet the manner of going which is peculiar to it, must wear out its claws as much as in animals which run, for it rubs them all against earth singly and one after another; so that when it puts down one paw, it rests at first only upon the hindermost nail, then on the next, and so passes to the others, even to the fore-claw by turning its paw, which is round and bordered with nails like a chariot which moves its wheels, and imprints the heads of the nails with which their circumference is bordered, and makes them to enter into the earth one after the other.

The tail of the tortoise of Pondicherry was large, having at its beginning six inches diameter. It was fourteen inches long, and terminated in a point like an ox's horn. Cardan calls it a nail, which he likens to the spur which is behind a cock's foot, and thinks that it is callosity engendered at the end of the tail of tortoises, which have been formerly cutoff: which is not probable; a callus not being able to obtain a figure so regular, and so exactly rounded as it was in the tail of Pondicherry tortoise. This tail after the death of the tortoise was turned on one side, and so inflexible, that it could never be made strait, what force so ever was used. The same inflexibility was found in the muscles of the jaws, which could not be opened otherwise than by cutting the muscles. Aristotle has observed that of all animals, the tortoise is that which hath most strength in his jaws, for its force is such, that it cuts in sunder whatever it lays hold on, even to the hardest flints. We have taken notice, in a small tortoise that its head, half an hour after its being cut off, did make its jaws to clack with a noise like to that of Castanetts. The stiffness has a great deal of strength in this part to strike with, and that this horn which it has at the end may serve instead of an offensive weapon.[7]

After having sawed on both the sides, the bon which in manner of a skull makes the cavity in which the entrails are enclosed as has been said. And after having quite cut away a membrane adhering to the part of this bone which is underneath, and which makes the belly, (this membrane supplying the place of the peritoneum towards the bottom and of the pleura towards the top) the internal parts which presented themselves to view, were the ventricle, liver and bladder, whose greatness was such, that it covered the intestine, and all the other parts of the lower belly.

The ventricle was placed underneath the liver, to which it was fastened by means of several vessels. It was nine inches long and three diameters. Its tunicles were very thick, its orifices strait and the membrane which makes the velvet was folded and bearing forms like leaves extended according to its length, It has the figure of the ventricle of a dog. Severinus attributes to it that of the ventricle of a man.[8] There is description about the intestine, liver, spleen, pancreas, kidneys, testicles, bladder, penis, heart and the lungs which had been examined and minute details had been reported.[9] Comparisons of the parts of the body had been made with dog and fish.[10] The report further goes on explaining the brain which was very small, the membranes, the medulla spinalis, the globe of the eye, the ears, the neck and the head.[11]

It is mentioned that they have frequently observed that as soon as a tortoise was put into the water it casts forth through the mouth or nostrils several bubbles which were in all likelihood formed by the overmuch air that is has in its lungs, for the keeping itself in a just equilibrium, which puts it in a condition of being heavy enough to sink to the bottom, at the least compression which its muscles do make upon its lungs, just as the little figure descends in the water at the smallest effort that is made to compress the air that it encloses, and it is easy to comprehend that if the tortoise being at the bottom of the water relaxes the muscles that did compress its lungs, the air by the virtue of its spring returning into its first state, can give again to its whole body, the extent which it had when it did swim upon the water. The probability of this arguing has been confirmed by experience.[12] The legends of the various parts of the body of the tortoise had been furnished in the drawing as follows.[13]

1. The trunk of the left vena cava
2. The trunk of the right vena cava,
3. The Trunk of the aorta at the going out of the heart, forming two crosses.
4. The left aorta
5. The right aorta
6. The conjunction of the two aortas
7. The carotids
8. The artery of the lungs
9. The veins of the lungs which are discharged into the axillares
10. The artery which goes to the stomach
11. The artery which goes to the liver, pancreas spleen etc
12. The artery which goes to the intestines
13. The heart in its natural situation
14. The anterior ventricle of the heart
15. The artery of the lungs opened, to show its three valvulae sigmoides
16. The heart out of its natural situation being raised upwards and separated from its auricles AA which are in their place
17. The two posterior ventricles of the heart
18. The two posterior ventricles of the heart

19. The aorta proceeding from the right ventricle. It is opened to represent its three valvuae sigmoides
20. The three valvulae sigmoides which are at the entrance of the auricles of the heart

Thus Duverney and Perrault in the *Memoirs pour servir a l'histoire des animaux* in 1676 wrote the way they examined and did comparative anatomy in new ways. The illustration of the tortoise (Figure 8 given in the printed book) broke new ground in the depiction of the animal. The tortoise though originated from the Coromandel Coast in the Tamil tropical landscape, its image had been given by the artist in France with a classical temple, obelisk, and bridge in an environment as the animal was found moving in Paris.

Elephants of Africa and Dissection by the Surgeons in London and Paris, 1681-1706

Queen Elizabeth in London received an elephant as a gift from Henri IV in 1591. King James I had been presented with a live elephant in 1623 as diplomatic tribute from Philip II, the king of Spain. However a young male elephant arrived at Whitefriars, London on 3 July 1675 and it was taken to Garraway's Coffee House. It was exhibited to a large crowd for an entrance fee of three shillings. This elephant according to his keepers would punch either man or beast that angered him, and came within his reach with his trunk.[14] A tract was printed in July 1675 to broadcast the arrival of this elephant in London and it was not exaggerating when it claimed that few persons amongst them, but such as travelled the Eastern world, ever saw one of them.[15] While on exhibition in Dublin, the booth in which this elephant was stabled caught alight in the early hours of 17 July 1681. Therefore the elephant was burnt alive and had broken a tusk in attempting to escape. Mr Wilkins had protected his property the carcass of the elephant. He sent for the butchers, but the Irish physician Allan Moulin offered his services. That night in a temporary wooden shed in Dublin city centre Moulin undertook the first British dissection of an elephant, boiling bones and cutting into parboiled organs by candlelight.[16]

The anatomists in Paris had evinced interest to dissect an elephant and their work was possible in 1681 because Louis XIV the king of France gave an elephant which died in the royal menagerie at Versailles to the Paris Academy of Sciences. Joseph–Guichard Duvernay received this dead African elephant (brought from Congo which was gifted by the king of Portugal in 1668) at the age of seventeen. Duvernay dissected it at Versailles in January 1681.[17] The account of description of the elephant is interesting.[18] Louis XIV the king of France had visited the laboratory to watch the dissection of the elephant. The sketch of elephant dissected by Duverney is now found at the Galerie de Paleontologie in the Muséum National d'Histoire Naturelle, Paris. The anatomical report of the elephant was later printed in 1733.

Another young female elephant arrived in Britain in 1683 and it was exhibited for some time at Edinburgh before she made her way to Dundee. Collapsing of fatigue on the road to Dundee in 1706, the elephant drowned after a ditch that had been dug to support her weight was filled with water during torrential rain. The bloated carcass attracted the attention of the locals who stole away with the elephant's forefoot—a body part that had to be recovered by force. Patrick Blair, the Dundee surgeon and apothecary performed the dissection and the anatomical account had brought him into the network of correspondence and acquaintance with Sir Hans Sloane and the Royal Society of London for the Promotion of Natural Knowledge. Blair had meticulously recorded both the process by which he prepared his specimen skeleton and skin, and the manner in which Moulin mounted his. The elephant deteriorated rapidly when exposed to the elements, in lieu of much extant soft tissue the preservation of the salted skin and skeleton took precedent. The skin of the earlier Dublin elephant had been incinerated in the booth fire increased the significance of the later Dundee specimen. Blair prepared and delivered four large copper plates depicting the skin, mounted skeleton, soft tissue and other osteological observations. The stuffed skin of the elephant stood in the Hall of the Royal Society of London.[19]

It is mentioned in records that a white elephant had toured British towns in the first decade of the eighteenth century was trained to take off his hat to the company and made reverence on his knees. His master then asking where he loves Queen Anne, then he pointed with his trunk to his heart, and what he must do for her, he sounded for her on the trumpet.[20] This elephant also took ten passengers on his back, two on his head, and two on his ears. Similarly a young elephant came to London in 1720 and it was reported in Mist's Journal as both-bending her knees to the ground to drink his majesty's George I health and-paying her compliments to company at their entrance.[21]

Dissection of an Elephant at Fort St. George in Madras by A. Suply the French Surgeon, 1715

Elephants in India had been associated with the god Ganesh depicting wisdom and learning in Hindu culture. The elephants had also symbolic use in terms of military deployment and the legitimization of royal power. This characteristic animal had continued to be of great interest to Europeans and they had learnt that the Indian elephant in size and form was different and they were less malicious than the African elephant.[22] In India from ancient times the people tamed the elephants to work especially to carry loads and it was astonishing to note what they perform and how skillfully and willingly did the work. Giovannio Borghesi the Italian physician in Pondicherry in 1703 had mentioned the use of elephants.[23]

The English in Madras were also interested to study the elephant because they desired to use the Indian species that had not been found in England. This they felt would help to dispel fanciful ideas about the animal and would provide a neat and better understanding of the functions of the bodily parts. The work in anatomy was also considered important which could be used to support research in physiology.

According to English records, dissecting an elephant was successfully carried out by A. Suply the French Surgeon at the English settlement of Fort St George in Madras in November 1715 and it lasted for twelve hours. The elephant which had died twenty-four hours ago had not yet begun to rot. However, it had been stated that the weather and climate were very unpleasant due to drizzling rain at that time.[24] The French surgeon was helped by a group of 20 *Paraiyars* who were Tamil speaking and the *Malas* the Telugu speaking untouchables to become a part of the autopsy. These natives were skilled workers for they handled the dead in the cremation ground.[25] The English Governor of Fort St. George had arranged these men for executing the autopsy who were well armed with a great hooked knife to help the surgeon open and separate the parts as the French surgeon thought fit to examine. It has been mentioned that the place of work was the house of the surgeon.

The surgeon in his report remarked that the autopsy of the elephant to be conducted was often similar to what he had done earlier upon a frog with pleasure during his training as a surgeon in France.[26] However he stated that it was not necessary to tell the audience that such a dissection had been given to him a person who was so weak and sickly.[27]

The account of autopsy mentions that the surgeon examined the carcass of a massive specimen and mused upon its inner workings. Regarding the animal he exclaimed 'What colour! and what vast intestines, bigger than the body of a man'.[28] He had an enthusiasm for anatomical knowledge and dissection and so had meticulously recorded the process of dissection and preserved the samples.[29]

While cutting across the kidney he observed a visible cavity, filled with a brown and viscous liquor.[30] Further he stated that the *Paraiyars* and *Malas* found a great heat issuing from the entrails and viscera. It was somewhat singular and diverting to see these savage anatomists went in and out of the belly of this animal, like Jonas, to wash themselves from the blood and filth in a little river that ran by our slaughter-house before they refreshed themselves when they came almost suffocated out of their Trojan Horse looking like so many infernal furies laden with their prey.[31]

The twenty-two pages account drafted by A. Suply had been written in the form of a letter addressed to the chief surgeon at Fort St David in Cuddalore, the English trading settlement on the Coromandel Coast. It had been made clear that the account was meant for a wider European audience and this fact is evident because the French Surgeon wrote another letter to Sir Hans Sloane in London to advertise his efforts.[32] He also sent to Sloane the full dissection account in manuscript form, and the elephant's tissues preparations.[33]

The observations and the findings of the surgeon had been revealing. He was more happy than to critique previous accounts of elephant anatomy. He wrote that Dr Dureen the author of the natural chemistry had been mistaken in affirming that the elephant had four ventricles like other ruminating animals.[34] The French surgeon offered reasons for the elephant's distinct heart structure, and was thus contributing not just descriptive and observational data, but also speculatively to the study.

The surgeon concluded his report with some observations in relation to the sentiments and instincts of the elephants, and some particulars which perhaps had not come to the knowledge of the Europeans.[35] He said that he had been repeating what he had heard, and leaving the judgment to the reader. He said that Indians saw elephants as personable creatures, with high intelligence, excellent memory and vast wisdom.[36] They seriously believed that elephants understand love and flattery etc., for which reason they invent and compliment them with most magnificent titles to cajole and render them tractable and gentle.[37]

The French surgeon also reported that when an elephant died on ship-board the crew did not throw him whole into the sea. They were forced to cut him in pieces as privately as they could, and to convey him away, for the fear of other elephants which would die out of sympathy and the elephants were so lively in their instinct, and so tendered towards their own kind.[38]

The Significance of the Report of Elephant Dissection at Madras for the Study of Comparative Animal Anatomy

It is important to note that the report of A. Suply from Madras had been helpful to many anatomists in Europe like Sir Hans Sloane and William

Stukeley who dissected in London an elephant originated from Africa. This elephant had arrived in West Smithfield London and it was reported in Mist's Journal on 2 July 1720. A mere four months later Mist's Journal informed its readers that Hans Sloane, that curious inspector of the works of nature was then dissecting the same elephant shown at West Smithfield. It was dissected on the lawn of Sloane's London residence and it was reported by his colleagues William Stukeley and Dr Douglas that the elephant had died mainly for want of a suitable and proportionate method of food, and from the ignorance of the keepers, who exposed it to cold and moisture. A fever had been exacerbated by a broken tusk, the great quantities of ale the spectators continually gave it.[39] Intestinal purges and the failed medical intervention of a farrier had hastened the eventual death of the elephant on 4 October 1720. Sir Hans Sloane and Dr Douglas who dissected the elephant also removed specific anatomical parts for further examination and collection. Stukeley informs us that Sir Hans Sloane stretched out the plexus of the arteries that ran along the exterior of the brain onto paper for this purpose, and that Dr Douglas took home-those organs pertaining to generation in a female.[40] Further Stukeley wrote that Pliny's tale of a learned elephant learnt to read and write the Greek alphabet was proverbial. It was invoked by Stukeley mainly to convey the structure of the elephant brain which he found-so fine and perfect. Stukeley's elephant anatomy was published as an appendix to his work of the spleen, its description and history in 1723. For Stukeley the spleen maintained the balance between solids and fluids in the body and so was of service in vomiting, menstruation, fever and digestion.[41]

It is interesting to find that William Stukeley had compared his observations and the anatomical observations of the Indian elephant made by A. Suply at Fort St. George in Madras. The surgeon later conducted tests on the samples—for example, filling a length of intestine with water in order to test its porosity—and included the results of these experiments in his account.[42] William Stukeley said that Suply the French Surgeon after the dissection of the elephant had sent the outer and the thinner of the two bones between the knee and ankle of the leg (fibula) to the Royal Society of London.[43]

Curiosity of the Germans and Collecting More Details on the Elephants from Tranquebar, 1779

Carl von Linné (Linnaeus) the Swedish botanist and naturalist gave in 1758 in his binominal classification for the elephant (*Elephas maximus*) and he considered the African and Asian elephants to belong to a single species. People in early modern Europe were very curious to learn a lot more on elephants. They had understood that the absence of tusk indicated that elephant was a female. Further, they also learnt that the relatively small ears make clearest that the elephant was not from Africa but from India. Balthasar Kohlhoff and Daniel Zeglin the two German missionaries in Tranquebar therefore had collected the details in a question-answer format from the mahout in Thanjavur. The answers they got in Tamil from the elephant caretaker of the ruler of Thanjavur were communicated in German to a knight, who sought certain clarifications about the elephant too.[44] Some of these interesting questions and the replies are furnished below:

Question: How many people can an elephant carry?

Answer: Twenty-eight

Question: How do the 28 persons sit on the elephant?

Answer: On the top of the elephant one builds a structure, on which seven persons sit to the left and seven to the right. Two planks under its belly take six persons these on each side. Near the tail one makes a construction for a person who can stand and for another person behind the two legs.

Question: How is it possible for the elephant to carry?

Answer: An adult elephant could do this. It is very difficult to find such an elephant. Tej Singh the great king of Gingee had such an elephant and some of the descendants of that elephant are still found in the country.

Question: How do they send an elephant into a battlefield? How do they make him so furious? Do they use red juice or anything else?

Answer: Nothing is known about red juice but they use different means that are similar to narcotic and intoxication. Such things make the elephant drunken or lose his senses and make him furious. Some other things are also made into powder and given to the elephant to eat before it goes to the battlefield. They tie at his trunk two torches (made from sulphur and sulphate which had been noiseless and hand–held match stick) in the daytime and two in the night through the smoke of it the vision becomes dim and the elephant cannot see what was going on in the war.

Johann David Michaelis (1717-1791) in Germany was inspired by his desire to recapture the biblical natural world and so he sent a questionnaire to the missionaries in Tranquebar who could answer the questions concerning several animal descriptions found in the Old Testament. One of the questions was about the behemoth, a large animal mentioned in the book of Job. Michaelis thought the behemoth was an elephant. But after reading the book of George Louis de Buffon's natural history he began to doubt this. To find out what the behemoth was, he asked the missionaries about the habitat of the elephant, its fond and its reproduction habits.[45]

Michaelis had also contacted Johann Christopher Wolf who was employed in the services of the Dutch East India Company in Sri Lanka to know about the elephant. Today this large animal the behemoth is thought to be the hippopotamus and not the elephant. The intensive study of the elephants led the German naturalist and anatomist Johann Friedrich Blumenbach in 1797 to assign the African elephant a separate binominal, *Loxodonta africana*.

To conclude it may be said that dissection of living and dead animals had become a widespread technique in Europe. It developed as a standard method of obtaining new knowledge, and an important focus of the new experimental science. The intertwined practices of anatomy and natural history had hinged chiefly on the distinction between historia and scientia. The ideas, events, and practices in Europe took their cue from humanist anatomy and natural history produced new knowledge that was not necessarily the causal knowledge of the exact sciences, but it was nonetheless both experimental and experiential knowledge and not merely with description. It must be pointed out that Duverney and Perrault in Paris could not distinguish between tortoises and turtles. It shows that the experiments they performed had described were most likely on European turtles rather than tortoises. However we have learnt that they dissected in Paris the tortoise from the land sent by the French East India Company in Pondicherry from the Coromandel Coast. The birth of the experimental method in natural history had largely helped in the reconfiguration of the animal body. There was no anesthesia or reliable means of reducing pain while dissecting the live animals in Europe. We find that dead animals were mostly dissected. The dissection of the dead elephant in Madras by the English East India Company had helped for the study of comparative anatomy of Indian and African elephants. Printing, publishing, and illustrations of the dissected animals helped for wider circulation of knowledge. It is known that a new curiosity about the Tamil natural world of animals had begun to explode particularly on Indian elephants in Europe and the people had understood properly and it helped to change the long-held beliefs. It should be noted that anatomy in this period referred both to what we now call anatomy—that is, the study of structure—and to what we now call physiology, the study of function. Indeed, disentangling the relationship of structure to function was a major goal of anatomical study in this age.

Notes

1. Claude Perrault, 'The anatomical description of a great Indian tortoise' in *Memoirs for a natural history of animals containing the anatomical description*

of several creatures dissected by the Royal Academy of Sciences at Paris, trs., Alexander Pitfield, London, 1688, p. 3.

2. Linda Hall Library of Science, Engineering and Technology, University of Missouri, Kansa City USA, *Memoires pour server a l'histoire animaux, Dresses par M. Perrault de l'Academie Royale des Sciences & Medecin de la Faculte de Paris*, Paris, MDCLXXVI, pp. 192-205; See also, British Library, London, *Memoires pour server a l'histoire animaux, Dresses par M. Perrault de l'Academie Royale des Sciences & Medecin de la Faculte de Paris*, Paris, MDCLXXVI, shelf-mark 74/C 128.k.6.
3. Claude Perrault, The anatomical description of a great Indian tortoise, pp. 250-267, see p. 252.
4. *Ibid.*, p. 253.
5. *Ibid.*
6. *Ibid.*, pp. 253-4.
7. *Ibid.*, p. 254.
8. *Ibid.*, p. 255.
9. *Ibid.*, pp. 255-262.
10. *Ibid.*, pp. 262-3
11. *Ibid.*, pp. 263-267.
12. *Ibid.*, pp. 263-4.
13. *Ibid.*, p. 251.
14. Allan Moulin, *An Anatomical Account of the Elephant Accidentally Burnt in Dublin*, London, 1682, p. 35.
15. *A True and Perfect Description of the Strange and Wonderful Elephant Sent from the East Indies*, London, 1675.
16. Alan Moulin, An Anatomical Account of the Elephant Accidentally Burnt, p. 4.
17. Anita Guerrini, *Courtiers' Anatomists: Animals and Humans in Louis XIV's Paris*, Chicago, 2015, p. 202.
18. Archives Academie des Sciences, Paris (AASP), Proces-verbaux, vol. 10, fl.83v, Decembre 1681.
19. Patrick Blair, 'The Anatomy and Osteology of an Elephant, being an exact Description of all the Bones of the Elephant which died near Dundee, April the 27th, 1706, with their several dimensions', *Philosophical Transactions*, vol. XXVII, 1710, p. 53; See also, Patrick Blair, *Osteographica Elephantina: Or a Full and Exact Account of the Bones of an Elephant which Died near Dundee*, London, 1713, pp. 18, 104.
20. Bodleian Library, University of Oxford, John Johnson Collection, 1702-1714, *The Great White Elephant Alive: Is to be seen in this Town*, Single Sheet Folio.
21. BL, Lysons Collection, *Mist's Journal*, 1720 Microfilm: 20452.
22. John Corse and Joseph Banks, 'Observations on the Different Species of Asiatic Elephants, and Their Mode of Dentition', *Philosophical Transactions of the Royal Society of London* (hereafter Philosophical Transactions), vol. 89, 1799, pp. 205-236.

23. Giovanni Borghesi, *Lettera Scritta da Pondischeri*, p. 206.
24. BL, London, Western Manuscripts Collections, Sloane, MSS 3916, A. Suply, '*Anatomical Remarkes Upon an Elephant open'd att Fort St George in November 1715*. This manuscript contains also French version titled 'A. Suply, *Remarques anatomiques sur un elephant ouvert au fort Saint-Georges, 1715*'. I have used the English version.
25. China Rao Yagti, 'Medieval Telugu Literature and the Untouchables in Society', ed., S. Jeyaseela Stephen, *Literature, Caste and Society: The Masks and Veils*, Delhi, 2006, pp.103-118. See, pp.111-112. Mala is one of the two major untouchable communities in Andhra. The text of the poem runs thus: 'Why revile a mala again and again. Are not his flesh and blood same as yours, You plunge into the water after you touch a Mala, When you depart to the cremation ground the Mala burns your body the filth that touched you, then; where did it go'.
26. A. Suply, Anatomical Remarkes Upon an Elephant, p. 15.
27. *Ibid.*, p. 1.
28. *Ibid.*, p. 4.
29. *Ibid.*
30. *Ibid.*, 5.
31. *Ibid.*, pp. 10-11.
32. BL, Sloane MS 4045, fol. 282, see the letter of A. Suply to Hans Sloane dated 8 January 1719/20.
33. A. Suply, Anatomical Remarkes upon an Elephant, p. 1.
34. *Ibid.*, p. 8.
35. *Ibid.*, p. 18.
36. *Ibid.*, p. 22.
37. *Ibid.*
38. *Ibid.*
39. William Stukeley, 'An Essay Towards the Anatomy of the Elephant, from one dissected at Fort St George Oct. 1715 and another at London Oct.1720', in William Stukeley, *Of the Spleen: To Which is Added Some Anatomical Observations in the Dissection of an Elephant*, London, 1723, p. 18.
40. *Ibid.*, p. 16.
41. *Ibid.*
42. *Ibid.*, p. 95.
43. *Ibid.*, pp. 90-93.
44. Georg Christian Knapp et al., eds., *Neuere Geschichte der Evangelischen Missions-Anstalten zu Bekehrung der Heiden in Ostindien aus den eigenhändigen Aufsätzen und Briefen der Missionarien erausgegeben*, Waisenhaus, Teil 1–8 (Stück 1–95), Waiserihaus, Halle, 1770–8/95, 1848 (hereafter NHB), 1779, pp. 293-4; see also, NHB 2, p. 793.
45. NHB, 3, pp. 136-44.

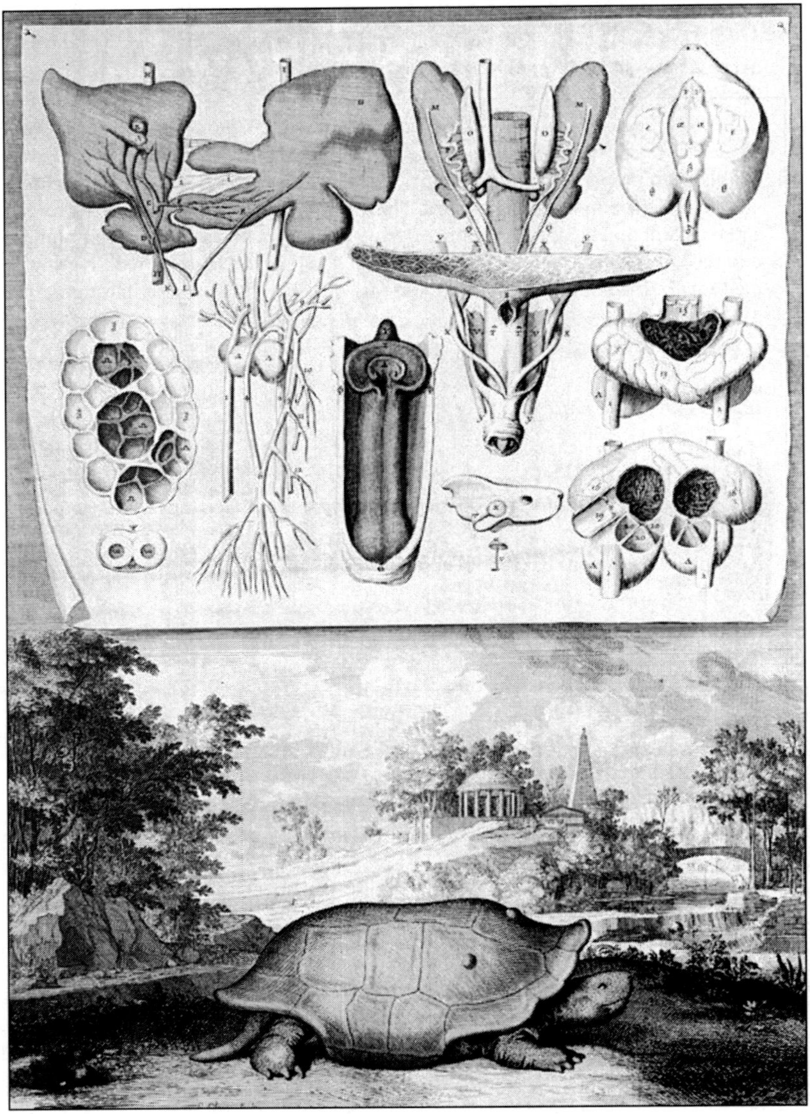

4.1. The tortoise sent from Pondicherry to Paris in 1674 and the anatomical drawings of its parts of the body after dissection.

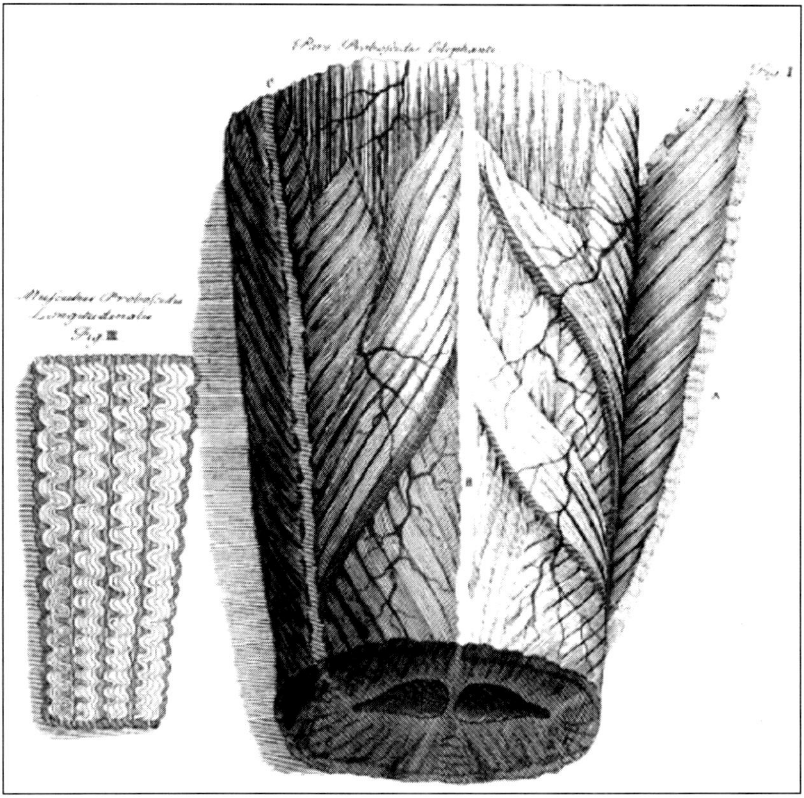

4.2. The anatomical drawing of an elephant's trunk dissected at Fort St George, Madras by Dr. A. Suply in October 1715 and another elephant at London in 1720 by William Stukeley

5

Exploring the Exotic: Entomology and Herpetology, 1690-1853

The Portuguese traders who came to the Tamil coast in the sixteenth century were mainly interested in the overseas trade of Asia. The Padroado missionaries who came were only interested in the conversion of the Hindus to Catholicism. Therefore these early Europeans were not all interested in any way to undertake studies on nature and living things. Claudio Acqua Viva (1543-1615), the fifth superior-general of the Society of Jesus elected in 1581 in Rome, demanded that no Jesuit defend, or even study, any opinion or principle that contradicted the received theology or philosophy. Though the scientific study by the Jesuits was significant in Europe but it was controversial as the conflict between scientific reasoning and religious faith had continued to plague with those Jesuits in Tamil country who wished to study the former while living a life of the latter.

The commercial ambition and activities of the servants and officials of the newly formed United East India Company, the English East India Company and the Danish Asiatic Company in Europe in the early seventeenth century had been completely opposite in nature to the Portuguese expansion. Further a new spirit was added with the advent of the German and Danish-Halle Protestant missionaries on the Tamil coast in preaching the gospel to the natives at the beginning of the eighteenth century. The northern Europeans evinced interest in the study of fauna though they were equally eager to conduct maritime trade and to convert the Hindus. They were very well aware of the development in Europe and keen to do things valued such as modern science, its reading and writing.

The New World information poured into Europe at increased rates had called for self reflection. The natural historians of Europe desired to redirect their gaze towards the rapidly expanding world around the globe particularly on the Tamil coast. Thus the culture of collecting the fauna gradually asserted itself in the realm of natural history and gained momentum. Various types of insects and their poisonous bites and medicines administered were interesting to the Europeans on the Tamil coast. Hence they learnt the details gradually and described them in their accounts sent to Europe.

Instructions Issued for Collecting and Sending Insects and Natural Things from Madras to London

The Royal Society of London (RSL) for the Promotion of Natural Knowledge (founded on 28 November 1660) provided a forum for the scientists in Europe to communicate with each other through its publication of the journal 'Philosophical Transactions'. Since collecting flora and fauna from various parts of the world had developed, the impulse to catalogue the natural world outside of Europe developed and it could be traced from the earliest efforts of the Royal Society, as evident in 1665 with the lists of instruction and inquiry produced under its auspices, including 'Directions for Sea-Men, Bound for Far Voyages' which continued for next thirty years till 1696.[1] James Petiver in London sent instructions on what sort of material and information he wanted, and on the best ways to preserve samples for the long sea voyage. These correspondences have survived in a manuscript and found in the consolidated standard manual which he published in London in 1709.[2]

James Petiver gave directions to persons engaged in the overseas who were collecting the curiosities for him. This he did for the easy making and preserving collections of all natural curiosities. He mentioned that with regard to fauna that all small animals, as beasts, birds, fish, serpents, lizards, and other fleshy bodies capable of corruption, were certainly preserved in rack, rum, brandy or any other spirits; but where these were not easily to be had, a strong pickle, or brine of sea water might serve; to every gallon of which, put 3 or 4 handfuls of common or bay salt, with a spoonful or two of alum powdered, if they had any, and so sent them in any pot, bottle, jar, and close, corked and rosined. He added that they might often find in the stomachs of sharks, and other great fish, which they caught at sea, diverse strange animals not easily to be met with elsewhere; which prey look for, and preserve as above. As to fowls, those that were large, if they could not have their cases whole, their head, legs, or wings, would be acceptable, but smaller birds were easily sent entire, by putting them in spirits as above, or if they brought them dry, they must take out their entrais; which was best done by cutting them under their wing, and then stuff them with tow, mixed with pitch or tar; and being thoroughly dried in the sun, wrap them up close, to keep them from moisture, but in long voyages, they must bake them gently, once in a month or two, to kill the vermin which often breed in them.[3] Thus curiosities collection had been very much encouraged in this age.

There was also a sense of sharing the materials collected with the leading scholars and it developed over a period of time. We find insects, moths and beetles particularly the Indian marbled butterfly, Madras yellow tricolor, Madras Prittillary and Madras ring coffin sent from Fort St. George at Madras by Edward Buckley to James Petiver in London and these had been shared with Joseph Pitton de Tournefort (1656-1708) the French naturalist in Paris.[4]

Description of Insects found in Pondicherry by Louis Le Comte, 1690

Louis Le Comte the French Jesuit who visited Pondicherry in 1690 had mentioned in his letter to Monsieur Abbe Jean-Paul Bignon (1662-1743) in Paris that there were a prodigious number of insects that might deserve the most serious reflections. He said that were certain flies that nature hath painted of such a lively yellow, so polished and shining, that the most curious gilding does not come near it. Some other insects were but points of light, that always glow and emitted rays all night long and all the air appeared as if set on fire with it when they flew and when they light upon leaves or branches/ the trees resembled, afar off, those fireworks they made in the India for solemn illuminations. Thus he had written on the glow worms called *minmini puchchi* in Tamil.[5]

Information on the Long Worm of Madras Received by Martin Lister in London, 1695-97

Martin Lister (1639-1712) the English naturalist and one of Her Majesties principal physicians in London received information from English men at Fort St. George in Madras about the fauna of the place. Therefore he narrated the details on the long worm which had not been known for the knowledge of the English audience in London. He reported that on 2 May 1695 after arriving at Fort St George Madras an English man in a few days after saw a little below the instep of his left foot, a worm put out his head which afterwards cost him much trouble. He stated that he learnt that these worms were bred by the water, and they came out in any part of the body, and were very troublesome and dangerous; because he had known those who have kept their bed for them, some, six, some ten months, and some there were who have lost sometimes their legs, sometimes their lives by them. These worms came out sometimes to the length of six or seven yards and when they came first out were small like a thread, and afterwards growing bigger and stronger by degrees they wrapped them up upon a little bit of stick or cotton, and put upon them onions and flower of rice boiled in milk. The chief care was to be taken not to break them, for then it was that they do mischief. When it first came out for about forty or fifty days it came out every day by little and little, without putting the English man too much pain, but that he could go up and down till it came out a yard and a quarter. Afterwards, one day stirring too much he hurt the worm and it got raged, and so it broke off itself, and going in, caused his foot and leg to swell till the skin was ready to burst, which kept him sleepless. This had also cast him into a fever. Therefore the English man had the surgeon of Fort St. George and kept his bed for about twenty days, in which time had several fits of the said fever. The worm was broken into pieces, and came out in several parts of his foot; but the surgeon applied the medicine and killed the worm. The surgeon lanced his leg a little above the ankle, and another place of his foot, and drew it all out. The English man had said that he had been by God's blessing clear altogether of that troublesome creature and the English company surgeon in Madras left him ten days later.[6]

Treatment to Poisonous Insect Bites Described by Samuel Brown in Madras, 1700

Samuel Brown the surgeon entered into the services of the English East India Company and reached Madras in 1688. He was the principal surgeon at Fort St. George from 1688-1697. He noticed the treatment of poisonous insect bites by Tamils and so he had elaborated the details in 1700. According to him the whole plant of *Balsamina aquat indiae oriental* was ground with water and rubbed on the body to cure the bites of venomous insects. The powdered bark of *cheerean* was taken in hot water for treating bites of venomous insects.[7] The powdered root of *cachakaillille* (*gatchki chittu* in Telugu) drunk with water was good for rat bites and venomous creatures. The whole plant of *chetamucan* ground with water and drank cured the venomous insects. A dram of the powdered bark of *shala maram* (*Shorea robusta*) was taken to cure the bites of a venomous horse-fly, which the Tamils called *wandoo-kadi*. It was also good against the bites of other insects.[8]

Butterfly Sent by Edward Buckley from Madras to James Petiver in London, 1701-02

Edward Buckley (1651-1714) was employed as the surgeon and coroner at Fort St George in Madras. He became the principal surgeon in 1692 and remained in the post till 1709. He collected and sent a number of the objects to James Petiver in London. We find the drawing of *Papilio madraspatanus* the singular butterfly sent from Fort St. George in a publication printed in London in 1702.[9]

Johann Gerard Koenig in Tranquebar and his Study of Thirteen Insects, 1770-77

Johann Gerard Koenig (1728-85) was appointed surgeon at Tranquebar the Danish settlement on the Tamil Coast. He arrived there in 1768 as successor of Samuel Benjamin Knoll.[10] Koenig conducted a study of insects in Tranquebar and he had communicated the details to Europe. In 1792 Johann Christian Fabricius (1745-1808) the Danish zoologist had thanked him.[11] Further he also thanked I.K. Daldorf the Danish Naval officer in Tranquebar for the help he extended to the study of insects.[12] J.C. Fabricius had named one insect *Cryptocephalus koeinigi* after Koenig and honoured him for his help.[13] *Scarabaeus koenigii* the insect was named after Johann Gerard Koenig who had sent the insect specimen. The specific character of the insect had been that it was without scutel, unarmed, black; shield of the head bidentated: thorax scabrous: wing-cases dotted with cinereous.[14]

Chrysis oculata was found in Tranquebar by Johann Gerard Koenig and the specific character of the insect had been that it was shining green, with an ocellated golden spot on each side of the abdomen. The tail was blue and armed with six teeth. This insect is distinguished for the peculiar brilliancy of its colours. J.C. Fabricius stated in 1781 that he had described this insect from a specimen sent by Koenig found in the collection of Sir Joseph Banks in London.[15]

It is mentioned that a charming insect was found in Tranquebar and it was uncommonly rare and the specific character of this insect *Chrysis fasciata* had been that the thorax was green, with a blue band, anterior part of the abdomen blue faciated with violet, golden in the middle, posterior end was red, with four teeth. J.C. Fabricius had said that he had found this specimen only in the cabinet of Sir Joseph Banks.[16]

It is recorded that Johann Gerard Koenig had discovered the insect *Chrysis splendida* in Tranquebar. The specific character of the insect had been that it was shining blue, with four teeth at the tail. J.C. Fabricius had said that he had described this insect from a specimen in the cabinet of Sir. Joseph Banks.[17]

Vespa cincta the insect was found in Tranquebar and the specific character of the insect had been that it was black, throax obscurely spotted, and the body was black with a ferruginous band.[18]

Chrysomela palliata the insect was found in Tranquebar. It was pale yellow and the shells were black.[19]

Chrysomela cincia the insect found in Tranquebar was pale and the edge all round the shells had been black. The antennae singular, the second joint minute was globular, three spinous each side, and marginal line was interrupted and behind the colour was black.[20]

Scarbaeus seniculus the insect was found in Tranquebar. It had thorax on the fore-part and shield on the hind-part two-horned. The shells were substriate, black, crossed with two ferruginous stripes composed of dots at the base. The legs were short and ferruginous.[21]

Scarbaeus pygmaeus the insect was found in Tranquebar. Its thorax was two-toothed, brassy: shield unarmed and emarginated. The shells were testaceous, spotted with black. The shield was round, widely emarginate before and the shells substriate and the body was black.[22]

*Scarbaeus dionysius*the insect was found in Tranquebar and its thorax had been excavate: horn of the head recurved, depressed, thicker at the tip and the shells had been substriate.[23]

Scarbaeus hircus the insect was found in Tranquebar and the thorax was rough, head with a transverse carinate line, shield was two-toothed.[24]

Scarbaeus nanus the insect was found in Tranquebar and its thorax was with a double prominence; horn of the head erect, simple, as long as the head. The shield was rounded: thorax was with an impressed point each side and the shells striate.[25]

The Study of Five Insects by Johann Gerard Koenig in Madras, 1778-85

Johann Gerard Koenig became the English East India Company's natural historian in 1778 in Madras. He continued his study of insects and sent the details to Sir Joseph Banks in London. *Vespa arcuata* the insect was found by Koenig in Madras. The specific character had been that it was black, variegated with yellow, petiole of the abdomen incurved and it had been with four yellow spots.[26]

Buprestis sternicornis the insect was brought from Madras. The specific character had been that it was entirely shining green, with grey impressed spots. Wing cases serrated and terminated in three teeth. A conic projecting horn was on the breast.[27]

Cimex uniguttatus was a curious species from Madras. Its special character had been that its thorax with acute spines, ferruginous; scutel marked with a large white dot.[28]

Papilio idaeus the butterfly was brought from Madras to London. Its specific character had been that the wings dentated, black. A short yellow dash was across the anterior margin of the first pair. Second pair spotted with red: a palmated mark of three red spots in the middle.[29]

Phalaena figura the insect was brought from Madras to London and its specific character had been that its anterior wings whitish, with brown and black spots; in the middle a black character: posterior wings cinereous.[30]

Six Scarce Insects Reported from the Coromandel Coast to Johann Christian Fabricius in Denmark

Vespa petiolata was the insect found in Tamil country and the specific character is that the insect had been ferruginous and yellow varied; abdominal petiole incurved and ferruginous with a black band. It had been described by J.C. Fabricius.[31]

Scarbaeus rhadamistus the small insect was found on the Coromandel Coast and its thorax was found deeply excavate with a recurved horn before: head unarmed: the shells rufous, with a black future and two spots. The shield rounded, brassy and whitish before thorax longer than the shells, brassy, pale at the sides with a brassy dot: Shells were striate.[32]

Scarbaeus sabaus the insect was found on the Coromandel Coast and its thorax had been with a double prominence: horn of the head erect, simple, as long as the thorax. The shield was rounded, scarcely emarginate: thorax black, polished, with an impressed lateral point each side: shells striate, black, polished.[33]

Scarabaeus spinifex the insect had been found on the Coromandel Coast and its specific character had been that it was without scutel, thorax roundish, unarmed: a recurved spine on the back of the head. J.C. Fabricius referred to this insect which he found in the collection of Sir Joseph Banks in London.[34]

Buprestis aenea the insect was found on the Coromandel Coast. Its specific character had been that it was shining, bronze, wing-cases terminated in three teeth. J.C. Fabricius had mentioned that he had studied and used it from the cabinet of Sir Joseph Banks in London.[35]

Fulgora festiva (the handsome fire fly) was found on the Coromandel Coast. The specific character of the insect was that its trunk conic, wing cases brown: anterior margin green with five black spots, semi-circled with orange, wings red at the base.[36]

The Study of Hover Flies and Stilt-legged Flies by Christoph Samuel John in Tranquebar Communicated to Denmark and Norway, 1780-1805

Christoph Samuel John (1747-1813) the Protestant missionary succeeded Johann Gerard Koenig as doctor in the Danish mission in Tranquebar in 1771.[37] He noticed many types of flies (called by the Tamils Ee) and fleas (known *Naay Ee* or *Thellu puchchi*). He also found the hover flies (Syrphidae: Diptera) that played a crucial role in pollination. He sent the details and specimens of *Platycheirus albimanus* (1781), *Phytomia errans* (1787) *Phytomia zunatum* (1787) *Lathyrophthalmus arvorum* (1787) *Lathyrophthalmus quinquestrrialtus* (1794), *Paragus bicolor* (1794) and *Metasyrphus corollae* (1794) to Denmark. The paragus serratus and Ischidon scutellaris were the first species reported by Johann Christian Fabricius (1745-1808) the Danish zoologist in 1805 which he received from Tranquebar. Thus we find nine varieties were mentioned by J.C. Fabricius.[38] Vidua Wiedemann from Norway was the first to describe a species of Micropezidae (insect: dipteral) the stilt-legged flies which he received from Tranquebar in 1840.[39] Thus the study of entomology received an impetus in Europe and the missionaries of Tranquebar had played a crucial role.

Import of Cochineal Insect from South America to Madras and the English Experiments in Dyeing at Saidapettai, 1786–1812

The English desired to conduct studies on the natural dyes of the Tamil coast, and also began to import dyes of foreign origin. Cochineal, an insect found in the Spanish colony of Mexico, was used for dyeing cloth. For a long time Spain had monopolized this article. It was a shield insect native to Central and South America, and was reared on the leaves of the nopal cactus. Hundreds of eggs were laid by the female insect on the nopal plant, which hatched thirty five to forty days later. Five months later the young insects were gathered and placed under the sun or heated over a low fire, and later crushed to produce a dye of brilliant crimson red. This method was discovered by the Spaniards in Mexico in 1518 and made known to Europe in 1523. Herman Cortes, the Spanish conquistador in Mexico, was the first to learn of it. Cochineal was used as a dyestuff by the Aztec and Mexican Indians. The merchants of Antwerp started buying cochineal in raw and powdered form, and used it in dyeing cloth. The move for the establishment of a farm was initiated by James Anderson, a physician of the English Company and an amateur botanist. The work was chiefly carried out to weaken the Spain's monopoly in the production of the expensive cochineal dye, but it was not very successful. Anderson experimented with American cactus grown in plantations for breeding cochineal, and established this farm in 1786 to cultivate the nopal plant in Saidapettai.

Anderson hoped to obtain cochineal dye by feeding local cochineal insects on the cacti, as he believed that the quality and colour of carminic acid was influenced by what the insects fed upon. He sent specimens of scale insects he collected on the grass (*Elikunchi pul* in Tamil, *Spinifix littoreus*) that grew on Madras beaches and the dye the people produced to Joseph Banks for verification. The insect Anderson found in grass in Madras appeared to correspond with the descriptions of the cochineal insect mentioned in the various earlier works of Leeuwenhek, Rueamur, Linnaeus and Hans Sloane. Anderson, therefore, began to do some research. By softening a number of these insects in a solution of wine and water, he obtained a colour that he claimed was similar to the one of the Mexican cochineal. Further, without much delay, he planted in a plot in his garden the grass that harboured the insect. He later sent thousands of opuntias and also the specimens of the insect to Joseph Banks.[40] The Madras Government supported Anderson's experiments and in their letter assured the Court of Directors in London that Anderson's project merited support. However, a chemical analysis of the specimens sent to London indicated that the project was commercially worthless. Nonetheless, Anderson was commended for his efforts and he was given the responsibility of maintaining the botanical garden at Marmelon (modern Saidapettai) in Madras. His nephew Dr Andrew Berry was appointed the superintendent of the garden of the Honourable Company. In the botanical garden, Anderson continued to cultivate and experiment with cochineals. He sent a specimen of a new species of cochineal lately discovered on the Coromandel Coast in 1787 to his friend and it was placed before the Royal Society of Edinburgh.[41]

James Anderson found an insect which he believed to be a kind of cochineal, and with which had had dyed pieces of flannel, shawls and satins. He forwarded the specimens to the Court of Directors in London, which was ordered for various experiments, but they were found to be entirely useless for the purpose of dyeing. Joseph Banks, who obtained similar results in May 1787, opined that the insect was a species of coccus. Anderson's finding was a case of mistaken identity.

However, Joseph Banks concluded then that the true cochineal might easily be cultivated on the Coromandel Coast as the climate was very similar to that of the West Indies.[42] Thus, the English, after identifying the climatic suitability, began to introduce cochineal in the Tamil coast. This was carried out with a view to promote the English needs, since cochineal had commercial value in England. The Company in Madras was trying to integrate the Tamil textile producing region into the world market, and transferring cochineal to the English settlement was felt to be a worthy endeavour.[43]

In 1788, the English East India Company gave sealed orders to a ship's captain proceeding to Brazil to procure cochineal. A consignment of the insects was brought from Brazil in a ship under the care of Commodore Phillips and delivered to Anderson the same year. The Court of Directors did not want the specific instructions relating to the care and preservation of the cochineal insect at sea to be made public, the operation was carried out in secret.[44] Anderson established the English Company's farm for the cultivation of the several kinds of cactus, on which the true cochineal feeds. He was assisted in this venture by his nephew, Andrew Berry. Cactus plants were obtained with considerable difficulty from Canton, Manila and Mauritius as well as from the Kew gardens. In a short period of three years, there were over two thousand opuntia plants in the Company's nopal plantation.

Anderson carried out his work as best he could and wrote to Campbell that he had devised a method of sheltering the plants from high winds by fences of plants. He reported that there were many suitable plants on the coast, but a thick hedge and mirgora tree would prove sufficient; the acrid juices of the one and bitterness of the other would not admit the generation of any insect that would prejudice the cochineal.[45] In 1795, Andrew Berry wrote that they had achieved some degree of certainty regarding the success of breeding cochineal in the Tamil coast, that the climate seemed most congenial, and the insects thrived in all situations both sheltered and exposed–even to the direct rays of the sun.[46]

In 1807, the English encouraged and developed cochineal cultivation in the areas of Nagapattinam and Madras.[47] The Company offered the cultivators of cochineal one *pagoda* per pound in order to encourage production. However, the selling price of Madras cochineal in London was only a little more than its prime cost.[48] By 1812, cochineal and colours for printers were imported from London to Madras.[49] Thus, the early efforts of developing commercial products by the English in the Tamil coast had failed. This made the Company adopt a different policy later for the commercialization of agriculture, and they were successful in transforming Tamil coast into a region producing raw material to serve the English industries.

The object of the English Company was to transfer European natural history enterprise to India for purely commercial purposes. The establishment of farm and the botanical garden at Madras had been the representative programme of research in economic botany. This persuaded the English to set up the Royal Botanic Gardens at Sibpur near Calcutta in 1787. The assigned task of Robert Kyd, the first official botanist, was to establish a stock for disseminating botanical articles which tended to the extension of English commerce and riches.

Reptiles of the Tamil Coast: Centipede Noticed by the Missionaries in Tranquebar

Europeans took abiding interest in herpetology. Reptiles which included the phylogenetic roots of all terrestrial vertebrates and amphibians of the Tamil country had attracted the attention of the Europeans since they were new to them. Hence they reported the physical features of the reptiles as they had not seen such creatures in Europe. The missionaries understood that the early classification of animals by the Tamils, including amphibians and reptiles in the region was based on form, medium occupied (earth, air or water), the presumed number of sensory powers possessed, besides noting whether they were wild or domesticated.

The Protestant missionaries in Tranquebar in 1718 noticed several reptiles and so they were interested to know the details of these tropical reptiles. According to them *sevi puraan* in Tamil was the centipede. It crept into the ears of children and caused them much pain. There was no special treatment for this and the people were asked to be careful when sleeping on the floor on mats.[50]

Four Types of Scorpions Mentioned by Johann Christian Wiedebrock and Kohlhoff in Tranquebar, 1763-65

Johann Christian Wiedebrock and Johann Balthasar Kohlhoff the two Protestant missionaries arrived Tranquebar on 19 August 1737 and worked in the Danish mission.[51] They mentioned the deadly poisonous types of scorpions in their report of 7 September 1763. It was said that the ordinary scorpion was called *thezhl* in Tamil. *Saramandali* had been another type of scorpion and it had a long tail, which had hairs at the end. The tail had eight joints, which were called *mani* by the Tamils. This special scorpion had eight folders while the ordinary scorpion had only seven. Samuel Benjamin Cnoll, the Danish missionary doctor in Tranquebar treated the patients who were bitten by scorpions with a special type of oil. It was applied on the bitten spot which had soothed and helped to remove the pain. The missionaries also stated that there were two more types of scorpions. One was called *Sidemandali*, which was white in its back. The other scorpion was called *Reththamandali* and it was said that if it had bitten people would sweat blood. The missionaries reported that Gnanamuthu an employee in the Danish mission in Thanjavur was bitten by *Saramandali* scorpion and he died in the month of August in 1763.[52]

The Study of Scorpions by Christoph Samuel John in Tranquebar Communicated to Prof. J.R. Forster in Germany, 1793

Scorpion was called *thezhl* by the Tamils. Christoph Samuel John also evinced keen interest in the study of scorpions. He wrote the details in his report to his fellow missionaries in Halle. Professor J.R. Forster who read it desired to know more details from C.S. John and so Forster had raised some questions for which C.S. John had answered them as follows:

Questions: Are the scorpions poisonous? How many varieties are there in India? What anti-poison had been used against them?

Answers: The small white yellow and brownish scorpion caused severe pain for several hours and the best way to reduce the pain was to put oil on the wound. The Tamils know some plants with which they could remove the pain. The physicians used to bite some betel leaves with pepper corns and they blew on the bite through which the pain was soothed. But the big black scorpions were considered by the Tamils more poisonous than the worst snakes and were feared. The biggest was larger than one span and had broad scissors. But C.S. John said that he not heard that anybody died out of this bite though the Tamils were taking the strongest anti-poison like in the case of snakebites. The big scorpions did not live in the houses like the small ones but in the fields, in the heaps of stones and under the roots of trees. The Tamils have given different names to these scorpions. The small one was called *thezhl*. The big one was black in colour and it was called *nanduwakali* (*nanduvaaykaali*).[53]

Thus the Europeans had spent much of their time in acquainting themselves with the tropical zoological species and especially the poisonous ones. In all probability this had been carried out with a view to know the respective medical prescriptions. Another reason was to save themselves also against poisonous bites and to inform those engaged in Europe to learn Tamil medicine.

The Study on the Beetle and its Bites by Christoph Samuel John in Tranquebar Communicated to Prof. J.R. Forster in Germany, 1793

C.S. John developed an interest in the study of reptiles. He noticed the bee called *theni* by the Tamils, the beetle known as *vandu* and wasp called *kuzhlavi*. C.S. John communicated the details on the beetles found in Tranquebar to Prof. Johann Reinhold Forster (1729-1798) in Germany and he stated that there were several poisonous insects and the Tamils got rashes for which they explained that they got it through a bite of a *puchchi* (worm/ an insect which cannot fly but will bite or sting), or *vandu* (which can fly and bite or sting). The locals could not identify and tell the various types of insects. C. S. John said that he was bitten by an insect at night and got his hand swollen besides fingers and the eyes, but the pain had only slowly disappeared. He was also bitten again by an insect on the thigh when he was returning to Tranquebar from a solitude place. A severe burning, itching and swelling had developed and it spread for several inches long. He applied fine white limestone powder on it and it was healed step by step. He remarked that limestone was also used for the bites of poisonous snakes with success especially in the case of water-snakes.[54] It is interesting to note that missionary himself had narrated his personal experiences of poisonous insect bite.

Leeches Noticed and Exported from Pondicherry to Mauritius and Paris, 1833-48

The French in Pondicherry noticed the leech called *attai* in Tamil. *Attai vidal* (the use of leeches by the Tamils) and bloodletting in medicine (applying leeches to areas of blood concussion to drink the obnoxious blood, so that pain was alleviated and the inflammation reduced) was well known to the natives.[55] The French exported a large quantity of leeches from Pondicherry to France to treat patients. A. Moquin-Tandon in Paris received 'hirudo granulose', a medicinal leech employed by Tamil doctors in Pondicherry.[56] The examination of patients, classification of diseases and the observation of their natural causes, assumed great importance in France under the direction of the famous physician P.C.A. Louis. He made extensive and systematic use of record keeping and data analysis and insisted on their indispensability to medical nosology. In 1834 he developed guidelines to be followed in designing prospective studies for evaluating different modes of treatment.[57] Louis's most famous application was the practice of bloodletting which he published in 1836.[58]

As the practice of blood-letting or phlebotomy was a dominant feature of French medicine, a large number of leeches were exported by the French Company from Pondicherry to Mauritius. Local pharmacists in Mauritius developed a long-standing attraction for medicinal leeches and imported these from Pondicherry. We find advertisements for the sale of leeches from Pondicherry placed by the pharmacists in Port Louis in 1833 and 1848.[59] Fifty Indians who had migrated from Madras and Pondicherry to Mauritius, arriving on the island on 15 April 1833, brought with them many leeches for sale along with other commodities like rice and merchandise. Various ships that sailed from Pondicherry brought leeches to Mauritius on 31 May 1833, 14 June 1833 and 22 February 1848. Shipments of leeches continued for several years and the application of leeches was considered a mild form of blood-letting, became well developed in Mauritius.[60] Thus we see that the medical practices of Tamil doctors had spread from Pondicherry to other French colonies. Many natives who were involved in various businesses and jobs practised medicine privately in Pondicherry. Sonnerat, the Commissioner of the Marine and Naturalist to king Louis XVI observed that physicians in Pondicherry mostly comprised of individuals who were washermen, weavers and blacksmiths and they were pretenders to some knowledge of medicine. It must be stated that the caste system in Tamil country was so strong that some men of each caste learnt and practiced medicine in order to help their fellow caste members. Sonnerat also pointed out that the Tamil physicians had no understanding of anatomy.[61]

Seven Types of Lizards Mentioned by Thomas Caverhill Jerdon and Walter Elliot, 1853

Thomas Caverhill Jerdon (1811-1872) entered into the service of the East India Company in 1835 as an assistant surgeon. He arrived in Madras on 21 February 1836 and he was posted on 1 March 1837 to second light cavalry at Tiruchirapalli. After his marriage in July 1841 he went to Nilgiris. Later he was in-charge of the dispensary at Madras. He again moved over to Nellore when he was posted in January 1842 as the civil-surgeon of Nellore. Lord Canning patronized him and so Jerdon's services were transferred to the Government of India on special duty for preparing major works on Indian natural history. Finally Jerdon left India for Europe in 1864. Jerdon had developed interest in the study of reptiles.

Lizard was called *palli* by the Tamils. According to Jerdon *Calotes nemoricola* the lizard had one detached spine in front of two or three small ones on each side of the nape. A fold of skin on the shoulder was found, scales of the sides very large, not keeled, and those of the abdomen much smaller, keeled. The dorsal crest extended only about one-third along the back. The colour was green. Jerdon had procured one specimen of this lizard near the foot of the Coonoor ghats in Nilgiris. Compared with versicolor, the large smooth scales were the most prominent feature of distinction. The scales at the base of the tail above were of rather large size, keeled and pointed. The tympanum was large, where the dorsal crest terminated, the scales of the ridge were pointed. The length of the lizard specimen was eighteen inches of which the tail was eight.[62]

Salea jebdoni, the lizard had the nuchal and dorsal crest formed of elongated compressed scales and had tail with a keeled crest. This pretty lizard was described by Mr. Gray from specimens sent to London by Jerdon. This lizard was only found in the Nilgiris where it frequented the bushes, hedges and gardens. Its colour was a bright grass-green marbled with brown, some red marks on the head and nape, and a few white scales on the sides.

It did not appear to possess the faculty of changing its colours. The length of one lizard was nine and a half inches, of which the tail was six and a half inches.[63]

Sitana ponticeriana the lizard was fawn-coloured with rhomboidal dark spots on the back, and a pale longitudinal streak from ear to tail. This had been the common ground lizard. It was rare in the forest districts, frequenting the open country and fields. On the approach of danger, it ran with great rapidity, tail erect, and concealed itself in any crack in the ground or hole, or under a stone or bush. Notwithstanding its activity, it was the common prey of harriers, buzzards, hawks and eagles. Jerdon had not seen the beautiful dewlap (blue black and red) developed and exhibited during the pairing season, and it then became larger than previously. At this time, too, some blue marks were observable on the nape and back, that on the nape indeed forming a kind of crest more conspicuous now, the colours in general too were deepened, and the quadrangular marks was found on the back and barring of the limbs very distinct. The name *Sitana*, said by Cuvier to be the name by which it was known at Pondicherry, is a Latin termination of the word *shaitan* (devil) a name applied to it by the Muslims.[64]

Calosattra lescheisattltii the lizard had dorsal scales rhomboidal, keeled six rows of longitudinal scales on the abdomen. Its colour was reddish brown above, pale yellow beneath, and the sides were dark brown with two pale yellow bands, tail red. This pretty little ground lizard is somewhat locally distributed. Jerdon had seen it in Salem and Coimbatore areas only, especially near the banks of the Cauvery. It frequented bushy ground, hedges of Euphorbia and clumps of cactus, under which it rapidly took shelter, as also among rocks.[65]

Varanus dracaena the species of Monitor appears generally spread throughout the whole of India. It was chiefly nocturnal in its habits and frequented jungles. It was by no means confined to the neighbourhood of water, though perhaps it preferred such a locality. It defended itself most vigorously by striking with its tail. It could climb well both trees and walls, and it was popularly believed that thieves made use of it to have an entrance into a building. It was eaten by the natives, who considered it highly nourishing and aphrodisiac, and many Europeans used it for soup. It could be always procured in the market in Madras.[66]

Acanthodyactylus nilgherrensis the lizard, had apparently belonged to a genus new to India, and it was purchased by Walter Elliot near Coonoor. Jerdon himself had not been fortunate enough to observe it, and knew nothing of its haunts. Its colours in spirit were of a pale pearl grey with a row of black spots on its back, another row on its sides somewhat larger and white, edged black. The anterior edge of ear toothed scaly, collar transverse, scales of back had been somewhat larger behind than in front, an occipital plate.[67]

Mocoa bilineata the scink had front-parietal plates two, separate; ears round, moderate, with two very indistinct minute scales in front; the drum sunken; scales six or eight rowed, thin, smooth. The colour was above shining olive, whitish beneath, a dark broad line on each side from nostril to end of tail; two narrow dark lines on back from neck to end of tail. In the young and half grown animal, the tail was of a beautiful violet colour. Jerdon had only found this scink under stones on the summit of the Nilgiris.[68]

To conclude it may be said that European physicians and surgeons like Samuel Brown in Madras, Johann Gerard Koenig and Christoph Samuel John in Tranquebar had mainly conducted studies on insects to know the poisonous bites and medical treatment. The details of the uncommonly rare and scarce insects reported from the Coromandel Coast had caused a deep impact into the study of insects by zoologists like Johann Christian Fabricius in Denmark. Further the details communicated on hover flies and stilt-legged flies by C.S. John from Tranquebar helped to develop studies by Vidua Wiedemann in Norway. The study of scorpions by Christoph Samuel John in Tranquebar was communicated to Prof. J.R. Forster in Germany. He also made a study on the beetle and its bites and the information was circulated to Prof. J.R. Forster in Germany. Leeches noticed by the French in Pondicherry were exported because of medicinal use from Pondicherry to Mauritius and Paris. The English in Madras imported cochineal insect from South America and conducted experiments in dyeing at Saidapettai. Thus there developed communications on zoology and medicine linking the local to the global.

Notes

1. Robert Boyle, 'General Heads for a Natural History of a Countrey, Great or Small', *Philosophical Transactions*, vol. 1, 1665, pp. 1-22; John Woodward, *Brief Instructions for Making Observations in All Parts of the World as Also, for Collecting, Preserving, and Sending over Natural Things*, London, 1696.
2. British Library (hereafter BL), London, Sloane MS 3332, fols. 1-6, see James Petiver, 'Directions Concerning Plants'; See also, James Petiver, 'Brief Directions for the Easie Making, and Preserving Collections of All Natural Curiosities', *Monthly Miscellany or Memoirs for the Curious*, no. 3, London, 1709. In this pamphlet James Petiver had encouraged his correspondents to disseminate copies of his instructions as widely as possible.
3. British Museum (hereafter BM), London, 456. e. 11 (9). This is a single printed sheet in the collection of James Petiver's works in the museum. It is obviously the directions with which Petiver supplied his correspondents who were in the

overseas or to those who were setting out on a voyage. A manuscript copy of the above with printer's instructions is also available. See, BL, Additional Manuscripts, 4448, fol. 5.

4. BL, Sloane MS 3333, fols. 181-2; See also, 'An Account of a Book: Musei Petiveriani Centuria Prima', *Philosophical Transactions*, vol. 19, 1697, p. 399; see also, Jacobus Petiver, *Gazophylacii Naturæ & Artis: Decas Prima*, Londini, MDCCII, pp.85-6.

5. Louis Le Comte, *Nouveau Mémoires Sur L'état Présent De La Chine*, Paris, tome II, 1696, pp. 512-13. The text runs thus: Mais comme Dieu n'est pas moins admirable dans les petites choses que dans les grandes, il y a dans les Indes une infinité d'insectes, qui mériteraient les réflexions les plus sérieuses. On y voit des mouches que la nature a peintes d'un jaune si vif, si poli & si éclatant, que la plus belle dorure n'en approche pas; d'autres sont proprement des points de lumière, qui brillent de tous côtés durant la nuit; ainsi, comme elles vont par essaim, tout l'air en paraît enflammé quand elles volent; & quand elles s'arrêtent sur les feuilles ou sur les branches, les arbres ressemblent de loin à ces beaux feux d'artifice, qu'on fait dans les Indes pour les illuminations publiques. See, also, *Memoirs and Observations: Topographical, physical, mathematical, mechanical, natural and ecclesiastical made in a late journey through the empire of China and published in several letters, by Louis Le Comte, Translated from the Paris edition and illustrated with figures*, London, 1697, p. 515.

6. Martin Lister, Part of a Letter from Fort St. George, in the East-Indies, Giving an Account of the Long Worm which is Troublesome to the Inhabitants of Those Parts, Communicated by Dr. Martin Lister, Fellow of College of Physicians and Royal Society, *Philosophical Transactions of the Royal Society of London*, 1683-1775 (hereafter *Philosophical Transactions*, vol. 19 (1695-1697), pp. 417-8.

7. *Philosophical Transactions*, vol. 22, p. 850, 852.

8. *Ibid.*, pp. 702, 714. Brown had recorded with regard to Shevanar calunga that 'this cures, they say, all sort of venomous bites and Vonda guddee: but against that of the Cobree de Capello 'twill do no good, as I have tried'. See, Petiver, 'An Account of Mr Sam. Brown His Sixth Book of East India Plants, with Their Names, Vertues, Description, Etc. To These Are Added Some Animals, Etc.', *Philosophical Transactions*, 1702-1703, vol. 23, pp. 1055-65, see p. 1061.

9. Jacobus Petiver, *Gazophylacii Naturæ & Artis: Decas Prima*, Londini, MDCCII, Tab. IV, see the image item no. 3. The text runs thus: Plan-Orbis INDICA, ex castaneo siboque triaro, N°t Ve umbilico patulo. This was brought from Fort St. George, to my Curiou Friend Dr. Grey; Schænanthus Avenaceus procumbens MADRASPATANUS Beupleuri facie Muf. nost. 577. The heads of this Camels-hay are much smaller and shorter than any other Species. I have yet seen, as are its Leaves and its Sheaths; Pápilio MADRASPATÄNUS m°dius, flavedine & fusco mixtus, liturâ cæruleâ infignitus. This singular Butterfly Mr. Edwr. Bulkley sent me from Fort St. George, see, pp. 7-8.

10. S. Jeyaseela Stephen, *A Meeting of the Minds: European and Tamil Encounters in Modern Sciences, 1507-1857*, Delhi, 2016, pp. 120-2.

11. Johann Christian Fabricii, *Entomologia Systematica emendate et aucta secundum classes, ordines, genera, species, adjectis, synonimis, locis, observationibus,*

descriptionibus (hereafter Entomologia Systematica), Hafniae, MDCCXCIII, Tome I, p. IV.

12. *Ibid.*, See also, I. K. Daldorf, 'Uddrag af Hr. Daldorfs Dagbog Paaen Reise fra Kiobenhavn til Tranquebar fidst o Aaret 1790 og forst I Aaret 1791', *Skrivter af Naturhistorie Selskaber*, 2 (2), 1793, pp. 147-173.

13. Johann Christian Fabricii, *Species Insectorum Exhibientes Erorum Differentias Specificas Synoynma Auctorum, Loca Natalia, Metamorphosin Adjectis Observationibus Descriptionibus* (hereafter Species Insectorum), 1781, see, Insecta Cryptocephalus koeinigi, 45.

14. E. Donovan, *An epitome of the natural history insects of islands in the Indian seas: Comprising upwards of two hundred and fifty figures and descriptions the most singular and beautiful species, selected chiefly from those recently discovered, and which have not appeared in the works of any preceding author. The figures are accurately drawn, engraved and coloured, from specimens of the insects; the descriptions are arranged according to the system of Linnaeus; with references to the writings of Fabricius, and other systematic authors by E. Donovan, Author of the natural history of the insects of China*, London, 1800, See the illustration no. 3.

15. Johann Christian Fabricii, Species Insectorum, p. 455 SP. 4. J.C. Fabricius had described thus in Latin: Viridis nitens, abdomine utrinque macula ocellari aurea, ano sexdentat coeruleo.

16. *Ibid.*, J.C. Fabricius had described thus in Latin: Thorace viridi fascia cyanea abdomine antice cyaneo-violaceoque faciato; medio aureo, postice rubro quadridentato.

17. *Ibid.*, p. 454, SP. 1.

18. Johann Christian Fabricii, Entomologia Systematica, 1792-1799, Tome 2, p. 253, Sp. 1. J.C. Fabricius had described in Latin thus: Nigra thorace obscure maculato, abdomine atro: fascia ferruginea.

19. Sir Charles Linne, *A General System of Nature: through the three kingdoms of animals, vegetables and minerals systematically divided into their several classes, orders genera, species and varieties*, Swansea, 1800, vol. II, p. 162.

20. *Ibid.*

21. Sir Charles Linne, *A General System of Nature: through the three kingdoms of animals, vegetables and minerals systematically divided into their several classes, orders genera, species and varieties, vol. II, Animal Kingdom, Insects, Part I*, Swansea, 1806, p. 20.

22. *Ibid.*

23. *Ibid.*, p. 25.

24. Sir Charles Linne, A General System of Nature, 1800, vol. II, p. 25.

25. Sir Charles Linne, A General System of Nature, 1806, vol. II, Animal Kingdom, Insects, Part I, p. 25.

26. Johann Christian Fabricii, Entomologia Systematica, 1792-1799, Tome 2, p. 276, SP. 83 Fabricius had described in Latin thus: Nigra flavor variegate abdominis petiole incurvo: maculis quatuor flavis.

27. Johann Christian Fabricii, Entomologia Systematica, Tome 3, Part 1, p.194, Sp. 35.
28. E. Donovan, An Epitome of the Natural History, see Cimex uniguttatus.
29. Johann Christian Fabricii, Entomologia Systematica, Tome 1, Part 1, p. 16, Sp. 48.
30. E. Donovan, An Epitome of the Natural History, see Phalaena figura.
31. Johann Christian Fabricii, Entomologia Systematica, 1792-1799, Tome 2, p. 278, Sp. 87. He records in Latin thus: Ferrugineo flavoque varia abdominis petiole incurvo ferrugineo, fascia atra.
32. Sir Charles Linne, A General System of Nature, Swansea, 1800, vol. II, p. 25.
33. Sir Charles Linne, A General System of Nature, Swansea, 1806, vol. II, Animal Kingdom, Insects, Part I, p. 25.
34. Johann Christian Fabricii, Species Insectorum, Tome 1, p. 29, Sp.131.
35. Johann Christian Fabricii, Entomologia Systematica, Tome 3, Part 1, p. 193, Sp.31.
36. Johann Christian Fabricii, Entomologia Systematica, Tome 4, p.5, Sp.17.
37. S. Jeyaseela Stephen, A Meeting of the Minds, pp. 120-21.
38. Johann Christian Fabricii, *Systema Antilabrum Secundus Ordines Genere, Species*, Brusvigae, 1805.
39. Vidua Widemann, *Ausser Europaischez Weiflugelige Insekten Zuseiter Theil Schulz*, Hamm, 1830.
40. Ray Desmond, *The European Discovery of the Indian Flora*, Oxford, 1992, p. 209.
41. British Library (hereafter BL), London, Oriental and India Office Collection (hereafter, OIOC), MSS Eur.85, folio.1. James Anderson wrote to Joseph Banks about the cochineal, but Banks referred to them as imaginary. See the letter of Sir Joseph Banks dated 22 May 1787 to James Anderson in Madras.
42. BL, OIOC, MSS Eur. 85, see Correspondence for the Introduction of Cochineal Insects from America, Madras, 1791.
43. BL, OIOC, E/4/873, *Madras Dispatches*, See the letter dated 21 July 1787; Tamilnadu State Archives (hereafter TNSA), Chennai, *Commercial Department*, Dispatches from England to the President and Council of Fort St. George, 10 May 1788.
44. TNSA, *Public Consultations*, 187A/42, Extract from the minute dated 22 July 1789: TNSA, Commercial Department, Dispatches from England to the President and Council of Fort St. George, 10 May 1788.
45. TNSA, *Public Consultations*, 187A/42, see the letter of James Anderson dated 6 January 1789 to Archibald Campbell.
46. TNSA, *Letters to the Board of Revenue*, see the letter of Andrew Berry dated 26 August 1795 to Lord Hobart, the Governor and Council of Fort St. George.
47. M. Legoux de Flax, *Essai Historique Geographique et Politque sur l' Indoustan avec le Tableaux de Son Commerce*, Paris, 1807, p. 156.
48. Arvind Sinha, 'Implantation of Commercial Crops: Cochineal Culture and the Regional Ecology in the Eighteenth Century Coromandel', in *Coastal Histories:*

Society and Ecology in Pre-Modern India, ed. Yogesh Sharma, Delhi, 2010, pp. 1–13, see, p. 10.

49. BL, OIOC, P/174/13; see also, P/339/123 (No pagination).
50. Arno Lehmann, 'Hallesche Mediziner und Medizinen am Anfang Deutesch-Indischer Beziehungen' in *Mathematische–Naturwisssenchaftliche Reihe*, vol. 5 (2) 1955, pp. 11-32, see p. 120.
51. Johann Christian Wiedebrock was born at Minden in Westphalia on 9 February 1713, studied at Halle, was ordained and arrived at Tranquebar on 19 August 1737, married on 27 January 1740, and laboured at Tranquebar for nearly 30 years. He died on 7 April 1767 and was buried in the New Jerusalem Churchyard. See, J. Ferd Fenger, *History of the Tranquebar Mission: Worked out from the Original Papers*, tr. Emil Francke, Tranquebar, 1863, p. 314. Johann Balthasar Kohlhoff was born at Neuwarp in Western Pomerania on 15 November 1711, studied at Rostock and Halle, was ordained and arrived at Tranquebar on 19 August 1737, married for the first time on 15 February 1741, and for the second time in September 1760, laboured at Tranquebar for more than 53 years. He died there on 17 December 1790 and was buried in New Jerusalem Churchyard. J. Ferd Fenger, History of the Tranquebar Mission, p. 314.
52. Gotthilf August Francke ed., *Der Königl. Dänischen Missionarien aus Ost-Indien eingesandter ausführlichen Berichten, Von dem Werck ihrs Ams unter den Heyden, angerichteten Schulen und Gemeinen, ereigneten Hindernissen und schweren Umstanden; Beschaffenheit des Malabarischen Heydenthums, gepflogenen brieflicher Correspondentz und mundlchen Unterredungen mit selbigen heyden*, Teil 1–9, (Continuationen 1–108) Waiserihaus, Halle, 1710–1772 (hereafter Hallesche Berichten = HB), see, 100th Continuation des Berichts der Königliche – Dänischen Missionarien in Ost Indien, 1766, p. 419.
53. Georg Christian Knapp, et.al., eds., *Neuere Geschichte der Evangelischen Missions-Anstalten zu Bekehrung der Heiden in Ostindien aus den eigenhändigen Aufsätzen und Briefen der Missionarien erausgegeben*, Waisenhaus, Teil 1–8 (Stück 1–95), Waiserihaus, Halle, 1770-8/95, 1848 (hereafter Neuere Hallesche Berichte = NHB), see, Anstalten in Ostindien aus den eigenhändigen Aufsätzen und Briefen der Missionare, 1793, p. 656.
54. *Ibid.*, p. 657.
55. Attai Vidal was known to Tamils who practiced Ayurveda. It had been described in Sushruta Samhita vide Chapter XIII.
56. A. Moquin-Tandon, *Monographie de la Famille des Hirudirees*, Paris, 1846, p. 361.
57. P. C. A. Louis, *Essay on Clinical Instruction*, Paris, 1834, tr. P. Martin, London; repr. 1910.
58. P. C. A. Louis, *Researches on the Effects of Bloodletting*, Paris, 1836, tr. C.G. Putnam, Boston, 1918.
59. National Archives of Mauritius, DB Complex, Petite Riviere, see, 'Le Cerneen' in *Journal de L'Ile Maurice*, 1833, 1848, 1864 and 1872.
60. Roy T. Sawyer, 'The Trade in Medicinal Leeches in the Southern Indian Ocean in the Nineteenth Century', *Medical History*, vol. 43 (2), 1999, pp. 241–5.
61. Pierre Sonnerat, *Voyages aux Indes Orientles et a la Chine*, Paris, MDCCCVI.

62. Thomas Caverhill Jerdon, 'Catalogue of reptiles inhabiting peninsular India', *Journal of the Asiatic Society of Bengal*, vol. XXII, 1853, pp. 462-79, see p. 471.
63. *Ibid.*, p. 473.
64. *Ibid.*, pp. 473-4.
65. *Ibid.*, p. 476.
66. *Ibid.*, pp. 475-6.
67. *Ibid.*, pp. 476-7.
68. *Ibid.*, p. 477.

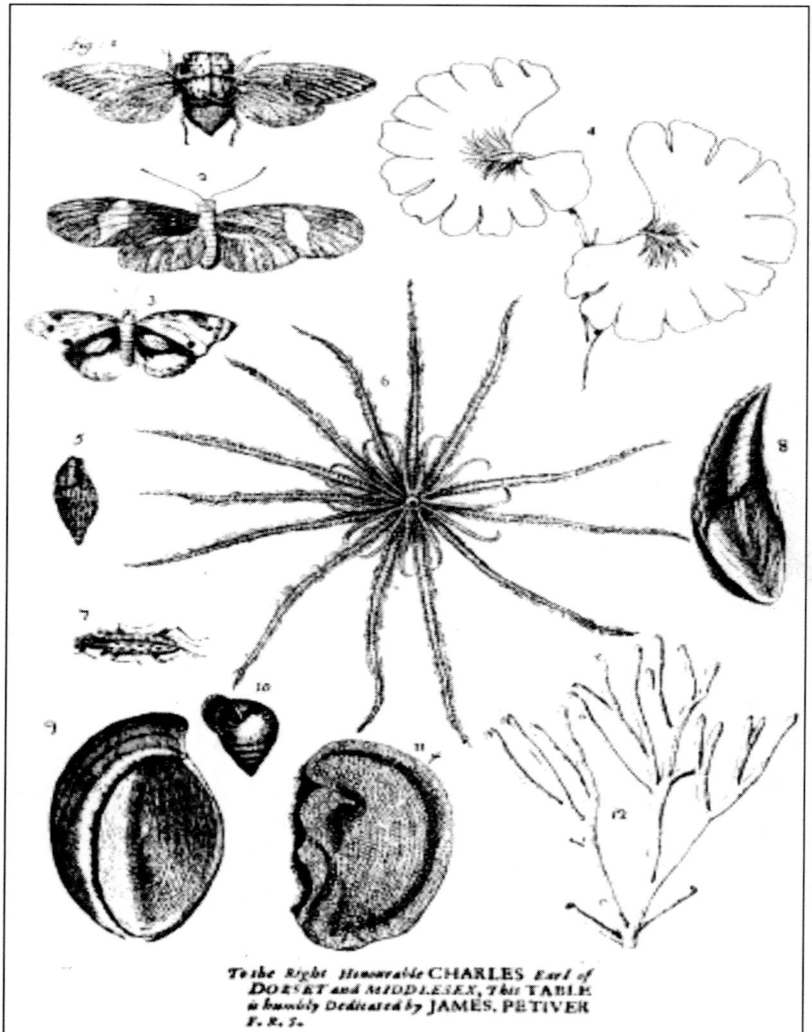

5.1. Insects sent from Madras found in a plate printed in London, 1702.

5.2. Scarabaeus spinifex from Madras.

5.3. Scarabaeus koenigii noticed in Tranquebar.

5.4. Buprestis sterniconis found in Madras.

5.5. Buprestis aenea from Madras.

5.6. Fulgrava festiva from Madras.

5.7. Cimex uniguttatus found in Madras.

5.8. Papilio idaeus found in Madras.

5.9. Chrysis fasciata noticed in Tranquebar.

5.10. Chrysis splendid noticed in Tranquebar.

5.11. Chrysis oculta noticed in Tranquebar.

5.12. Vespa cincta noticed in Tranquebar.

5.13. Vespa petiolata from Madras.

6

In to the Sky of Tamil Landscape: Avifauna and Ornithology, 1701-1847

Science in Europe in the beginning of the seventeenth century found its natural way into the study of the New World objects owing to the abundant collections of the flora and fauna rather than the distant possessions of the East. The Dutch who arrived in India in 1605 had taken some interest in birds and we notice that Hendrick Arentsz the Dutch Company's upper merchant in Surat in 1625 was asked to present Jahangir the Mughal emperor (1605-1627) a casuwari bird to win the support for the Dutch company to get the *farman* renewed since the old one issued was four years old.[1] This casuwari bird was a curious one in India and it was found only in the island of Ceram island and in Moluccas called emen/eme. Rare birds were also asked to be collected by the directors of the Dutch East India Company in Amsterdam for the Prince of Orange and so an order was passed in this regard. The Dutch company servants in Surat therefore took steps to obtain some curious birds and animals. Four pigeons received as presents in Agra from Mukarrab Khan the head of the Mughal royal treasury were sent to Jakarta for onward transmission to the Netherlands.[2]

The European travellers were also struck with wonder to see the strange and beautiful birds. Peter Mundy first saw the Mauritius Dodo (*Raphus cucullatus*) in Surat when he visited the English factory in 1628.[3] The missionaries and the East India Company servants and officials also showed interest in the study of birds because many such birds were new and not found at all in Europe. Therefore the westerners began to describe the colour of the birds, size, food habits etc in their writings. Thus there emerged the new era of documentation of the birds and development of ornithology.

Edward Buckley in Madras and the First Record of Bird Watching, 1701-10

Edward Buckley (1651-1714) was employed as the surgeon and Coroner at Fort St George in Madras. He became the principal surgeon in 1692 and remained in the post till 1709, when he was transferred to the civil services as member of the council.[4] Buckley watched several birds with various tails, bills, crest and feet besides bright colour birds and sober colour birds. Hence he conducted a study of birds at Madras @ Chennaipattinam in 1701 where the English East India Company had established a trading factory and built Fort St. George. The report prepared in Latin was sent to James Petiver in London in 1711. We find mention of 27 birds and these details were published by John Ray in 1713.[5]

The List of 27 Birds and Drawings Sent from Madras to London

1. Himantopus Maderaspatanus
2. The partridge snipe
3. The black and white wag tail
4. The forked wag tail
5. The sea crow
6. The Madras rail-hen
7. The buff jay
8. The yellow jay
9. The motled jay
10. The green jay
11. The small blue jay
12. The Madrass jay
13. The pied bird of paradise
14. The broad tailed Madras dove
15. The parrot dove
16. The red jay-dove
17. The small red pied dove
18. The Madras ring-dove
19. The cock saulary
20. The hen saulary
21. The sanguillo
22. The red tooracca with a black head

23. The red and white tooracca
24. The whitish tooracca
25. The black tooracca
26. The magpy tooracca
27. The magpy tooracca with red spots

Buckley felt the importance of the birds in visual form so that the English audience could observe and benefit. Hence he engaged a native artist to do the drawings. These drawings of the birds sent in manuscript original are available in the British Library, London.[6] The names with serial numbers of the birds are found in the these paintings.[7]

It may be mentioned that *Himantopus maderaspatanus* the bird was named by Edward Buckley himself. He also noted about Pliny's description (vide his book 10, chapter 47). Buckley called the bird in English the red legged crane.

Buckley provides some Tamil names of the birds too. He says that the *Avis Maderaspatana* major is the bird which had been called *kadal kaakka* by the Tamils. He stated that the same bird was also called *Samudhira Kaakai*. He recorded the bird *Kaannagkozhi* and in English he called it The Madras Rail hen.[8]

Further Buckley also mentions the birds with Telugu names. He had collected the information from Telugus who had migrated and settled in Madras. The list follows with eight names.

English name—Telugu name

The Buff-Jay — Vanga paandu

The Yellow-Jay — Pedda vanga paandu

The Motled-Jay — Sundai vanga paandu

The Green-Jay — Pasaaikaaye

The Small Blue-Jay — Peachcaye

The Pied Bird of Paradise —— Thella yekku naarai

Madras Ring Dove — Woorulla ponnunky

Sanguillo — Gulla kavalla

The Identification of birds with different names in Tamil corresponding to the English names given by Buckley had been provided below with zoological names.

English name of Buckley — Zoological name — Tamil name

No English name — Himantopus maderaspatanus — Pavazhakaal ullaan

The partridge snipe — Gallinago gallinago — Korai kuththi

The black and white wag tail — Motacilla maderaspatensis — Kulathu kuruvi

The forked wag tail — Motacilla cincrea — Kodikaal vaalaaati

The sea crow — Avis maderaspatensis major — Kadal kaaka, Samudhira kaakai

The Madras rail-hen — Amaurornis phoenicurus — Kaanaang kozhi

The buff jay — Ixobrychus sinensis — Manal Naarai

The yellow jay — Oriolus oriolus — Manjal kuruvi

The motled jay — Motacilla flava — Manjal Vaalaati

The green jay — Phaenicophoeus virdirostris — Pachchai Vaayan kuil

The small blue jay — Columba livia — Maada puraa

The Madras jay — Pitta brachyuran — Arumanai kuruvi

The pied bird of paradise — Terpsiphone paradise — Vethivaal kuruvi

The broad tailed Madras dove — Schoenicola platyunus

The parrot dove — Psittaeula krameri — Kizhli

The red jay-dove — Streptopelia senegalensis — Thavittu puraa

The small red pied dove — Streptopelia chinensis — Mani puraa

The Madras ring-dove — Accipiter badius — Vallooru

The cock saulary — Gallus gallus domesticus

The hen saulary — Gallus gallus domesticus

The sanguillo — Passer domesticus

The red tooracca with a black head — Vanellus indicus — Azhlkaati

The red and white tooracca

The whitish tooracca — Mesophyx intermedia — Vellai kokku

The black tooracca — Dupetor flavicollis — Karungkurugu

The magpy tooracca — Copsychus saularis — Vannathi kuruvi

The magpy tooracca with red spots — Saxicoloides fulicata — Vannathi kurivi

The Nightingale and Other Birds Reported by Christoph Theodosius Walther in Tranquebar, 1726-33

The Protestant missionaries who arrived in Tranquebar had shown abiding interest in the study of birds in that region. Various missionaries who had noticed the birds gave details in their reports sent to Denmark and Germany. Christoph Theodosius Walther (1699-1744) reached Tranquebar in 1725.[9] He observed the birds flying in the region and wrote the details. As he had contacts with Theophil Siegfried Bayer at St. Petersburg he mentioned the details in his report dated 16 October 1726.[10] He stated that the bird which the Germans call *Paradies-vogel*, the Tamils called it *Umakkuruwi*. The Tamils also called the same bird as *Aagasapadschi* (*Luft vogel*). He explained that the term *Aagasam* meant empty space between the heaven and earth and the word *padschi* meant bird. According to Tamils this bird was always flying high in the air and remained there.[11] It is interesting to note that a small bird, flying very high in the air had caught the fancy of Christoph Theodosius Walther and his comparison with a similar bird in Germany is highly laudatory. The missionary had continued his study of birds later too. In his letter of 22 October 1733 he described the birds and given the German and Tamil names of birds. He also indicated the Hebrew, Arabic, Persian and Sanskrit names of birds. He noted the additional literature on birds and the earlier mentions of those birds in his letter.[12]

Swans, Ducks, Kingfisher and Other Birds Noticed by Christian Friedrich Pressier in Tranquebar, 1729

Christian Friedrich Pressier (1697-1738) the Protestant missionary reached Tranquebar in 1725.[13] He took interest in the study of birds and he reported especially of the swans and ducks. Pressier in his observation of tropical ornithology wrote about a wide-beaked tropical aquatic bird and a colourful one which he observed in Tranquebar and he wrote the details to Joachim Sentzke in Halle. Pressier stated that in the Danish colony of Tranquebar there was a bird which stayed in lakes and ponds. God has given in its beak as a net so that it could catch fish easily. The beak was very long like an arm and it had the breath of two fingers. The upper part was fully bony and on the lower was partly bony while the sides were of bones and between them there was strong skin in folds. Because of that, the lower part of the beak could be stretched by the bird. The upper part of the beak in front was bent like a hook. The bird if it fished, it went deep with the beak into the water, opened the beak and stretched the skin. Therefore it collected a good quantity of water along with the fish. The water and the fish were then collected in the skin, like in a sack. The bird kept the fish and let the water go. Its feet were like the feet of the goose.[14] There were three kinds of such fish called *meenkoththi* in Tamil and it included the white breasted kingfisher (*Halcyon smyrnensis*), the small blue kingfisher (*Alcedo atthis*) and the lesser pied kingfisher (*Ceryle rudis*).

Pressier wrote that the birds in Tranquebar were of many colours. He said that the very beautiful bird was the worse in its singing. These birds were flying and they moved about freely everywhere and quite daring because no one killed them except the Europeans. Pressier said that there was a small bird in Tranquebar like the *Zaunkoenige*, which likes to be in crowd. The people also kept them in cages, sometimes as many as twenty four. They were quite peaceful. They looked as if they were painted with beautiful red, black, grey and other colours but they do not sing better than the sparrows.[15] The bird that sang was called *vaanambaadi* in Tamil. It included various types such as the eastern skylark (*Alauda gulgula*) Jerdon's bushlark (*mirafra affinis*) and the ashy-crowned sparrow-lark (*Eremopterix grisea*). There was yet another variety of bird which also sang and it was called *kuyil* in Tamil and the varieties also included the Asian koel (*Eudynamys scolopacea*) and Indian treepie called *maangkuyil* (*Dendrocitta vagabunde*) in Tamil.

Carl Linnaeus in Europe and Introduction of Binomials to Birds, 1735-1766

Francis Willughby (1635–1672) in Europe classified birds by habit. John Ray (1627-1705) expanded this system by distinguishing species through anatomical and other differences—in plumage, or in the structure of beaks and claws. Over 230 species were described in his study of birds from personal observation. The illustrated and descriptive list of known bird species in Madras reported by Edward Buckley was published by John Ray and it had helped in a way while expanding the work on birds by Carl Linnaeus (1707–1778). Though Ray had separated birds into species that lived on land and those that ventured into water, the taxonomy adopted by Linnaeus was different and we find it in his great work of *Systema Naturae* published in 1735. Linnaeus later in his *Systema Naturae* published in 1758 mentioned the division of animal kingdom into six classes. It included (a) mammalia (b) Aves (c) Amphibia (d) Pisces (e) Insecta and (f) Vermes. Linnaeus had collected the details of the then known birds and he had mentioned several birds found in Tamil country as follows by 1758.

Tamil name — Zoological name — English name

Chinna kottaan — Charadrius alexandrines — Kentish plover

Chola kuruvi — Sturnus roseus — Rosy starling

Kanni kokku — Bulbulcus ibis — Cattle Egret

Kaatu kuruvi/ Pey kuruvi — Lanius schach — Rufous backed shrike

Kotaan — Actitis hypoleucos — Common sandpiper

Kuyil — Eudynamya scolopacea — Asian koel

Kuruvi valluru — Accipiter nisus — Eurasian sparrow hawk

Kondai kozhuththi — Pycnonotus jocosus — Red-whiskered bulbul

Komban aanthai — Bubo bubo — Eurasian eagle owl

Maarkkaliyan — Anas acuta — Northern pintail

Manjal thirudi — Neophron percnopterus — Egyptian vulture

Mayil — Pavo cristatus — Indian peafowl

Marangkoththi — Dinopium benghalense — Lesser golden-backed wood pecker

Meenkoththi — Alcedo atthis — Small blue kingfisher

Meenkoththi — Ceryle rudis — Lesser pied kingfisher

Naamak kozhi — Fulica atra — Common coot

Neer Kozhli — Porphyrio porphyries — Purple moorhen

Nellu kuruvi — Lochura malabarica — White throated munia

Pavazha Kaaalullan — Himantopus himantopus — Black winged stilt

Panagkaadai — Coracias benghalensis — Indian rover blue jay

Periya vellai kokku — Casmerodius albus — Large Egret

Poo Naarai uriyan — Phoenicopterus ruber — Greater flamingo

Saambal Naarai — Ardea cincerea — Grey horn

Sigappu valluru — Falco kinnunculus — Common kestrel

Thaneer kozhi — Gallinula chlorpus — Common moorhen

Thosi kokku — Butorides striatus — Little green heron

Ur kuruvi/Adaikalaan kuruvi — Passer domesticus — House sparrrow

Vakka — Nycticorax nycticorax — Black crowned night heron

In the 12th edition of *Systema Naturae* published in 1766 we find that birds from Tamil country had continued to be cited.[16] The list included many more new birds.

Tamil name — Zoological name — English name

Anril — Plegadis falcinellus — Glossy Ibis

Arumani kuruvi — Pitta brachyuran — Indian pitta

Chinna minchittu — Pericrocothus cinnamomeus — Small minivet

Chinna vellai kokku — Egretta Garzetta — Little Egret

Kadal kaakai — Larus ridibundus — Black headed gull

Kondai kuruvi — Pycnonnotus cafer — Red-vented bulbul

Manipuraa — Streptopelia chinensis — Spotted dove

Naaganavaay — Aeridotheres tristis — Common myna

Neerkaakagam — Phalocrocorax niger — Little cormorant

Sennaarai — Ardea Purpurea — Purple horn

Thavittupuraa — Streptopelia senegalensis — Little brown dove

Birds Found in Pondicherry, Gingee and Coromandel Coast Reported to Europe, 1756-1789

Pierre Poivre (1719-86) joined the Foreign Mission Society of Paris in 1739. He left for Cambodia and China for missionary work. After many years of service he desired to return to France. While returning his ship was attacked by the English in Banca Straits on 5 February 1745. A bullet had carried off his right arm and he was taken prisoner. Later he was deported to Pondicherry where he remained for some time and left for France via Mauritius and reached in June 1748. Poivre again returned to Pondicherry in June 1749 and stayed in Pondicherry for many years.[17] At that time he evinced interest in the study of birds. He again returned to France in 1757.[18] The birds he observed in Pondicherry were reported and they were made known to the natural historians in France and Europe. Pieter Boddaert (1730-1795) who published his work '*Table des Planches Enlumineez d' histoire naturelle de M. D'Aubenton*' in 1783 had noted these birds. We find also mention of many birds observed by Pierre Sonnerat the French traveller during 1775 and 1780 in Pondicherry and Gingee.[19] Some birds are mentioned just with the name of Coromandel Coast without specific locality since these birds were found scattered all along the coast. The list of birds is as follows:

English name — Tamil name — Zoological name

Asian openbill — Naththaikuththi Naarai — Anastomus oscitans

Black kite — Kal Parundhu — Milvus migrans

Black Drongo — Coromandel

Blue tailed bee-eater — Coromandel

Cuckoo crested — Coromandel

Common myna — Coromandel

Duck — Coromandel

Flycatcher — Coromandel

Falcon — Gingee

Gallimule — Madras

Hornbill — Gingee

House crow — Coromandel — Corvus splendens

Herons — Coromandel

Jungle crow — Coromandel

White breasted kingfisher — Coromandel

Kite — Garudan — Haliastur Indus

Lark — Gingee

Owl — Coromandel

Rose ringed Parakeet — Gingee

Partridge — Gingee

Partridge — Pondicherri

Partridge — Coromandel

Pratincok— Madras

Pied kingfisher — Coromandel

Red wattled lapwing Vulture — Aal Kaati — Vanellus indicus

Runner Curiosus — Coromandel

Snipe — Madras

Thrush — Gingee

Titmouse — Malabar

Vulture — Pondicherri

Wabler — Coromandel

Yellow wattled lapwing — Aal Kaati — Vanellus malabaricus

Source: Pierre Sonnerat, *Voyages aux Indes Orientles et a la Chine*, Paris MDCCLXXXII, vol. II, plates 104, 113, 114, 118, 119, 121, 219; Pieter Boddaert, *Table des Planches Enlumineez*, 239, 416, 872, 892, 910, 932, 949. 950.

Some interesting and rare birds had been described very well. It is stated that the eagle in Pondicherry was a handsome one. In size the bird equalled the Jerfalcon. The length was one foot and seven inches. The bill was cinereous, with the tip yellow and the cere was bluish. The colour of the body was chestnut. The shaft of each feather was blackish and the head, neck, and breast, are white, with a longitudinal brown line down the middle of each feather. The end half of the fix first prime quills was black and the tail-feathers chestnut. The fix middle feathers were of a palefulvous colour at the tip. The three others have narrow blackish bands on the inner webs and the legs luteous and the claws were black. This eagle species found in Pondicherry was held as a sacred bird and it was worshipped by the natives.[20]

The moustache parrakeet was found in Pondicherry and it was about eleven inches in length. The forehead, from one eye to the other was black, from the under jaw on each side arose a black stripe, which passed to the fides of the throat, where it was wider than at its origin, and appeared like a moustache. The left of the face was white and bluish. The back was of a deep green, the wing coverts were marked with yellow and the quills were deep green. The breast was the colour of lilac. The tail was about half the length of the bird and above green and beneath straw colour.[21]

The falcon bird was found in Gingee and it measured twenty-one inches in length and the colour was crimson and round the eyes was a naked reddish skin. The plumage above was of a deep olive green, and beneath of a pale green, with a mixture of yellow. The throat and fore part of the neck inclining was to ash and the wing coverts nearest the body of a dull red, while the others green. The quills were green, edged with black and the tail was thirteen inches in length; the two middle feathers nine inches and three quarters longer than the two outer ones. The colour was green, with brown shafts. The wings, when closed, reached one-third of the length of the tail. The legs were reddish and the claws black.[22]

The blossom-headed parakeet was found in Gingee. The total length of the bird was eleven inches. The bill was reddish, the head red, with a shade of light blue; partaking most of this colour at the hind head. The chin was black, narrowing into a slender line from the corners of the mouth to the hind head, beneath the black was another slender line of a very pale green, both making a kind of collar and the rest of the plumage was green. The under parts had a tinge of yellow and on the wing coverts was a dull red spot. The tail was six inches and a quarter long; green above, with the inner margins yellow; the outer feather shorter than the middle ones by four inches. The legs and claws were grey.[23]

The little horn owl found in Tamil country was an elegant piece of bird. It represented of its natural size. The irides were scarlet. The horns took their origin from the base of the bill, and pointed to the sides of the head on their inner side. They were dusky, on their exterior white. The bill was dusky, surrounded with long bristles. The circle of feathers round the eyes was of a very pale ash color, the external circle was of a yellowish brown. The head was of a deep ash-color, the back dusky, the coverts of the wings grey, marked with narrow lines of black, pointing downwards. The quill-feathers regularly barred with black and white, the bread buff-coloured marked with small fagittal black spots. The legs feathered half way down and the naked part was of a reddish yellow.[24]

In France the *Cabinet du Roi* (King's Cabinet) with natural curiosities began to develop and it contained the collection of rare and strange birds and animals of the world. The first detailed account of the King's Cabinet was made in 1789 at the time of French Revolution and it reported 460 birds and 75 mammals but the identities were not specified. The specimens from Pierre Poivre (1719-1786) had been included. Later the Muséum National d'Histoire Naturelle, Paris (MNHNP), was founded in 1793 and under able administration of its various directors the collection grew very steadily. Pierre Sonnerat (1748-1814) the travelller's second voyage collection of birds from China to India (1774-1781) were included with a collection of 300 birds in total but we find 16 birds from Pondicherry acknowledged to Pierre Sonnerat by Georges-Louis-Leclerc de Buffon (1707-1788) at the Muséum National d'Histoire Naturelle in 1813. The list of birds is as follows:

English name — Zoological name

Blue-naped Parrot — *Tanygnathus lucionensis*

Caica Parrot — *Pyrilia caica*

Dusky Parrot — *Pionus fuscus*

Great Barbet — *Megalaima virens*

Great Potoo — *Nyctibius grandis*

Greater Painted Snipe — *Rostratula benghalensis*

Green-and-rufous Kingfisher — *Chloroceryle inda*

Long-tailed Parakeet — *Psittacula longicauda*

Northern Fulmar — *Fulmarus glacialis*

Red-bellied Macaw — *Orthopsittaca manilatus*

Red-footed Falcon — *Falco vespertinus*

Spot-breasted Woodpecker — *Colaptes punctigula*

Spotted Puff bird — *Nystactes tamatia*

White-naped Woodpecker — *Chrysocolaptes festivus*

Yellow-breasted Crake — *Porzana flaviventer*

Yellow-shouldered Parrot — *Amazona barbadensis*

Johann Friedrich Gmelin (1748-1804) who published the 10th edition of *Systema Naturae* of Part IV in 1789 had mentioned the birds from Tamil country.[25] He gave the bird names and also the places from where they were observed like Madras and Pondicherry. Further he also noted carefully the bird that was mainly found in the Hindu temples and so he used the term *pagodarum*.

Tamil name — Zoological name — English name

Aatru aala — Gleochelidon nilotica — River tern

Koudaari — Francolinus pondicerianus — Grey francolin

Kulaththu kuruvi — Motacilla maderaspatensis — Large pied wag tail

Manal naarai — Ixobrychus sinensis — Yellow Bittern

Maadapuraa— Columba livia — Blue rock pigeon

Paapathi naaganavaay — Sturnus pagodarum —– Brahminy starling

Sengkurugu —– Ixobrychus cinnamomeus — Chestnut Bittern

Uppukoththi/ Kottaan — Plurialis fulva — Pacific golden plover

Valluru — Accipiter badius — Shikara

Storks, Cranes and Other Birds Observed by Christoph Samuel John in Tranquebar, 1781-1793

Christoph Samuel John (1747-1813) the Protestant missionary reached Tranquebar in 1771.[26] He showed interest in the study of birds and wrote about the storks and cranes found in the region to Professor Johann Reinhold Forster (1729-98) in Germany. He mentioned the tropical birds like the *nellu kuruvi* in Tamil (paddy kokku), the white throated munia (*Lochura malabarica*) and the spotted munia (*Lonchura punctulata*) were found at Poraiyar and Tranquebar. He said that there were birds which would come to the rice fields and these were actually water birds. The list included the common moorhen (*Gaalinula chloropus*) the *kulaththu kuruvi* in Tamil, the large pied wag tail (*Motacilla Maderaspatensis*) *vayal ullan* or *kottaan* in Tamil besides the wood sand piper (*Tringa glareola*) which ate only the fish which the fresh water brought into the field. These birds trembled over the fresh seeds but snakes and crabs did more harm and damage. C.S. John said that what the sparrows and other birds ate the grain did less harm to the field than the theft of the *Taleiaren* (*Thalayaari* in Tamil, petty village official) who were hired to watch the paddy. The missionary also said that the *kokkus* were migrating birds which had been in Tranquebar only when the fresh water came in during the rainy season. After that they flew to the Malabar Coast where there was rainy season. The ordinary chickens were found in the Tondaimaan kingdom of Pudukottai and they were found in the thorny bushes. C.S. John added that the turkey had been raised in Tranquebar as domestic bird like in Europe. The price of one cock was one *pagoda* and a hen fetched half a *pagoda* in the market.[27] The bird called *Periya vellai kokku* in Tamil was also noticed by C.S. John and he mentioned that the egg of this bird he saw was similar to that of an ostrich only longer and greener in colour.[28]

Prof. J.R. Forster in Germany who received the communication from C.S. John had identified *pulli mooku vaathu* in Tamil (the spot bile duck) and he had named it scientifically *Anas Poecilorhynche* in his work *Indische Zoologie* published in 1781. Regarding the characters and size he said that the spot bile duck was of domestic duck; large body with buff gray and dark brown feathers; the wings spectrum was green with black and white margin. A broad white bar was conspicuous more prominent in flight; and the dark bill was tipped with yellow and a reddish-lores found on the base of bill. Further it had been said that the bird occurred in small flocks: inhabited wetlands, paddy field and marshlands and fed only on vegetable matter and cultivated grain. Thus knowledge transferred was useful universally to ornithologists. It is very significant to note that the immense curiosity developed by the Protestant missionaries in Tamil country for they reported the matter with minute details to Europe. Hence it may be said that the missionaries served as vehicles of transfer of the natural history knowledge to Germany and other parts of Europe. C.S. John mentioned that he engaged the drawing teacher of the Danish mission school who did the drawings of the birds and animals which he sent to Halle along with the description.[29]

The Native Response to the European Study of Birds: Serfoji's Collection in Thanjavur, 1803-1821

The impetus to the bird study was not restricted to Europeans for we find Serfoji II (1777-1832) the ruler of Thanjavur who had developed abiding interest. He established contacts with the missionaries and East India Company officials who devoted time and labour by taking interest in procuring birds. Therefore he got a similar interest and began to collect and maintain the birds besides studying in detail. Serfoji purchased birds of prey such as hawks. Annasami the hunter was paid five *phulivaragan* in 1803 for the purchase of a bird called behari (Brahminy kite, *Haliasatur*

Indus, called *Garudan* in Tamil).[30] Again we find five *phulivaragan* was paid to procure a beshwara (*Accipiter besra* — The besra hawk) the bird of paradise.[31] A darter (*Anhinga melanogaster* called *Paambu thaaaraa* in Tamil) was purchased through Umer Khan.[32] Wild hens were procured by Thimmathi Dharma *chetti* and many others.[33]

Knowing the interest of Serfoji II in the purchase of birds, many people came to Thanjavur to supply and make the sale of birds from distant places. According to records three persons had come from North India with a curious bird for the Raja.[34] Serfoji had also purchased a bauze (a kind of hawk) from the British Resident of Hyderbad.[35]

Exotic and rare birds were purchased through Serfji's commercial agent Arbuthnot & Co in Madras. In 1821 Serfoji purchased sarus cranes during the pilgrimage to Benares.[36] Captain Twady the English resident in Thanjavur had shot dead one of these cranes and so orders were immediately placed with Arbuthnot & Co for the purchase of the same bird from Calcutta accompanied by an illustration for its proper identification.[37] In a few months two birds were supplied to Serfoji and they were reared safely in the palace.[38] Serfoji also had other birds like *Pancha Varana Kizhli*, the five coloured parrot.[39] He also had mentioned a kind of elegant bird called *patte chittoo* or honey bird.[40]

Serfoji was kind enough to donate some birds to a few individuals of his own choice. We find mention of a curious bird that he sent to Blackburne the English resident of Thanjavur.[41] Similarly Charles Harris the Collector of Thanjavur was also supplied with a pair of hawks.[42]

Serfoji's Album of Drawings and Paintings of Birds with Description, 1812

All beautiful and rare birds maintained in the royal menagerie were asked to be painted by the artists in Thanjavur. Serfoji had specially commissioned Venkatadass the artist to make portraits of the birds. A portrait of the bauze was painted by one of the artists in the royal court and it is reported that the painting was well admired by all those who visited the royal palace.[43]

Serfoji who collected birds was also keen to furnish the description in detail. He stated that a bird called shamah was found common only in the region of Kashmir. The singing of the bird was said to be very melodious like that of agun and chundole. He stated that shamah lived upon the food which consisted of a spoonful of flour of a kind of pea mixed with two cloves well floured and the yellow of an egg. All of these items were well roasted with ghee and it was fed to the bird.[44] The bird came to the menageries in Thanjavur via Hyderabad. It has been recorded that the bird was fond of grasshoppers.[45]

Serfoji had similarly given the description of a bird called *thony kalamban*. The bird ate small insects. The small hawks were very fond to prey upon this bird. A man could catch it by at little trouble because the bird could not run much. When a single bird was caught all this kind of birds too will fell in that place about 20 or 30 of them out of sympathy and the birds were so lively in their instinct. The Muslims said that the flesh of the bird was very tasty and so they liked to eat.[46]

Serfoji had further described a bird called casuwari found in Ceram island in Moluccas called emen/eme. Its length from foot to neck was three feet and two and a half inches. From neck to the tail it was two feet and five inches. From neck to the bill it was one foot to ten and a half inches. The bird ate some guva fruits and plantains. A quarter measure of rice boiled with milk in a day was also given as food. She likewise swallowed garlic, and onion. She had laid an egg after it came to the palace of Thanjavur and the colour of the egg was yellowish like the papaya fruit.[47]

The Study of Birds and the Collection Sent from Pondicherry to Paris, 1807-1825

Jean Baptiste-Louis-Claude-Théodore Leschenault de la Tour (1773-1826) was sent to Pondicherry to establish a botanical garden. He travelled to India in May 1816 and returned to France in 1822. During his stay at Pondicherry he made a visit to Nilgiris and he collected birds and delivered 196 birds (both from Bengal and Coromandel) on 29 April 1819, out of which 131 birds were from Pondicherry which added to the Muséum National d'Histoire Naturelle Collection. J.B. Leschenault de la Tour again delivered 17 birds from Pondicherry on 5 June 1822, followed by 556 specimens from Ceylon and the Coromandel Coast on 1 July 1822 after his arrival to France. He was awarded the Legion d' Honneur. It may be pointed out that the collection of Javanese birds of Leschenault de la Tour was earlier described by Georges Cuvier. However a number of birds were named after Leschenault de la Tour and the birds include Greater sand plover (*Charadius leschenaulti*), White-crowned forktail (*Enicurus leschaulti*) and Sirkeer malkoha (*Phaenicophaeus leschenaultii*).

It is recorded that J.J. Dussumier who lived in the city of Bordeaux in France gave 28 birds that arrived from India on 3 June 1824. Again he gave 9 birds that came from Pondicherry on 17 July 1824 which he had received. Some birds from India were again donated by A. Duvaucel in 1825. Thus the collection of birds in the Muséum National d'Histoire Naturelle, Paris had been enriched from time to time. A detailed study of the various collections to understand the numerous bird specimens sent from Pondicherry to Paris would be interesting. An in depth investigation into the taxonomy is also needed and important.

The Study of Birds by Thomas Caverhill Jerdon in Madras, Nilgiris and Nellore, 1837-1847

Thomas Caverhill Jerdon (1811-1872) the assistant surgeon of the English East India Company in 1837 studied the birds and he began to publish his catalogue of the birds in 1839 in the Madras Journal of Literature and Science.[48] Two parts issued that year were succeeded by four more in the next year.[49] In 1842 he sent some bird specimens to William Jardine in Scotland, but these were so badly infested with moth that they had to be destroyed on arrival. Further specimens were later sent and these are kept among the collections of the Natural History Museum in London.

During 1842 to 1844 Jerdon presented the bird specimens to the Museum of the Asiatic Society in Calcutta and later some duplicates were given to the India Museum in London.[50] In 1843 the first of four parts of Jerdon's Illustrations of Indian Ornithology appeared, with the second publication in 1845.[51] Jerdon in the beginning bestowed an English name to all the birds largely based on British analogies. Later he used the Linnaeus system by adopting the binominals.

Birds Reported from the Tamil Region

Jerdon well knew the geographical limits of the then Tamil country for he had included the region of Travancore and Nellore which are presently included in the states of Kerala and Andhra Pradesh. In my earlier study of the historical geography of the sixteenth century I had also found these regions were then located within Tamil country and the work is based on the study of inscriptions and Portuguese records.

Jerdon had listed 38 birds and given some names of the birds in Tamil language as known to locals in the region. Perhaps these were informed to him as he asked for names and details from the natives. 1. *Nisaetus grandis* — Large hawk-eagle (*Rajaali* in Tamil); 2. *Muscipeta paradise* — Paradise flycatcher (*Wal kondaathee* in Tamil); 3. *Pterocles quadricinctus* — Painted rock grouse (*Kul-koudaree* in Tamil); 4. *Falco shaheen* — The shaheen yellow (*Wuloor* in Tamil) and 5. *Otis aurita* — The black florikin (*Mayil* in Tamil)

Jerdon had just indicated three birds that were found common throughout the Tamil country. 1. *Malacocircus* — White headed babbler;

2. *Chloropsis jerdoni* — Common green bulbul and 3. *Falco luggur* — The luggur falcon.

Jerdon mentioned the various localities such as Coimbatore, Pondicherry, Madras, Travancore, Nellore, Arcot, Carnatic, Connor, Nilgiris and Madurai where he found the particular birds and he had listed them as follows:

Coimbatore

Zanclostomus viridirostris — Green billed cuckoo

Pondicherry

Francolinus hardwickii — Female painted spur-fowl

Madras

1. Ardea flavicollis — Yellow necked black heron
2. Scops sunia — Red scops owl

Travancore

1. Brachypus rubineus — Ruby throated bulbul
2. Mirafra erythroptera — Red winged lark
3. Hemicircus cordatus — Heart-spotted woodpecker

Nellore, Arcot and Carnatic

1. Vinago bicincta — Purple and orange breasted green pigeon
2. Dendrocygna major — Large whistling teal
3. Ceyx tridactyla — Purple three-toed kingfisher
4. Anas caryophyllacea — Pink headed duck
5. Pycnonotus xantholaemus — Yellow throated bulbul

Conoor

1. Accipiter besra — The besra hawk
2. Crateropus delesserti — White breasted babbler
3. Strix candida — long legged grass owl
4. Branchypodius poiocephalus — White eyed bulbul

Nilgiris

1. Prinia cursitans — Grass wabler
2. Turdus wardii — Pied thrush
3. Scolopax nemoricola — Wood snipe

4. Phaenicornis flammeus— Fiery red bird
5. Muscicapa albicaudata — Nelgheery blue flycatcher
6. Palaornis columboides — Blue winged parakeet
7. Petrocincla pandoo — Indian blue rock thrush
8. Caprimulgus indicus — Large Indian nightjar
9. Bucoo viridis — Green barabet
10. Buteo rufirenter — Rufous buzzard
11. Dicaeum concolor — Olive flower pecker
12. Anthus similis — Mountain titlark
13. Parus nuchalis — White naped titmouse
14. Columba elphinstoni — Neelgherry wood pigeon

The Methods and Means Adopted by Jerdon for the Study of Birds

Jerdon mentioned that in Madurai a Common Barn Owl he caught. The text runs thus: 'Whilst at Madura lately, one flew into my room at an open window after a rat that was running, and I secured it alive'.[52]

It is mentioned by Jerdon that he had often purchased birds for his study. He added that he bought the bird *Pernis cristata* at Niligris for the purpose of study.[53] A specimen of the bird Goshwak was procured in the Nilgiris.[54] A single specimen of the beautiful bird *Pharee tees* (hill tessa) in the valley of South Pennar river near Lalapettai was obtained.[55] He procured a species of the female of Goshwak shot dead at Khunda range of the Nilgiris and he gave the length and details of the same bird.[56] He procured an owl in Nilgiris which he called the Neilgherry wood owl and stated that it was quite nocturne in its habits.[57] He purchased *Thimalia poioicephala* (small grey-headed wabbler) in Conoor.[58] He also procured *Thimalia platyura* and *Musicicapa rubricula* at Gudalur.[59] The bird *Pallus porzana* was obtained in a swamp on the Nilgiris in April 1844.[60]

Jerdon had often travelled and got engaged himself in hunting for the study of birds besides purchase. He had given the dimensions of the bird *Colomba badia* that he shot dead at Khunda.[61] Further he had collected information about the birds from the hunter Meer Shikhar about the bird *Spizaetus milvoides*.[62] Jerdon went out for hunting and reported he had successfully killed *Buteo longiper* the bird.[63] Jerdon had also shot dead a specimen of buzzard seated on the ground near a small brook on the swampy ground in Nilgiris.[64] Black-eared buzzard was killed by Jerdon during hunting at the foot of the Nilgiris.[65]

Jerdon prepared a catalogue of all the birds of the peninsular India of which he had wide knowledge. He divided the regions of the bird locations in his work into four zones (a) Northern Circars, (b) Carnatic (c) West Coast and (d) The great central table land.[66] We shall see the birds of the Tamil region alone mentioned by him. The following birds and the places had been neatly recorded.[67]

Name of the Bird — Place/Region

Acceipter fringillarius (Sparrow hawk) — Nilgiris

Acceipter palumbarius — Nilgiris and Conoor

Bulcea Sinensis — Palayamkottai

Crested honey-buzzard — Nilgiris

Eagle — Nilgiris

Eagle buzzard — Tiruchirapalli

Falcon Peregrinus — Ramnad and Tiruchirapalli

Haliaetus Pondicherianus (Garudan in Tamil) — Brahminy kite of Europeans

Indian horned owl— Nilgiris and Conoor

Little spotted owl — Carnatic

Serpent eagle — All over Tamil country

Strix flammea (White owl) — Madurai

Strix longimembris — Conoor

Vulture Pondicherinaus (Black Vulture) — Pondicherry

Vulture — Nilgiris

Jerdon in his voluminous study of birds had mentioned at large the names of the birds in English and he tried his level best to provide the scientific names by following Linnaeus. He was again very keen to mention the places where they were found noticed.

Name of the Bird — Place/Region

Ash-coloured wren warbler — Kotagiri

Alauda gulgula — Nilgiris

Alauda rufescens — Nilgiris

Buceros caveats (Large hornbill) — Conoor

Black headed tit — Nilgiris

Chif-chaff of Europe — Nilgiris

Crypsirina vagabandula (Indian magpie) — All over Tamil country

Crypsirina sinensis — Nilgiris

Cryptolopha poidicephala (Grey headed flycatcher) — Nilgiris

Euplecta philippensis (Weaver bird) — All over Tamil country

Indian black and white wagtail — All over Tamil country

Jungle wren warbler — Nilgiris

Leucocirca fuscocentris — Nilgiris

Muscipeta paradisa (Long tailed white flycatcher) — Carnatic

Musicicapa caerulea (Black naped blue flycatcher) — Conoor

Musicicapa pallipes (White billed blue flycatcher) — Conoor

Musicicapa banyuma (Red breasted blue flycatcher) — Carnatic

Musicicapa albi-caudata (Niligiri blue flycatcher) — Nilgiris

Musicicapa poonensis (Indian Grey flycatcher) — Tiruchirapalli

Musicicapa hirundinaces (Black and white flycatcher) — Nilgiris

Pastor pagodarum (Brahminy myna) — Carnatic

Pastor roseus (Chola kuruvi) — Carnatic

Pastor tirstis (Common myna) — All over Tamil country

Pastor fuscus (Hill myna) — Nilgiris

Pastor malabaricus (White headed myna) — Carnatic

Small brown finch — All over Tamil country

Spermestes malacca (Black headed finch) — Carnatic

Spermestes nisoria (Chestnut throated finch) — Nilgiris

Word or jungle wagtail — Nilgiris

Yellow checked tit — Nilgiris

Zosterops maderaspatensis —Nilgiris

Source: Catalogue of birds of the peninsular India, *Madras Journal of Literature and Science*, vol. XI, Madras, January-June 1840, pp. 1-38, see pp, 3-4, 6-8,10,12-17, 19- 23, 25-28, 30, 34, 37

The Zoological Naming of Birds

Jerdon began to follow the Linnaean system and he mentioned the following birds which he found in the Nilgiris since 1840. He gave the zoological names for most of them as follows:

Palaeornis columboides

Dicaeum conclor

Bucco viridis (Jungle barbet)

Psittaculus vernalsi (Dwarf parrot)

Picus strictus (Scarlet backed woodpecker)

Dendrocopus maharattensis (Red bellied woodpecker)

Malacolophus squamatus (Scally bellied woodpecker)

Brachylophus bengalensis (Orange and black woodpecker)

Dendrophila frontalis (Velvet-fronted blue nuthatch)

Xanclostomus sirkee (Red billed cuckoo)

Common red-ringed parakeet

Source: Catalogue of birds of the peninsular India, *Madras Journal of Literature and Science*, vol. XII, Madras, 1840, pp. 207-238, see pp. 207, 209-214, 217, 218, 223, 227

Jerdon noticed some birds at Conoor and had mentioned them too with zoological names.

Chrysonotus tiga (Crimson backed woodpecker)

Xanclostomus viridirostris (Green billed cukoo)

Merops quinicolor (Chestnut headed bee-eater)

Merops cyano-gularis (Blue throated bee-eater)

Cuculus himalayanus (Small bay cuckoo)

Source: Catalogue of birds of the peninsular India, *Madras Journal of Literature and Science*, vol. XII, Madras, 1840, pp. 207-238, see 216, 220, 223, 227.

Jerdon had also observed a few birds in the Carnatic region and in Madras which he had mentioned them with zoological names.

Oxylophus coronus

Oxylophus edolius (Black and white crested cuckoo)

Cinnyris sola (Honey sucker)

Cinnyris polita

Merops philippensis (Blue tailed bee-eater)

Source: Catalogue of birds of the peninsular India, *Madras Journal of Literature and Science*, vol. XII, Madras, 1840, pp. 207-238, see pp. 222, 225, 227.

The Drawings of Birds by Jerdon: Role of Krishna Raju the Native Artist of Nellore in Litho Printing

Jerdon favoured the drawing of birds by local artists. In 1847 he published a selection of 50 lithographs with descriptive letterpress titled 'Illustrations of Indian Ornithology'.[68] 21 of the 50 lithographs were drawn by C. V. Krishna Raju (spelt as Kistnarajoo) the artist and they were printed. The excellence and faithfulness of the drawings have been appreciated universally.

Krishna Raju worked under Jerdon's superintendence, and set up the colour templates, and had executed the colour plates. It is significant to note that he worked on pencil sketches made by Jerdon. These were then drawn on stone and made into lithographs, which were used to make imprints on paper. Lithography had arrived in Madras as early as in 1827. Krishna Raju's lithography has been much admired over the years, both for its light touch, and the use of water-colour along with lithography. The following twenty one plates had been found with his signature.

Birds Name on Plate	**Zoological name**
1. Nisaetus Strenuus	Aquila fasciata
2. Zanclostomus viridirostris	Phaenicophaeus viridirostris
3. Accipiter besra	Accipiter virgatus
4. Prinia cursitans	Cisticola juncidis
5. Muscipeta paradisea	Terpsiphone paradisi
6. Turdus wardii	Geokichla wardii
7. Scolopax nemoricola	Gallinago nemoricola
8. Pterocles quadricinctus	Pterocles indicus
9. Phænicornis flammeus	Pericrocotus flammeus
10. Falco Shaheen	Falco peregrinus
11. Crateropus delesserti	Garrulax delesserti
12. Muscicapa albicaudata	Eumyias albicaudatus
13. Ardea nigra	Ixobrychus flavicollis
14. Palaeornis columboides	Psittacula columboides
15. Malacocircus griseus	Turdoides affinis

16. Petrocincla manillensis	Monticola solitarius
17. Vinago bicincta	Treron bicinctus
18. Dendrocygna major	Dendrocygna bicolor
19. Caprimulgus indicus	Caprimulgus indicus
20. Ceyx tridactyla	Ceyx erithaca
21. Hemicircus cordatus	Hemicircus canente

Assistance Sought for Printing the Birds by Reeve Brothers in London

While the 21 plates of Krishna Raju were lithographed and printed at Nellore the other remaining 17 plates were executed by Reeve Brothers firm in London. The names of the birds are as follows:

Birds Name on Plate	**Zoological name**
1. Bucco viridis	Psilopogon viridis
2. Buteo rufiventer	Buteo buteo
3. Strix candida	Tyto longimembris
4. Brachypodius poioicephalus	Alcippe poioicephala
5. Otis aurita	Sypheotides indicus
6. Anas caryophyllacea	Rhodonessa caryophyllacea
7. Pycnonotus xantholæmus	Pycnonotus xantholaemus
8. Brachypus rubineus	Pycnonotus melanicterus
9. Mirafra erythroptera	Mirafra erythroptera
10. Dicæum concolor	Dicaeum concolor
11. Scops sunia	Otus sunia
12. Francolinus hardwickii	Galloperdix lunulata
13. Chloropsis jerdoni	Chloropsis jerdoni
14. Falco luggur	Falco jugger
15. Anthus similis	Anthus similis
16. Parus nuchalis	Machlolophus nuchalis
17. Columba elphinstonii	Columba elphinstonii

Jerdon became very impatient with delays in the publication of part two of the book on ornithology. The reason was the extreme slowness of colourists.[69] Jerdon's book had been reprinted in 1862, 1863 and 1864.[70] His book on birds epitomizes the knowledge up to that period based largely upon the publications of the several other illustrators and field naturalists. Thus through the pioneering efforts of the Europeans the study of birds in Tamil country had significantly scaled new heights.

To conclude it may be said that the birds had come to be classified over a long period of time in Europe into six orders such as (a) *raptores* (birds of prey) (b) *incessores* (perching birds) (c) *gemitores* (pigeons) (d) *rasores* (game birds) (e) *gralltores* (wading birds) and (f) *natatores* (swimming birds). Tamil country had possessed several species of birds unknown to the rest of the world. John Ray was the first in Europe to publish the birds of Madras at Fort St George noticed by Edward Buckley. Later many Protestant missionaries of Tranquebar emerged as ornithologists and they had reported many birds and types. However T.C. Jerdon published extensively on the birds of Tamil region in the Madras Journal of Literature and Science between 1839 and 1844. In fact these bird studies were distinguished by deep research and great acumen and very full in details of structure. Jerdon's printed plates of birds stand a great success and forms a significant milestone by playing a vital part of the complex network of specimens and drawings that came to be circulated widely among the European scientific community. Eventually various bird specimens from Tamil coast found way to the museums in England, Scotland, France and at Calcutta in India.

Notes

1. Om Prakash, *The Dutch Factories in India: A Collection of Dutch East India Company Documents Pertaining to India*, Vol. I, (1617-1623) New Delhi, Munshiram, 1984; Vol. II, (1624-1627), New Delhi, Manohar, 2007, see vol. II, p. 142.
2. *Ibid.*
3. Salim Ali, *Bird Study in India: Its History and its Importance*, Indian Council for Cultural Relations, New Delhi, 1979.
4. S. Jeyaseela Stephen, *A Meeting of the Minds: European and Tamil Encounters in Modern Sciences, 1507-1857*, Delhi, 2016, p. 94.
5. Joannis Raii, *Synopsis Methodica Avium & Piscium, opus posthumum quod vivus recensuit & perfecit ipse insignissimus Author: in quo multas species in ipsius ornithologia & Ichthyologia desideratas adjecit: Methodumque suam Piscium Naturae magis convenientem reddidit cum appendice & Iconibus*, Londini, Impenis Gulielmi Innys, ad Insignia principis in coementerio D. Pauli, MDCCXIII. London, 1713, pp. 193-198. Salim Ali is incorrect in saying that Edward Buckley had given description of 22 birds. In fact we find 27 birds.
6. British Library (hereafter BL), London, Western Manuscripts Collections, Sloane MSS 2346, 3332, 3348, 4066. See particularly on Birds, BL, Additional Manuscripts, 5266, *Icone Avium Maderaspatanarum*.
7. BL, Western Manuscripts Collections, Sloane MSS, 4020, fl.192, see, Edward Bulkley of Fort St. George, *Descriptions of East Indian Birds from His Paintings sent to James Petiver, Apothecary to the Charter House*. It is known that James Petiver left the bulk of his goods to Jane Woodstock, his sister from whom Sloane had purchased them.

8. Joannis Raii, Synopsis Methodica Avium, pp. 193-4.
9. S. Jeyaseela Stephen, A Meeting of the Minds, p. 115.
10. *Ibid.*, p. 702.
11. Gotthilf August Francke, ed., *Der Königl. Dänischen Missionarien aus Ost-Indien eingesandter ausführlichen Berichten, Von dem Werck ihrs Ams unter den Heyden, angerichteten Schulen und Gemeinen, ereigneten Hindernissen und schweren Umstanden; Beschaffenheit des Malabarischen Heydenthums, gepflogenen brieflicher Correspondentz und mundlchen Unterredungen mit selbigen heyden*, Teil 1–9, (Continuationen 1–108) Waiserihaus, Halle, 1710–1772 (hereafter Hallesche Berichten = HB), see, 24th Continuation des Berichts der Königliche – Dänischen Missionarien in Ost Indien, 1729, pp. 1037-8.
12. HB, 38th Continuation des Berichts der Königliche – Dänischen Missionarien in Ost Indien, pp. 221-31.
13. S. Jeyaseela Stephen, A Meeting of the Minds, p.114.
14. HB, 24th Continuation des Berichts der Königliche – Dänischen Missionarien in Ost Indien, 1729, pp. 1054-55.
15. *Ibid.*
16. Francis Willughby, *The Ornithology*, London, Printed by A.C. for John Martyn, 1678; Carl Linnaeus, *Systema Naturae per Regna Tria Naturae Secundum Classes, Ordines, Genera, Species cum characteribus, differentiis, synonymis, locis*, Tome 1, Stockholm, 1766.
17. S. Jeyaseela Stephen, *Oceanscapes: Tamil Textiles in the Early Modern World*, Delhi, 2014, pp. 543-44.
18. E. Stresemenn, 'On the Birds Collected by Pierre Poivre in Canton, Manila, India and Madagascar, 1751-56', *IBIS*, vol. 94, issue 3, pp. 499-523.
19. Pierre Sonnerat, *Voyages aux Indes Orientles et a la Chine*, Paris, MDCCLXXXII.
20. John Latham, *A General Synopsis of Birds*, London, MDCCLXXXI, vol. I, part I, p. 41.
21. Pieter Boddaert, *Table des Planches Enlumineez d'Histoire Naturelle de M. D'Aubenton*, Utrecht, MDCCLXXXIII, p. 25, see PL.416.E. see also, p. 30, see, PL.517.
22. John Latham, *Index ornithologicus, sive systema ornithologiæ; complectens avium divisionem in classes, ordines, genera, species, ipsarumque varietates: adjectis synonymis, locis, descriptionibus & c. Studie et opera*, London, 1790; John Latham, *Supplementum Indicis ornithologici sive Systematis ornithologiae*, London, 1802; Stuart Cary Welch, *Indian Drawings and Painted Sketches 16th through 19th Centuries*, The Asia Society, New York, 1976, see Gingi Vulture, figure 26, p. 64.
23. John Latham, A General Synopsis of Birds, p. 209.
24. Thomas Pennant, *Indian Zoology*, London, MDCCXC, second edition, p. 34.
25. Johann Friedrich Gmelin, *Systema Naturae, per Regna Tria Naturae Secundum Classes, Ordines, Genera, Species, cum Characteribus, Differentiis, Synonymis, Locis*, 13th edition, Tome 1, Pars I, Lyon/Leipzig, 1788; Johann Friedrich Gmelin, *Systema Naturae, per Regna Tria Naturae Secundum Classes, Ordines, Genera, Species, cum Characteribus, Differentiis, Synonymis, Locis*, 13th edition, Tome 1, Pars II, Lyon/ Leipzig, 1789.

26. S. Jeyaseela Stephen, A Meeting of the Minds, p. 126
27. Georg Christian Knapp et al., eds., *Neuere Geschichte der Evangelischen Missions-Anstalten zu Bekehrung der Heiden in Ostindien aus den eigenhändigen Aufsätzen und Briefen der Missionarien erausgegeben*, Waisenhaus, Teil 1–8 (Stück 1–95), Waiserihaus, Halle, 1770–8/95, 1848 (hereafter NHB), 1793, pp. 660-1.
28. Archiv der Franckeschen Stiftungen (hereafter AFSt), Halle, AFSt/M2 E27:18, Tagebuch von Christoph Samuel John, 12 December 1803 - 31 December 1804, See also, NHB, 6 Bd., 63, s.259.
29. NHB 43. st. 655.
30. Saraswati Mahal Library, Thanjavur (hereafter SMLT), *Modi Bundles* (hereafter MB), 105C/45-1; see also, P. Subramanian, Venkataramaiyaa and Vivekananda Gopal, *Thanjai Maraattiyar Modi Aavana Thamizhaakamum Kurippuraiyum* (Modi Records of the Mahratta Rulers of Tanjore in Tamil Translation), 3 vols, Tamil University, Tanjore, 1989 (hereafter MDT), vol. I, part I, p. 19.
31. K. M. Venkataramaiyaa, *Thanjai Marattiya Mannarkaala Arasiyalum Samudhaaya Vaazhkaiyum* (Administration and Social Life under the Maratha Rulers of Tanjore), Tamil University, Thanjavur, 1984, p. 368.
32. SMLT, MB, 160C/9; see also, MDT, vol. I, part VIII, p. 389.
33. SMLT, MB, 31C/29; see also, MDT, vol. I, part VIII, p. 326.
34. Tamilnadu State Archives (hereafter TNSA), Chennai, *Tanjore District Records* (hereafter TDR), vol. 4353, p. 38, 24 March 1803.
35. TNSA, TDR, vol. 3479, p. 511, 20 April 1804; TDR, vol. 3417, p. 67, 20 April 1804.
36. TNSA, TDR, vol. 4432, pp. 249-50, 20 December 1824.
37. TNSA, TDR, vol. 4455, p.149, 28 March 1828.
38. TNSA, TDR, vol. 4436, pp. 200-1, 3 April 1828.
39. British Library (hereafter BL), London, *Natural History Drawings of the India Office Collections* (hereafter IOL, NHD), 7/1031.
40. *Ibid.*, 7/1033.
41. TNSA, TDR, vol. 3418, see 17 January 1805.
42. TNSA, TDR, vol. 3492, p. 211, 25 May 1807.
43. TNSA, TDR, vol. 3492, p. 51, January 1807.
44. SMLT, MB, 31C/ 44-1-11; see also, MDT, vol. I, part VIII, p. 345.
45. BL, IOL, NHD, 7/1330.
46. *Ibid.*, 7/1032.
47. *Ibid.*, 7/1029.
48. Thomas Caverhill Jerdon, 'Catalogue of the birds of the peninsula of India arranged according to the modern system of classification, with brief notes on their habits and geographical distribution, and descriptions of new, doubtful and imperfectly described species', *Madras Journal of Literature and Science*, 1839 (a), vol. 10 (24), pp. 60-91; T. C. Jerdon, 'Catalogue of the birds of the peninsula of India arranged according to the modern system of classification, with brief notes on their habits and geographical distribution, and descriptions of new, doubtful and imperfectly described species' *Madras Journal of Literature and Science*, 1839 (b), vol. 10 (25), pp. 234-269.
49. Thomas Caverhill Jerdon, 'Catalogue of the birds of the peninsula of India arranged according to the modern system of classification, with brief notes on

their habits and geographical distribution, and descriptions of new, doubtful and imperfectly described species', *Madras Journal of Literature and Science*, 1840 (a), vol. 11 (26), pp. 1-38; T. C. Jerdon, 'Catalogue of the birds of the peninsula of India arranged according to the modern system of classification, with brief notes on their habits and geographical distribution, and descriptions of new, doubtful and imperfectly described specie', *Madras Journal of Literature and Science*, 1840 (b) vol. 11 (27), pp. 207-239; T. C. Jerdon, 'Catalogue of the birds of the peninsula of India arranged according to the modern system of classification, with brief notes on their habits and geographical distribution, and descriptions of new, doubtful and imperfectly described species', *Madras Journal of Literature and Science*, 1840 (c) vol. 12 (28), pp. 1-15; T. C. Jerdon, 'Catalogue of the birds of the peninsula of India arranged according to the modern system of classification, with brief notes on their habits and geographical distribution, and descriptions of new, doubtful and imperfectly described species', *Madras Journal of Literature and Science*, 1840 (d), vol. 12 (29), pp. 193-227; See also, T. C. Jerdon, *Catalogue of the birds of the peninsula of India arranged according to the modern system of classification: with brief notes on their habits and geographical distribution, and descriptions of new, doubtful and imperfectly described species*, 1st ed. Madras, J.B. Pharaoh, 1839, pp. i–xxiv, 1–203.

50. 'The King of Tanjore — Drawings of Birds from Southern India Presented by John Torin, Esq, 1812', and 'A Collection of Birds, Made by the Company's Naturalist at Fort St. George, 1829' in M. Thomas Horsfield & Frederic Moore, *A Catalogue of the Birds in the Museum of the Honourable East-India Company*, WM. H. Allen & Co., London, 1854, p. 3.
51. T. C. Jerdon, *Illustrations of Indian Ornithology*, 1st ed. Madras, J. B. Pharaoh, Vol. I of IV vols, 1843; T. C. Jerdon, 'Supplement to the catalogue of birds of the peninsula of Indi', *Madras Journal of Literature and Science*, 1844, vol. XIII (30), pp. 156–174; Anonymous, 'Jerdon's Illustrations of Indian Ornithology', *Calcutta Journal of Natural History*, 1844, vol. IV (16), pp. 534-536; T. C. Jerdon, Illustrations of Indian Ornithology containing 50 figures of new, unfigured and interesting birds, chiefly from the South of India, Madras, 1845 (a); T. C. Jerdon, 'Second Supplement to the Catalogue of the birds of Southern India', *Madras Journal of Literature and Science*, 1845 (b) vol. 13 (31), pp. 116-144; H. E. Strickland, 'Bibliographical Notices: Illustrations of Indian Ornithology by T.C. Jerdon', *Annual Magazine of Natural History*, 1845, vol. (1) 15, pp. 274-275; T. C. Jerdon, *Illustrations of Indian Ornithology*. Church Street, Vepery, India, R. W. Thorpe, Christian Knowledge Society's Press, Vol. II of IV vols, 1845; T. C. Jerdon, 'Second supplement to the catalogue of the birds of southern India', *Madras Journal of Literature and Science*, 1846 (a), vol. 13 (31), pp. 116–144; T. C. Jerdon, *Illustrations of Indian Ornithology*, Church Street, Vepery, India, Reuben Twigg, Christian Knowledge Society's Press, Vol. III of IV vols. 1846 (b).
52. T. C. Jerdon, 'Catalogue of the birds of the peninsula of India, arranged according to the modern system of classification; with brief notes on their habits and geographical distribution, and description of new, doubtful and imperfectly described species', *Madras Journal of Literature and Science*, 1839, vol. X (24), pp. 60–91.
53. T. C. Jerdon, 'Supplement to the catalogue of birds of the peninsula of Indi', *Madras Journal of Literature and Science*, 1844, vol. XIII (30), pp. 156–174, see p.159.

54. *Ibid.*, p. 162.
55. *Ibid.*, p. 165.
56. *Ibid.*, p. 163.
57. *Ibid.*, pp. 167-8.
58. *Ibid.*, p. 169.
59. *Ibid.*, pp. 170-1.
60. *Ibid.*, p. 174.
61. *Ibid.*, p. 164.
62. *Ibid.*, p. 160.
63. *Ibid.*
64. *Ibid.*, p. 166.
65. *Ibid.*, pp. 166-7.
66. T. C. Jerdon, 'Catalogue of the birds of the peninsular India arranged according to the modern system of classification with brief notice on their habits and geographical distribution & description of new, doubtful and imperfectly described species', *Madras Journal of Literature and Science*, vol. X, July-December 1839, pp. 60-92, see, p. 61.
67. *Ibid.*, pp. 63-4, 68, 70, 72, 75, 79, 80, 82, 85-8, 91.
68. T. C. Jerdon, *Illustrations of Indian Ornithology*: *Containing fifty figures of new, unfigured and interesting species of birds chiefly from the South of India*, printed by P.R. Hunt, American Mission Press, Madras, vol. IV of IV vols, 1847. The author has given the place and date of his work as 3 November 1843. The work contains 47 distinct species of birds in 50 plates. We find 3 birds from the Himalayas and one bird procured by Lord A. Hay from Ceylon. See also, T. C. Jerdon, *The Birds of India being a natural history of all the birds known to inhabit continental India; with descriptions of the species, genera, families, tribes, and orders, and a brief notice of such families as are not found in India, making it a manual of ornithology specially adapted for India*, Calcutta, 1863.
69. T. C. Jerdon, *Illustrations of Indian Ornithology*. Church Street, Vepery, India, R. W. Thorpe, Christian Knowledge Society's Press, Vol. II of IV vols, 1845, See, Notice to subscribers.
70. T. C. Jerdon, *The birds of India being a natural history of all the birds known to inhabit continental India: with descriptions of the species, genera, families, tribes, and orders, and a brief notice of such families as are not found in India, making it a manual of ornithology specially adapted for India*, 1st ed. Calcutta: Published by the author at the Military Orphan Press, 1862, pp. i–xlv, 1–535; T. C. Jerdon, *The birds of India being a natural history of all the birds known to inhabit continental India: with descriptions of the species, genera, families, tribes, and orders, and a brief notice of such families as are not found in India, making it a manual of ornithology specially adapted for India*, 1st ed. Calcutta, Published by the author, Printed by the Military Orphan Press, 1863, vol. II-Part I of 2 vols, pp. 1–439; T. C. Jerdon, T. C., *The birds of India: being a natural history of all the birds known to inhabit continental India; with descriptions of the species, genera, families, tribes, and orders, and a brief notice of such families as are not found in India, making it a manual of ornithology specially adapted for India*, 1st ed. vol. II-Part II of 2 vols, Published by the author, Printed by George Wyman and Co, Calcutta, 1864.

6.1. Aandhai, Strix candida, Long legged grass owl from Conoor.

6.2. Sivappu Aandhai, Scops sunia, Red scops owl from Madras.

6.3. Chinna kombu Anadhai, The little horned Owl.

6.4. Aandhai, Tfuhua Pectoralis.

6.5. Rajaali, Nisaetus grandis, Large hawk-eagle/bauze.

6.6. Chinna Valluru, Accipiter virgatus, The besra sparrow hawk from Conoor.

6.7. Parundhu, Buteo rufirenter, Rufous buzzard from Nilgiris.

6.8. Kazhugu, Falco luggur, The luggur falcon

6.9. Karungkuyil, Zanclostomus viridirostris, Green billed cuckoo from Coimbatore.

6.10. Maang Kuyil, Indian Treepie and Sengkuil, Fiery red bird from Nilgiris

6.11. Kizhli, Blue winged parakeet from Nilgiris.

6.12. Pancha Varna Kizhli, Five coloured parakeet from Madras.

6.13. Neer Kozhi, Scolopax nemoricola, Wood snipe from Nilgiris.

6.14. Kaanang Kozhi, Ardea flavicollis, Yellow necked black heron from Madras.

6.15. Kozhi, Francolinus Hardwickii, Female painted spur-fowl from Pondicherry.

6.16. Meen Koththi, Ceyx tridactyla, Purple three-toed kingfisher from Carnatic region

6.17. Poong Koththi, Dicaeum concolor, Olive flower pecker from Nilgiris.

6.18. Marang Koththi, Hemicircus cordatus, Heart-spotted woodpecker from Travancore.

6.19. Marang Koththi from Madras, Picus Hodgsonii.

6.20. Blue flycatcher from Nilgiris, Muscicapa albicaudata.

6.21. Vaal kondaththi, Muscipeta paradisea, Paradise fly-catcher.

6.22. Sivappu Iragu Chittu Kuruvi, Mirafra erythroptera, Red winged lark from the Eastern ghats.

6.23. Malai Chittu Kuruvi, Anthus similis, Mountain tit-lark found in Nilgiris

6.24. Neer Vaaththu, Dendrocygna major, Large whistling teal from Nellore.

6.25. Ilang Sivappu Thalai Vaaththu, Anas caryophyllacea, Pink headed duck from Nellore.

6.26. Kul-kaudaari, Pterocles quadricinctus, Painted rock grouse/Rock patridge

6.27. Vallooru/Wuloor, Falco shaheen, The shaheen yellow.

6.28. Thaen sittu, Crateropus delesserti, White breasted babbler from Conoor.

6.29. Thavittu Kuruvi, Malacocircus Griseus, White headed babbler.

6.30. Branchypodius poiocephalus, White eyed bulbul from Conoor.

6.31. Pycnonotus xantholaemus, Yellow throated bulbul from Nellore.

6.32. Brachypus rubineus, Ruby throated bulbul from Travancore.

6.33. Chloropsis jerdoni, Common green bulbul.

6.34. Thaen sittu, Prinia cursitans, Grass wabler from Nilgiris.

6.35. Karung sittu, Turdus wardii, Pied thrush from Nilgiris.

6.36. Vinago bicincta, Purple and orange breasted green pigeon from Nellore.

6.37. Columba elphinstoni, Wood pigeon from Nilgiris.

6.38. Petrocincla pandoo, Indian blue rock thrush from Nilgiris.

6.39. Caprimulgus indicus, Large Indian nightjar from Nilgiris.

6.40. Bucoo viridis, Green barabet from Nilgiris.

6.41. Parus nuchalis, White naped titmouse from Nilgiris.

6.42. Neela mayil, Otis aurita, The black florikin.

6.43. South Indian Birds, Vier Zeichnungen auf Glimmer.

6.44. Birds found in the region of Fort St George, Madras.

6.45. Birds found in the region of Fort St George, Madras.

6.46. Icones Avium Maderaspatanarum.

6.47. A specimen from Icones Avium Maderaspatanarum.

7

Ophiology and Toxicology through Experience and Learning, 1701-1853

The scientific study of reptiles particularly about the snakes including their behavior in Tamil country had developed in the age of European expansion. Though snakes were found in Tamil country, the Europeans did not evince interest to know the various types in the beginning when they settled on the coast and began their trade. They also did not bother to have any knowledge of their descriptions. The Europeans were gradually drawn to the study of snakes to know the medicine administered by the natives to the snakebites. Since snakes were a problem mainly in rural Tamil country the native doctors administered siddha medicine to snakebites. They knew well to distinguish between the poisonous and the non-poisonous snakes. There were several Europeans who made some pioneering efforts in the study of snakes in Tranquebar, Madras and in various other places on the coast. We shall examine in this chapter their efforts and the importance in the dissemination of knowledge.

Snakes and the Treatment for Snakebites Observed by the Europeans on the Tamil Coast, 1701-1738

Samuel Brown was the principal surgeon at Fort St. George in Madras.[1] He mentioned in 1701 that venomous snakebites were treated differently by the Tamils. According to him the fruit, leaves and root of *yetti* (*Strynchnos nux-vomica*) tree were mashed and boiled, and the oil pressed from the kernels was applied externally and taken orally as a sovereign medicine against poisonous bites of venomous serpents by Tamils.[2] He also wrote that the juice of *punga maram* (*Crotalaria juncea*) taken timely had cured the bites of venomous serpents.[3]

Gaston Laurent Coeurdoux the Jesuit left France for Madurai mission in 1732 served at first in Pondicherry and in 1740 became the Jesuit Superior at Karaikal. In 1745 he was appointed the procurator at Pondicherry. In 1745 he became the Jesuit Superior there until replaced by Fr. Laud in 1751.[4] He came to know the *Sillarai Kovai* (Miscellaneous Collection) a medical text in Tamil that dealt with subjects such as toxicology, antidotes for poisons, and remedies for bites of various types of poisonous snakes and insects. He evinced interest in this branch of Tamil medicine since these were more effective than the medicines imported from France. Therefore Fr. Coeurdoux sent an excellent remedy against snakebite to Fr. Souciet in 1738.[5]

The Study of Snakes by Johann Christian Wiedebrock and Johann Balthasar Kohlhoff in Tranquebar, 1764

Johann Christian Wiedebrock and Johann Balthasar Kohlhoff the two Protestant missionaries worked in the Danish mission at Tranquebar since August 1737.[6] They evinced keen interest in the study of snakes at Tranquebar and communicated the details in a report dated 28 September 1764 to Halle. It was mentioned by them that there was a snake called *Woellandei* in Tamil (*Uzhavan Paambu*, *Eryx conicus*, Russell's Sand Boa) which was very fearful. One of their gardeners, a Christian had found this big snake dead in the garden and he brought it to them. The missionaries desired to learn about the snake and contacted a brahmin to make enquiries. They were informed that the snake was called *malai paampu* (mountain snake in Tamil, *Python molorus*) and it was usually found only in the mountains. This snake was of a brown colour and was as thick as an arm from head to tail. Only its tail was a little thinner. It was reported by the brahmin that this type of snake normally wound itself around the body of animals such as a goat, calf and fox and pressed so hard that the animals could not breathe easily and they died. The missionaries were informed of *vazhalai paambu* (*Echis carinatus*, the saw-scaled viper) another variety but it was non-poisonous.[7]

A Detailed Study of 22 Snakes by Christoph Samuel John in Tranquebar, 1785-92

Christoph Samuel John (1747-1813) the Protestant missionary doctor had been employed in the Danish mission in Tranquebar in 1771. He found his income very low and to earn some extra amount, he went out and collected curiosities which he sold to European collectors. In this way, he made some reasonable amount which enabled him to survive.[8] He found also a recurring way of supplementing his income and ran a private school for a better class of people, namely the half-caste children whose European fathers were anxious to see them well educated. These pupils in turn served as assistants for field work. In the afternoon, after school time, he took the children and they were occupied in gardening and also engaged in collecting plants and insects.[9]

C. S. John conducted an extensive and in-depth study of snakes. He wrote about twenty two types of snakes and their nature, besides the degree of their poison. We find interesting information in his report of 1785 sent to Halle from Tranquebar. According to him, *Udira wirien* was a blood snake and its bite caused blood to flow from the nose, ears and mouth of the victim. Further, the poison could be found in the pores of the body and a difference in the colour of the blood was noticed through-out the whole body. Those bitten by this snake could not be saved, for the snake's venom was deadly. *Karhudei wirien* (*Karuvazhlai*/Bridal snake) was a dark black snake which expanded itself, and owed its name because of its size which was non-poisonous. Another type of snake the *Mulagu wirien*, called the pepper snake, was very small. *Kadtu wirien* (*Bungarus caeruleus*, the common krait), *Kattu viriyan* in Tamil was another variety also called the band snake because its bite caused boils in the human body that were dangerous. *Nir wirien* (water snake) was a poisonous one. *Surudtu wirien* was called the coiled snake because it appeared mostly in the rolled position. *Peru wirien* (the Grand snake) was a big snake that owed its name to its severe poison. *Pori wirien* was called the scabies snake because its bite caused sparkles or small dots to appear all over the skin of the person who had been bitten. *Karu wirien*, was the (light) black snake, and owed its name to its colour. Its bite was deadly poisonous.[10]

Sentalei wirien was a red-headed snake. The bite of *Arhalei wirien* snake caused severe burning sensation and pain in the limbs. *Pillu wirien* (*Trimeresurus graminus*) was the grass-snake which was found commonly in the bushes amidst grass. The bite of *Tamarei Kaai wirien* snake caused marks to appear on the body which looked like the fruit of a lotus. *Kollei wirien* was a snake generally found in the backyards of the house or the garden and its bite caused boils all over the body. The bite of *Kurei wirien* snake worked slowly but it later quickly affected the fingers and toes of the person who became paralyzed step by step. *Yettu Adi wirien* was an eight feet long snake, owing its name to the length. Its bite could not be healed very easily. *Karhuttu Kol wirien*, the thin-necked snake, looked like a stick. It was approximately one inch in thickness but its venom was dangerous. The person bitten had to be treated within three hours of time.[11]

In his letter dated 20 September 1792 Christoph again mentioned a snake called *Komberi mukkan*, (*Dendrelaphis tristis*, the bronze-backed tree snake).[12] He mentioned also about the cobra in Tamil called *Nalla paambu* (*Naja–naja*, literally good snake), in an another letter sent by him from Tranquebar to Halle.[13] This snake had been also called *Karu naagam* (*Ophiophagus Hannah*, the king cobra). The brahmins did not allow this snake called *naagam*, *Cobra de Capello* to be killed since it was worshipped by the Hindus. C.S. John had observed an individual who distracted a snake with garlic.[14] He used the assistance of some natives to compile the description of the different kinds of cobras but the names of those persons are not mentioned. Christoph translated the details he heard and saw from the natives and these were included in his various reports sent to Halle from time to time.[15] In my opinion C.S. John should therefore be said as the father of Tamil ophiology for his pioneering efforts and contribution.

Christoph Samuel John had made a note on *Patschai paambu* (*Ahaetnlla nastua*) literally green snake in Tamil. He stated that the snake was also called *Kan-kuththi paambu*, for its bite was painful as an arrow shot in the eye.[16] C.S. John had kept a pet snake the two headed specimen called *Iruthalai naagam* in Tamil which he named *Boa biceps*.[17] This double-headed snake was sent by him from Tranquebar to Patrick Russell in Visakhapattinam.[18] Russell had also received another snake called *siddhil* from C.S. John in Tranquebar. It was said that its bite was held by the natives to be dangerous though not fatal. The bite of *siddhil* was said to have produced a burning heat all over the whole body. According to Russell, this snake had no venomous apparatus.[19]

The Opinion of William Petrie on the Identification of Snake in Madras, 1787

William Petrie (1784-1816), was an officer of the English Company in Madras in 1778. He became president of the Board of Revenue in Madras in 1800 and later acted as the English Governor of Madras for three months in 1807. He noted that the natives disagreed very much not only in their accounts of the *Cobra de manili* but also in the identity of snake itself.[20]

The Study of Snakes by Christian Pohle in Tranquebar, 1793

Christian Pohle the Protestant missionary arrived at Tranquebar in 1777 and he evinced interest in the study of snakes.[21] In his letter to missionaries in Halle dated 16 March 1793 he mentioned *Mannuli paampu*, the snake that hid itself in the soil. Pohle mentioned that it was about one span long, thin and ash grey in colour. One day, as it ran over his mat he attempted to hit its head. He learnt from the natives that its bite was not poisonous.[22] Twenty nine snakes in total were mentioned by the various Protestant missionaries of Tranquebar through their serious studies conducted.

It is very interesting to find that drawings and paintings of the snakes that had developed over a period of time. Serfoji II, the ruler of Thanjavur had commissioned the drawings of the snakes such as *Thaneer paambu* literally the water snake (*Xenochrophis piscatori*, the checkered keelback), the green snake (*Ahaetulla nastua*), the *kannaadi viriyan* (*Daboia russelii*, *Vipera russelii*, Russell's viper) and the *thudal naagam*.[23]

The Description of Sea-Snake by Walter Elliot in Mylapore, 1840

Walter Elliot (1803-1887) the Scottish civil servant of the English company arrived in Madras in 1820. It has been reported by him that a fishermen from one of the *kuppams* (fishing hamlets) at Santhome of Mylapore brought a box containing a sea-snake (*kadal paambu* in Tamil, *Enydrina valakadien*) which he said that he had picked up while floating in the sea when fishing in his catamaram. He perceived it to be of unusual size and it differed from the common kind of snakes in the distribution of colours. This snake was a new species of cobra (*Naaga paambu* in Tamil) but with the head scarcely broader than the neck, the crown depressed and slopping to the muzzle which was somewhat obtus and covered with fourteen more conspicuous plates or lamine.[24] A painting depicting the fight with the sea-snake by the fishermen at Tranquebar is preserved at the Nationalmuseet, Copenhagen.[25]

A Detailed Study of 15 Snakes Found in Madras and Nilgiris by T.C. Jerdon, 1853

Thomas Caverhill Jerdon (1811-1872) entered into the service of the East India Company in 1835 as an assistant surgeon and he served at Madras since March 1837. He made a detailed study of snakes. According to Jerdon *Bungarus candidus* the snake was called *Yenna viriyan* by the Tamils. It was up to three feet in length and was found very common all over South India, and was said to be fatal. This snake was distinguished from one or two harmless species that much resembled it in colour, by the sub-caudal scutellse being in one row, not double.[26]

Naia lutescens, the cobra was called *Naaga paambu* or *Nalla paambu* by the Tamils. It was also found all over India.[27]

Trigonocephalus Elliotti was olive-green above and pearl-white beneath. Its poison-fangs being small the head was covered with plates. It was up to two feet and upwards long. T.C. Jerdon had only procured this on the Nilgiris towards the lower portion of the plateau.[28]

Trigonocephalus (cophias) *neelgherriensis* snake was of small size, dark brown with black markings with twenty three rows of carinated scales. It was found in the woods on the Nilgiris.[29]

Jerdon noted that *Vipera russellii* was called *Kannaadi viriyan* by the Tamils. This well known and justly dreaded snake grew to a large size. He was strongly inclined to believe that the far-famed *cobra de manili* of some was merely the young of this species. The old orthography was *manili*, which simply meant a chain or necklace, and whoever looked at the markings of this snake, especially of the young one, must have struck with the resemblance thereof to a necklace. Jerdon said that he needed hardly to remind the reader that both *Cobra capella* and *Cobra de manili* were Portuguese names, and he had little doubt, that the latter name was given to this species by the Portuguese. It has however been forgotten as applied to this viper, and might be considered a fable; for everyone he met had been able, on their own showing, to point out the real *Cobra de manili* as quite distinct, and what was more remarkable, was that no two observers had described it alike. They only had agreed in its being a very small and a very deadly snake. Jerdon added that the carpet snake, another household word in the Madras army, appeared to him to be equally fabulous, as he had not been able to identify it among the venomous snakes. Several prettily marked innocent species had been, at different times pointed out to him as the carpet snake.[30]

Vipera echis the snake was called *Kutta viriyan* by the Tamils. This little snake was found very common in the Carnatic. Jerdon did not think its bite would prove fatal to man. He had known a dog bitten by one had recovered. The above are all the venomous land snakes he had met with. Of these the only ones at all common were the Cobra, the Chain Viper (*Vipera russelii*), the *Bungarus candidus*, and the little *Vipera echis*. Most of the others were peculiar to the forests of south India. The *Trigonocephali* were not usually fatal. He had known several cases of bites by *Trigonocephalus malabaricus*, and *Trigonocephalus nepa* and none proved fatal. Great pain was experienced, and swelling usually followed, but the patient had gradually recovered. Jerdon himself was bitten in the fore-finger by the *Trigonocephalus neelgherriensis* and he had applied ligature round the finger, and sucked the wound vigorously. In a minute or so the skin round the bite blackened, and in a minute or two more a perfectly circular bit of the skin came off in his mouth. He set off running immediately as he was bitten, and felt no further ill effects.[31]

Jerdon possessed *kadal paambu* (*Hydrophus colubina*) and it was apparently a variety of the species of sea-snake. It differed from the finished drawing of the species in Cuvier's in the black markings meeting on the back and abdomen, thus forming a series of light-coloured oval spots on the sides; the abdominal scutse commenced nearer the mouth, had only three or four series of small scales between them and the elongated mentals.

The scutse were above 300 in number, and the rows of scales were from 35 to 45—whilst in *Hydrophus colubrina* the scutae were only 246—and the rows of scales were twenty five. Jerdon's only specimen was a young one and he had procured it at Madras.[32]

Hydrus gracilis the snake had the number of rows of scales varied from 26 to 35 on the neck, and from 44 to 51 on the trunk. The scutse had been 350 to 450 and the scutellae was around 50 to 60. It had been found very common in Madras. It was very remarkable for the small circumference of head and neck compared to that of the body. It was up to four feet long. All the sea snakes are venomous, and their bite had been dreaded.[33]

Mannuli paambu (*Cylindrophis macroselis*) had differed from the sea-snake in its shorter, more triangular head and differed from both in the much larger scales. These small species of snakes were not very common. They are sometimes found on the surface of the ground in rainy weather, but were generally dug out of the earth. They were called earth snakes by the Tamils.[34]

Coronella taeniolata snake had fifteen rows of smooth scales. The scutse had been 185 and scutellse 41. This species was referred to Tropidonotus stolatus by Cantor, but a snake that Jerdon possessed and it answered tolerably well to Russell's description and figure. It appears to be a true *Coronella*. The snake was found common in Madras.[35]

Coluber blumenbachii was called *Saarai paambu* by the Tamils. It was the most common snake in the country and it grew to a large size, seven feet and upwards. It frequented chiefly the marshy-land and paddy-fields. It had seventeen rows of scales. Jerdon had seen it nearly three feet long.[36]

Dipsas trigonata was called the *Suruttai Paambu* by the Tamils. It was found common in the Carnatic.[37]

Leptophis pictus was called *Komberi mukkan* by the Tamils. It was found very common in all parts of the country.[38]

Dryinus nasutus was called the *Pachchai paambu* in Tamil the Green whip-snake. It was found common all over the country. Jerdon had seen one that had swallowed a parrot and became gorged.[39]

Wilhelm Friedrich Gericke in Tranquebar and his Observation on the Treatment for Snakebites, 1767

Wilhelm Friedrich Gericke the Protestant missionary came to Tranquebar on 6 June 1767 and worked in the Danish missions at Cuddalore and Nagapattinam.[40] He evinced interest in the study of medicine on snakebites and mentioned in his report of 1767 sent from Tranquebar to Halle that he had witnessed the native treatment given for venomous snakebite to Sathyanathan, the catechist. He reported that at midnight the catechist was bitten by a deadly snake while he was asleep. He woke up thereafter and asked everyone to pray to god. The village chief, with whose family the catechist had good contacts, rushed for help immediately and arranged for an experienced native doctor to attend the catechist. The doctor made a cut with a knife the spot on Sathyanathan's left foot where the snake had bitten. He had brought six chickens with him, and he pulled out the back feathers from the chickens and pressed the exposed back part of the chickens one after another on the wound. Five of the chickens died within a few minutes. The sixth one remained alive, and this was a sign that the poison had been removed from the body of the patient. The native doctor later informed Gericke that he had never known a person bitten by the snake during his sleep to have been saved and said that the catechist seemed to have the grace of god.[41]

Samuel, a catechist and a servant of Christian Friedrich Schwartz the missionary was an expert in treating snakebites. He had a prescription against the bite of cobra and also against the bite of rabid dogs with which he had cured many people in the presence of Schwartz. Some of these cures caused quite a sensation. He maintained a great deal of secrecy about the prescriptions. The Madras government, therefore, requested Schwartz to arrange to send Samuel to the English settlement in order to discover this secret. This was felt necessary for the cause of public good and they promised a suitable reward to Samuel. Schwartz finally arranged for Samuel's journey in 1789. On his arrival in Madras, Samuel either willingly or unwillingly revealed the secret of the medicine. He received 200 star *pagodas* for disclosing the formula.[42]

The Treatment for Snakebites Noticed by Pierre Sonnerat in Karaikal, 1775-80

Pierre Sonnerat, the French traveller who visited Pondicherry and Karaikal during 1775 and 1780 mentioned that the native doctors treated quite successfully and very efficiently many cases of snakebites.[43] The treatment of snakebite given to a patient in Karaikal the French settlement had caught his attention. He observed that the native doctor took a young fowl and applied its breech (buttocks) to the bite, which had almost the same effect as a cupping glass, and drew out the poison. The fowl expired soon after. A second fowl was applied, which also soon expired, and was replaced by a third one. Thus, thirteen fowls were successively applied and the last one did not die, neither did it appear disordered. Finally, the patient declared to be fully cured.[44] The information completely agrees with Wilhelm Friedrich Gericke's observation at Tranquebar on the treatment of snakebite mentioned earlier. It must be pointed out in these cases no antidote or anti-venom was injected into the patient's veins. The treatment was based on simple ornithological knowledge and experience that chickens were hot-blooded birds, and that their live anus parts helped in sucking out the venom when placed in contact with the bite wound. Thus, we see that the medical practices of the Tamils were not exotic tales rather they were eye witnessed by several Europeans and spoke to the genuine credit of indigenous medical knowledge. Such marvels of medical treatment should have convinced the Europeans of the superiority of native Tamil medicine. The opinion of Abbé Felice Fontana (1730–1805) that venom acted through blood was confirmed, we see that Tamil doctors had elaborated the same in their treatment of snakebites.

Christian Friedrich Schwartz and His Observation on the Native Medicine for Snakebites, 1788

Christian Friedrich Schwartz, the Protestant missionary settled at Thanjavur in 1778.[45] He evinced interest in the study of siddha medicine and was struck with wonder when he saw a Tamil doctor preparing pills for snakebites. This doctor was also skilled in the treatment of poisonous insect bites. Schwartz introduced the Tamil doctor to Dr Strange, the English surgeon stationed in Thanjavur in July 1788.[46] After discussion with the Tamil doctor and being personally satisfied with the medicine for snakebite and treatment given by the native doctor, both Schwartz and Strange agreed to write to Archibald Campbell, the English Governor in Madras. In his letter Dr Strange mentioned that the Tamil doctor and his snake pills should be examined by the English doctors in Madras. He wanted to make the best use of the situation and affirmed that the Tamil doctor who prepared the snake pills had cured many people. The Governor, in his reply, asked for the Tamil doctor's snake pills to be sent to Madras where the Hospital Board could make trials of the pills for the purpose of learning the merits of his medicines and also ascertain the truth.[47] Snake pills were obtained and dispatched to Madras and a thorough examination and analysis were carried out. William Duffin and other surgeons wrote to the Hospital Board in September 1788 that the results of repeated trials had proved highly successful. Hence, they recommended the pills to the government for treatment of snakebites and also allow every doctor to administer the remedies as per his own judgment in cases of treatment of venomous bites.[48] They pointed out that some of the components of the snake pills had raised certain queries but these could be clarified later. The government decided to publish the details of the report. William Duffin and other surgeons extolled the government's decision to do so since doubts regarding the ingredients had been raised by some medical experts.[49] In October 1788, after the preliminary analysis was completed, the Military Board approved and encouraged the use of the pills for snake and mad dog bites.[50] It requested medical storekeepers to maintain an adequate quantity of Thanjavur snake pills.[51]

The English Company doctors who prescribed the snake pills only as an option, conducted further analysis of the ingredients since some serious doubts were raised regarding the pills prepared by the Tamil doctor. The Physician-General of Madras and the hospital members without any loss of time began to make a detailed analysis of the pills, especially of the ingredients, and to draw up an accurate account of the names and proportions of articles composed of in the pills. They had to specify in a particular manner the Tamil and English names of each article, as well as the botanical names of such plants or roots as used in the composition of these pills and the manner of using the pills.[52] The Military Board desired to publish the same without delay in the Madras Courier. It wanted to provide details with regard to proper administration of the pills and a sufficient quantity of these pills to be immediately made available at every station in Tamil country.[53]

James Anderson, the Physician-General at Fort St. George, produced a detailed list of the ingredients of the pills vide his minute prepared in November 1788. He added that it was the inclusion of arsenic that put the usage in doubt. He demanded a ban on the internal use of the pills. He stated that such noxious drugs should be expelled from the British Materia Medica and also for the sake of humanity.[54] His view, however, was seriously contested by William Duffin, the Head Surgeon of the hospital in Madras. He wrote in his minutes that despite the presence of arsenic he found the snake pills had been beneficial in most cases. Duffin added that he had earlier transmitted the results to Patrick Russell, the physician and naturalist to the English East India Company, who had communicated the details to the Royal Society of London. Duffin also wrote that he was at that time still making experiments with the pills to corroborate the facts.[55] Duffin defended the native treatment, and stated that the English were still ignorant of the analysis of exotic plants and other vegetable matter which were compounded with those minerals. They should not hastily condemn a remedy where experience and demonstration had in many cases proved successful. The medicine could be given with great precaution, besides the internal use of arsenic was by no means prohibited. He mentioned that it was given in cases of cancer and intermittent fevers by the established practitioners in

Europe. Therefore, Duffin was of the opinion that the formula should be published in the Madras Courier.[56]

In 1789, Sir William Jones wrote to James Anderson about his own success with arsenic and mentioned that he was greatly interested to know the details mentioned in the papers Anderson had submitted regarding the snake pills. He admitted that till the time he saw Duncan's Medical Commentaries, he had the same abhorrence as James Anderson to the use of arsenic in medicine. He had to later resolve a paper of one Tamil physician concerning the cure of the elephantiasis by small quantities of arsenic that he had earlier suppressed. Jones stated that when he found that arsenic had been safely administered for treatment in England, he ventured to print the paper in the second volume of the journal of the Asiatic Society of Bengal. He stated that poisons must, no doubt, be administered with extreme caution, but if they were banished from practice, how would the human race survive without the three essential articles of medicine like antimony, mercury and opium.[57] He said that there was great probability that chemistry had been noted by Tamils and it must have flourished in the region for a long time.[58] In his reply to William Jones, James Anderson said that he only urged caution in the use of arsenic or any other poison in medicine. He added that Tamils were better acquainted with the use of simples than any other people in the world. Thus, we find a duality in the writings of Anderson. He evidently changed his opinion and took a different stand later with regard to the use of snake pills.

William Duffin, the surgeon of the garrison at Vellore and later Chief Surgeon at Fort St. George in Madras, had first drawn Patrick Russell's attention towards the Thanjavur pills. In a letter dated January 1788, Duffin mentioned that he had recently seen Russell's public memoir on the subject of snakes, and that he was sending him the formula of a remedy which had been used with success in the bites of all poisonous animals, even of mad dogs. He had procured it through the medium of C.F. Schwartz, who had persuaded a native of Thanjavur to impart it for a pecuniary consideration. Duffin wrote that the harmful quality of the arsenic was not the only objection to using the medicine; he was also given to understand that two of the other ingredients, *vellainaamai* (*Anogeissus latifolia*) and *nerivisham*, were poisonous roots; and the third, *nervaazham* (*Croton tiglium*), was a drastic purge. All of these three were found in every market in Tamil country, but, on account of their poisonous qualities, could not be purchased without the knowledge of an officer of the police. These herbs were indigenous to the Malabar Coast, and used in composition, by the native practitioners, in a variety of diseases, besides those from animal poisons. He stated that he had been assured by Schwartz that, to his knowledge, the medicine had been used repeatedly; that no alarming symptoms occurred from it; and that it never failed in effecting a cure, when given in time, before the poison had affected the whole system.[59] Duffin assured Patrick Russell about the efficaciousness of the pill by giving the histories in details of two cases of snake-poisoning in which he himself had successfully administered Thanjavur pills, and added that the cases were no longer attended by any alarming symptoms. He said that the pills generally occasioned nausea and purging, but seldom in a violent degree.[60] Duffin also mentioned another reference, communicated to him by James Ramsay, the assistant surgeon to the 3rd Regiment of Cavalry in the cantonment near Arcot, where the result of the application of the pills was somewhat alike.[61]

Russell then performed a series of experiments with the unknown articles of Thanjavur pill. He arrived at a preliminary notion that none of the unknown ingredients were deleterious, with the exception of *vellainaamai*.[62] Then he prepared in his own way, unlike indigenous method, a mass with all the above ingredients supplied to him by Duffin or collected from the local bazaar to form the pill. After making the preparation, he administered it in several experiments on sound dogs and chickens. Russell also gave the pills, with varying successes, at different times to patients bitten by mad dogs. He regretted not having the opportunity of trying out the Thanjavur medicine on human beings bitten by serpents.[63] Therefore, in case of snake-poisoning, he could not be sure about its remedial power and cautiously filed his own judgment that its efficacy was a difficult question to answer.[64] Thus, he described his experiments with the Thanjavur snake pills as inconclusive.

Communication on Snakes and Snakebites from Christoph Samuel John in Tranquebar to Prof. Johann Reinhold Forster in Germany, 1792

C.S. John in Tranquebar became a dependable informant for German naturalists because he conducted in depth study and had excellent knowledge of snakes. In 1792, Johann Reinhold Forster (1729-1798) in Germany wrote to him asking for a lot of information on poisonous snakes and traditional antidotes. John who had collected the data passed on the details to Prof. Johann Reinhold Forster through his letter dated 12 January 1792. Forster again raised eighteen queries with regard to this information received and he called for additional details. He particularly wanted to know the size of the various snakes and desired also to know of the antidotes provided by the doctors. In a letter to Forster dated 20 January 1792 C.S. John submitted answers to all the eighteen questions.[65] A few important questions and answers are as follows:

Question: Is it possible to preserve some varieties of snakes in arrack or spirit?

Answer: I have already preserved snakes in the spirit and sent some to Europe.

Question: Is it true that the poisonous snakes come out of their holes when they heard the horn?

Answer: The name of the snake catchers in Tamil is *pudurer* who used different means and arts for catching the snakes. The most dangerous snake, *Coluber Naja* (*Brillen Schlange*, the King Cobra) came out of its hiding place as soon as it heard the tune. The snake-charmers may be near or at some distance. Before blowing the horn the *pudurer* said some incantations which neither he nor the snake understood. In general such incantations were common.

Question: Do the snakes dislike the smell of onions and garlic? Do they leave the places where such things were placed?

Answer: The snakes lived in places where onion and garlic were growing. During the war a distinguished Dutch family lived with *malla* (Telugu speaking untouchable) slaves and they had been lodged in the house of C.S. John. Once when a snake-charmer let a *Brillen Schlenge* (the king cobra) danced in front of the door, the *malla* slave threw something on the snake unnoticed, which was considered as a piece of garlic. The nicely dancing snake got restless and stopped dancing. Also the snake-charmers became restless and they could not blow the horn anymore. They went away ashamed with anger. Among the onlookers only one noticed the *malla* and then it was asserted that it was not the throwing of the garlic but the chanting of some formulas had influenced the snake. In general all Tamils even the educated asserted the power of enchanting and believed it. There are books of magic and enchanting. To find out the truth, the European scientists should become the Tamils.

Question: Is it not possible to find out the ingredients of the anti-poison against the bites of the poisonous snakes? Are these anti-poisons always effective?

Answer: Samuel the servant of Schwartz the missionary had the recipe against the bite of *Brillen Schlange* (the king cobra) and rabid dogs. In the presence of Schwartz he had cured many. Some of his cases attracted attention and brought him great fame. Everyone purchased some pills from him and each cost half a *panam*. They were like a pea but black in colour and big. He used to give all the instructions how to use them. He kept the recipe as a secret till the government in Madras requested Schwartz to send the man to Madras to reveal the secret, which would be useful for the people for which he would get a reward. This happened and C.S. John had met him three years ago when he was returning from Madras. Samuel got two hundred star *pagodas* for his invention. It was then made known in the Madras Courier.

Question: Is one *Aristlochia* used as anti poison against snakebite in India?

Answer: The root of the plant *Aristlochia—Semper virens* (*Aadu Thinnaa Paalei* in Tamil—Goat that would not leaves) known also as *Aadaa thoda ilei* was the means through which one can find out with certainty whether you were bitten by a poisonous snake and by which one. If the taste was bitter you were not bitten. But if the taste was sweet you were certainly bitten by a *Coluber naga*. If the taste was savour you were bitten by *Woellandei* (*Uzhavan paambu*, *Eryx conicus*, Russell's Sand Boa). If it was salty, it was the *Pudei* snake bitten. If the taste was hot like pepper then it was the bite of the snake *Retta mandeli*. If the person felt itching on the tongue he was bitten by the snake *Komberi mukkan*.

Question: How big are the snakes in India? Can they swallow deer, gazelle and antelope?

Answer: The land in Thanjavur was flat and had no mountains. Therefore the snakes in the area do not have the size of those in the mountains. C.S. John had measured *Brillen Schlangen* (the king cobra) which was nine feet long and thick like a small hand. The *Saarei paambu*, which was considered to be the male of the cobra, had sometimes the same size, but it had neither the design on the face nor the poisonous teeth. In Tranquebar and Poraiyar area *Malai paambu* (Python) or mountain snakes were found. C.S. John had one that was more than nine feet long and it had the thickness of the fist of a man. It had many teeth without poison. C.S. John had it in his room where his children played with it without fear and harm. The conjurers and the snake charmers hanged this snake around their shoulders and went around attracting the people. This snake was a dangerous one for the ducks and chickens. One was found in the *Bruder Garten* (Garden of the Moravians in Tranquebar) and it was killed. It had several ducks in its stomach.

Question: Are there also harmless snakes? What are their names?

Answer: The water snakes in the rivers and ponds were harmless. The Tamils also considered them as harmless. All these types were called *Neer paambu* or water snakes. But C.S. John also considered all the snakes on the land, which do not have poisonous teeth, were not dangerous. But the Tamils were afraid of them. The sea snakes were considered poisonous though they did not have poisonous teeth.

C. S. John had thus explained in detail of the characteristics and behaviour of the snakes and also the preparations of anti-venoms for snakebites.[66] In a letter written from Tranquebar to Dr Roxburgh in Madras, he mentioned six ingredients used in the preparation of the medicine for the cure of a venomous snakebite, namely white arsenic, *nerivisham* bought in the local markets, *nervaazhlam* (*Croton tiglium*) purchased in the bazaars, *rasam* (mercury), black pepper, and milk extracted from white *erukkan* leaves (*Aschepia gigantia*).[67] Thus, we find that Europeans nearly found it hard to obtain medical secrets from Tamil professionals, and on receipt of these preparations the Europeans communicated them to each other.

It had been known that native doctors treated patients according to the type of snake that had bitten the person. Further, it was also necessary and essential for the native doctor to know how much time had passed since the patient was bitten by the snake. The native doctors, thereafter, carefully treated the patient by increasing the dose of medicine to get the desired result.

William Boag's Opinion on the Tamil Medicine for Snakebites, 1809

William Boag said that arsenic had long been employed by the Tamils since it formed the principal ingredient in the Thanjavur pills. The little experience collected by the Europeans did not enable them to form very exact judgment respecting the pill. It was, therefore, difficult to distinguish the effects of the remedy from the symptoms of the disease. He opined in 1809 that, it should probably be employed in desperate cases only and where no other powerful remedy could be procured.[68]

Thanjavur pills were used effectively for the treatment of the Europeans like Peter Francis a private soldier of the 3rd Regiment.[69] Europeans always had a great want for a useful drug against venomous bites. The multitude of experiments made in Europe to test the celebrated internal western remedies usually recommended against venomous bites, had confirmed their inefficaciousness.[70] The only remedy established in Europe by Fontana's experiments as effectual had been under certain limitations, with amputation and ligature.[71] The Thanjavur pill promised a cure for snakebites without any physical mortification and mutilation. Hence the search for an efficacious remedy against poisonous became both a universal therapeutic urge and a compulsion for the Europeans.

The Study on the Treatment to Snakebites by William Mackenzie in Madras, 1820

William Mackenzie (1754-1821) the Scottish army officer of the English company in Madras later became surveyor general of Madras in 1810. He accepted some indigenous systems of treatment with due respect. He made his remarks in 1820 explaining why salt was offered to the person bitten by snakes. He said that it was proper to add since it was an universal belief prevails amongst the Tamils, that salt tasted sweet to those who were under the influence of a powerful animal poison, and that when this morbid taste ceased, that the danger was abated or entirely over, and that all medicine may be safely discontinued.[72] This evidence suggests how in the rudimentary stage the colonial medicine sought to introduce, in many cases, the Tamil local cultural elements into Western medicine and had greatly opened up a creative potential for an inter-cultural assimilation and synthesis. Hence it may be said that the triumphal march of Western medical-zoology indiscriminately had not blinded all its practitioners to the merits of indigenous medical knowledge, Rather we find that there were some examples to manifest that Europe's encounter with Tamil medicine which was often a respectful dialogue, based upon a shared medical understanding.

The study of snakes and snake poisons in Europe had been well directed as early as in 1603, when John Ray, the English naturalist, pointed out various serpents and the distinguishing criterion of different dentitions. Linnaeus had not duly considered this in his methodological arrangement of serpents. Abbé Felice Fontana (1730-1805), the Italian physiologist, naturalist and renowned experimentalists in toxicology had worked in Tuscany on the venom of European vipers. He made great progress in his research and seldom met with an instance where envenomation proved lethal to human beings. In Fontana's hypothesis, a single bite could never be mortal to an adult. He witnessed a dozen cases himself and had heard of fifty more, and only two of which ended fatally. He reported that some very timid, delicate and nervous people died out of fear rather than from the effect of snake poison. He wrote that death may be brought on by very violent affections of the mind, without any internal disease.

The German missionaries in Tranquebar had given at length the classification of snakes according to the local traditions in Tamil country. The natives differentiated and named snakes by colour, size, nature and the places in which they preferred to live. Linnaeus epitomized the system of scientific classification of natural world into classes depending on structural resemblances and differences, thereby stimulating the study of natural history in Europe and overseas. The tenth edition of *Systema Naturae* is a monumental work and in this the binomial nomenclature for the whole animal kingdom had been introduced for the first time. The missionaries eventually named the snakes based on the *Systema Naturae* of Linnaeus. They classified at first amphibia that contained four orders, and the snakes formed the second order *serpentes*, which included six sub-orders—crotalus (rattle snakes), boa (boas), coluber (racers, vipers and cobras), anguis (slow worms and worm snakes), amphisbaena (worm lizards), and caecilia (caecilians). A unique aspect of the work of the Tranquebar missionaries was their preference for both the Tamil names of the serpents and their zoological ones.

The snake pills of Thanjavur had continued to be in use as an antidote for snakebites. T. Lauder Brunton and J. Fayrer wrote that while the pills enjoyed a large amount of popular confidence, when they were brought to test by careful experiments in 1873 they had failed to provide the desired results as expected.[73] Europeans were interested primarily in the medical efficacy of applied substances, an efficacy that could be exploited for healing or as a marketable commodity. Portable, profitable and, above all, the practical remedies that could be marketed and sold for application against specific maladies were in high demand. The exigencies of survival of the military personnel in the services of the English East India Company in Madras helped to foster inquiries and debate into Tamil medicine. However, snake specimens also found way to the India Museum in London.[74]

To conclude it may be said that the emergence of a medical-zoological discipline in Tamil country under Protestant missionaries of Tranquebar provided the impetus for confronting the issue of snakebites globally on a different scale. Though few snakes were said to be harmfully poisonous, the snakebites had always had been considered lethal since they had led to deaths. Snakes were considered to be the most dreadful of all living creatures in the world. Interestingly, in the early modern period, Protestant missionaries in Tranquebar had opened up the flood gates of siddha medicine and they were the pioneers who through their analytical and detailed studies on the snakes of Tamil country, pointed out the knowledgeable of their venom and power, and frequently witnessed the victims of deadly snakebites and poisoning. It may be also said that Tamils had their own traditional preventive measures and curative treatments. The snakes as well as the practice of treatment for snakebite were completely different in Telugu country, as observed by Patrick Russell who collected and examined 43 snakes at Visakhapatnam region. However he had also named a snake giving due credit to Christoph Samuel John and he called the *Iruthalai naagam* (the double-headed snake) as *Boa johnii*. The snakes and snakebites encountered in the various regions in India were entirely different and immensely perilous. The cases were widely different with respect to the poisons of the snakes found in India and Europe during the early modern age.

Notes

1. S. Jeyaseela Stephen, *A Meeting of the Minds: European and Tamil Encounters in Modern Sciences, 1507-1857*, Delhi, 2016, pp. 91-2.
2. *Philosophical Transactions of the Royal Society of London*, 1683-1775 (hereafter *Philosophical Transactions*), vol. 22, p. 588.
3. *Ibid.*, p. 1009. See also, *Philosophical Transactions*, vol. 20, p. 325.
4. S. Jeyaseela Stephen, *Oceanscapes: Tamil Textiles in the Early Modern World*, Delhi, 2014, p. 533.
5. Madurai Province Jesuit Archives (hereafter MPJA), Shenbaganur, *Documents de la Mission du Carnatic*, vol. III, no. 48, pp. 159–160, see the letter of Fr. Coeurdoux dated 29 September 1738.
6. J. Ferd Fenger, *History of the Tranquebar Mission: Worked Out from the Original Papers*, tr. Emil Francke, Tranquebar, 1863, p. 314.
7. Georg Christian Knapp et al., eds., *Neuere Geschichte der Evangelischen Missions-Anstalten zu Bekehrung der Heiden in Ostindien aus den eigenhändigen Aufsätzen und Briefen der Missionarien erausgegeben*, Waisenhaus, Teil 1–8 (Stück 1–95), Waiserihaus, Halle, 1770–8/95, 1848 (hereafter NHB) 43. St., 642.
8. J. Ferd Fenger, History of the Tranquebar Mission, p. 289.
9. *Ibid.*, p. 291.
10. NHB 32. St., 869–3.
11. *Ibid.*
12. Archiv der Franckeschen Stiftungen (hereafter AFSt), Halle, AFSt/M2 B1: 6; Berichte aus Zoologie und Botanik.
13. AFSt/ M2 B1: 5; Berichte aus Zoologie und Botanik.
14. NHB 43. St., 649.
15. NHB 32, St., 869–73; NHB 36. St., 1368.
16. AFSt/M2 B1: 5; Berichte aus Zoologie und Botanik.
17. Natural History Museum, London (hereafter NHML), Zoology Library, MSS JOHN, Additional Observations on Snakes by the Reverend Dr. John (undated).
18. Anonymous, 'Memoir of the Life and Writings of Patrick Russell, M.D. F.R.S.,' in Patrick Russell, *A Continuation of an Account of Indian Serpent; Containing Descriptions and Figures, from Specimens and Drawings, Transmitted from Various Parts of India*, W. Bulmer & Co. Shakespeare Press, London, 1801, pp. 18–9.
19. *Ibid.*, p. 14.
20. NHML, Botany Library: DTC 5, dated 20 May 1787, p. 167.

21. Christian Pohle was born near Luckau in Lower Lusatia (Brandenburg) on 9 March 1744, studied at Leipzig, was ordained at Copenhagen in 1776, and arrived at Tranquebar in 1777. Later he was sent to Tiruchirapalli, where he died after more than 41 years' labour on 28 January 1818. See, J. Ferd Fenger, History of the Tranquebar Mission, p. 318.
22. NHB 32. St., 962.
23. British Library (hereafter BL), London, *Natural History Drawings of the India Office Collections* (hereafter IOL, NHD), 7/1087-94.
24. Walter Elliot, 'Description of a New Species of Naga or Cobra Capello', *Madras Journal of Literature and Science*, 1840, pp. 39-41.
25. Nationalmuseet, Copenhagen (hereafter NMC), DU 452.
26. Thomas Caverhill Jerdon, 'Catalogue of Reptiles Inhabiting Peninsular India', *Journal of the Asiatic Society of Bengal*, vol. XXII, 1853, pp. 522-534, see, p. 523.
27. *Ibid.*
28. *Ibid.*
29. *Ibid.*, p. 524.
30. *Ibid.*
31. *Ibid.*, pp. 524-5.
32. *Ibid.*, p. 525.
33. *Ibid.*, p. 526.
34. *Ibid.*, p. 527.
35. *Ibid.*, p. 528.
36. *Ibid.*, p. 529.
37. *Ibid.*
38. *Ibid.*
39. *Ibid.*, p. 530.
40. W. Fr. Gericke was born at Colberg in Pomerania on 5 April 1742, studied at Halle, was ordained at Wernigerode 1765, came out via Hamburg and England, landed after a long and dangerous voyage at Point de Galle on 4 December 1766 and arrived at Tranquebar on 6 June 1767. He went to Cuddalore to assist Hiittemann, whose daughter he married, and laboured at various places especially at Nagapattinam until 1788. Later, he became the successor of Fabricius and chaplain of the Female Asylum at Madras. He died at Vellore on 2 October 1803 and was buried at Madras. See, J. Ferd Fenger, History of the Tranquebar Mission, p. 316.
41. Gotthilf August Francke, ed., *Der Königl. Dänischen Missionarien aus Ost-Indien eingesandter ausführlichen Berichten, Von dem Werck ihrs Ams unter den Heyden, angerichteten Schulen und Gemeinen, ereigneten Hindernissen und schweren Umstanden; Beschaffenheit des Malabarischen Heydenthums, gepflogenen brieflicher Correspondentz und mundlchen Unterredungen mit selbigen heyden*, Teil 1–9, (Continuationen 1–108) Waiserihaus, Halle, 1710–1772 (hereafter Hallesche Berichten = HB), see, 106th Continuation des Berichts der Königliche – Dänischen Missionarien in Ost Indien, p. 1524.

42. NHB 43. St., 649, See the letter from Christoph Samuel John to Johann Reinhold Forster dated 20 January 1792.
43. Pierre Sonnerat, *A Voyage to the East Indies and China*, 2 vols., trs. Francis Magnus, Calcutta, 1788–89, see vol. II, pp. 151–3.
44. *Ibid.*, pp. 153–4.
45. Christian Frederick Schwartz was born on 26 October 1726 at Sonnenberg in Brandenburg, studied at Halle, ordained at Copenhagen in 1749, reached Cuddalore on 30 July 1750 and worked for forty eight years in Tamil country. Schwartz worked as missionary for eleven years at Tranquebar and then established the Tiruchirapalli mission in 1762. He later settled at Thanjavur in 1778 where he continued his work until his death on 13 February 1798. See, J. Ferd Fenger, History of the Tranquebar Mission, pp. 199, 313.
46. Tamilnadu State Archives (hereafter TNSA) Chennai, *Surgeon General's Records* (hereafter SGR), vol. 3, fol. 175, see the letter from the Military Board to James Anderson, the Physician General and Members of the Hospital Board dated 17 September 1788.
47. *Ibid.*
48. *Ibid.*, fols.185–6, see the letter of the Hospital Board dated 26 September 1788.
49. *Ibid.*
50. *Ibid.*, fols. 223–5, see the letter from the Military Board to James Anderson, the Physician General and Members of the Hospital Board dated 22 October 1788.
51. *Ibid.*
52. TNSA, SGR, vol. 3, fol. 224.
53. *Ibid.*
54. *Ibid.*, fols. 230–1, see James Anderson's opinion dated 10 November 1788 on the pills.
55. *Ibid.*, fols. 238–41, see Duffin's opinion dated 17 November 1788 communicated to the Hospital Board.
56. *Ibid.*, fol. 241.
57. NHML, Botany Library, MSS ROX, see, the letter of William Jones from Crishnanagar dated 14 September 1789 to James Anderson at Fort St. George in Madras.
58. *Ibid.*
59. Patrick Russell, *An Account of Indian Serpents Collected on the Coast of Coromandel: Containing Descriptions and Drawings of Each Species; Together with Experiments and Remarks on their Several Poison*, London, W. Bulmer & Co., Shakespeare Press, 1796, p. 74.
60. *Ibid.*
61. *Ibid.*, p. 79.
62. *Ibid.*, p. 75.
63. *Ibid.*, pp. 75–6.
64. *Ibid.*, p. 77.
65. NHB 43. St., 648–9.
66. NHB 48. St., 1093.

67. AFSt/M2 B1: 5; Berichte aus Zoologie und Botanik.
68. William Boag, 'On the Poison of Serpents' in *Asiatic Researches Comprising History and Antiquities, the Arts, Sciences and literature of Asia*, 20 vols., 1788-1839, see vol. VI, 1809, pp. 103–26, see pp. 112–3.
69. Patrick Russell, An Account of Indian Serpents, p. 78.
70. *Ibid*., p. 67.
71. *Ibid*., p. 74.
72. William Mackenzie, 'An Account of Venomous Snakes on the Coast of Madras', in *Asiatic Researches Comprising History and Antiquities, the Arts, Sciences and literature of Asia*, vol. 13, 1820, pp. 329-336, see p. 336.
73. T. Lauder Brunton and J. Fayrer, 'On the Nature and Physiological Action of the Poison of Naja Tripudians and Other Indian Venomous Snakes–Part II', *Proceedings of the Royal Society of London*, 1873–74, vol. 22, pp. 68–133, see pp. 132–3.
74. NHML, Z Mss IND (ii) no. 29, Venomous Serpents Received from the Asiatic Society of Bengal, undated; Z Mss IND (ii) no. 32, Serpents: Honourable Company's Collection: Thomas Cantor, 1838; Z Mss IND (ii) no. 55, Jars of snakes, lizards and a snake-lizard preserved in spirits, War collection from Tipu Sultan, Cir. 1800; NHML, 'Patrick Russell, 47 numbered 1–60', Water colour drawings of Reptiles: an important collection of water colour drawings of reptiles, some being original, Company School drawings for Patrick Russell's book on Indian snakes, etc. sold at Sotheby's, Catalogue of printed books, Tuesday, 22 November 1977, Lot 325, Accompanied by memo regarding the sale by P.J.P. Whitehead and A.F. Stimson, Zoology Department, NHML, Zoology, 96Ao TR; 96Ao Tr (drawings).

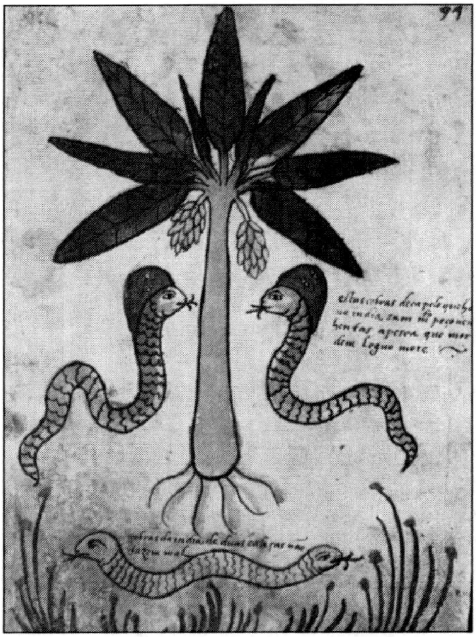

7.1. Two hooded rattlesnakes and a snake with two heads, colour drawing by an unknown artist.

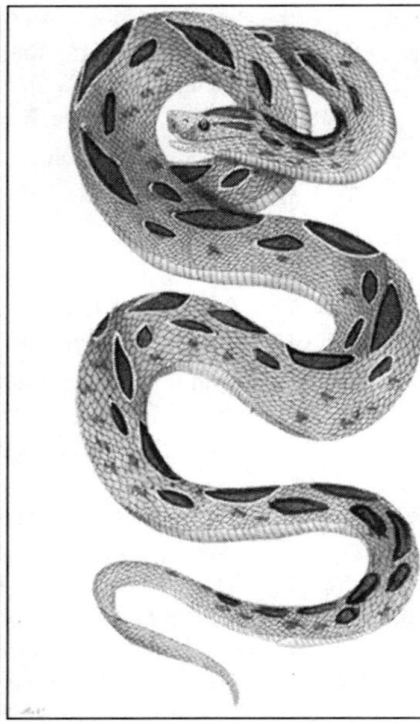

7.2. Kannaadi Viriyan, Russell's viper, Daboia russelli, 1797.

7.3. Bungarus semifaciantus, 1837.

7.4. Naia Vittata snake from Mylapore, 1840.

7.5. The snake charmer and his wife in Tranquebar, 1839.

7.6. A fight with the sea-serpent.

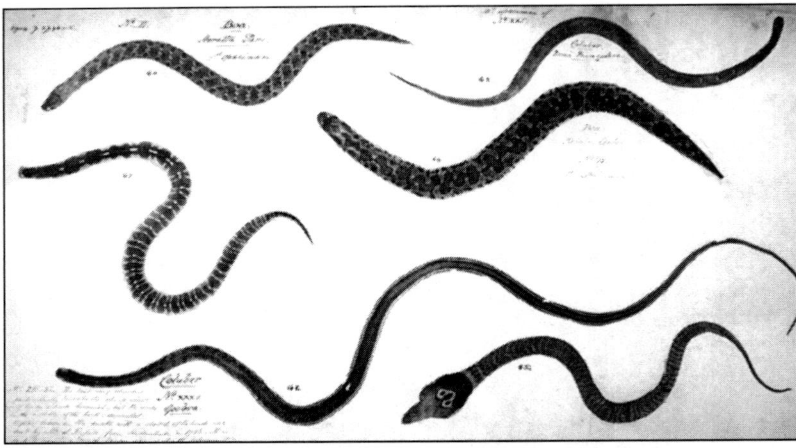

7.7 Snake skins.

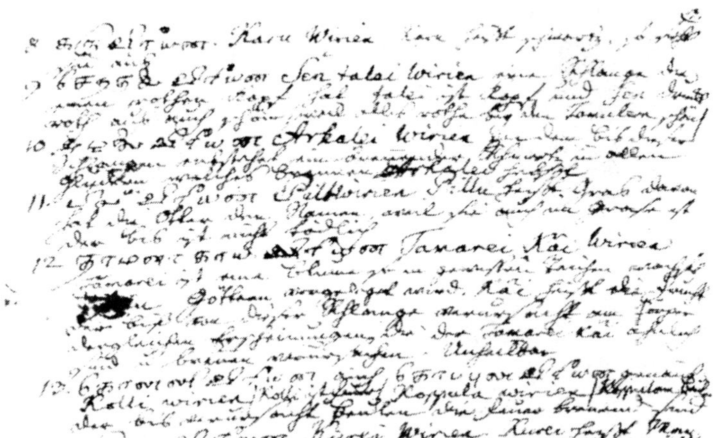

7.8. The letter of C.S. John from Tranquebar with details of snakes, 1785.

8

Ichthyology and Aqua-Fauna: Observation, Identification and Authentication, 1779-1853

European travellers visited the various coastal zones of India and met with societies and also wrote down the details. They particularly noted the different types of fish and the creatures living in water found in these regions. John Fryer recorded that Mazagon was a great fishing town peculiarly notable for the fish called '*bumbel*' and it was the chief sustenance of the poorer sort who lived on them.[1] Jon Olaffson in Tranquebar noted the sea was a major provider of wealth, prosperity and livelihood and so the local people held popular religious rituals and ceremonies. They conducted it before the commencement of the fishing season. He added that before Easter, three of their Hindu gods were conveyed down to the seashore with much drumming and music and the sea water carried upon in splendid gold vessels was poured over the gods. Then the same holy water was sprinkled over the people by the temple priest. This festival was held in Tranquebar so that there shall be better luck with fishing and greater safety for fishermen. Olaffson also mentioned that there were varieties of fish available for sale in the local market.[2]

When the study of fish in Europe began to make great strides the interest in the study of fish also commenced and coincided with the development on the Tamil coast. The difficulty of preserving the fish in the tropical climate presented in general the chief cause for transporting those varieties which were unknown in Europe. However, the Europeans collected details of fish in great number and in variety and forms. They reported the rich colours of many. They also attempted to arrange the fish in scientific order as done in Europe. They worked upon with the individuality of fish forms belonging to each genus and species. They used the then available scientific writings of the pioneers like Petrus Artedi (1705-35) the Swedish naturalist who investigated a large number of species and the book of Carl Linnaeus which appeared in five volumes. Further, the works of L.T. Gronow (a German resident in Holland who followed Artendi's example) published on fish were read by Europeans and they found them very useful because they threw new light for their study of fish on the Tamil coast.[3]

Johann Gerard Koenig in Madras and his Study of Fish, 1779-85

Johann Gerard Koenig (1728-85) was appointed as surgeon in Tranquebar in the Danish settlement of Tranquebar on the Tamil Coast. He arrived there in 1768 as successor of Samuel Benjamin Knoll. In the beginning he was engaged in the study of flora. In 1778 he became the English East India Company's natural historian in Madras.[4] As a student of Linnaeus, Koenig had also taken interest in the study of fish and so he collected fish and examined them carefully. Thereafter he communicated the details to Germany.

Patrick Russell in Madras had mentioned that he received valuable information from Koenig while describing the fish called *kakahsi* in Tamil also known as *seena vaarai* (Finned Bulls eye in English, *Priacanthus*). This fish had the body which was somewhat said to be ovate, but with a protuberance in the back; much compressed, without scales, was smooth and pellucid. The head was small, compressed, without scales; front declivous, carinated; the rostrum was short, truncated, the mouth in the middle had been a little oblique, wide; but no lips, the cheeks membranous. The jaws were extractile and the under moved freely, and had a small protuberance at the point, adapted to a cavity for its reception in the upper. The teeth had been setaceous and numerous, tongue short, awl-form, white; eyes in deep orbits, small, orbicular. The nostrils were double, in the middle between the orbit and rostrum. The opercula consisted of two laminae, sub-membranous, with four prickles on the edge of the second. The branchial membrane was half exposed while the aperture arched. The trunk, the back, gradually assurgent from the vertex, formed a hump in the middle, on the declivity of which, towards the tail, was situated the dorsal fin. The sides were much compressed the belly carinated and the breast prickly. The branchiae had been four-leaved, the exterior pectinated on the inside, with very long teeth. The lateral line was very slightly curved, high, smooth and faint. The anus was near the breast. On the ridge of the back before the dorsal, there were seven small prickles, equidistant from each other, unconnected, three pointing forward, three backward, the seventh, and anterior, was the longest, appeared like a crest, in the shape of the elephant's trunk. It was covered with a black coloured skin, above which appeared its curve point, but the direction of the crest was forward. On the concave side, it was connected by a very loose membrane. The lower towards the rostrum had two other prickles, erect and very minute. The dorsal fin had one spinous ray, the next ramous was an inch long, the last ray four lines. The pectoral was in the middle, lanceolate, short; the ventral rays resembled fingers, they covered the anus, and were placed a little more forward than the pectoral fins. The long anal fin mounted towards the tail in an arch, but the rays were nearly equal; the caudal forked, the lobes sub-falcate. The colour of this fish, when alive, was changeable, faint red, blue, and green, on a golden ground and that was on the upper part of the head and back; the rest a glossy white. All the fins were whitish, but powdered with minute dark points, as were also the shoulders. This fish described had been five inches in length. Though the position of its ventral fins had been scarcely more forward than the pectoral, their rays five in number, had been placed; but the under was strong of its belonging to the genus. Patrick Russell noted the hump on the back raised a suspicion of its being allied to the new genus *kurtus*, of which only one species had been sent from the Coromandel Coast by Johann Gerard Koenig which was thereafter known in Germany. But there were strong objections to such a conjecture.[5]

The Study of Fish by Christoph Samuel John in Tranquebar, 1779-1801

Christoph Samuel John the missionary in Tranquebar collected fish and studied them with the help of local fishermen. He mainly described the fish of Tranquebar region. He engaged some native professionals and prepared around 50 specimens of fish in pressing jars and sent them to Marcus Eliser Bloch (1723-99) the famous German ichthyologist in Berlin.[6] C.S. John had neatly mentioned the collection of his fish and the methods adopted in preservation before sending the same to Germany and Denmark. He added that fishes were treated with myrtle oil.[7] He stated in 1780 that the entire work of collecting and preserving fish in pressing jars was very tedious chiefly owing to the tropical climate of Tranquebar. Fish dissections were prepared by C.S. John and he sent them also to Germany. With the founding of the Humboldt University in1810 a museum came up and it was given a department structure. J.K.W. Illiger became the first director of the new zoological museum. The fish collections sent from Tranquebar reached have been now found in the collection of Marcus Eliser Bloch in the Museum für Naturkunde, Humboldt Universität, Berlin.[8]

C.S. John was of great assistance to Marcus Elieser Bloch for launching his study of fish. Bloch had emerged as the pioneering authority on fish with his well-illustrated work on the natural history of fish.[9] The twelve volumes were printed during 1785 and 1799.[10] Bloch wrote that his assertion respecting the generation of some fish, that the eggs were retained in the mouth till the young were hatched, had been confirmed by C.S. John, in his letters sent to him from Tranquebar during 1795 and 1796. C.S. John had said that this fact was already known to the fishermen of Tranquebar.[11] Therefore it is very interesting to note that the Tamil fishermen's common knowledge emerged as a European research finding. It is also important to note that the fish Red snapper in English has been variously known as sevvilzhai and sankara in Tamil (*Lutjanus campechanus*).

Bloch had named three fish in honour of C.S. John. We find it in his splendidly illustrated work on fish where the species were dedicated to John in 1792 and 1793.

Year — Zoological Name — Name given by Bloch — English Name

1792 — Lutjanus johnii — Anthias johnii — Golden snapper

1793 — Johnius carutta — Johnius carutta — Bearded Croaker

1793 — Johnieops aneus — Johnius aneus — Big eye croaker

Source: Marcus Elieser Bloch, *Allgemeine Naturgeschichte der auslandischen Fische*, Plates 318, 356 and 357.

Johann Gottfried Klein in Tranquebar and his Study of Fish, 1789

Johann Gottfried Klein (1766-1821) was born in Tranquebar in 1766. His father was Jacob Klein (1721-1790) a Lutheran missionary who worked in the Danish mission at Tranquebar nearly for forty-four years and died on 18 May 1790, and buried in New Jerusalem church-yard. Johann Gottfried Klein went to Copenhagen to study medicine and he returned to Tranquebar in 1789 as the mission doctor.[12] He developed interest in the study of fish and he communicated the details to Marcus Eliser Bloch who named two fish in Klein's honour in his work in 1790 and 1793.

Year — Zoological Name — Name given by Bloch — English Name

1790— Chaetodon kleinii — Chaetodon kleinii — Black lip butterfly

1793— Caranx kleinii — Scomber Kleinii — Razor belly scad

Source: Marcus Elieser Bloch, *Allgemeine Naturgeschichte der auslandischen Fische*, Plates 218 and 347.

The Study of Fish by Johann Peter Rottler in Tranquebar, 1791

Johann Peter Rottler (1749-1836) the Lutheran missionary arrived at Tranquebar on 5 August 1776 and worked there till 1803.[13] He was mainly interested in the study of plants but also showed some interest in the study of fish. He sent the details of fish to Marcus Elieser Bloch and as a result Bloch had named one fish in Rottler's honour in his work in 1793.

Year — Zoological Name — Name given by Bloch — English Name

1793 — Caranx rottleri — Scomber Rottleri — Torpedo scad

Source: Marcus Elieser Bloch, *Allgemeine Naturgeschichte der auslandischen Fische*, Plate 346.

Thus Bloch received help from the three missionaries of Tranquebar. He had sincerely acknowledged them for assistance extended by naming some of the fish after them for having helped him the most.

An Exploration into the Study of Marcus Elieser Bloch's Fish Collection sent from Tranquebar now in Germany, 1786-1795

Bloch produced his work of ichthyology based on Linnaean principles. He carefully described and illustrated so many of the then known fish species, some of which were introduced to a wider audience in colour for the first time. He gave full descriptions of every species known to him, and illustrated them with high quality drawings. It had thus resulted as the most magnificent publication on fish in Europe. The names of the fish were given in several languages, including names in Latin to settle any classification problems. Bloch had built up a steady collection of fish and the descriptions and illustrations drawn were from actual specimens received from Tranquebar.[14]

Bloch's collection of fish specimens preserved at the Museum für Naturkunde, Humboldt Universität, Berlin (MNB), are with Bloch's handwritten catalogues. The following fish of Tranquebar and their details have been culled his writings from time to time.

Year — Zoological Name — Name given by Bloch — English Name

1786 — Rhinecanthus aculeatus — Balistes aculeatus — White branded trigger fish

1793 — Seriola fasciata — Scomber fasciatus — Lesser amber jack

1793 — Channa punctata — Ophicephalus punctatus — Spotted snake head

1793— Channa striata — Ophicephalus striatus — Butter fish/Striped snake head

1794 — Heteropneustes fossilis — Silurus fossilis — Emerald shiner

1794 — Pseudeutropius atherinoides — Silurus atherinoides — Indian potasi

1794— Mystus vittatus — Silurus vittatus — The striped dwarf catfish

1794 — Hoplias malabaricus — Esox malabaricus — Wolf fish/ Tiger fish

1795 — Clupea athernoides — Cyprinus clupeoides — The silver stripped herring

1795 — Labeo fimbriatus — Cyprinus fimbriatus — The fringed-carp

1795 — Cirrhinus cirrhosus — Cyprinus cirrhosus — The cirrhated-carp

1795 — Labeo falcatus — Cyprinus falcatus — The sickle-carp

1795 — Etroplus maculatus — Chaetodon maculatus — The maculated chetodon

1795 — Thryssa malabarica — Clupea malabaricus — The herring of Malabar

Source: Marcus Elieser Bloch, *Allgemeine Naturgeschichte der auslandischen Fische*, Plates 149, 341, 358, 359, 370, 371, 371, 392, 408, 409, 411, 412, 427, 432.

It is also found mention that *Cyprinus clupeoides* (*Salmostoma acinaces*) was called in English as silver razor-belly minnow. The fish Channa punctata was called in English as green snake-headed murrel (spotted snake head) and it was found in the rivers and lakes of the Coromandel Coast. *Heteropneustus fossilis* was called in English as stinging catfish. *Labeo fimbriatus* was called in English as Fringed-lipped peninsula carp and it was found all over the Tamil coast.

Bloch in 1794 described certain catfishes of Tranquebar such as *Silurus vittatus* and it was called striped dwarf catfish in English. Again we find *Colisa fasciatus* from Tranquebar called banded colisa in English. It is interesting to note that Bloch had stated in the description that *Ophicephalus striatus* (plate 359) was called by the Tamils as *viraal* in their language (butter fish/murrel in English). Similarly Bloch stated that *Cyprinus fimbriatus* (plate 408) fish was called in Tamil *solkondei* (*Kendai* in Tamil, greas carp in English). *Cyprinus cirrhousus* (plate 411) the mrigal carp was also called *Woen koenndy* (*Thullu kondai/kandal* in Tamil, perch in English) and *Cyprinus falcatus* (plate 412) as *Karpfen* (*karuppan*). It is certain that the missionaries of Tranquebar would have communicated the Tamil names of the fish.

Since most of the fish found around Tranquebar were sent as these were unknown to the audience in Europe, the descriptions of the fish were found necessary. Hence the detailed descriptions were furnished in German by Bloch in his nine volumes of *Allgemeine Naturgeschichte der auslandischen Fische* published in 1785, 1786, 1787, 1790, 1791, 1792, 1793, 1794 and 1795, and the fish names were only written in Latin.

The diagnosis of *viraal* fish in Tamil (*Ophiocephalus striatus* plate 359) had been recorded thus in 1793: Seventeen scales present before dorsal fin; lateral line scales 56. Dark oblique bands pass from ventral surface up to the lateral line; caudal fin with two distinct vertical bands at its base.

The diagnosis of *Heteropneustes fossilis*, the stinging catfish (plate 370) had been mentioned thus in 1794: Head depressed; median frontal groove on head limited to a round depression between and backwards of eyes; occipital process short and not extending to base of dorsal fin; rayed dorsal fin is short and without a spine; anal fin long based, separated by a distinct notch from caudal fin; pectoral fin with strong serrated spine; caudal fin rounded.

The diagnosis of *Cyprinus cirrhosus* fish, the mrigal carp (plate 411) had been recorded thus in 1795: Dorsal profile convex but ventral profile straight; dorsal fin located far ahead of ventral fin and inserted nearer to snout tip than caudal base; anal tip reach near to caudal base; lateral line straight; mouth sub terminal and cresentic; one pair of small and delicate maxillary barbels which never reach eyes.

C.S. John mentioned of a new species of star gazer (*Pisces, Uranoscopidae*) in his report in 1801 immediately following Lebeck's description of the Ganges dolphin.[15] Here, C.S. John named the new star gazer after Lebeck with the following justification: 'One of them (the marvellous fish book by Dr Bloch) has been received by my most active and to the natural history most committed friend Mr. Lebeck, the crown of my education college, who continued and enriched his science under a famous Thunberg in Uppsala and who will make the best use of it. After he has travelled part of the Cape of Good Hope, Ceylon, Bengal and the Coromandel Coast, he is now bound for Java. Naturalists therefore will not blame me for honouring him by naming this fish '*Uranoscopus Lebeckii*'. C.S. John's name and description were acknowledged by Schneider under the name *Uranoscopus Lebeck.*[16] John had sent drawings and notes on the star gazer as well as the Ganges dolphin to Marcus Elieser Bloch. Schneider ascribed the picture and note on *Delphinus gangeticus* to Lebeck and forwarded the plates and manuscripts to the *Gesellschaft naturforschender Freunde zu Berlin.*[17]

C.S. John and Rottler had mentioned the fish *kaanangeluthi/ Kaanagkaaththan* in Tamil (Indian mackerel in English, *Rastrelliger kanagurta*), *Waiangadei Parei* (*Thengaa Paarai* in Tamil, Horse mackerel in English) and gave the details to Bloch. The Tamil classification of the system of fishes had been carefully noted by C.S. John who wrote to Bloch and mentioned the names in Tamil besides giving the descriptions of the several names of fish in Tamil. It includes ten types of *Kattalai* fish (*Kaaththaalai* in Tamil, Jaw fish in English): (1) *Seng Kattalei* (2) *Wang Kattalei* (3) *Karung Kattalei* (4) *Turuatie Kattalei* (5) *Kari Kattalei* (6) *Wari Kattalei* (7) *Walang Kattalei* (8) *Sotu Kattalei* (9) *Kura Kattalei* and (10) *Anei Kattalei*. Further C.S. John had also mentioned and written about the various other fish in Tamil like *Taleipi sedtei* (Tilapia in English, *Jilebi* in Tamil) *Tumbi*, *Aralmin*, (eral meen in Tamil, Shrimp/Prawn) *Otemin* (in English, Dropt chaeton), and *Narikaendai*. (*Kendai* or *Katlaa* in Tamil, Bengal carp in English).[18] Bloch expressed that C.S. John and Klein had furnished several names of fish like *Woolra min*, (*Oozhaa meen* or *Sheela* in Tamil, Barracada in English) *Jede Walen Parei*, (*Paarai* in Tamil, Blue fin trevally or Malabar trevally) *Murtschi karel* (In English Tooth B Mackrel) *Pilitschei* (*pilinjan* in Tamil, in English Little Mackrel), *Tombili* and *Kolamin* (*Kola meen* in Tamil, Saw fish/Gar fish in English) in Tamil and gave the descriptions.

Patrick Russell in Madras and His Study of Fish, 1788-1805

Patrick Russell (1727-1805) reached Madras in 1781 and he later succeeded Johann Gerard Koenig as naturalist to the English Company. During his stay in Madras since 1788 he collected marine as well as freshwater fish assiduously. He mentioned that the fish varieties of scomber and clupea which he found at Santhome of Mylapore were new and unknown in Europe.[19] The large collection he made was deposited in the Company's Museum at Fort St. George before his departure from Madras. Notes on this collection and specially commissioned paintings by an unnamed Indian painter were brought back to Britain, and this had provided material for the future work on ichthyology.[20]

Patrick Russell conducted the study of the fish called *vaaval* or *vowvaal* in Tamil particularly on the white pomfret (*vellai vaava,* The silver pampel), the black pomfret (*karu vaava*, also known as *ney meen*, *kadal vaaval,* The black pampel) and the grey stromale (grey mullet, *Chelon lobrosus*). Bloch had also referred to these fishes in his work published in 1795 vide *Stromateus argenteus* (Plate 421, The silver pampel), *Parastromateus niger* (Plate 422, The Black Pampel) and the *Stromateus cinereus* (Plate 420, The grey stromale). Russell said that the fish *Stromateus cinereus* had the body nearly orbicular, much compressed and scaly. The scales were small, round and close, less tenacious than in the other species. The head was round, compressed, short, the rostrum obtuse, like that of the white pomfret, and the crown and part of the front had been squamous. The mouth was small, capable of little extension; the jaws were short, nearly of equal length, hardly extractile, the under one only moveable and obtuse; the teeth were unlike those in the other species. The upper jaw was rough to the finger like a file, the under was a bone distinctly pectinate. The tongue was roundish, thick, smooth, bridled; the palate also smooth. The eyes were small, round, not protuberant. Nostrils were double, and close to the nose the posterior was large and oval but the anterior was smaller and round. The opercula could scarcely be called two-leaved; they were not so pointed as in the white pomfret, and more confined, while the branchial aperture was so small that the membrane was completely hidden. The trunk and the back and belly arched, carinate while the sides were compressed. The tail grew narrow where the dorsal and anal fins end, but again expanded to receive its own fin. There were no spiculi on the back or belly. The lateral line conspicuous, supreme, carinate, arched; but towards the end straight, and terminates not exactly at the middle of the caudal fin. There was no second line. The anus was much nearer the head than the tail. The fins, the dorsal and anal were placed more forward than in the white pomfret; they were nearly alike in shape, and terminated opposite to each other, at the narrowest part of the tail. The first rays in both, were shorter, and rose more gradually to form the crescent. The caudal was less deeply divided, the lobes nearly of equal length: but all the three fins were more remarkably distinguished, by being squamous almost to the margin of the membrane. The pectoral was broad, descending, the point a little curve. No ventral fins were found. Regarding the colour, the whole fish was of a cineritious colour, the belly only being somewhat lighter, and here and there marked with very minute black dots. According to Patrick Russell this species was very rare. He first he saw this fish in May 1788, and it was very seldom brought afterwards. In quality for the table it was very inferior to the white or black pomfret. Though alike in colour, this fish was very different from the *Stromateus cinereus* of Bloch which was specifically characterized, by the length of the lower lobe of the caudal fin.[21]

Russell gave elaborate description of fish and according to him *Stromateus argenteus* was with a squamous rhomboidal body; the dorsal and anal fins falcate; the pectoral fins lanceolate. It was called *vavval* in Tamil (white pomfret in English). This fish had the body nearly rhomb-form, much compressed, smooth, covered with small orbicular scales, close, imbricate, tenacious. The head was small, much compressed and obtuse without scales, the front declivous. The mouth was under the blunt nose, small, a little oblique; the lips simple. The lower jaw somewhat extractile, the upper immoveable, both short and set with numerous small teeth. The tongue was roundish, short, smooth, tied, the palate smooth. The eyes were middle, near the rostrum, orbicular, moderate size. Nostrils were near the edge of the rostrum, double, the posterior (which was the biggest) oval, the anterior round. The branchial opercula, smooth, ciliate at the edge, bridled so as hardly to be moveable, or to admit seeing the membrane. The trunk, the back ass urgent, carinate, and on the ridge, before the dorsal fin, five or six spiculi under the skin, might be felt by the finger; the throat and abdomen declivous, ridged, the sides and tail compressed, the former a little convex: five spiculi between the anus and the anal fin, rather more perceptible than those on the back, were found just piercing the skin. The lateral line rising from the upper edge of the opercula, formed an arch over the pectoral fin to the end of the dorsal, and was then continued straight along the upper part of the tail: another line but less conspicuous rising with the first ran straight to the middle of the caudal fin. The anus was small, considerably nearer the head than the tail. The fins, the dorsal rising from the highest point of the back, consisted at first of eleven or twelve longer rays, disposed in somewhat of a crescent-form, and then becoming narrow and equal, was continued along the declivity, to where the tail grew narrowest. The anal of the same length, rose opposite to the dorsal; the pectoral nearer the belly than the back, long, sharp, lanceolate, or acuminate in the middle; the caudal fin deeply forked. The colour was of the back dark, with a bluish or purplish cast; the rest a silver gray; the dorsal and caudal fins a little lighter than the back. The anal had a very pale yellowish cast.[22]

The fish *Parastromateus niger* called *karu vavval* in Tamil (black pomfret in English) had the body ovate, much compressed; scales oblong, roundish, close, smooth and tenacious. The head was much compressed, as in the former fish, but the nose less blunt, or round; the lower part of the face covered with scales. The mouth was small, and capable of more extension, both jaws being in some degree extractile, and the rostrum was not projecting as in the former. The teeth had been numerous, but larger; the eyes were proportionally larger also and more distant from the rostrum; the nostrils were found as in the former. The opercula ciliated as in the former, but it was rounder: in some parts covered with scales, and not being tied down- behind, left the membrane visibly exposed. Regarding the trunk the back was arched, carinate; the throat, belly, and tail, also carinated, but the dorsal and anal fins terminated, became very small and round, the sides hardly convex. The two exterior branchial were pectinate and tuberculous, the interior tuberculous only. The lateral line gently curved, but from the end of the pectoral fin ran straight along the middle of the tail. There was no appearance of a second line. The spines before the fins, in the former fish, were here wanting; and the anus was placed still nearer the head, on a line with the pectoral fin. The dorsal and anal resembled those of the former fish, in their situation, but had less of the crescent-form; the pectoral had been long and falcate, There were no ventral fins; the caudal forked, though not very deep as in the white pomfret. The colour was universally dark, tending to black, except the throat and belly, which were some shades lighter. The skin, as also the membranes of the fins were remarkably thick. The length from the nose to the caudal fin had been seven inches and the greatest breadth had been four inches.

In his remarks Russell added that *vavaal* in Tamil, the white and the black pomfret had been the esteemed two of the most delicious fish on the Coromandel Coast. But they must be eaten when caught fresh, as they were injured greatly by being kept only a few hours. The black, though a less firm fish, was by some preferred to the white. In the latter fortnight of March, and during part of April, pomfrets were in most plenty. It was remarkable that they were never caught in abundance for more than two or three days successively; after which they, in a manner, disappeared for a like number of days, and again returned. The pomfrets which Patrick Russell saw both at Visakhapatnam and Madras, agreed exactly with the descriptions given above; but there were other species on that part of the coast, of which notice had to be taken. The figure of one species of this genus has been given by Sir Hans Sloane in his history of Jamaica, where it was known under the name pampus, or pampel, probably the name pomfret among the English in the East Indies: sometimes pronounced pomplet, or pomflet.[23]

Patrick Russell mentions the fish called *vanjaram* in Tamil (seer fish or king fish in English, *Scomber pinnulis*) and described it. The body of this fish was lanceolate, compressed, without scales and smooth. The head was small, ovate, sharp, and smooth. The front was very gently declivous, somewhat flattened. The mouth was large, oblique, with hardly any lips. The jaws had been extractile, of equal length; the teeth had been numerous, close, regular, conical, somewhat larger in the under than in the upper jaw. The tongue was small, ovate, and a little rough in the middle, scarcely moveable. The palate and fauces had been rough. The eyes in middle, near the rostrum, had been large, orbicular; iris silvery and yellow. The nostrils were double, distant from each other, and the posterior was close to the orbit. The branchial opercula had been large, rounded, smooth, hardly more than one lamina. The membrane of seven rays, covered; aperture arched. The back, breast, and abdomen, somewhat convex, but carinate also; the sides were convex and compressed. The lateral line was supreme, gently arched to the beginning of the pinnulse, then straight to the middle of the caudal fin, carinated to near the end, where it had a fin-like edge. There were two dorsal fins besides the pinnulse: the first spinous, consisting of fifteen or sixteen soft spines, of which the last six, (connected by a very tender membrane and lying in a groove) might easily escape notice if not raised; the second had eighteen or twenty ramous, declining rays, the last three with somewhat the appearance of pinnulae: the pinnae spuria varied from eight to nine. The pectoral fins middle, broad, acuminate above; the ventral of the same shape but not half so long; the anal of the same form with the second dorsal; the pinnulae varied from seven to eight; the caudal completely falcate, and all the fins were somewhat of a falcate form. The colour in the upper part of the head was a changeable dark green and blue, the ridge of the back of the same colour, but changed to a polished leaden, which, from the lateral line growing gradually lighter, terminated on the belly in a bluish white. Above, but parallel to the line, a row of small, round spots, nearly black; and on the sides were several similar spots. The fins were darkish, the ventral and anal except which were of the same colour with the belly. The length of the fish was one foot and five inches. Russell made a remark that this *vanjaram* fish was esteemed by the Europeans. It was reckoned best when about the size of two feet. When it exceeded two feet and a half, it was coarse and insipid. The figure presented by Patrick Russell had differed considerably from the figure of the same fish given by Bloch, particularly in the shape of the first dorsal fin and the tail. Bloch makes the reference to the figure which was without the first dorsal fin. Hence in the opinion of Patrick Russell the drawing was probably made from a dried fish.[24]

The fish called *suraa* in Tamil (shark in English, *Ophicephalus punctatus*, Bloch, plate 358) was rather oblong than lanceolate, rounder at the shoulders, more compressed near the tail, and bended from the anus gently upward to the end of the anal fin. The scales were larger, orbicular, and all, except on the abdomen, marked with a cluster of small black dots on the anterior part. The body of the fish was lubricous. There was little difference in the shape of the head; but the scales on the crown were here only larger than those on the trunk, of the same form, and imbricate. The marginal row of teeth had been more complete. The tubuli on the edge of the rostrum was less conspicuous. The first lamina of the operculum was obtusely angular, the second acuminated. The pectoral and caudal were pointed as well as round; while the ventral had been more obtuse, and proportionally longer. The colour was less dusky, with an obscure tinge of green. A regular row of angular marks, of a colour lighter than that of the back, formed a denticulate border to the lateral line, from its infraction to its end. Beneath these the colour was a yellowish white. The dorsal, anal, and caudal fins, with a greenish cast, were less dusky than the back; the pectoral and ventral were of a yellowish dusky white. The length of the fish was one foot and six inches. Russell remarked that this fish had survived many hours even out of water.[25]

Russell had stated that the fish types of *Ophicephalus* were unknown to Carl Linnaeus. It was also not found in Gmelin's edition of the *Systema Naturae*. From the specimens received from Tranquebar, the new genus was formed by Bloch. Patrick Russell had therefore borrowed the generic character and he had cited in his work which he had admitted.[26]

The Native Response and the European Impact: Serfoji in Thanjavur and his Collection of Fish from Adirampattinam, 1805-1821

Serfoji II, the ruler of Thanjavur evinced interest in the collection and study of fish for he had contacts with C.S. John the missionary in Tranquebar. In 1805 Serfoji sent the coloured illustrations of the fish that he had found during his stay at Adirampattinam with a brief account of the place, together with the virtues of the fish that were drawn by the artist to Benjamin Torin the English resident of Thanjavur.[27] We find that a large turtle was sent by Blackburne the English Resident in Thanjavur to Serfoji which also got illustrated at that time.[28]

Thomas Caverhill Jerdon in Madras and His Study of Fish, 1837-1849

Thomas Caverhill Jerdon (1811-1872) the assistant surgeon of the Madras establishment of the English East India Company turned his attention leaving aside the sea fish. He confined his study largely to the fish found in tanks, ponds, lakes and rivers in the Carnatic region. He obtained many species apparently new, which he briefly described; and aimed to make a catalogue of fish. He also planned to introduce all those fish earlier described by Georges Cuvier (1769-1832) and Achille Valenciennes (1794-1865) and aimed to compare the fish found in the Carnatic.[29] This he did so with a view that in the future the inquirers could at once ascertain a fish, if they meet with a known fish, or a non-descript fish.[30]

The Types of Fish Found in the Rivers of Cauvery and Bhavani

Jerdon travelled widely in Tamil country and found a new species of fish and he called it *Pristolepis marginatus* (Malabar leaf-fish in English). Its scales were on the pre-opercule large, those on the opercule smaller. The colour was sap green, palest beneath; dorsal fin with a streak of-orange on the membrane of the spinous portions of the dorsal and anal fins. Some small scales were there at the base of the tail. Pectoral fin rather large, somewhat rounded; soft parts of the dorsal and anal fins much higher than the spinous, and rounded; tail rounded and lateral line parallel with the back for the length of the dorsal fin nearly, and distant a quarter of the height of the body. The head to the body was in the proportion of 1:3; and the height of the body was about half the length, not counting the dorsal fin. Jerdon's specimens were only about four inches long, but he was told that it grew considerably larger. He was much puzzled with this fish on first purchasing it, and he even undecided if he was right in placing it in a new genus. It is allied to Dules, Centrarchus, Pomotis, and Cychla, but appeared to differ from all. From Dules it differed in its general habit, interrupted lateral line, shape of caudal fin, &c., from Centrarchus in its serrated pre-opercule; from Cychla which was said to have an interrupted lateral line, in its spined operculum, and from Pomotis in wanting the prolongation of the opercule, and its interrupted lateral line–Centrarchus, Pomotis and Cychla. Jerdon had purchased the specimens from the river flowing into the Cauvery. He had placed the species later in the genus Cyprinus.[31]

Cyprinus kontius (pig mouth carp in English) was a new species. Its muzzle blunt, truncated; snout with mucous pores, head was small. The profile rose abruptly to front of dorsal, thence gradually drooping; the dorsal fin high in front, low behind, with spines, the third strong, broad, simple. The colour was dusky greenish, brighter beneath; fins dashed with reddish. It had 38 or 39 scales along the lateralline in thirteen rows. Jerdon had found this fish in the Cauvery and its tributaries, growing, it was said to be of a considerable size and his specimens were only a foot long.[32]

Cirrhinus rubro punctatus (pig mouth carp in English) was a new species and its cirri minute; head to the body was 1 to 44; the height was to the total length as 1:3. It had 40 scales along the lateral line in fifteen rows. The colour was greenish above, dusky silvery beneath, many of the scales in the centre of the body had been red spotted and the fins red tipped. Jerdon had purchased this handsome fish in the upper portion of the Cauvery river and in several of its tributaries. His specimens were about a foot long. It was said to grow to a larger size however.[33]

Cirrhinus fasciatus (melon bar in English) was a new species and its snout covered with mucous pores; cirri very long and thin, head large, being to the body as 1 to 44. The scales were 20 along the sides in six rows. The colour was reddish yellow, with four black bands, sometimes interrupted, on the sides; viz., one behind eye, one beneath the dorsal fin and another between the dorsal and caudal fins, and the fourth close to the tail. This was an active little fish found in the higher branches of the streams that run into the Cauvery. It lived chiefly on vegetable matter, but also took worms. Jerdon had kept it alive for some months, and he observed it to be extremely active and pugnacious.[34]

Leuciscus acanthogramme was the fish which had head rather smaller than the length of body; dorsal was a very little behind the middle of the body; lateral line curved; about 30 scales along the sides in eleven or twelve rows. The lower lobe of caudal was longer than the upper one; eye rather small, about five times in head; green above, silvery beneath; a yellow stripe on the side from opercule to tail. Jerdon possessed a sketch of another Leuciscus from the Cauvery river of which he had lost his specimen, which appeared to differ from any of these. It was nearly allied to *Leuciscus Caverii* in form, but has a much larger eye, and the depression in the crown more marked, muzzle in front of the depression continuing straight, parallel with the back; profile of abdomen a good deal arched; lateral line much curved. Jerdon was unable to give the number of fin rays or scales.[35]

Systomus tristis was a new species and it had two cirri; 24 scales along the sides in seven rows and the body had been compressed. The colour was plain olive green above, silvery beneath and the fins were plain and it was three inches long. Jerdon had purchased a single specimen of this fish in the Cauvery river.[36]

Gobio Gotyla had four small cirri; snout was thick, divided by a deep transverse fissure and covered with prominent mucous pores. The head to the whole body was 1 to 54. It had 34 scales along the body in seven rows. The colour was dark olive green above, yellowish beneath, some of the scales red edged; fins yellowish green, tipped with orange. The length was about eight or nine inches. Jerdon had obtained this fish in the Bhavani river at the foot of the Nilgiris. It was only found where the bed of the river was stony, and kept always close to the bottom, living apparently on the vegetable matter adhering to the stones. This species in Telugu was called *korava* (murrel in English).[37]

Gonorhynchus stenorhynchus was a new species and the muzzle was more acute and ending in a blunt rounded projection studded with large and prominent mucous pores. It had four longish cirri; the head to the whole body was 1 to 44, height was four times in the length. It had 34 scales along the body in seven rows and was about 10 inches long. Jerdon had only found this well marked species in the Bhavani river at the foot of the Nilgiri hills.[38]

Systomus carnaticus was a new species, very closely allied to the *Systomus dorsalis* and it differed in having much longer cirri, and in its dorsal fin being lower, and had only two instead of three entire rays and the lateral line was more curved, had scales 24 along the sides in seven rows. The colour was bluish green above, yellowish on the cheeks and sides, and reddish beneath, a large black spot was found on each side of the tail and the dorsal fin was reddish, stained with black; other fins were pale yellow. Jerdon had obtained the specimens of this fish in the Bhavani river at the foot of the Nilgiris and also in the Cauvery river.[39]

Pimelodus carnaticus was a new species. Its head was broad, muzzle blunt, eye small, situated far back. The dorsal spine was smooth; pectoral spine strongly toothed and the maxillary cirri had been barely as long as the head and all the others short, slender. Its colour was yellow ochre, blotched and marbled with brown about four to five inches long. Jerdon had only found this curious fish in the Bhavani river. It did not exceed six inches or so in length.[40]

Gobio hamiltonii (violet gilled shark in English) was a new species had scales along the body and ten or eleven in its depth. The colour was green above and silvery beneath. The snout was concave between eye and muzzle. Dorsal and anal fins were colourless, the pectoral and ventrals orange margined and the caudal pale yellow. Jerdon had procured this fish, of some small specimens, five or six inches long, in the Cauvery river and its tributaries. He did not notice any cirri in this but they might exist notwithstanding, as his only specimen of the first was destroyed, and his present one was in such bad order that he could not make them out. He was strengthened in the supposition of his present species not having cirri by having lately obtained in the Bhavani river, a tributary of the Cauvery, a large Gobio which might be identical with it, but of which unfortunately he lost his only specimen. It was of large size 20 inches long, head small, being to the rest of the body as 1 to 5; and had 39 or 40 scales along the body in eleven rows. The colour was green above, silvery on the sides and beneath; all the fins dusky, edged with red. Should, on a further comparison, this could be found a distinct one which Jerdon proposed the name of *Gobio bovanius*.[41]

Barbus carnaticus called *soorai meen* in Tamil (little tuna in English, *gedare* in Kannada) was mentioned by Jerdon. It was a new species and its head was small, being rather more than one-fifth of whole body; obtuse; body not much compressed, and the eye was about one-fourth the length of the head. It had about 32 scales along the sides in eight rows, cirri was of moderate length; and the profile of back ascending to the dorsal. The colour was dark glassy olive green above, silvery beneath; fins yellowish dusky. The spine was stout, simple. This fish was found in the Cauvery river and all its tributaries, frequenting the streams, and rising to the fly. Jerdon had heard of some fine fish of this species having been taken in the Bhavani river at the foot of the Nilgiris and in other parts of Tamil country. It grew to three feet and more in length, and was then a very heavy fish.[42]

The Fresh Water Varieties of Fish Found in the Inland Tanks and Ponds

Cirrhinus Belangeri (orange fin labeo in English) had the cirri rather small; head to the body was 1 to 43. It had 45 or 46 scales along the body in 15 or 16 rows. The colour was dusky green throughout, many of the scales red spotted and the fins dark. Jerdon found this fish in most of the large tanks of the Carnatic and his specimens were about 14 inches long, but it was said to grow much larger.[43]

Systomus sophone had no cirri and the dorsal spine was smooth. Its head was four times in body and its height is two times and two-thirds its total length. The colour was dusky green above, cheeks orange, silvery beneath and a streak of fine red along the sides and the dorsal fin sometimes stained with black; usually a black spot was found on the tail; ventral and anal fins were often tinged with red. There were 23 scales along the sides in nine rows. This fish was found common in the tanks in the Carnatic region.[44]

Systomus chola had two cirri and 24 scales in nine rows and the dorsal spine was smooth. The colour was green above, silvery beneath and the dorsal fin was reddish, stained and spotted with black, other fins yellowish and a large black spot was found on the root of the tail while the cheeks had been golden. The height was about 24 times in the length. Jerdon had procured this fish from the tanks in the Carnatic.[45]

Pelecus cultellus was the fish that had its head 53 times in total length of body, equal to the height of the body; eye one-fifth of its head; profile slightly rising from the nape to the middle of the body, thence gently concave; abdomen slightly curved; lateral line very little bent, dorsal small, placed slightly in front of anal; pectoral large; ventral and caudal small. It had 100 scales along the sides. The colour was greenish with a tinge of red above, silvery beneath; fins yellowish; six to seven inches long. The fish was found common in the tanks of the Carnatic.[46]

The Fish Types Found in the Inland Towns of Coimbatore, Salem and Erode

Opsarius dualis was a new species and its head was four times in the length of body. The eye being small; profile of back barely arched to the dorsal; thence concave; that of abdomen regularly arching; dorsal fin was behind the middle. It had 42 scales along the sides in eleven rows. The colour was green above, golden on the sides with transverse bars; silvery beneath; fins white, tipped with orange; all the scales with a small black spot on the middle, about four to five inches long. Jerdon had found this fish in tanks and the rivers at Coimbatore. This was one of the few fish which he had found in rivers running both to the east and west coast, and it occurs just in that part of the country where the two districts are most nearly connected without the intervention of hills, viz., in the gap of Coimbatore. Jerdon had procured some small specimens, of what he imagined was the young of this species, in a river in the Salem district.[47]

Bagrus aorides was a new species and its head was three times in the body, flat, depressed, narrow, its width being three times in its length, eye four times in the length of head, so situated that its posterior edge was more than half the length of the head from the muzzle; not quite one diameter between the two eyes. The maxillary cirri long, reached to the tail and the posterior, lower cirri was equal to the head. The length was about one foot. The colour was greenish, iridescent above, silvery iridescent beneath; upper fins greenish, with a black spot on the posterior edge of the adipose fin. Jerdon procured some specimens of this remarkable looking fish in the Cauvery river at Erode.[48]

The Fish Varieties Found in the Coastal Cities of Tranquebar, Pondicherry and Madras

Colisa fasciata (*Trichogater fasciata,* giant gouram in English) was of eight or ten vertical dark bands on sides of body. It was found at Tranquebar. Jerdon knew nothing of this species, but as several of the genus had been stated to inhabit fresh waters, so he had included them in this list.[49]

The fish *Bagrus vittatus* (Bloch) was called *keluththi* in Tamil (catfish in English, *Mystus vittatus*). It had its head about four times in the length of body; height not quite so much. The eye was four times in the head, and with two diameters between them. The occipital spine was moderate, approaching to the dorsal. The dorsal spine was with two or three fine teeth in front and seven or eight very fine ones behind; the pectoral spine was strong, flat with about thirteen strong teeth. The maxillary cirri reached to end of ventrals. The colour was coppery brown above, yellowish beneath, with two longitudinal whitish stripes on the sides of the body. The length was about four inches. Jerdon had only found this fish in the neighbourhood of Madras where it was tolerably common. He opined that it is most probably the species so named by Bloch, who received it from Tranquebar.[50]

Clarias batrachus (Philippine catfish in English) was called *Tali* in Tamil and it was brought from Tranquebar. Its maxillary cirri reached the ventrals and lower cirri the pectorals and covered with white spots.[51]

Colisa Ponticeriana described by Cuvier (*Trichogaster fasciata,* giant gouram in English) was opercule rounded with a black spot near its lower edge; oblique brown lines on its body. The fish was found at Pondicherry.[52] Mastacemblus ponticerianus was of a row of 18 spots along the back, and 12 along the edge of the anal fin. Jerdon had not personally seen this fish which appears very similar to the Bengal *Mastacemblus armatus*.[53]

Barbus subnasutus the fish had its head one-fifth of the total length. The eyes were small; muzzle was smooth; the height was three times and a third on the total length. It had 29 scales along the side in twelve rows. It was found at Pondicherry and the size was nearly 6 inches long.[54]

Barbus roseipinnis the fish had cirri long, thin; and toothed dorsal ray slightly bent, of moderate size. The eye was large and had 22 scales along the side. The caudal, anal, and ventral fins were strongly tinged with red and it was found at Pondicherry.[55]

Cirrhinus fimbriatus described by Bloch (*Labeo fimbriatus*, fringed-lipped peninsula carp in English) had the cirri very minute; head short, broad, five times and one-third in the total length; many mucous pores on the snout, which was rounded. The height of the body was one quarter of its length and had 45 scales along the body and this fish was found at Pondicherry.[56]

Cirrhinus Cuvierii (*Cirrhinus cirrhoses*, mrigal carp in English) had the labial cirrus which was fine, maxillary one fleshy; both short; body elongated; head short, and it was one-sixth of the total length of the body. The eye was large and it had 40 scales along the body. The colour was greenish above, silvery beneath and fins yellowish. Jerdon had purchased this fish from the neighbourhood of Madras. It resembled the specimen of Valenciennes which was from Pondicherry called as *Dangila Leschenaultii*, a genus he characterized as having an edging of conic papillae on the upper lip.[57]

Nandus marmoratus (*Nandus nandus*, Asian leaf-fish in English) had the height one-third of its length and the head was with the same thickness of one-third of height. The colours were olive green marbled with brown. The length was about 5 or 6 inches. Jerdon had found this curious fish only in tanks in the neighbourhood of Madras and in other parts of the Carnatic.[58]

Gobius neglectus was called *kora meen* in Tamil (*korah* in Telugu, Murrel snake-head in English). Its profile was of head sloping from the eye to muzzle, head a quarter of total length, eye one-fifth of length of head, and distant barely one diameter from each other. The scales were small, about 50 along the body. Until Jerdon had actually compared his fish with the description given by Cuvier, he had no doubt of his fish being the Gobius Russelii, to which he refers Russell's figure; but there are too many points of difference to allow of this. In Gobius Russelii the eyes were small and distant, their diameter was one-eighth the length of the head, and they were distant two diameters from each other. The colours of this fish were nearly uniform fulvous, with occasionally some dark markings on the back; and the second dorsal and caudal fins spotted. Jerdon had purchased this fish from the vicinity of Madras.[59]

Gobio limnophilus had been very closely allied to the *Gobio hamiltoni* and perhaps indeed identical. It had 36 scales along the sides and 12 scales across and had two small cirri. The colour was reddish yellow above, silvery beneath; fins dusky greenish yellow. The head was little more than a sixth of total length of body. It was found in the tanks and rivers near Madras, and other parts of the Carnatic.[60]

Systomus conchonius (*Puntius conchonius*, Rosy barb in English) had the body rather arched beneath, its depth two times in the length; head five times in total length. The second dorsal spine was strongly serrated, not so long as the next soft ray. The colour was green above, silvery beneath, fins yellowish. It had 25 scales along the body in 8 or 9 rows. The fish was two inches long. This little fish was from the tanks near Madras.[61]

Bagrus atherinoides (Bloch) was the Indian potsai in English (*Pseudeutropius athernoides*). This fish had its head six times in total length; depth 4 times in the same; maxillary cirri reached beyond the ventrals while the others all longer than the head. The eye was small and the dorsal spine finely serrated and the pectoral spine was with ten or eleven strong teeth. The colour was reddish yellow above; white abdomen, and a broad silver streak was found from head to the tail. The dorsal, pectoral, and ventral fins was of black colour and the caudal and anal had been pale yellow, the former was with a black spot at its base. The length was about four inches. Jerdon had obtained this pretty little fish from tanks in the neighbourhood of Madras.[62]

The fish *Bagrus albilabris* was called *kezhluri* or *keluththi* in Tamil (catfish *Nanobagrus fuscus*). It had its head which was four times in length of body and the height five times in the same. The eye was one-sixth of length of head, and three diameters distance between the two. The dorsal spine was moderately strong, short, toothed; first and second soft rays were much longer, the pectoral spine was strongly toothed; adipose fin was opposite the anal. The maxillary cirri reached somewhat beyond the ventrals. The colour was olive brown above, yellowish beneath, and the lower fins tinged red. The length was about five inches. Jerdon had purchased this fish at Madras from the rivers and backwaters, living both in fresh and brackish waters.[63]

Reporting the Tamil Names of Fish

According to Jerdon the fish *Etroplus maculatus* (orange chromide in English, *Psepetroplus maculatus*) was of a dusky green colour with vertical dark bands, ventral and anal fins inky black; a black band at base of tail. This fish was very common in the tanks in the Carnatic, when it was called *Nalla thanni Sipeli*, i.e., fresh water spell, which was the name of the *Scatophagus argus*. It was said by the natives to be good eating, but from its small size—not exceeding three inches—it was not sought after. Jerdon knew nothing of its habits. The fish was however sent to Marcus Elieser Bloch in Germany from Tranquebar, and Schneider had described it accurately.[64]

Tamils called the fish *Anabas scandens* as *kurukaruppan* (Grunter in English, *korakka* in Telugu as noted by Jerdon, *Anthias testudineus*, Bloch; *Amphiprion scansor*, Schneider; *Coius cobojius*). The same fish was also called *panaiyeri* by the Tamils (climbing perch in English). It was very variable in colour, usually greenish, marbled or speckled with darker, occasionally quite black, fins reddish usually, and in the young spotted. The Tamil name, Panaieri, meant climber of palmyra trees. In order to conduct a study Jerdon had kept small ones in a vase of water. They, in general, were very sluggish, but every now and then rose slowly to near the surface of the water, then made a dash to the top, and down to the bottom again with all speed. Some young ones had the tail and soft part of the dorsal fin much lengthened, thus approximating some of the species of Macropodus, but the prolongation did not appear to be persistent. This fish abounded in all the ditches, pools, and tanks throughout Tamil country, but was not in general found in the rivers. Jerdon had not seen this fish longer than six inches, usually less.[65]

Koduvai the fish called in Tamil (known as *muttah* in Telugu said by Jerdon, convict surgeon fish in English) was also known as *kozhi meen* and *vaazhai meen* in Tamil (emperor mula in English). Its body was compressed behind the pectorals; muzzle semi-circular and eyes near the end of the muzzle. The colour had been dusky green above, whitish beneath, with obscure markings on the back, dorsal, anal, and caudal fins. Jerdon had not seen any spots in the marked manner as described by the earlier writers. The rays of the dorsal fin were sometimes 30, and those of the anal 21, 22, and 23. This fish was called *korave* by the Tamils. It was exceedingly common in all the sluggish rivers, and also in almost every tank, ditch, and wells. It was not usually met with longer than 6 or 8 inches, but was said to reach a foot and more. It was very easily taken with a hook baited with worm. The fish was said to be good eating.[66]

Koravai the fish called in Tamil (murrel snakehead fish in English) had its head shorter, broader, and more round than the last; ventrals very small, of uniform dusky green color, lighter beneath; dorsal and caudal fins margined with orange; the former, and pectoral, with a tinge of the same colour throughout. Jerdon mentioned that this species was most abundant in rivers and tanks found in the Carnatic. He had not seen it longer than 6 inches. The natives applied the name *korave* to it and as to the earlier specimen, which indeed it very closely resembled in pronunciation.[67]

The fish called *viraal* (Butter fish in English, *Ophicephalus striatus*) by the Tamils had its head depressed and rounded in front and the colours were dusky green above, white beneath, with bars of the former colour extending into the white of the lower parts. Belly often spotted; fins sometimes uniform in tint, at other times barred and spotted. It abounded in all large rivers and tanks, and was highly esteemed both by Natives and Europeans, and as it was the only good fish to be procured at many inland stations was much sought after. It attained a large size. Jerdon had seen it nearly three feet long. It was very voracious, and had been easily taken with a frog or small fish as a bait.[68]

The fish called *eral* by the Tamils (shrimp or prawn in English, *Rhynchobdella aculeate*) was brown above and on the sides, yellowish beneath, fins with a sienna tinge, and the dorsal with three black spots or eyes; caudal barred, and length about 9 or 10 inches. This species was the only one of its genus, had been common enough in the rivers and tanks of the Carnatic; but Jerdon had not seen it anywhere else. The number of spots on the dorsal fin varied. It was said to be good eating.[59] Thus six fishes in total had been well studied and described by Jerdon and he had furnished the Tamil names which he collected from the locals.

The fish called *theera* in Tamil (leather skin fish in English, *Silurus ruallagoo*) by the natives had its head that was about five times in total length. The eye was one-seventh of the length of head, and with five diameters between them. The muzzle was depressed, parabolic and the maxillary cirri reached nearly to the anal fin; the lower cirri had been minute. The caudal was lobed deeply and the upper the lowest. It was of a leaden color throughout, darkest above; dorsal and caudal fins greenish dusky; pectoral, ventral and anal reddish yellow and the latter edged with dusky; up to three feet and upwards. It was found in the rivers and tanks throughout south India. It had been much esteemed by the natives and it was by no means a bad fish. It was very voracious, and was often taken with a fish or frog as bait. It was a sluggish fish in its habits, and when taken did not afford much sport to the angler. It may be considered as the pike of Indian fishing.[70]

The fish called *vaalai* in Tamil also known as *Yeri vaalai* (Ribbon in English, *Clarias marpus*) and this had its head that was one-sixth of total length and sides of head but slightly arched; and the casque had been very rough; maxillary cirri reached to the end of the pectorals. It was up to one foot long. The colour purplish was black or brown and paler beneath. It was found in rivers and tanks throughout the Tamil country and was said to be good eating.[71]

Butirinus Maderaspatensis (also called *Chanos Chanos* by Jerdon later) called *moram kende* (*Kendai*) was a new species. The head was one-fourth of whole body and had no elongated scales at base of dorsal, anal or caudal fins. It had 75 scales along the sides in 21 rows; and the body was deeper than the other fishes and it was green above, white beneath, silvery throughout, fins tinged with yellowish. Jerdon possessed some small specimens of this fish which appeared to differ from the west coast of India and it was found in the tanks in Madras. He was informed, that it was chiefly an estuary fish in Madras.[72]

There was a fish called *Oozhaa* or *Gola* in Tamil (sea pike in English) found at Madras. Jerdon found also this fish at Tiruchirapalli which ascended in the Cauvery river during the freshes for the purpose of spawning, and it was caught for the sake of its roe, which was highly esteemed.[73]

Etroplus maculatus fish was called *kasimarrah* in Telugu and it had been mentioned by Jerdon. This fish was called pearl spot in English and also variously called in Tamil such as *pattai*, *palincha* and *setha kendei*.

The Rare and the New Varieties of Fish Noticed by Jerdon

The fish *Ambassis baculis* had the length about twice and a quarter the height. It was silvery and diaphanous. Jerdon stated that he was by no means certain that this fish was Buchanan's fish, or Cuvier's Ambassis alta; to both of which it had some resemblance. According to Jerdon it was possible that, on comparison, his species had been distinct; in which case he suggested the name of *Ambassis carnaticus*. It was found in most of the permanent tanks throughout the Carnatic and did not exceed one and a half inch in length in general.[74]

Jerdon in 1849 had reported a collection of fresh water fishes from south India and described 16 species of bagrus of which 8 were referable to mystus. Jerdon's descriptions were very brief and they were without any illustrations. We find mention of *Puntius dorsalis* (long snouted barb in

English) fish by Jerdon (*Systomus dorsalis*) which he had stated that they were found in the tanks and rivers in the environs of Madras. This fish in English was called the long snouted barb.[75]

Systomus dorsalis was a new species and the head was three times in total length and the height was also three times of the same. The snout was irregular and had 26 scales along the sides in eight rows. There were two labial cirri; profile rising to dorsal and descending rapidly to the end of that fin, thence nearly straight. The colour was bluish above, yellowish on the sides, silvery beneath with a black spot on each side of the tail occasionally and the fins were with a yellowish tinge, the dorsal fin with a black spot on its base behind. The fish was four to five inches long and it was found common in all the tanks and rivers in the neighbourhood of Madras and Jerdon had not seen it anywhere else.[76]

Leuciscus flavus was a new species and the head of the fish was equal to the height of the body, one-fourth of the total length; eye rather large, dorsal medial; scales about 30, very caduceus. The colour was greenish yellow above, silvery beneath; a yellow streak along the sides, fins yellowish; caudal tipped with black; lateral line straight. It was about three inches long and found in the tanks in the Carnatic.[77]

Leuciscus microcephalus was a new species and its head was small, one-fifth of length of body; eye close to muzzle; opercule large, pointed; profile of back rising from the crown, and gently arching to the dorsal, thence concave to the tail; abdomen much curved to the anal, nearly straight thence. The dorsal fin was behind the middle, over the interval of ventral and anal. It had 30 scales along the body in seven rows and the lateral line curved. The colour was yellow green above, silvery beneath with a bright burnished silver streak along the sides, fins pale yellowish. It was found in the tanks and rivers near Madras.[78]

Bagrus affinis (catfish in English) was a new species, very nearly allied to *Bagrus vittatus* and differed in its more depressed head. The eye was smaller; occipital and the spine was more triangular. The dorsal spine was barely toothed; the pectoral spine less strongly toothed, and had only twelve teeth. It was broader and the head was about three times in the body; the maxillary cirri reached to the ventrals. The colour pale was bluish above, yellowish on the sides, whitish beneath and the fins yellowish. The length was about four inches. Jerdon purchased this fish from the neighbourhood of Madras. He opined that it may be perhaps be Bloch's vittatus.[79]

Systomus Maderaspatensis was a new species and also very closely allied. It differed in its colours chiefly, and in wanting (occasionally) the prolongation of the dorsal rays. The dorsal fin was reddish, stained with black; caudal edged broadly with fine red, and a black tip to each lobe; anal red; other fins reddish. Jerdon had purchased this fish from the tanks near Madras and its usual length was about four inches. Jerdon had also later purchased one specimen in the tank at Sriperumpudur not far from Madras, which had the dorsal rays prolonged, but which appeared to belong to this species.[80]

Pearl fishing on the Tamil Coast and the Study of Marine Fauna by the Europeans

Pearl fishery was conducted in the Gulf of Mannar from time immemorial and the Portuguese, the Dutch and the English in the early modern age noticed the activities. On this pearl fishery coast the fishing was conducted to gather pearls from oysters. Temporary camps were set up on the seashore at particular times of the year, under license from the Portuguese captain of the region to generate revenues and also to prevent excessive pearl diving which could denude the oyster and pearl stocks. Caesar Frederici the Italian traveller in the 1570s mentioned that every year in the month of March or April pearl fishing time began and after fifty days or so the pearl season was over. The pearl fishery was held one year in one place and another year in another place of the same sea.[81]

An account of pearl fishery held in March and April 1797 had been reported and it is said that it was remarkable to see some of the sea animals that were as red as blood, and that the inside of the shell had the same colour, with the usual pearly lustre. Though the servant of Henry Le Beck the Dutch Governor had found a reddish pearl in an oyster of this colour, yet such an event was very rare. The divers attributed this redness to the sickness of the pearl-fish, though it was most probable, that they had it from their first existence. In the shade they would live twenty-four hours, after being taken out of the water. This sea animal was eaten by the lower class of Tamils either fresh in their carries, or cured by drying, in which state they were exported.[82]

It had been stated that within a mother of pearl shell it was found thirteen *Murices undati* the largest of which was three quarters of an inch long, but as many of them were putrid and the pearl-fish itself dead, Hence Henry Le Beck could not ascertain whether they had crept in as enemies, or were drawn in by the animal itself. At any rate turtles and crabs were inimical to the animals, and a small living crab was found in one of them.[83] It had been said that the pearls were only in the softer part of the animal, and never in that firm, muscular column above mentioned. They found them in general near the cardo and on both sides of the mouth. The natives entertained the same foolish opinion concerning the formation of the pearl, which the ancients did. They suppose them formed from dew-drops, in connection with sun-beams.[84]

It could be judged with greater or lesser probability by the appearance of the pearl-shell, whether they contain pearls or not. Those that had a thick, calcareous crust upon them to which Serpula (sea tubes), Tubuli marini irregulariter intorti. Crita-galli, Chama lazarus, Lepas tintinabulum, Madrepora, Millipora, Cellipora, Gorgonia, Spongiae, and other Zoophytes were fastened have arrived at their full growth, and commonly contain the best pearls; but those that appear smooth, contain either none, or small once only. Henry Le Beck the Dutch Governor mentioned that indeed, no place in the East Indies abounded more with rare shells, than these in the Gulf of Mannar for there they remain undisturbed, by being sheltered from turbulent seas, and the fury of the surf. He had mentioned just a few names viz. Tellina foliacea (Linnaeus, The Golden Tong), Telina spenglerii, Arca cuculatat, Arca Noae, Solen anatinus (Linnaeus), Ostrea Isognomum, Terebellum albidium striatum, Turbo scalaris (Royal staircase), Bulla volva (Linneaus, Weaver's shuttle), Vexillum nigritarum. Amongst the beautiful Conch-shells Henry Le Beck noted Conus Thalassarchus, anglicanus lullatus (Red English Admiral), Amadis Thasslarchus, Con. Generalis (Linnaeus), C. Capitaneus, C. Miles (Garter stamper), C. Stercus muscarum (Great sand stamper), C. reteaureum, C. glaucus (Caps Gottw), C. cereola, Regia corona, Murus lapideus, Cauda erminea, Societas cordium. He said that there were many other besides those already mentioned, equally valuable and curious.[85]

Description of Oysters, Pearl-fish, Jellyfish and Corals

It is known that millions of pearl-producing bi-valve mollusks (*Margaritifera vulgaris*) had populated the low-lying shoals and rock and coral formations on the south eastern coast of India. In 1800 Eudelin de Jonville had provided an account of the fauna of the Gulf of Mannar including descriptions and drawings of pearl oysters that brought specific knowledge about the habitat and life-cycle of the species to the attention of people.[86]

We find details of various sea creatures such as oysters, pearl fish, jellyfish and corals. In 1805 the contract signed between the English East India Company and Manali Chinnaiah Mudaliar, the renter of the pearl fishery at Tuticorin, stipulated that a servant belonging to the superintendent shall be placed in each boat to take an account of the number of oysters fished in the course of each day.[87] At the 1807 the pearl fishery at Tuticorin had over seventy-one million oysters that were fished during thirty days.[88]

Further, from the pearl fishery held in 1822, the head native accountants at the Kutcheri received 5,240 oysters from the divers' share. 23,849 had been the government's share, thus amounting to a total of 29,089 oysters.[89] The workers normally left the oysters to rot in the hot tropical sun, which killed the animal, and left nothing but the dried flesh of the organism and its shell.

Henry Le Beck the Dutch governor and naturalist wrote that the boat owners and purchasers often lost many of the best pearls while the boat was still returning from the pearl bank; for, as long as the animal was alive, and untouched, the shells were frequently opened near an inch; and if any of them contained a large pearl, it was easily discovered, and taken out by means of a small piece of stiff grass, or bit of stick, without hurting the pearl fish. In this practice they were extremely expert. Some of them were discovered while he was there, and received their due punishment for such an act.[90] It is reported that women sat aligned in rows on the floor of the huts, working five to a team, picked at oysters shells and sifting sand, making sure that no pearls, even those of the smallest were not missed out.

In 1834, the *jati thalaivan* of Tuticorin submitted a curious report in which a village inhabitant stumbled across some discarded oyster shells and broken diving stones. According to this report the discovery of the old shells and the diving stone induced him to suppose that there were oysters on the banks and that there had been fishery carried once. He picked some pieces of corals found scattered.[91]

The jellyfish was a sea-creature that presented a real and recurring threat to the safety of pearl divers on the Tamil coast. It had brought a halt to the pearl fishery by preventing divers from plunging below the water's surface. In AD 1800 the superintendent of the pearl fishery at Tuticorin wrote, that the duty of a diver was known at all times to be dangerous and that danger increased towards the latter end of the months of April and the beginning of May when the land winds brought the blubbers towards the shore.[92] An unfortunate bunch of divers sustained very serious injuries from a jellyfish bloom and some even had died. Rama Chetti and Venkatachalam Chetti the two native agents of the principal renter submitted a petition to the Collector of Ramnad, the official superintending the pearl fishery in 1800 and wrote, that the blubbers had begun to be much frequent in touching the divers and upon some dead, and many wounded, these reasons absolutely had frighten any man to do their duty properly.[93] The government officials remained indifferent believing that deaths by jellyfish had been either an occupational hazard or just the stuff of rumor. Collector Lushington reported that jellyfish attack had become excited in the minds of the other divers.

Diving was known at all times to be dangerous when the land winds brought the blubbers towards the shore and under such conditions nothing but the fear of punishment compelled them to go on with it.[94] In a dispatch from Tuticorin to the Board of Revenue at Fort St. George, Lushington confirmed that the sting of a jellyfish had killed at least one diver, curtailing diver operations. He remarked, that the southerly winds blew with such violence and the blubber which caused the death of one man collecting in such quantity upon the pearl bank that the boats only attempted going out three days.[95] Thus pearl divers faced with natural enemies such jellyfish, and venomous sea-snakes.

Sending Shells from Madras to London by Edward Buckley, 1706

Edward Buckley the English company surgeon at Fort St George in Madras received a collection of items to be sent to England that came in a box from Macao in China in a ship in 1706 for onward transmission to London. The box on arrival at Madras was found broken and so Buckley had repacked it. While doing so, he added shells such as black and yellow streak Madras shell, Black and white girdled Madras olive, Thick Madras stamper, Warry Madras stamper, Madras reddish stopple, Madras furrow-wavel tellen, Madras smooth-waved tellen and Madras broad-headed tellen. These were sent in 1688 from Madras to James Petiver in London.[96] Some of these objects from this cabinet could be still be seen in the British Museum, London. However, the study of shells became a favourite subject amongst the Europeans on the Tamil coast of all the branches of natural history much later.

Johann Gerard Koenig and his Study of Shells in Tranquebar, 1770-71

Johann Gerard Koenig developed interest in the study of mollusca (sea-shells) the soft-bodied animals. As the shell is built of calcium carbonate and a good example of architectural skills of the animals, Koenig collected and dutifully sent them to Europe. On 20 December 1771, Linnaeus wrote to John Ellis his friend that Koenig had found a lot of new things in Tranquebar. There are three shells now preserved in the collection of Linnaeus marked Tranquebar. However, the name of the sender is not mentioned.[97] Living organisms in water in Tamil country had attracted the attention of the Europeans. Hence they conducted the study of the creatures. Johann Wilhelm Gerlach (1738-91) on arrival in Tranquebar in 1772 wrote to Christian Gottlieb Kratzenstein (1723-1795) the doctor and Physicist in Europe and gave an account of the animals that he saw at sea.[98]

Christoph Samuel John and his Study of Shells and Conches from Rameswaram and Tuticorin, 1779-1797

Christoph Samuel John the Protestant missionary in Tranquebar developed interest in the study of shells and conches. A letter written by Johann Peter Rottler the Protestant missionary in Tranquebar to a friend in Ramanathapuram in 1779 had mentioned that if Wisnarasy had still some cash from him in hand and if he would be pleased to send him for making a collection of shells from Rameswaram, it would give great pleasure and satisfaction to C. S. John.[99]

C.S. John took the help of many persons to collect the shells and conches. It is reported that with the assistance of Gerard van Angelbeck, the Dutch Governor along with the help of a local boat and divers at Tuticorin he was able to collect so many shells and conches in 1797. The prime collections were made by his agents, who afterwards sent them with the necessary instructions and apparatus. These shells are found mention in Chemitz's elegant Cabinet of Shells in quarto (with illuminated plates), where so many new species of zoophytes he had discovered.[100] We also learn the details from the work of Esper the German interested in shells living at Erlangen, where the third volume of the book was completed.[101] Thus we find C.S. John's shell collections were of great importance. We find conch shells of Tranquebar named *Cantharus tranquebaricus* found in the works of Gmelin in 1791 and Rodling in 1798.

Johann Christian Fabricius in Denmark and his Study of Crabs, Crayfish and Lobsters from Tranquebar

The Protestant missionaries of Tranquebar supplied the creatures living in water such as *nandu* (crab), *naththai* (snail) to European scholars who were interested in the study of fauna. The mud crab *Scylla serrata* had become a subject of importance for carcinologists. In 1755 Petrus Forskal described the species as *Cancer serrtus* but did not mention the type of locality.[102] Later Johann Christian Fabricius (1745-1808) the Danish zoologist in 1793 described *Portunus tranquebaricus* a specimen obtained from Tranquebar.[103] It is the olive ridley turtle (*Lepidochlus olivacea*). According to him the colour in carapace was olive. The frontal teeth had been blunt in shape but levelled. The length of cheliped was more than twice that of carapace. The size had not been mentioned.

Carl Linnaeus had mentioned in his work of 1758 three species of Astacus such as (a) *Astacus marinus* — *Homarus gammarus*; (b) *Astacus fluviatilis* — *Astacus astacus* and (c) *Astacus norwegicus* — *Nephrops norvegicus*. Johann Christian Fabricius in Europe had made a study of the crayfish and the lobsters which he received from the missionaries of

Tranquebar. He in his various studies conducted between 1775 and 1798 had recognized five species within that genus of Astacus, such as (1) *Astacus fulvus*, (Fabricius 1775: 415); (2) *Astacus scaber* (Fabricius 1793: 480); (3) *Astacus coerulescens — Hippolyte coerulescens* (Fabricius, 1793); (4) *Astacus fulgens* (Fabricius 1798: 408) and (5) *Astacus Bartonii — Cambarus bartonii* (Fabricius, 1798).[104]

Astacus fulvus was first described by J.C. Fabricius in 1793 and he gave a short Latin diagnosis and a slightly longer Latin description. The same species has also been mentioned by Johann Friedrich Wilhelm Herbst (1743-1807) the practical entomologist in 1796 who gave the diagnosis in Latin and translated the description in German.[105] Fabricius did not mention the colour of his specimen other than in the specific name fulvus (tawny or reddish-yellow). Fabricius in 1793 and 1798 had described the type specimen of Astacus fulaus as middle-sized. The type locality of *Astacus fulaus* was mentioned as ocean.[106]

J.C. Fabricius stated in 1798 that *Astacus scaber* was smaller than *Nephrops norvegicus*. The locality indicated by him was the Indian Ocean. Though the specimen of *Astacus modestus* had come from Tranquebar, Johann Friedrich Wilhelm Herbst in 1796 mentioned that his *Cancer modestus* from the East Indies. However Herbst had cited the name of C.S. John in Tranquebar and thanked him for this specimen in 1794.[107]

Fabricius had received crabs from Tranquebar and he mentioned *Leucosia fugax* (*Myra fugax*) in 1798.[108] Earlier J. F. W. Herbst had mentioned *Cancer punctatus* in 1783. We find the holotype, 26.0 mm carapace length crab, at the Zoological Museum, in the University of Copenhagen (ZMUC) recorded as sent from *India Orientalis*, by I. K. Daldorff, the Danish Naval officer in Tranquebar.[109] We find also another crab of 24.5 mm carapace length sent from Tranquebar and noted by H. Krøyer at the Zoological Museum, in the University of Copenhagen. The description of *Leucosia fugax* by Fabricius very well fits many Myra species. Indeed, Fabricius himself had failed to take notice of fugax that differs from the species (*Cancellus Anatum Tertius*) depicted by George Eberhard Rumphius (1627-1702) who had received it from Amboina in Indonesia.[110] It must be stated that the type specimen of Fabricius is an adult male, and its examination had allowed long lists of synonymies and during 1816-17 we find that K.M.H. Lichtenstein and W. E. Leach had established Myra for *Leucosia fugax* of Fabricius. Myra had been a source of systematic and nomenclatural confusion because of the subtle variants on its deceptively uniform morphology and also may be because of specific characters, or sex and age dependent.[111]

The Study of Tortoise and Turtle in Madras

Creatures living in water found in Tamil country attracted the Europeans and so they conducted studies. According to T.C. Jerdon in Madras, the fresh-water tortoise had been an extremely common species in Tamil country and it was found in tanks, rivers, wells, and pools of water, burying itself in the mud with great celerity. It was frequently brought to the market in Madras for sale and was eaten by many of the people there.[112]

Chelonia maculosa (Cuvier) the turtle was caught by the fishermen on the Tamil coast. This had vertebral plates larger than broad, marked with yellow in an olive brown ground.[113]

Six Types of Frogs Mentioned by Walter Elliot and Jerdon, 1853

Frog was called *thavazhlai* by the Tamils and there were various varieties found in Tamil country. *Rana nilgirica* the frog differed in its much longer limbs. The length was two inches. Jerdon had only seen this frog in marshes in the Nilgiris.[114]

Polypadates leucomystax was the Chunam frog of Europeans. It was found very common all over Tamil country.[115]

Polypadates variabilis was the green frog of the Nilgiris. Its colour was green, sometimes unspotted, at other times with gold spots or blackish spots; at times golden yellow with brown spots; at other times brown with darker spots. It was found in the banks of streams and in shrubs.[116]

Phyllomedusa tinniens was the tinkling frog of the Nilgiris. The fingers opposable; feet webbed at base only; yellowish red, or sometimes blackish above; side of head dark and inner fingers yellow. It was found in grass and among bushes on the Nilgiris. It had a peculiar loud clear metallic tinkling call.[117]

Engystoma ornatum had been the very handsome frog and it was only once purchased by Walter Elliot in Nilgiris.[118]

Engystoma rubrum frog had the Indian red above and some black marks on the legs. It was found in the sandy banks near rivers in the Carnatic region.[119]

The Study of Crocodile in Vellore Fort

Crocodile was called *muthalai* by the Tamils and they were found in rivers and ditches of the fort. *Crocodilus porosus* was the larger and fiercer of the crocodiles, found in various localities on the Tamil coast. This species was so abundant in the fort ditch at Vellore. It was of very rapid growth. An egg brought from Vellore to Walter Elliot was hatched in the Government house compound, and in eight years had increased to the length of eight or nine feet, becoming so powerful as to destroy a full grown buck antelope which had come to drink water at the tank where it usually resorted to. Jerdon mentioned that the species of crocodile were almost universally called alligators by the English in India and erroneously so, of course, as no alligators had as yet been found in India.[120] Colonel Walter Campbell mentioned that the crocodiles in the Vellore fort ditch were in the habit of sinking to the bottom and hid themselves in the mud for some time after morning and evening guns were fired from the fort.[121]

To conclude it may be said that the Europeans on the Tamil coast had neatly understood the various types of fish and sea animals. They included *vilangu* (Indian mottled eel in English, *Anguilla bengalensis*), *kanavaay* in Tamil (cuttle fish in English) and *oosi kanawa* (squid in English) as sea animals. The new knowledge on fish and the marine fauna of the Tamil coast that emerged had shaped the natural history knowledge of Europe and the networks developed were truly global. With the descriptions provided in the early modern age it may be possible to know the fish and its type even now. It may be also easy to trace whether it is extinct or not, though the international code of zoological nomenclature had been changing from time to time. Global travel had increased exponentially and the European society and culture came to transform in response. The exotic and the related writings had inspired the individuals to learn. The strange and marvelous things of the Tamil sea strongly influenced the continued development of ichthyology and the study of marine fauna. Knowledge production in the orbit of marine science had thus provided space to dissemination and reception of knowledge in Europe. Though most of the knowledge gathered were descriptive it was essential to building the animal science. Many elements of knowledge about the fish of the Tamil coast were not changed or forgotten during the transformation from empirically gained knowledge into knowledge compilation stored in memory media like encyclopedias. The three forms of representation of fish generation, namely printed engravings, colour plates, and verbal descriptions had in a large measure contributed immensely to the study of fish.

Notes

1. William Crooke, ed., *A New Account of East Indies and Persia, 1672-1681*, London, 1909, repr. Delhi, 1992, vol. I, pp. 173-4.
2. R. C. Temple, ed., *The Life of Icelander Jon Olafsson Traveller to India*, London, 1931, p. 143.
3. Laurence Theodor Gronow, 'Animalium Rariorum Fasciculus Pisces', *Acta Helvetica, Physico-Mathematico-Anatamico-Botanico-Medica*, Basile, 1772, pp. 43-52.

4. S. Jeyaseela Stephen, *A Meeting of the Minds: European and Tamil Encounters in Modern Sciences, 1507-1857*, Delhi, 2016, pp. 120-2.
5. Patrick Russell, *Descriptions and Figures of Two Hundred Fishes; Collected at Vizagapatam on the Coast of Coromandel, Presented to the Honourable the Court of Directors of the East India Company*, London, 2 vols., 1803, see, vol. 1, no. 48.
6. C. S. John, 'Einige Nachrichten von Trankenbar auf der Kuste Koromandel: Aus einem Briete von dem Missionarius Hrn John an Hrn Doktor Bloch in Berlin', *Berlinische Monatsschrift*, vol. 20, 1792, pp. 585-96. The letter is partly published in the introduction of a book. See, Marcus Elieser Bloch, *Allgemeine Naturgeschichte der Auslandischen Fische*, Den Konigl Akademischen Kunsthandlern J. Morino & Comp, Berlin, 1793, vol. VII, pp. viii-x.
7. Arthur Macgregor, 'European Enlightenment in India: An Episode of Anglo-German Collaboration in the Natural Sciences on the Coromandel Coast, Late 1700 and Early 1800s', in ed., Arthur Macgregor, *Naturalists in the Field: Collecting, Recording and Preserving the Natural World from the Fifteenth to the Twenty-First Century*, Leiden, 2018, pp. 365-392, see p. 381.
8. Hans-Joachim Paepke, *Bloch's Fish Collection in the Museum für Naturkunde der Humboldt Universität zu Berlin–An Illustrated Catalog and Historical Account*, Liechtenstein, A.R.G. Gantner Verlag KG, 1999; Hoppe Brigittee, 'Vonder Naturgeschchite zuden Naturwissenschaftern-die Danisch-Halleschen Missionare als Naturfurschen in Indien em 18 bis 19 Jahrhundert' in Heike Liebau, Andreas Nehring and Brigitte Klosterberg, eds. *Mission und Forschung: Translokale Wissenproduktion Zwischen Indien und Europe im 18,und.19 Jahrhundert*, Halle, 2010, pp. 141-166; see also, 'Eine Fischsammelung aus Tranquebar die Berliner Gesellschaft Naturschender Freunde und deren Mitgliel Marcus Eliser Bloch', in Heike Liebau, Andreas Nehring and Brigitte Klosterberg, eds. *Mission und Forschung*, pp. 167-180.
9. Marcus Elieser Bloch was born in Ansbach in 1723. His father held a high religious position as a Torah writer in a Jewish community. As his salary was low Bloch's early education suffered and he was almost illiterate till the age of nineteen. However, Bloch worked hard on his education and with some knowledge of Hebrew and rabbinical literature he got a job as a teacher at a Jewish surgeon's house in Hamburg. During this time he learnt German and Latin. Bloch thereafter began studying the fish found in Germany. Later he sent his son to Switzerland, England, Holland and Denmark to gather fish specimens. In 1797, Bloch travelled to Paris and Holland and met scientists like Georges Cuvier, Achille Valenciennes and other great scientists. He died of a stroke at Carlsbad (Karlovy Vary) on 6 September 1799.
10. Bloch published Naturgeschichte der Maraene, his first work on Ichthyology in 1779. It was followed by Oeconomische Naturgeschichte der Fische der Preußischen Staaten in 1780. He published Oeconomische Naturgeschichte der Fische Deutschlands the three volume work on German fish during 1782 and 1784. This was followed by his work on fish from other parts of the world, the nine-volume Naturgeschichte der Ausländischen Fische during 1785-1795. At about the same time, he combined the last two multi-volume works such as Allgemeine Naturgeschichte der Fische in twelve folio volumes, illustrated with

432 coloured copperplate engravings, and providing detailed descriptions of about 500 fish species. The copy of this work is a six-volume French translation with the title Ichthyologie; ou, Histoire Naturelle des Poissons, produced in a reduced octavo format in 1796 with 216 plates. Bloch's Systema Ichthyologiae contains descriptions of 1,254 fish species and it was planned as his crowning achievement but did not live to see its completion. It was later revised and published by his friend Johann Gottlob Schneider (1750-1822) in 1801.

11. *The Analytical Review or History of Literature, Domestic and Foreign*, London, 1796, vol. XXIII, p. 219.
12. J. Ferd Fenger, *History of the Tranquebar Mission: Worked out from the Original Papers*, tr. Emil Francke, Tranquebar, 1863, pp. 297-8.
13. S. Jeyaseela Stephen, A Meeting of the Minds, p. 134.
14. Marcus Elieser Bloch, Allgemeine Naturgeschichte der Auslandischen Fische 1793, pp. 86-9, 132-7.
15. C. S. John, 'Beschreibung und Abbildung des Uranoscopus Lebeckii', Der *Gesellschaft Naturforschender Freunde zu Berlin Neue Schriften*, vol. III. 1801, pp. 283-287.
16. J. G. Schneider, M. E. Blochii, *Systema Ichtyologiae iconibus CX illustratum*, Bibliopolio Sanderiano, Berolini, 1801, pp. 47-9. The text runs thus. 'Eins (Dr. Blochs Herrliches Fischbuch) hat mein thätigster und für die Naturgeschichte brennender Freund Hr. Lebeck, die Krone meiner Erziehungsanstalt, der unter einem berühmten Thunberg in Upsala seine Wissenschaften fortsetzte, und so sehr bereicherte, erhalten, der darmit aufs beste wuchert. Nachdem er einen Theil von Cap de bonne Esperance, von Ceylon, von Bengalen und von der Küste Coromandel bereiset, gehet er nun nach Java. Die Naturforscher werden es mir folglich nicht verdenken, wenn ich ihm zu Ehren diesen Fisch Uranoscopus Lebeckii genannt habe'. For details see also, Plate 163 and the illustration in Museum fur Naturkunde der Humboldt-Universitat zu Berlin; Historische Bild- und Schriftgutsammlungen: GNF Christoph Samuel John. See also, Uranoscopus scaber Linnaeus, 1758 Uranoscopidae Der Sternseher Bloch, 1786: 90; Uranoscopus Scaber; Bloch, 1786, pl. 163, Der Sternseher, Le Boeuf, The Star Gazer; Uranoscopus scaber, Bloch, 1787: 124; Uranoscopus Scaber, Bloch, 1795: 120.
17. *Der Gesellschaft Naturforschender Freunde zu Berlin Neue Schriften*, vol. 3, see the preface. The text runs thus: 'Picturam et notitiam misit Johnius, et piscem pulcherrimum ab ardentissimo historiae naturalis amatore Le Beck cognominavit, cui picturam et notitiam delphini Gangetici debebat Blochius, quanquam aquis Caroliniensibus immortuus, antea quam literae Johnii cum picturis huc advenissent'.
18. Marcus Elieser Bloch, Allgemeine Naturgeschichte der Auslandischen Fische 1795, pp.109-113.
19. Patrick Russell, Descriptions and Figures of Two Hundred Fishes, vol. I, p. vi.
20. Anantanarayanan Raman, 'Patrick Russell and Natural History of the Coromandel', *Journal of the Bombay Natural History Society*, 107 (2), 2010, pp. 116–121.

21. Patrick Russell, Descriptions and Figures of Two Hundred Fishes, vol. I, no. 44.
22. *Ibid.*, vol. I, no. 42.
23. *Ibid.*, vol. I, no. 43.
24. *Ibid.*, vol. II, no. 134.
25. *Ibid.*, vol. II, no. 153.
26. *Ibid.*, vol. II, no. 152.
27. Tamilnadu State Archives (hereafter TNSA), Chennai, *Tanjore District Records* (hereafter TDR), vol. 3417, p. 168, 4 March 1805.
28. TNSA, TDR, vol. 3479, pp. 218-9, 1 September 1805.
29. Georges Cuvier, *Le Regne animal ditribue d'après son organization pour servir de base a l'historie naturelle des animaux et introduction a l'anatomie compare*, 4 vols, Paris, 1817; Georges Cuvier, *The Animal Kingdom, Arranged after Its Organization, Forming a Natural History of Animals and an Introduction to Comparative Anatomy*, Williams S. Orr, London, 1840; Georges Cuvier & Achille Valenciennes, *Histoire Naturelle des Poissons*, 22 vols, Paris, 1828-1848.
30. T. C. Jerdon, 'On the Fresh Water Fishes of Southern India', *Madras Journal of Literature and Science*, vol. XV (1), 1848, pp. 139-149, see p. 139.
31. *Ibid.*, pp. 141-2. T.C. Jerdon, 'On Pristolepis Marginatus', *Annual Magazine of Natural History*, (3) 16, 1865, p. 298.
32. T. C. Jerdon, 'On the Fresh Water Fishes of Southern India', *Madras Journal of Literature and Science*, vol. XV (2), pp. 302-346, see p. 302.
33. *Ibid.*, p. 303.
34. *Ibid.*, pp. 305-6.
35. *Ibid.*, p. 321.
36. *Ibid.*, p. 316.
37. *Ibid.*, pp. 309-10.
38. *Ibid.*, pp. 310-1.
39. *Ibid.*, pp. 315-6.
40. *Ibid.*, p. 341.
41. *Ibid.*, p. 307.
42. *Ibid.*, pp. 311-2.
43. *Ibid.*, pp. 303.
44. *Ibid.*, p. 316.
45. *Ibid.*
46. *Ibid.*, p. 326.
47. *Ibid.*, p. 330.
48. *Ibid.*, pp. 336-7.
49. T. C. Jerdon, 'On the Fresh Water Fishes of Southern India', *Madras Journal of Literature and Science*, vol. XV (1), p. 145.
50. T. C. Jerdon, 'On the Fresh Water Fishes of Southern India', *Madras Journal of Literature and Science*, vol. XV (2), p. 338.
51. *Ibid.*, p. 342

52. T. C. Jerdon, 'On the Fresh Water Fishes of Southern India', *Madras Journal of Literature and Science*, vol. XV (1), p. 145.
53. *Ibid.*, p. 147.
54. T. C. Jerdon, 'On the Fresh Water Fishes of Southern India', *Madras Journal of Literature and Science*, vol. XV (2), p. 313.
55. *Ibid.*, p. 314.
56. *Ibid.*, p. 304.
57. *Ibid.*
58. T. C. Jerdon, 'On the Fresh Water Fishes of Southern India', *Madras Journal of Literature and Science*, vol. XV (1), p. 141.
59. *Ibid.*, pp. 148-9. See also, 'Ichthyological Gleanings in Madras', *Madras Journal of Literature and Science*, vol. XVII, 1851, pp. 128-151.
60. T. C. Jerdon, 'On the Fresh Water Fishes of Southern India', *Madras Journal of Literature and Science*, vol. XV (2), p. 308.
61. *Ibid.*, p. 317.
62. *Ibid.*, p. 336.
63. *Ibid.*, p. 338-9.
64. T. C. Jerdon, 'On the Fresh Water Fishes of Southern India', *Madras Journal of Literature and Science*, vol. XV (1), p. 142.
65. *Ibid.*, p. 144.
66. *Ibid.*, p. 145.
67. *Ibid.*
68. *Ibid.*, p. 146.
69. *Ibid.*, p. 147.
70. T. C. Jerdon, 'On the Fresh Water Fishes of Southern India', *Madras Journal of Literature and Science*, vol. XV (2), pp. 333-4.
71. *Ibid.*, p. 342.
72. *Ibid.*, p. 344.
73. *Ibid.*, p. 345.
74. T. C. Jerdon, 'On the Fresh Water Fishes of Southern India', *Madras Journal of Literature and Science*, vol. XV (1), p. 140.
75. T. C. Jerdon, 'On the Fresh Water Fishes of Southern India', *Madras Journal of Literature and Science*, vol. XV (2), p. 314.
76. *Ibid.*, pp. 314-5.
77. *Ibid.*, pp. 320-1.
78. *Ibid.*, p. 321.
79. *Ibid.*, p. 338.
80. *Ibid.*, p. 319.
81. Richard Hakluyt, 'The voyage and travel of M. Caesar Fredericke, merchant of Venice into the East India, and beyond the Indies, 1563', in *The Principal Navigations, Voyages, Traffiques and Discoveries of the English Nation*, vol. V, Glasgow, 1907; S. Jeyaseela Stephen, *Portuguese in the Tamil Coast: Historical*

Explorations in Commerce and Culture, Pondicherry, 1998, pp. 72-81; S. Jeyaseela Stephen, *Expanding Portuguese Empire and the Tamil Economy, Sixteenth-Eighteenth Centuries*, Delhi, 2009, pp. 85-91.

82. 'An Account of the Pearl-Fishery in the Gulph of Manar, in March and April 1797—by Henry J. Le Beck, Esq. communicated by Doctor Roxburgh', *Asiatick Researches*, Calcutta, vol. V, pp. 393-411, see p. 407.
83. *Ibid.*, p. 407.
84. *Ibid.*, pp. 407-8.
85. *Ibid.*, p. 410.
86. British Library (hereafter BL), London, Sloane MS 3321, fol. 191, see the letter of Edward Buckley to James Petiver dated 23 February 1705/6; see also, Jacobus Petiver, *Gazophylacii Naturæ & Artis: Decas Prima*, Londini, MDCCII, p. 88.
87. S. P. Dance, 'Report on the Linnaean Shell Collection', *Proceedings of Linnaean Society London*, vol. 176 (1), 1967, pp. 1- 34, see p. 8.
88. Georg Christian Knapp et al., eds., *Neuere Geschichte der Evangelischen Missions-Anstalten zu Bekehrung der Heiden in Ostindien aus den eigenhändigen Aufsätzen und Briefen der Missionarien erausgegeben*, Waisenhaus, Teil 1–8 (Stück 1–95), Waiserihaus, Halle, 1770–8/95, 1848 (hereafter NHB) 2, pp. 716-38.
89. T. Foulkes, 'Biographical Memoir of Dr Rottler', *Madras Journal of Literature and Science*, New Series, 1861, pp. 1-17, see p. 4.
90. Friedrich Martini & J. H. Chemnitz, *Neues Systematisches Concylie-Cabinet*, Nurenberg, 11 vols., 1769-1795.
91. An Account of the Pearl-Fishery in the Gulph of Manar, p. 411.
92. Petrus Forskal, *Descriptiones animalium, avium, amphihiorum. insectorum vermium quae in itenere orientali observavit*, Hafniae, MDCCLV.
93. Johann Christian Fabricii, *Supplementum entomologiae systematicae*, Hafniae, MDCCXCVIII.
94. Johann Christian Fabricii, *Entomologia systematica, emendata et aucta. Classes, ordines, genera, species adjectis synonymis, locis, observationibus, descriptionibus*, Hafniae, MDCCXCIII.
95. BL, MSS Eur. E80-82, *Quelques notions sur l'Isle de Ceylan*.
96. TNSA, *Tirunelveli Collectorate Records*, (hereafter TCR), vol. 3565, p. 39 (22 March 1805).
97. TNSA, TCR, vol. 3582, pp. 153-7 (14 May 1807).
98. TNSA, TCR, vol. 4696, pp. 228-34 (21 December 1822).
99. An Account of the Pearl-Fishery in the Gulph of Manar, pp. 404-5.
100. TNSA, TCR, vol. 4708, pp. 121-2 (27 June 1834).
101. TNSA, *Madras Presidency: Board of Revenue Proceedings*, (hereafter BORP), vol. 251, p. 3958 (8 May 1800).
102. *Ibid.*, p. 3955.
103. *Ibid.*, pp. 3957-8.
104. TNSA, TCR, vol. 3582, pp. 212-3 (8 August 1807).

105. Johann Friedrich Wilhelm Herbst, *Versuch einer Naturgeschichte der Krabben und Krebse nebst einer systematischen Beschreibung ihrer verschiedenen Arten*, vol. 1 (1782-1790), vol. 2 (1791-1796), vol. 3 (1799-1804).
106. Johann Christian Fabricii, *Systema entomologiae, sistens insectorum classes, ordines, genera, species, adjectis, synonymis, locis, descriptionibus, observationibus*, Hafniae, MDCCLXXV.
107. Johann Friedrich Wilhelm Herbst, *Versuch einer Naturgeschichte der Krabben und Krebse nebst einer systematischen Beschreibung ihrer verschiedenen Arten*, 1794, vol. 2, p. 150. The text runs thus: 'Am meisten bin ich vom Herrn Missionarius John in Tranquebar mit einigen ganz neuen seltenen Arten beschenkt worden'.
108. J. C. Fabricius, *Supplementum Entomologiae Systematicae*, Hafniae, 1798, 351. Fabricius described Leucosia fugax thus: Thorace oblongo postice tridentato: dente medio longiore recuruo, digitis dentatis.
109. J. F. W. Herbst, Versuch einer Naturgeschichte der Krabben und Krebse, vol. I, 1783: 89, pl. 2, figures 15 and 16; I. K. Daldorf, 'Uddrag af Hr. Daldorfs Dagbog Paaen Reise fra Kiobenhavn til Tranquebar fidst o Aaret 1790 og forst I Aaret 1791', *Skrivter af Naturhistorie Selskaber*, 2 (2), 1793, pp. 147-173.
110. George Eberhard Rumphius, *D'amboinsche Rariteitkamer, Behelzende eene Beschyvinge van allerhande zoo weeke als harde Schaalvischen, te weeten raare Krabben, Kreeften, en diergelyke Zeedieren, als mede allerhande Hoorntjes en Schulpen, die men in d'Amboinsche Zee vindt: Daar beneven zommige Mineraalen, Gesteenten, en soorten van Aarde, die in d'Amboinsche, en zommige omleggende Eilanden gevonden worden*, Amsterdam, third Edition, 1741, pl.10, fig C.
111. K. M. H. Lichtenstein, Die Gattung Leucosia: als Probe einer neuer Bearbeitung der Krabben und Krebse, *Magasin der Gesellschaft Naturforschender Freunde zu Berlin*, 7 (2), 1816, pp. 135-144; W.E, Leach, *The Zoological Miscellany, Being Descriptions of New or Interesting Animals*, London, 1817, vol 3, pp. i-vi.
112. T. C. Jerdon, 'Catalogue of reptiles inhabiting peninsular India', *Journal of the Asiatic Society of Bengal*, vol. XXII, 1853, pp. 462-79, see p. 464.
113. *Ibid.*, pp. 464-5.
114. T. C. Jerdon, 'Catalogue of reptiles inhabiting peninsular India', *Journal of the Asiatic Society of Bengal*, vol. XXII, 1853, pp. 522-534, see p. 532.
115. *Ibid.*, p. 532.
116. *Ibid.*
117. *Ibid.*, p. 533.
118. *Ibid.*, p. 534.
119. *Ibid.*
120. T. C. Jerdon, 'Catalogue of reptiles inhabiting peninsular India', *Journal of the Asiatic Society of Bengal*', vol. XXII, 1853, pp. 462-79, see p. 465.
121. Colonel Walter Campbell, *My Indian Journal*, Edinburgh, MDCCCLXIV, p. 54.

8.1. Appai, Balistes aculeatus, White branded trigger fish, 1786.

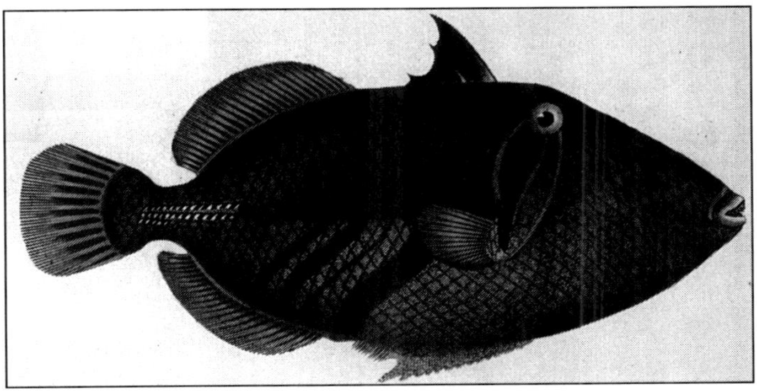

8.2. Seruppu Appai, Chaetdon kleinii, Black lip butterfly, 1790.

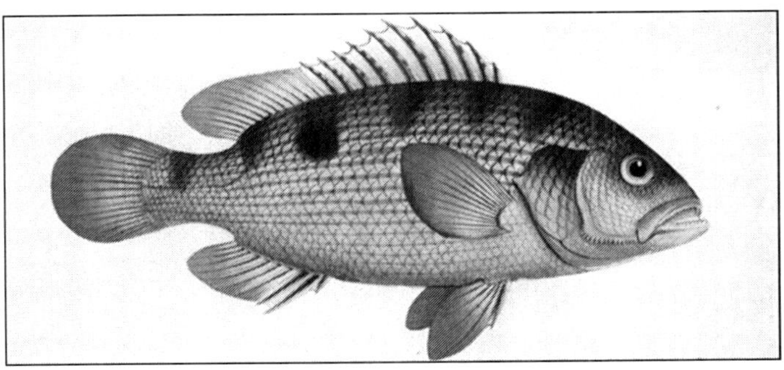

8.3. Keechchaan, Anthias johnii, Golden snapper, 1792.

8.4. Varipaarai, Scomber ruber, Mackerel, 1793.

8.5. Velampaarai, Scomber Rottleri, Torpedo scad, 1793.

8.6. Sathuppunangkaarai, Scomber Kleinii, Razor belly scad, 1793.

8.7. Karuththa Viraal, Johnius carcutta, Bearded croaker, 1793.

8.8. Aanai Viraal, Johnius aneus, Big eye croaker, 1793.

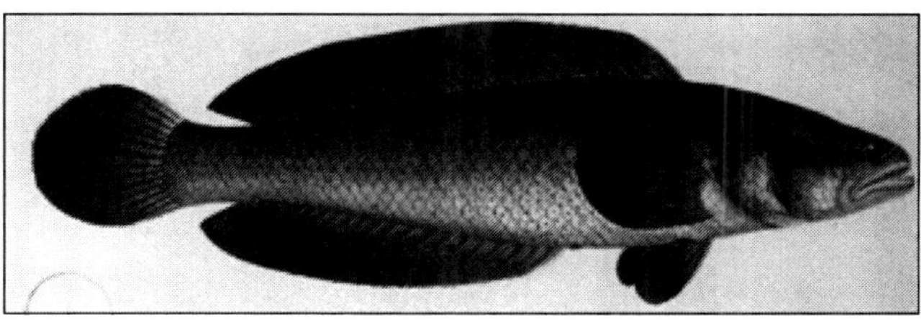

8.9. Surrah, Ophicephalus punctatus,
Shark/Spotted snake-head, 1793

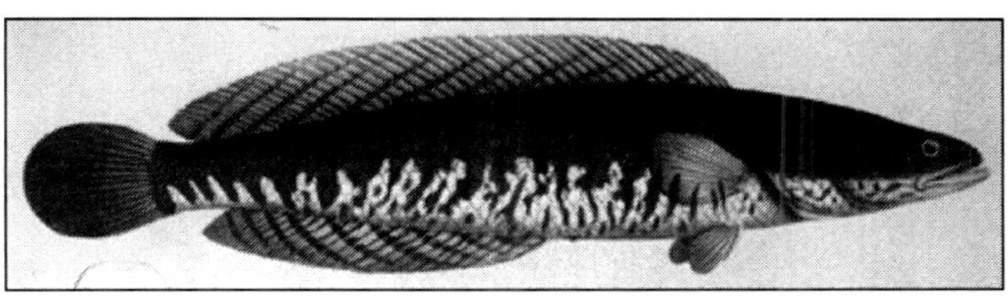

8.10. Viraal, Ophicephalus striatus, Butterfish/Murrel, 1793.

8.11. Kuzhlaththu Kezhluththi, Heteropneustus fossilis, Emerald silver, 1794.

8.12. Kezhluththi, Silurus atheinoides, Indian potsai, 1794.

8.13. Irung kezhluththi, Silurus vittatus, The striped dwarf catfish, 1794.

8.14. Aathu kendai, Esox Malabricus, The malabar brochet, 1794.

8.15. Sozha kendai, Clupea athernoides, The silver stripped herring, 1795.

8.16. Meththai Paarai, Cyprinus fimbriatus, The fringed-carp, 1795.

8.17. Sangu munchi karuvaa/Kandal/Thullu kendai, Cyrinus cirrhosus, The cirrhatedcarp, 1795.

8.18. Allaaththi Karuppan, Cyprinus falcatus, The sickle-carp, 1795.

8.19. Seruppu, Chaetdon maculatus, The maculated chetodon, 1795.

8.20. Allaaththi, Clupea malabricus, The herring of Malabar, 1795.

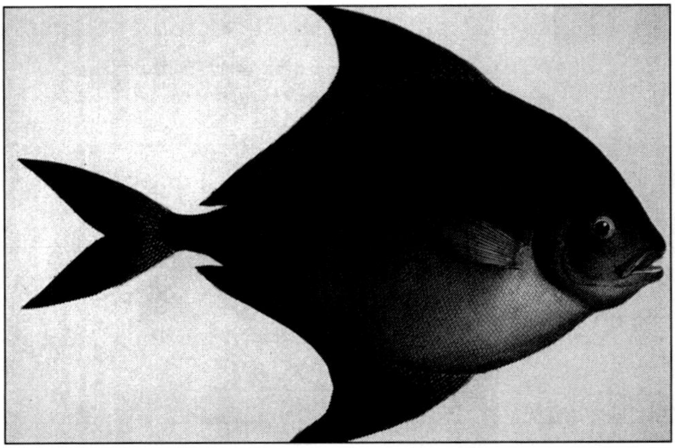

8.21. Vellai Vavvaa, Stromateus Argentes, The silver pampel/White pomfret, 1795

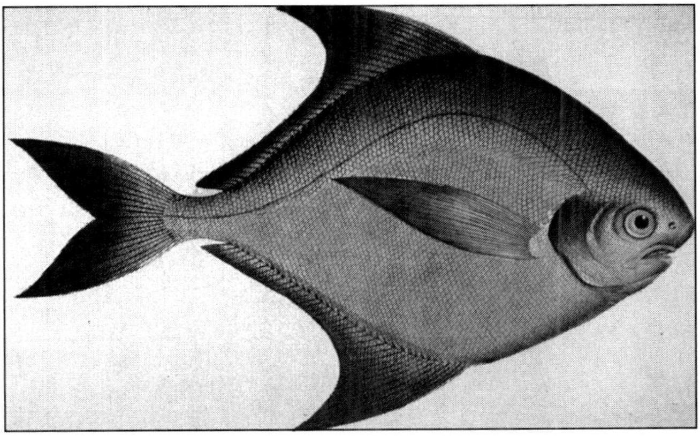

8.22. Karuppu Vavvaa, Stromateus niger, The black pambel/Black pomfret, 1795.

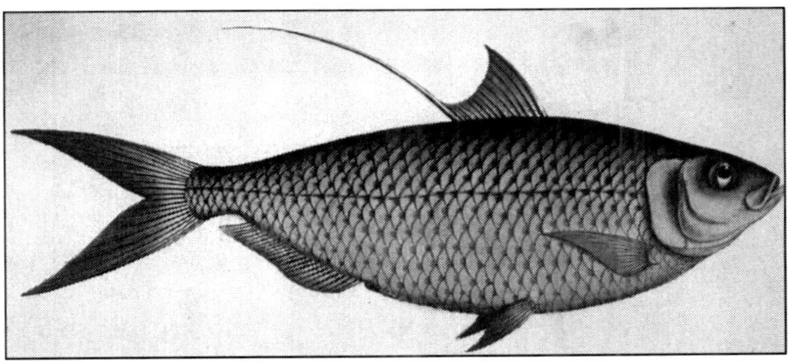

8.23. Katlaa, Clupea trissa, The sprat/ Bengal carp, 1795.

8.24. Suudai, Clupea nasus, The nose herring, 1795.

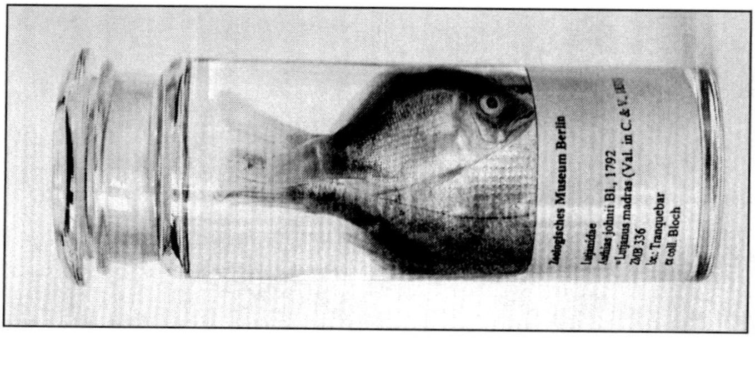

8.25. Vudangkanni, Anthias Johnii named by Bloch in 1792 the fish sent from Tranquebar by Christoph Samuel John.

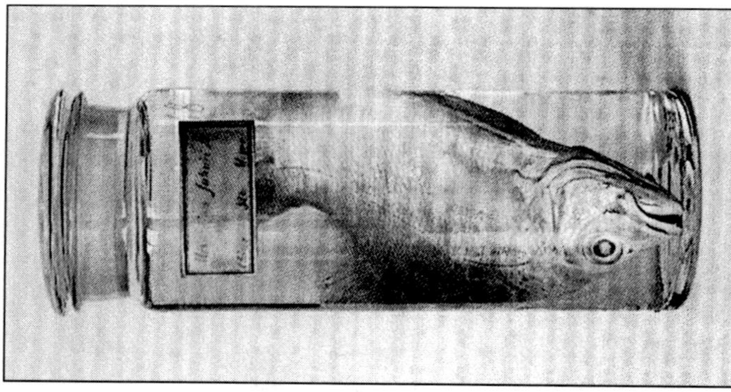

8.26. Koduvaa, Exocoetus mesogastor, The deep water fish, 1795.

8.27. Chenna Avaraa/Sevvizhlai/ Sankara, Mesoprion Johnii, Red snapper/The mulatto, 1787.

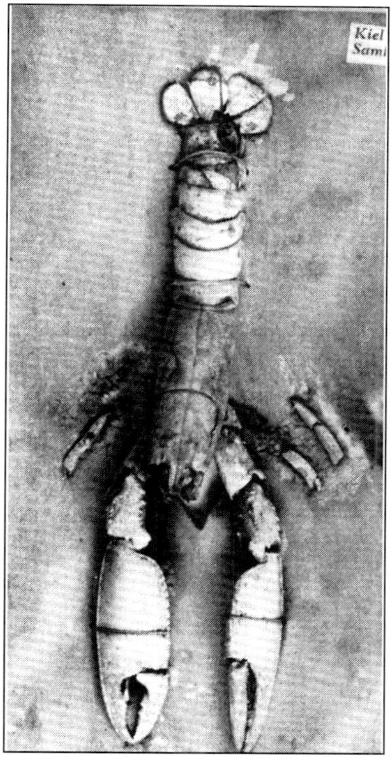

8.28. Madakku Iraa, Astacus the specimen sent by C.S. John from Tranquebar to J.C. Fabricius in Denmark in 1793.

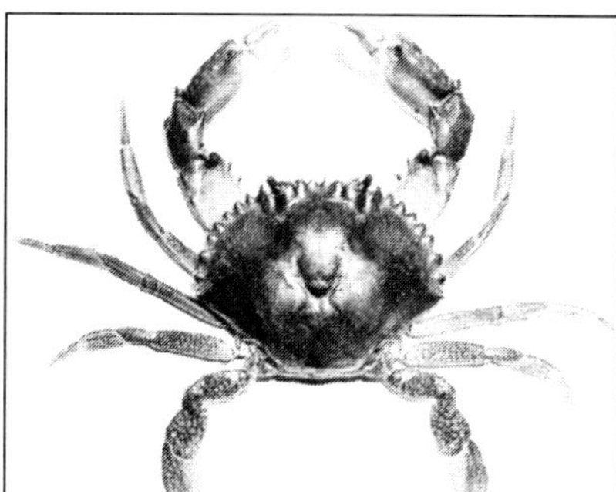

8.29. Paar Nandu, Scylla tranquebarica, the specimen sent by C.S. John from Tranquebar to J.C. Fabricius in Denmark in 1798

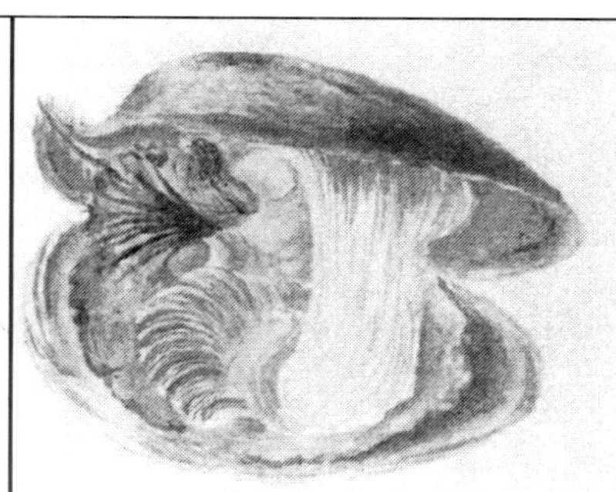

8.30. Muthu Chippi, Pearl-Oyster noticed by Eudelin de Jonville in 1800.

8.31. Chippi/Mattikkal, Oyster noticed by Eudelin de Jonville in 1800.

8.32. Pavazham, Coral reef by noticed by Eudelin de Jonville in 1800.

9

Conclusion

The Dutch, the Dane, the English and the French who arrived on the Tamil coast in the seventeenth century developed a great curiosity strikingly on the fauna. It was initially linked to their commerce very closely and it gradually and greatly resulted into in depth studies. The desire for novelties in Europe had already developed as a stimulus to trade, and the objects of curiosity at that time were treated mostly as luxuries. We find three main methods by which Europe in this period received abundant knowledge of the Tamil coast. It included the extensive information passed on through the secular travel accounts, the missionary activities of the Catholics and Protestants and by the officials and servants of the East India trading companies who added new facts and stimuli to investigators in Europe. This led to the rejuvenation of natural science and Europe came to know of the vast range and diverse kinds of animals, reptiles, birds, insects, snakes and fish found in the Tamil environment. Thereafter identifying the useful, as well as harmful living beings developed, in addition to differentiating and grouping and giving the names to living things in a scientific manner came as an important activity of the newly encountered on the Tamil littoral. The European scholars at that point of time thought it is very necessary to deal with such enormous diversity of life forms and they also wanted to do proper classification.

The curiosity of the New World and the East had increased at a tremendous speed in the age of discoveries along with the circumnavigation of the globe which contributed flow of information and various objects into Europe. The focus thereafter began to shift from how the natural world might inform and reflect the world of men and how men might reflect on and order the natural world. Many living things in Tamil country were found to be rare, new, unknown and some were very imperfectly known to Europeans in the field of general science. Hence it was realized that each would contribute some very interesting supply to the extensive results of enquiry. The Christian missionaries opined that nature was supposed to be a bounty created by god for his creation endowed with the power of knowledge. Christianity was thus known for appropriating nature for man. From the age of renaissance to enlightenment in Europe, curiosity and wonder were the only two most commonly used words and they meant to describe the contemporary responses to new objects particularly those that were brought back from the small pocket of the Tamil coast in the planet earth as the Europeans began to study and acquire the knowledge of fauna.

I

Insects of the Tamil coast attracted the attention of the European investigators. They desired to know the internal anatomy of the insects and found it very complex when compared to that of the larger animals. The interplay between techniques of investigation and representation of insects in the early modern age had been very difficult because insects posed unusual problems because of their diminutive size and esoteric nature. Anatomists had to render figures of the peculiar body parts intelligible and the readers in the beginning had to grapple with images of insects produced that had no correspondence to their own experience. The use of microscope in this early modern age though revealed unexpectedly complex organisms, yet it posed also considerable problems both to technical and interpretive. The invention of a simple microscope by Galileo Galilei (1564-1642) helped to study the compound eye of insects. Marcello Malpighi (1628-1694) another Italian micro-anatomist used a microscope to study the organ tissues of animals.

An interesting and a systematic work titled '*Synopsis Methodica Animalium Quadrupedum et Serpentini Generis*' was published by John Ray (1627-1705) in England in 1693 wherein he classified the animals based on gills, lungs, claws, teeth and other structures. Carl Linnaeus (1707-1778) the naturalist of Sweden in 1758 published his book *Systema Naturae* and first introduced the hierarchic system, both in animal and plant kingdoms and followed four categories namely class, order, genus, species for the animal world. Lamarck (1744-1829) made the first attempt to improve Linnaean system and he published seven volumes of his *Histoire Naturelle des Animaux sans Vertebres* and arranged animals according to evolution. He displayed the groups of animals in the form of a branching tree. With such developments and progress, the Europeans on the Tamil coast began to engage themselves very seriously in the study of fauna by coining zoological/scientific names.

In the course of living and trading in Tamil country besides doing religious activities, the Europeans saw the Tamil cosmos not a safe place (certainly not dangerous) because of its hot climate, many endemic and epidemic diseases with high mortality rate. They learnt that forests of the tropical Tamil land were filled with various kinds of dangerous animals, like wild elephants, rhinoceroses, tigers, snakes, crocodiles and poisonous insects. The fear of danger had made them to engage in the study of zoology and medicine very seriously. The Roman Catholic missionaries however had completely ignored at large the study of fauna as they were not encouraged by the superiors in Europe. But the Protestant missionaries in Tranquebar had combined preaching with pleasure, and without detracting from their devotion to duty and conversion to Christianity, they focused their attention heavily on the study Tamil fauna.

The elephant was a strange and wonderfully multifarious animal to the notice of the Europeans. It became increasingly an object of study and they desired to know the anatomy and render its prodigious qualities. Natural histories and anatomies in Europe at that time had wrestled with the challenge of constructing the elephant as a tangible animal from a mythological beast. Elephant anatomies were therefore made as an attempt to separate empirical natural knowledge from a classical understanding of this animal. The anatomizing of the elephant therefore became more than the dissection and representation of constituent elephant tissues, organs and bones by anatomists.

Europeans wrote of the diversities of the fauna types found at different environmental locations in Tamil country such as coastal plains, valleys, mountains and hills, the woods and forests. Further comparing one set of animal species with another, and determining quantitatively which of those were diverse had been well noted. They made it clear that a set of five species such as a crow, a woodpecker, a pigeon, a parakeet, and a hawk, was more diverse than another set of five species, all of which were bulbuls though the real-life bird communities were found to be more complex.

Scientific names were simply coined by using different types of criteria. What struck me in this investigation was the number of names that have originated from the Indian region and found their way into scientific nomenclature with generic and specific names. We find four main types followed in the process. (a) Birds and animals named by their appearance; in honour of a person, whether an ornithologist or not (such a word being called an 'eponym'); (b) named after the place where a taxon was discovered (known as a 'toponym') based on the native name of a species; (c) based on habitat, behaviour, food or, voice. (d) latinized words from Tamil and used them in scientific nomenclature. It may be mentioned that only much later i.e., in 1842, Strickland had proposed a system of International Code of Zoological Nomenclature. Since then, there has been a gradual acceptance and recognition of the validity of names that were not in Greek or Latin.

Birds found in Tamil country were named as Coromandel after the coast. We find coromanda / coromandelianus / coromandelica / coromandelicus /and coromandus had been used by the Europeans:

1. *Anas coromandelianus*, Gmelin, 1789, *Nettapus coromandelianus*
2. *Tetrao coromandelicus*, Gmelin, 1789, *Coturnix coromandelica*
3. *Charadrius coromandelicus*, Gmelin, 1789, *Cursorius coromandelicus*
4. *Strix coromanda*, Latham, 1790, *Bubo coromandus*
5. *Alcedo coromanda*, Latham, 1790, *Alcyon coromanda*

The study of natural history had begun on the Tamil coast with its bird species and watching by Edward Buckley the English company surgeon who lit the flame from his arrival at Fort St. George in Madras. Birds came to be named since 1766 by the Europeans after places where the species were found till 1847.

1. Madras: *Zosterops maderaspatanus*, Linnaeus, 1766; *Motacilla maderaspatensis*, Gmelin, 1789
2. Pondicherry: *Muscicapa pondiceriana*, Gmelin, 1789; *Tephrodornis pondicerianus*, Gmelin, 1789
3. *Gingee*: *Turdus ginginianus*, Latham, 1790; *Acridotheres ginginianus*, Latham, 1790
4. Tranquebar: *Columba tranquebarica*, Hermann, 1804; *Streptopelia tranquebarica*, Hermann, 1804
5. Nilgiris: *Reocincla neilgherriensis*, Blyth, 1847; *Zoothera dauma neilgherriensis*, Blyth, 1847 Various types of fish also came to be named by the Europeans after places such as Madras and Nilgiris where the species were found.

Esomus (Nuria) madraspatensis
Gobius madraspatensis
Pricanthus madraspatensis
Paradanio neilgherriensis
Glyptosternum madraspatanum
Priacanthichthys madraspatensis
Danio neilgherriensis
Rasbora neilgherriensis

The varieties of Fish noticed by T.C. Jerdon and Walter Elliot in Tamil country were named after them because they introduced and identified the new and rare fish varieties.

Amblypharyngodon jerdoni	Barbus jerdoni
Barbodes jerdoni	Hrachyhramma jerdonii
Brotula jerdoni	Garra jerdoni
Hara jerdoni	Mugil jerdoni
Pomacentrus jerdoni	Apogen ellioti
Balistes ellioti	Carcharias ellioti
Eleotris ellioti	

The Tamil coast-based European naturalists had decided to give names by themselves. This shows their level of confidence and knowledge. What they lacked by way of access to current scholarship and publications of Europe was more than made up by the novelty of the material in their own hands. The East India Companies had not provided any stimulation to its servants by showing an active interest in zoology. Most of the early initiatives were found to be private in nature. With the large scale exploration of the fauna on the Tamil coast, Europe's cabinets and menageries came to be filled up with curiosities.

II

Zoological illustrations and the development of natural history art in Tamil country and Europe in the early modern age had been studied in detail. The art of Tamil country in the ancient and medieval times was chiefly directed by the Hindu, Jain and Buddhist religious beliefs. It was also influenced by the thoughts of the elite, rich connoisseurs and rulers of the Tamil kingdoms. However, with the advent of the Portuguese in India the Indian artists were asked to make paintings on the themes that appealed to a European eye. We find 141 water colours prepared (dated between 1533 and 1546) and the illustrations depict customs and costumes of the Indians. This album is preserved now in the Biblioteca Casanatense, Roma. Paintings had continued to be prepared in Tamil country during the early eighteenth century. We find 78 paintings that depict Hindu Gods and Goddesses, the religious ceremonies and festivals of the natives besides the social groups particularly men and women of the various castes. These were made by an Indian artist (between 1685 and 1705) for Niccolao Manucci (1639-1717) the Italian traveller in Madras who wanted illustrations for his book 'Storia do Mogor'. These paintings are preserved at Bibliothèque Nationale, Paris and also in Biblioteca Nazionale Marciana, Venice. The illustrations have certain characteristics of Golconda paintings and that of Europe with mixed style. They were executed on European paper in water colour in shades of grey, brown, red and dull green.[1]

European taste and curiosity on the fauna of Tamil country when developed in due course of time, we find Europeans were collecting paintings made by native artists and commissioning works from them. These drawings, paintings, sketches and engravings became important for printing which had become a new form of natural history knowledge in the age of European commercial expansion. Scholars have not paid adequate attention to this and there is a curious gap in the existing historiography of art which straight away begins with British. It had been stated that British were extensively interested in the natural history drawings and by emphasizing emphasis particularly on Tilly Kettle (1735-1786) who came to Madras in 1769. It is said that he initiated the British art movement receiving patronage from the Arcot palace in Madras. Mildred Archer in her writings thus had overstated that artists had adopted British techniques and she flatters also the British taste by justifying the British's domination of India.[2] She has failed to take note of the links between natural history drawings and the enlightenment project of systematizing knowledge that was going on at that period of time.

This book had therefore presented the collection of data especially on the zoological drawings, sketches, paintings and illustrations prepared then which had been now scattered in the various repositories all over Europe. We find these pictures, each capturing a certain need or function, of the Europeans engaged in the study of fauna in Tamil country at that time. Two main types of art had developed on the Tamil coast while some were prepared by the native Tamil and Telugu artists while other paintings done by the European artists. Thanjavur became an important centre of art and the *muchis* (painters/artists) produced paintings for Europeans. Though the style and techniques were predominantly Indian in the beginning but as British power increased, European style had begun to influence the paintings. Serfoji, the ruler of Thanjavur himself had assisted in the spread of European influence. He engaged Danish tutors from whom he learnt to draw in the European manner.[3] Serfoji himself had used to present these sets of paintings made under his supervision to his guests and British residents. Shivaji (1832-53), the son of serfoji had also continued this practice.[4]

Tamil country's growing contact with Europe enabled the establishment and growth of natural history art in the urban centres like Madras, Tranquebar, and Thanjavur which marked to some extent the beginnings of modern art in Tamil country. It indicates a subtle change in the cultural environment; and the emergence of new trends in taste and patronage, new attitudes towards art training and new categories of art practice. Europeans painted animals, reptiles, insects, birds, snakes and fish in the realistic style and made life like paintings. Some natives like Krishna Rao from Nellore made drawings, lithographs and engravings of the local fauna and scene for printing in Madras. Working with the Europeans some of the artists got introduced to their techniques. Printing presses that appeared in Madras and Europe started producing illustrated books of Tamil fauna to meet the demands of the zoological publications.

Pictures of the birds of the Tamil coast were depicted by the natives and Europeans in the traditional way, from the side perched on a branch or stump of a tree. There are also drawings in which they were portrayed in flight or in a posture signifying themselves that the animal was taken by surprise in its natural situation. The virtuosity of these drawings, the component handling of the textures of feathers or their careful colouring had shown how talented the Tamil artists were. We are unable to know how many Tamil artists were employed by the Europeans at various intervals including the first set of the pictures of birds done for Edward Buckley in Madras. It is to be mentioned that most of the studies were research oriented and also kept in mind for the future publications.

Drawings at that time had become an easy means of retaining a visual recollection of animals from the distant destination of Tamil littoral. In Tamil country drawings were mostly drawn from living animals, not as so many others in Europe that were drawn from museum specimens only. Several of the collection of animals sent became part of the so called Wunderkammer or Kunstkammer (Chamber of wonders or chambers of art). The marine fauna of Tuticorin and Rameswaram, fish types from Coimbatore, Salem, Erode from the rivers of Cauvery and Bhavani, fresh water fish found in the inland ponds and tanks at various places, besides the avifauna of Madras, Tranquebar, Pondicherry, Coimbatore, Conoor, Nilgiris, Tiurchirapalli, Madurai and Travancore contributed greatly to an improvement in knowledge in Europe. We find mounted animals and bottled fish sent to Germany and Denmark. The Europeans who studied live models of animals also used the dead snake skins as models for their drawing.

A new understanding of the natural world had come to be reconstructed at the knowledge production level in Europe. New ideas which were assimilated and disseminated in animal sciences found way into the printed books. Displaying of strange animals in coffee houses and zoological gardens had become a way public manifestation and it was in reality done with a purpose to dominate the world. On the Tamil coast, missionaries took interest in educating the Tamils on zoology. We find a text book printed in Tamil titled *Urthiri vilangiyal* (domestic animals) at Nagercoil in 1836. Thus we find a move from a largely amateur natural history to a professionalized science of zoology propagation.

The active search and research conducted around the fauna of the Tamil world became very rich in Europe with a large number of endemic species and genera. The study of natural science also included logic and reason, inference and derivation. Herschel in Europe had pondered on what he called the 'mystery of mysteries', the replacement of extinct species by others' and he speculated that 'the origination of fresh species' could it ever become under the cognizanic world found to be a natural contradistinction to a miraculous process. Charles Darwin thereafter chose Herschel's phrase the origination of fresh species as he had been inspired. In 1859 Darwin published his famous work titled 'Origin of Species' and the new evolutionary concept of his had an immediate acceptance among biologists. Due to the influence of evolutionary ideas, taxonomy was studied and the taxonomists were encouraged to learn that evolution theory of Darwin gave meaning to their classifying activities. A large number of species were discovered and described. Darwin's great achievement was to discover how new species can arise naturally without miraculous creation. He discovered how evolution happens. Darwin at the end of his book said 'endless forms most beautiful and most wonderful have been, and are being evolved'.[5] Thus Darwinism was based on observation of life around and its scientific analysis based on logic and reason besides cause and effects later came to be introduced in Tamil country from Europe.

III

The existing literature of science and empire had shown interest in European knowledge production outside of Europe and emphasized the importance of global networks to scientific practice.[6] A few writers have developed Euro-centric view and tendency to take the perspective of Europe looking out to the rest of the globe, often through the centre-periphery model of empire. Some writings have pointed out the limitations of such an approach, and they had called for within the conceptual framework of 'nodes of empire' where manifold imperial activities had intersected.[7] As these works had ignored to pay attention to the view from local colonial contexts, we are unable to properly understand the exact and true mechanisms of empire. Writers have also introduced the concept of the contact zone laying emphasis on the interactive, improvisational dimensions of cross-cultural exchange within a colonial space, without simultaneously diminishing the often brutal realities of conquest and domination. Kapil Raj had demonstrated how scientific knowledge about the natural world was forged in the crucible of the 'contact zone' of colonial cities and can therefore be seen as the product of an encounter between European and local knowledge systems. Challenging the diffusionist model of scientific knowledge, he adopted the term contact zone from Mary Louise Pratt and persuasively showed that vernacular knowledge systems and local knowledge-producing methodologies in South Asia circulated alongside European approaches.[8]

Global historians opine that one of the greatest intellectual challenges by maritime historians is to simultaneously address the dynamics that integrated maritime regions without losing sight of either local experiences or of the global interactions that sometimes conditioned the experiences of the regions themselves. The seas and oceans have enormous potential as frameworks to analyze complex historical processes, and to bringing into focus cultural, biological, intellectual, and commercial exchanges between the societies.[9] Knowledge in transit has been termed by James Secord which is a narrative framework that understands science as a form of communication characterized by movement, translation and dissemination. Here texts, images and objects are the traces of acts of communication with receivers, producers and modes of convention that erase the distinctions between making and communicating knowledge. Linnaean binomial classification in this period had though become increasingly dominant it was not the only classificatory method for ordering nature. Likewise what was appropriate in constituting valid knowledge about a species like the elephant was disputed and changed over the course of the long eighteenth century. Knowledge from colonized lands were appropriated and reinvented, but they did not disappear powerless in the face of conquest, and neither were they isolated to colonial territories. James Secord therefore urges the importance of applying to our historical practice the well-established theoretical insight that there is no genuine separation between the making and the communication of knowledge. Questions of how knowledge travelled, to whom it was available, and how agreement was achieved are fundamental to the making of knowledge, and in this sense the process of knowledge making involves communication, rather than merely being followed by it.[10]

We have established through this book that Europeans in Tamil country have gathered and transmitted much of the information that they did with the help of Tamils and the Telugu migrants and that the knowledge they produced was thus often jointly-produced or hybridised. However, the specific nature of these interactions and especially the mechanisms of this process of hybridisation are unclear from the sources and so it has been less well understood. However, the hybridisation of natural knowledge produced at Madras, Pondicherry, Tranquebar etc., is very significant because the local Tamil information was made part of the European knowledge tradition and they came to understand the natural world through applying the experimental natural philosophy. In practice, selectively recorded information from Tamil coast reached Europe and thereafter by discarding or diminishing the local Tamil traditions and the explanations improvements were made in due course of time.

The dynamic of knowledge production relates to the changing ways in which Europeans understood the natural world within the context of natural science. There was no such thing as the scientific revolution in Europe. European naturalists in Tamil country conducted extensive travels and explored the fauna through field experience. They gathered specimens and also adopted a wide variety of practices such as reading, note-taking, compilation besides observation and contributed for understanding the world of natural history from local to global. However, many individuals in Europe like Sir Hans Sloane, James Petiver and Carl Linnaeus played multiple roles such as orchestrators, integrators by attracting their well-wishers, students and disciples whom they redeployed throughout the Tamil country and received letters and zoological specimens. All the correspondences were assembled, filed and cross-checked. Thus the bulk of natural history data called the stuff of science including the specimens, observations, data, and information of many kinds helped for trans-disciplinary approach to unlock global natural history which became the then need of the hour. The amount of new information gathered from the Tamil coast and communicated to Europe between 1639 and 1857 was staggering, and it is very important to trace the transfer of natural history knowledge now preserved in museum collections.

Tamil coast has been mainly represented by travellers, missionaries, East India Company officials, servants and artists. They helped to grow European knowledge of the wider world in myriad ways but chiefly in exoticist, magisterial and curatorial the three ways in the western writings.[11] Ronald Inden has categorized the western writings as possessing descriptive and commentative aspects which claim to represent the thought and acts of the Indians to the reader.[12] Writings in the history of modern science in India had largely been dominated by the view that scientific practice in late eighteenth and early nineteenth century was wholly shaped by the mercantilist motivations of the East India Companies. Such a view fails to acknowledge the percolation of 'enlightenment' ideas in India made possible through a generation of colonial naturalists and other officials who saw much value in the practice of disinterested science even when compelled to achieve mercantilist goals. The rulers of Tamil country like Serfoji II, the

Raja of Thanjavur came to be aware of the intellectual developments in Europe by his links to missionary and colonial networks. Inspired by the enlightenment's idea of progress, he generated a revolutionary intellectual ferment in response to colonial or the non-western Tamil context.

It has been argued that the animal sciences and its various branches in this period underwent dramatic changes particularly from the emergence of new empirically oriented and data-intensive disciplines to the multiplication of science societies and organizations in Europe. The expansion of professionalization to the invention of new methodologies had developed both in Europe and Tamil country. This puts an end to talking about centers and peripheries but focuses instead on the systems of circulation. It may be firmly concluded that the study of natural history became typically the colonial one way traffic in transmission, translation of knowledge and the improvement and transformation of the world. Missionaries and their scientific achievements besides the officers of the East India Companies and their study of animals and birds were indefatigable in their researches in collection, figuring and describing these interesting fauna of Tamil country. Their works and collections thus provide the unshakable foundation for modern study of zoology.

Notes

1. Mildred Archer, 'Company Painting in South India: The Early Collections of Niccolao Manucci', in *Apollo*, 1970, pp. 104-113; See also, Mildred Archer, *Company Paintings: Indian Paintings of the British Period*, London, 1992, pp, 12-15.
2. Mildred Archer and W. C. Archer, *Indian Paintings for the British, 1770-1880*, Oxford, 1955; Mildred Archer, *Natural History Drawings in the India Office Library*, London, 1962.
3. Mildred Archer, *Company Paintings: Indian Paintings of the British Period*, p. 44.
4. Mildred Archer, *Company Drawings in the India Office Library*, London, 1972, p. 23. Shivaji had interest in architecture and he became a founder member of the Royal Institute of British Architects in 1836. He presented the Institute ten drawings of his palace and of the local temples, which were executed in a mixed Indian-British style.
5. Charles Darwin, *The Origin of Species by Means of Natural Selection*, First edition, 1859, rep., Penguin, 1968.
6. James Delbourgo and Nicholas Dew, eds., *Science and Empire in the Atlantic World*, New York, 2008.
7. Simon Schaffer et al., eds., *The Brokered World: Go-Betweens and Global Intelligence, 1770-1820*, Sagamore Beach, 2009.
8. Marie Louis Pratt, *Imperial Eyes: Studies in Travel Writing and Transculturation*, London, 1992, pp. 1-12; Kapil Raj, *Relocating Modern Science: Circulation*

and the Construction of Scientific Knowledge in South Asia and Europe, 17th-19th Centuries, Delhi, 2006.

9. Jerry H. Bentley, 'Sea and Ocean Basins as Frameworks of Historical Analysis', *The Geographical Review*, vol. 89, no. 2, 1999, p. 222.
10. James A. Secord, 'Knowledge in Transit', *Isis*, 95, 2004, pp. 654–672.
11. Amartya Sen, 'Indian Traditions and the Western Imagination', *Daedalus*, vol. 126. no. 2, Spring 1997, pp. 1-26.
12. Ronald Inden, *Imagining India*, Oxford, 1990, p. 38.

Appendices

Appendix 1

A Report in Latin on 27 Birds Found in the Region of Fort St George, Madras, by Edward Buckley, 1701-10

Mantissam Hanc Avium Maderaspatanarum Addidit peritissimus Naturalis Historiae Cultor D. Jacobus Petiverus, S.R.S. Quarum Descriptiones ex Iconibus elegantissime pictis, Sibi a D. Edvardo Buckley, Ab Arce Maderaspatana (vulgo Fort St George) missis, desumptae sunt.

1. Himantopus Maderaspatanus e nigro albente cruribus rubris; Nobis. An Himantopus Plinii lib 10. cap. 47? The red legged Crane. Fig. 3. Rostrum longum, gracile, nigrum. Dorsum, Alae (quae ultra caudam extenduntur) Vertex, Cervicis pennae (usque ad Scapulas crispatae) eodem colore: inde usque ad caudae finem albo. Femora nuda; Crura longissima, gracilia; Digiti tres (Postico enim caret) membranulis connexi, rubro. Ungues acuti, adnuci, nigro. Cum Aldrovandi descriptione bene convenit.
2. Gallinago Maderaspatana Perdicis colore. The Patridge-Snipe. Fig. 2. Coloribus variis, maculisque elegantibus undique ornatur. Venter & Pectus (quod linea lata transversa nigra dividit) albescunt. Caput, Tempora, & margo Alarum superior maculis nigrofufcis asperguntur. Remiges alarum, & Cauda luteo, griseo, nigroque eleganter interstinguuntur, Rostrum longum (apice craissiusculo) rufescit. Digitus posticus (ungue adunco) longitudine anteriorem aequat.
3. Motacilk Mader. nigro alboque mixta, The Black and White Wagtail. Fig.3.
4. Motacila Mader. ex albo cinerea, cauda forcipata, The forked Wagtail. Fig. 6. Hunc & praecedentem Marem efle & Fisminam exiftimo, Utrique (prsefertim huic) cauda forcipata, quae ex 4 tantiim pennis constare viderur, exterioribus albis, mediis nigris.

5. Avis Maderas major, Novaculae facie, Coddel Cauka, sive Summoodra Cauky Malabaricis. The Sea Crow, Fig. 5. Nigrescunt Verrex & Alae, quarum extremitates longissimae, tenues, recurvae. Collum, Pectus, Venter albicant, lineolis subfuscis striata. Rupectus Crura brevia, Digiti (usque ad medium membranulis intercedentibus juncti) & magna pars Rostri. Maxilla superior inferiore multo brevior, & in eandem ut novacula in Manubrium suum incidit. Hujusmodi Rostrum e Carolina olim accepi, cujus Icon in Gazophi. Nat. & Art. Tab. 76. Fig. 2. exhibetur.
6. Crex Indica ex albo cinerea, nigroque mixta, Caunangoly, Malabarensibus: Bollu Cory, Gentilibus: The Maderas Rail-Hen. Fig. 4. Capite, Corporis magnitudine & figura, Anati similis: Rostrum autem habetacutum, teres, longiusculum; Pectus album, maculislunulatis nigrusculis respersum; Pennas alarum cinereas, marginibus nigris: Caudam brevissimam; Digitos & Ungues (aduncos) longos.
7. Pica Maderaspatanus. fulva alis pene nigris, Vanga Pandooe ; Gentil, The Buff-Jay. Fig. 9. Magnitudo circa Picae glandariae nostratis. Caudae superior pars, nigra, apice excepto, qui flavus: pars inferior, alba fiavo mixta. Ductus niger obliquus oculos cingit. Alae nigrae, apicibus, & areola circa mediam, flavis, Caetera fulva, lineolis ruffo-fuscis interstincta.
8. Pica Madraspatana flavicans. Vanga Pandooe Pedda; Gent. The Yelloe-Jay. Fig. 8. A praecedente differt colore dilutiore flavo: Pectore usque ad anum lineolis obliquis sinuosis (pellium Armenianarum instar) insignito; Alis integris, & Macula ovali Oculos ambiente, nigricantibus: Dorso & Gutture flavo.
9. Pica Madraspatana. Sturni ad instar maculata. Cundoe Vanga Pundooe; Gent. The Motled-Jay: Fig. 7, a praecedente differ Pectore & Dorso miscelli coloris; Capite & Cauda in hac nigrescente. quae in illa flavo.
10. Pica Maderaspatana. virescens cauda tricuspide, Passary Caye. Gent. The Green-Jay. Fig. 10. Magna exparte viridis; Dorso & cauda intensius Cauda tricuspis notabilis, apicibus nigricantibus, cuspide media longissima.
11. Pica Maderaspatana. mimma e caeruleo nigrescens. Peach Caye; Gent. The small blue jay. Fig. 11. Caput & Alae coeruleo intensiore quam Cauda. Caetera nigra aut cinerea; Cruribus & Rostro exceptis, quae rufescunt.
12. Pica Indica vulgaris: Ponnunky pitta; Gent. Ponnandutty; Maderaspatanensibus : The Madras Jay. Fig. 10. Nostrati Picae

glandariae affinis est. Linea arcuata albida supra oculos. Alarum regetes virescunt Scapis flavescentibus: juxta basin alarum macula caerulea: Remiges & Cauda nigrescunt: Uropygium coeruleo maculatur: inter femora usque ad caudam rubescit.

13. Manticodiata cristata ex albo nigroque variata: Tella yeaco narry; Gent. The Pied Bird of Paradise. Fig. 13. Hanc elegantissimam rariisimamque avem ejusdem speciei esse credimus, ac ea quam irr Hollandia inter Hermanniana, Anno 1711. pro Clariss. Sloanio emi. In D. Hermanni catalogo, p 13. No. 184. vocatur, Avicula Paradisaea Zeylanica barbata ex albo & nigro variegata, cauda 2 longissmis pennis Constructa: Walluhora, Zeylanensibus, i. e. Gossypium furata: Het Catoen Diefje ; Belgis. Rostrum, Crista, & totum Caput nigra. Castera alba, lineis arcuatis, sive lunulatis respersa. Cauda insignis, pennis 2 longissimis Apud Hollandos in magno pretio habetur, & inter rarissima numeratur. Nec quicquam ex Clariss. Hermanni Musaeo refertissimo pluris vendebatur.

14. Columba Maderaspatana. cauda 3 pennis latis conflate. The Broad-tailed Maderas Dove. Fig. 14. Pars maxima coloribus albescit. At alarum bases colore fulphureo, maculis rufescentibus fimbriatae extremitates Remigum nigrae. In Uropygio 3 pennae miniaceae acutae. Rostrum & Crura lutea. Huic proprium & peculiare, Cauda tribus rantum pennis longis latis, albis, nigro undulatis, scapis rubris, constructa ; quarum extrimae breviores, seta longa nigra inter fingulam pennam interposita.

15. Columha Maderaspatana. variis coloribus eleganter depicta. The Parrot-Dove. Fig 15. Variis coloribus perfunditur: Pectus sanguineo flavi umbra; Caput & Venter obscure viride pallescente; Alae fusco viride tincto; marginibus viride & luteo undulatis: Remigum apices, & pors Caudae superior nigro; inferior rufescente. Femora lanugine obducuntur. Crura brevissima, crassa, rufescentia. Pedes longi ejusdem coloris. Rostrum breve, crassum, prope apicem torosum.

16. Columba Maderaspatana. e rubro alboque mixta: The red jay-dove. Fig.16. Temporibus, Pectore & Ventre albis; Rostro & Vertice rubris, lineis duabus ejusdem coloris ; una colium cingente, altera pectus & ventrem dividente. Bases alarum cancellatae, ut in Pica glandaria, tantum rubro: Caeterae Alarum pennae albae, marginibus nigrescentibus, Remigibus exceptis, rubris albo tinctis. Cauda eodem colore, apice & lineis latis transversis rubris.

17. Columba Maderaspatana. minor, ex albo rufescens: The small red pied dove. Fig.17. Buccae, Pectus, Venter, Femora alba: Alae, Cauda,

Vertex, subrubra. Supra Oculos linea lata nigra: eodem colore pedes, Crura longa, nuda, gracilia.

18. Avis Maderaspatana. e cinereo-rubente, Madras Ring-Dove. Fig.8. Woorulla Ponnunky; Gent. Magnitudine Turdurm aequare viderur; cinereo colorc perfunditur, praesertim capite, collo, dorso, alis, & portiuncula caudae: pectore autem, ventre, & majore caudae parte, incarnato colore: vertice, alarum apicibus, & linea transversa sub maxilla inferiore, nigro; rostri apice flavescente.
19. Saulary masculina Maderaspatana. ex albo nigroque mixtus. The Cock Saulary. Fig 19. Magnitudo Sturni. Pectus, venter, femora, pars caudae inferior, & areola in alis albissima; caetera nigricantia.
20. Saulary femina Maderaspatana. fusco alboque varia, The Hen Saulary. Fig. 20. A Mare distinguitur cauda acuminata, & colore, qui in hac fuscus, ubi in illo niger.
21. Sanguillo Maderaspatana. capite caudaque nigris. Fig.20. Gulla Cavalla; Gent. Magnitudo picae variae. Vertex elatus, Rostrum, collum, & cauda, nigerrima. Alae, scapulae dorsum, & uropygium, rubra. Venter & semora alba Hujus avis nota characteritica est Vertex acuminatus, & cauda 3 pennis latis, in acumen definentibus, constructa; media penna ultra extimas protenditur, & Tragulae formam caudae tribuit.
22. Tooracca Bigaly Maderaspatana. e rubro alboque mistis, capite acuminato nigro, The red Tooracca, with a black head. Fig. 22. Huic Avium generi nota characteristic setae quaedam tenues in cervice. Multae sunt earum Specics, quae coloribus praecipue inter se distinguuntur. Huic pectus, venter, femora, & inferior pars caudae, alba: Scapulae, dorsum, alae, caudae pars superior, & anus, rubra. Haec & sequentes a Sanguillo differunt, Setis in cervice, & quod Sanguillo dimidio minores fint.
23. Tooracca Maderaspatana. e rubro alboque partitis. The Red and White Tooracca. Praecedenti similis, capite excepto, huic ruso, iili nigro.
24. Tooracca Maderaspatana. albida, ano rubente. The whitish Tooracca. A praecedente differt colore, huic cinereo albo, ubi illi rubro.
25. Tooracca Maderaspatana. nigrescens. The black tooracca. Fig. 23. Totum sere corpus nigrum apice caudae excepto, albo. In hac notatu dignum, Podicem, seu potius pennulas caudam sustinentes, nigricare, in omnibus aliis rubere.
26. Tooracca Maderaspatana. e nigro alblcans. The Magpy Tooracca. Pectus (nigris lunulis conspersum) venter & caudae pars inferior, alba, Pectoris colore, & ani rubicundia a praecedente differt.

27. Tooracca Maderaspatana. Auribus & macula in basi alarum sanguineis. The Magpy-Tooracca, with red spots. Fig. 24. A praecedente differt maculis sanguineis juxta aures, & alarum bases.

    Source: Joannis Raii, *Synopsis Methodica Avium & Piscium, opus posthumum quod vivus recensuit & perfecit ipse insignissimus Author: in quo multas species in ipsius ornithologia & Ichthyologia desideratas adjecit: Methodumque suam Piscium Naturae magis convenientem reddidit cum appendice & Iconibus*, Londini, Impenis Gulielmi Innys, ad Insignia principis in coementerio D. Pauli, MDCCXIII, pp. 193-198.

Appendix 2

The Description in German on the Types of Fish Received from Tranquebar by Marcus Elieser Bloch in Germany in 1793

1. *Scomber Rottleri, Die Rottlersche Makrele*

Die hervorstehende Unterkinnlade, und die zehn kleine Flossen, die sowohl Die Rottlersche Makrele. Bauchflosse sechs, über als unter dem Schwanze sitzen, machen die Kennzeichen dieses Fisches aus. In der Kiemenhaut zählt man fünf, in der Brustflosse funfzehn, in der ersten Afterflosse zwey, in der zweiten acht, in der Schwanzflosse zwanzig, in der ersten Rückenflosse ieben, und in der zweiten acht Strahlen. Der Körper ist gestreckt, der Kopf zusammen gedrückt und schuppenlos; die Kinnladen sind nur mit kleinen, spitzigen Zähnen bewaffnet; die Zunge ist platt, und der Gaumen vorn rauh. Die Lippenknochen sind breit; die Nasen löcher einfach; die Augen haben einen schwarzen Stern und einen silberfarbenen Ring. Die Kiemendeckel sind glatt; die Kiemenöffnung ist weit, und die Kiemenhaut bedeckt. Am Rumpfe sieht man kleine weiche Schuppen, und am Bauche und Rücken eine Furche zur Aufnahme der Flossen. Die Seiten linie bildet bey ihrem Anfange einen Bogen, und geht darauf in einer geraden Linie mitten über den Körper weg. Dieser Theil ist mit Schildern besetzt, welche mit einem nach unten zu gebogenen Haken versehen sind. Der erste Strahl in der Bauch-und Afterflosse und die sämmtlichen in der ersten Rücken flosse find hart, die übrigen aber weich. Die Seiten und der Kopf sind silberfarben, der Rücken grau, die Bru t-und Bauchflossen ind roth, und die übrigen Flossen grau. Von der nehmlichen Farbe sind auch die am Schwanze befindlichen zwanzig Bü chelflossen. Auf Malaisch heisst er Warangada Borei, auf Deutsch die Rottlersche Makrele, und Französisch Le Rottler.

2. *Karutua Kattolei, Iohnius Carcutta*

Man erkennt diesen Fisch an dem hervorstehenden Oberkiefer. In der Kiemenhaut zählt man fünf, in der Brustflosse sechszehn, in der Der Bauchflosse sechs, in der Afterflosse neun, in der Schwanzflosse achtzehn, und Karutt in der Rückenflosse vierzig Strahlen. Der Kopf iß abgerundet, zusammen gedrückt, und ganz mit Schuppen bedeckt. Die Kinnladen sind mit mehreren Reihen kleiner dünnen und spitzen Zähnen be etzt. Der Gaumen ist rauh, die Nasenlöcher sind doppelt; die Augen stehen nahe am Scheitel und haben einen schwarzen Stern, den ein orange farbener Ring umgiebt. Der vordere Kienendeckel ist schmahl, der hintere breit, die Kiemenöffnung weit, und die Kiemenhaut bedeckt. Der Rumpf ist zu ammen gedrückt; der Rücken rund, die Se tenlinie breit, gerade, und dem Rücken nahe. Der After ist der Schwanzflosse näher als dem Kope. In der Rückenflosse sind eilf, in der Bauchflosse einer, und in der Afterflosse zwey harte Strahlen vorhanden. Die weichen Strahlen sind vierzweigg. Der Rücken und die Seiten sind stahlblau, der Bauch und die Seitenlinie gelb, die Rücken-und Schwanzflosse bläulich und die übrigen braunroth. Auf Malaisch heisst dieser Fisch Karutua Kattolei.

3. *Anei Katuli, Johnius aneus*

Dieser Fisch unterscheidet sich von dem vorhergehenden durch den hervor ftehenden Unterkiefer. In der Kiemenbaut zählt man fünf, in der Brustflosse vierzehn, in der Bauchflosse sechs, in der Afterflosse neun, in der Schwanzflosse achtzehn, und in der Rückenflosse vier und dreissig Strahlen. Der Kopf ist zusammen gedrückt, ganz schuppig, und nur wenig abschüs fig. Die Mundöffnung ist weit; die Kinnladen sind mit kleinen dünnen und spitzen Zähnen versehen; die Lippenknochen sind schmahl; die Nasenlöcher doppelt, und dicht an den Augen befindlich. Diese sind gross, stehen nahe am Scheitel, und haben einen orangefarbenen Ring, der einen schwarzen Stern einschliesst. Der vordere Kiemendeckel ist schmahl, der hintere breit; die Kie menöffnung weit, und die Kiemenhaut bedeckt. Der Rumpf ist gestreckt; die Seitenlinie gerade, in der Nähe des Rückens, und der After dem Schwanze näher als dem Kopfe. Die Rückenflosse ist aus neun einfachen harten, und aus vier und zwanzig weichen und vierzweigigen Strahlen zusammen gesetzt. In der Afterflosse sind zwey von ersterer, und sieben von letzterer Art vor handen. Die Bauchflosse hat nur einen steifen Strahl, alle übrigen find weich und zweimal getheilt. Der Rücken ist schwärzlich, die Seiten ind weiss, die Brust-und Bauchflossen braunroth, der vordere Theil der

Rückenflosse ist schwärzlich, die übrigen Flossen sind roth, und blau eingefaßt. Auch dieser Fisch ist in den malabarischen Gewässern einheimisch. Auf Malasch heißt er Anei Katuli.

4. ***Ophicephalus punctatus***

Die schwarzen Punkte, die man fast am ganzen Körper wahrnimmt, dienen I zum Merkmal dieses Fisches. Der In der Kiemenhaut zählt man fünf, in der Brustflosse sechszehn, in der P° Schlangen Bauchflosse sechs, in der Afterflosse zwey und zwanzig, in der Schwanzflosse kop vierzehn, und in der Rückenflosse ein und dreissig Strahlen. Der Kopf ist flach, und wie erwähnt, mit ungleichförmigen Schuppen be deckt; die Mundöffnung ist weit; die Kinnladen sind gleich lang, und mit kleinen spitzen Zähnen versehen. Der Gaumen ist rauh, die Zunge glatt, die Lip penknochen sind sehr schmahl, die Nasenlöcher einfach, röhrenförmig und dicht an den Augen sichtbar; letztere sind klein, und nahe an der Mundöffnung be sindlich, ihr Stern ist schwarz, und der Ring blau. Die Kiemenöffnung ist weit, und die Kiemenhaut liegt verborgen. Der Bauch ist kurz, und der After nur halb so weit vom Kopfe als von der Schwanzflosse entfernt. Die Seiten linie macht hinter der Bru tflosse einen kleinen Ab atz und läuft, vom Rücken und den Bauche gleich weit entfernt, nach der Schwanzflosse. Der Rumpf ist lang und fleischig, der Rücken und Bauch rund. Die Brust-und Bauchflossen sind kurz und abgerundet. Die sämmtlichen Strahlen sind weich und vierzwei gig. Die Grundfarbe dieses Fisches ist schmutzig weiss; die vom Rücken und den Flossen schwarz. Dieser Fisch ist ein Bewohner der Gewä er an der Malabarischen Küste. Ich erwarte mit dem zunächst von daher kommenden Schiffe die Naturgeschichte, sowohl von diesem als von den übrigen in diesem Theile beschriebenen Fischen, die mit diesem ein gleiches Vaterland haben.

5. ***Wrahl* in Tamil, *Ophicephalus striatus***

De braunen Streiffen, die man sowohl am Rumpfe als an einigen Flossen wahr-2. nimmt, sind ein Merkmal, wodurch dieser Fisch von den vorhergehenden leicht. Der zu unterscheiden ist. Gestreifte Schlangen In der Kiemenhaut zählt man fünf, in der Brustflosse fiebzehn, in der kopf. Bauchflosse sechs, in der Aftersflosse sechs und zwanzig, in der Schwanzflosse siebzehn, und in der Rückenflosse drey und vierzig Strahlen. Der Kopf ist flach und mit Schuppen von verschiedener Gestallt bedeckt. Die Kinnladen sind gleich lang, und mit feinen spitzen Zähnen besetzt. Der Gaumen ist rauh, die Zunge frey und glatt. Die Nasenlöcher sind einfach, rund, und dicht an den

Augen befindlich. Beide stehen nahe an der Mund öffnung, und letztere haben einen schwarzen Stern und einen hochrothea Ring, der nah dem Sterne zu ins Grüngelbe fällt. Die Kemendeckel sind dergestalt von den Schuppen bedeckt, dass man nicht unterscheid kann, obeiner oder zwey vorhanden sind. Die Kiemenhaut liegt innerhalb der weiten Kiemenöffnung. Der Rumpf ist gestreckt; die Schuppen sind rauh und dünn; die Seitenlinie ist von dem schwarzgrünen Rücken und dem weissgelben Bauche gleich weit ent fernt; die Strahlen in der braunge treifften Rücken- und Afterflosse sind einmal, und die in den übrigen Flossen zweimal getheilt. Was die Naturgeschichte dieses Fisches anbelangt, so will ich hier dem Herrn Missionair John, dem ich sowohl den Fisch als auch eine da selb t gemachte Zeichnung zu verdanken habe, selb t erzählen lassen. Seine Worte sind: Die er Fisch heisst auf malabarisch Tamulici Wrahl. Die grö sten werden eine Elle lang und dicker als ein Arm. Er hält sich in Teichen im Schlamme auf, und wird deswegen nicht mit Netzen, sondern mit einem aus Rei ern geflochtenen Fischreu e gefangen, welches rund, unten anderthalb Fuss weit und zwey Fuss hoch ist, schmahl zugeht, oben aber eine Oeffnung hat, wodurch der Fischer einen Arm stecken kann. Dieses stürzen sie von einem Orte zum andern, um zu sondiren, wobey sie sogleich an der Bewegung des Fisches mer ken können, ob sie einen überdeckt haben. Er wird sehr gern gegessen, und bey der Diät empfohlen.

Source: Marcus Elieser Bloch, *Allgemeine Naturgeschichte der auslandischen Fische*, vol. VII, Berlin, Den Konigl Akademischen Kunsthandlern J. Morino & Comp, 1793, plates no. 346, 356, 357, 358 and 358.

Appendix 3

The Description in German on the Types of Fish Received from Tranquebar by Marcus Elieser Bloch in Germany in 1794

1. *Heteropneustus fossilis* (*Silurus fossilis*)

Die kurze Rücken-die lange After-und die runde Schwanzflosse Der sind Merkmale, woran man diesen Fisch von den übrigen leicht unterschei Schlamm wels. den kann. Der Kopf ist flach und schmahler als der Rumpf; die Knochenhülle desselben endiget sich in drey Spitzen. Die Mundöffnung ist Klein, die Kinnla den sind gleich lang, und von sehr kleinen Zähnen rauh, welches auch der Gaumen vorn ist. Die Zunge ist kurz, dick und glatt; die Nasenlöcher sind röhrenförmig und stehen dicht an der Oberlippe. Die acht Bartfa ernitzen paarweie beisammen. Die Augen stehen an der Seite nahe am Scheitel, haben einen blauen Stern, der von einem braunen Ringe einge hlossen wird. Die Kiemendeckel öffnen sich sowohl an den Seiten, als auch unten, wo man die Kiemenhaut ausgebreitet siehet. Auf der obern Seite des Kopfes nimmt man eine längliche Vertiefung wahr. Die Seiten sind zu ammen gedrückt, der Bauch kurz, der Rücken rund; die Seitenlinie hat bis gegen die Bauchflosse eine schiefe Richtung, und läuft dann in gerader Linie mitten durch die Seiten nach der Schwanzflosse zu, von welcher der After noch einmal so weit, als vom Kopfe entfernt ist. Die sämmtlichen Strahlen sind weich, kurz, an den Spitzen getheilt, und nur der erste Strahl in der Brustflosse ist hart. Die ser Fisch ist so mager, dass man die Zwischenräume der Muskeln durch die Haut sehen kann. Eine Choccolade-Farbe überzieht den ganzen Körper. Auch dieser Fisch ist ein Geschenk des Herrn John in Tranquebar.

2. *Silurus Atherinoides*

Der ist ein Ficheres Merkmal für unsern Fisch. Silberstreiff In der Kiemenhaut, in der Brust-und in der Bauchflosse zählt man in jeder sechs, in der Afterflosse sechs dnd dreissig, in der Schwanzflosse Der Silberstreiff, den man der Länge nach auf beiden Seiten wahrnimmt, zwanzig, in der ersten Rückenflosse fünf Strahlen, und die zweite ist nur eine Fettflosse. Der Kopf ist klein und beinahe viereckig; die Mundöffnung eng; die Kinnladen sind gleich lang, und die darin befindlichen Zähne kaum merk bar. Etwas grö ser aber sind die im Gaumen. Die Nasenlöcher sind doppelt, und unweit der Oberlippe. Dicht daran sind zwey Bartfasern, und von den übrigen sechsen sind zwey am Winkel des Mundes, und viere am Kinn sichtbar. Die Kiemenöffnung ist weit, und die Kiemenhaut grössten theils bedeckt. Der Bauch steht hervor; der After ist dem Kopfe viel näher als der Schwanzflosse, und die Seitenlinie in einer geringeren Entfernung vom Rücken als vom Bauche. Die Strahlen sind weich und vielzweigig, und nur der erste Strahl in der Rücken-und Bru tflosse ist hart, stark und gezähnelt. Eine hellbraune Farbe überzieht diesen Fisch. Der Bauch, und der vom Kopfe bis nach dem Schwanze sich erstreckende Streiff ist silberfarben. Letzterer hat mir Gelegenheit zu seiner Benennung gegeben. Auch diesen Fisch treffen wir in den üssen Wassern auf den malabarischen Küsten an. Ich habe ihn meinem Freunde, dem Herrn Missions-Prediger John in Tranquebar, zu verdanken.

3. *Silurus vittatus*

Man erkennt diesen Fisch an seinem, nach der Länge laufenden

Streifen. Der gestreiffte wels flosse in jeder sechs, in der Afterflosse acht, in der Schwanzflosse zwanzig, in In der Kiemenhaut zählt man fünf, in der Brustflosse und in der Bauch der ersten Rückenflosse neun Strahlen, und die zweite ist strahlenlos. Der Kopf ist abgerundet, vorn fach, und steigt nach dem Rücken zu etwas in die Höhe. Die Kinnladen sind gleich lang und feilenartig; der Gau men hat kleine Zähne, die einen B°gen bilden. Die Zunge ist kurz und glatt. Die Nasenlöcher sind doppelt, und die Anzahl der Bartfasern beläuft sich auf acht. Von letzteren sitzen zwey unweit der Ober-viere unweit der Unterlippe, und zwey in den Wilkeln des Mundes. Diese letztern sind die längsten. Die Augen stehen an den Seiten hinter dem Munde, und haben einen blauen Stern, der von einem weissen Ringe umgeben wird. Die Kiemenöffnung ist weit, und die Kiemenhaut liegt frey. Der Bauch ist dick, der After liegt in der Mitte, und die Seitenlinie läuft in gerader Richtung vom Kopfe bis nach der Mitte der Schwanzflosse. Die Strahlen sind bis auf den ersten in der Rücken- und Brustflosse weich, und an ihren Spitzen getheilt. Die harten Strahlen sind stark und am innern Rande gezähnelt. Der Kopf, der Rücken, und dessen Flossen, ingleichen die Brust-und Schwanzflosse sind kastanienbraun, der Bauch aschfarbig, die Streiffen hell blau, der mittelste gelb, die After- und Bauchflosse stahlfarbig. Auch diesen Fisch habe ich aus Tranquebar erhalten.

Source: Marcus Elieser Bloch, *Allgemeine Naturgeschichte der auslandischen Fische*, vol. VIII, Berlin, Den Konigl Akademischen Kunsthandlern J. Morino & Comp, 1794, plates no. 370, 371 and 371.

Appendix 4

The Description in German on the Types of Fish Received from Tranquebar by Marcus Elieser Bloch in Germany in 1795

1. Sölköndei in Tamil, Fringed-Carp in English, *Cyprinus fimbriatus*

Dieser Fisch ist leicht an seinen fransenartigen Lippen zu erkennen. Sie sind Der Fransen mund. breit, dick, beym Athemholen stösst sie der Fisch in Form einer Scheide her vor, und zieht sie bald wieder ein. Die Unterlippe ist lappiger als die obere, welche mit kleinen Warzen besetzt ist, und daher wie Chagrins aussieht. In der Brustflosse sind fiebzehn, in der Bauchflosse neun, in der After flosse eben so viel, in der Schwanzflosse fünf und zwanzig, und in der Rücken flosse achtzehn Strahlen. Der Kopf ist klein, glatt, zu ammen gedrückt; die Mundöffnung klein; die Zunge frey, und der Gaumen glatt. Der Aufenthalt dieses Fisches ist in den süssen Gewässern der Malabarischen Küste. Wenn er in den Teichen gehegt wird, erlangt er die Schwere von drey bis sechs Pfund. Die Zeichnung sowohl, als auch den Fisch selbst, habe ich dem Hrn. John zu verdanken. Auf Tamalaisch wird dieser Fisch Sölköndei, auf Französisch Frangé, auf Englisch Fringed-Carp, und auf Deutsch Fransenmund genannt.

2. *Voenkoenndey* in Tamil, Cirrhated-Carp in English, *Cyprinus cirrhosus*

Die zwey über der Mitte der Oberlippe herunter hangenden Fasern geben ein 34. Merkmahl für diesen Fisch ab. In der Brustflosse findet man fiebzehn, in der Bauchflosse neun, in der Wönkön dey Afterflosse dreyzehn, in der Schwanzflosse acht und zwanzig, und in der Rükkenflosse achtzehn Strahlen. Der Körper ist zusammen gedrückt; der Kopf, die Zunge und der Ganmen sind glatt, die Lippenknochen schmahl, die Nasenlöcher einfach, und dichtan den Augen befindlich. Die Seitenlinie läuft mitten über den Körper, und der After liegt in der Nähe der Schwanzflossse. Auch diesen Karpfen findet man auf der malabarischen Küste in den Flüf sen und Teichen. Er wird bis anderthalb Fuss lang, und steht den übrigen dasigen Karpfenarten an Güte nach; sein Genuss wird sogar denen, welche eine genaue Diät halten müssen, widerrathen. Auch diese Zeichnung nebst dem Fische und den dazu gehörigen Nachrich-ten habe ich dem würdigen Herrn John zu verdanken. Auf Tamalaisch und Deutsch heisst dieser Fisch Wönköndey; auf Franzö fisch Voncondre, und auf English Cirrhated-Carp.

3. The Sickle- Carp in English, *Cyprinus falcatus*

Man erkennt diesen Fisch an seiner fichelförmigen Rücken- und Afterflosse. In der Brustflosse achtzehn, in der Bauchflosse neun, in der Afterflosse 35. acht, in der Schwanzflosse vier und zwanzig, und in der Rückenflosse zwölf P° Strahlen. Karpfen. Der Kopf ist Klein, schuppenlos und zufammen gedrückt, oben roth und an den Seiten filberfarben mit blau gemischt; die Mundöffnung ist Klein, der Oberkiefer der längste, und seine Lippenknochen sind schmal; der Gaumen und die Zunge find glatt, die Nasenlöcher rund und einfach und zwischen der Mundspitze und den Augen in der Mitte. Diese haben einen schwarzen Stern und einen gelben Ring. Die Kiemenöffnung ist weit, und die Kiemenhaut fichtbar. Die Seitenlinie läuft in der Mitte, und der After ist noch einmal so weit vom Kopfe als von der gabelförmigen Schwanzflosse entfernt. Die Schuppen sind gross, die Strahlen weich und vielzweigig. Ueber der Bauchflosse ist ein Anhang oder Mittelflosse sichtbar. Der Rumpf ist silberfarben und schimmert ins Bläuliche, der Rücken ist blau, und die Flossen sind röthlich. In Frankreich heisst dieser Fisch Faucil, in England The Sickle-Carp, und in Deutschland Sichelkarpfen. Dieser Fisch hält sich in den süssen Gewässern der Malabarischen Küste auf. Ich habe ihn dem Herrn John zu verdanken.

Source: Marcus Elieser Bloch, *Allgemeine Naturgeschichte der auslandischen Fische*, vol. IX, Berlin, Den Konigl Akademischen Kunsthandlern J. Morino & Comp, 1795, plates no. 409, 410 and 412.

Bibliography

Primary Sources

Manuscripts

DENMARK

1. *Nationalmuseet, Copenhagen*

   DU 451; DU 452

   Fuglsang Collection no. D.1717

2. *Zoological Museum, University of Copenhagen*

   Fabricius Collection at Kiel, Specimen Astacus, 1793, Scylla Tranquebaria, 1798

FRANCE

3. *Archives Academie des Sciences, Paris*

   Proces-verbaux, vol. 10

4. *Muséum Nationale de L'Histoire Naturelle, Paris*

   Georges-Louis-Leclerc de Buffon, Catalogue

   Jean Baptiste-Leschenault de la Tour, Catalogue

GERMANY

5. *Archiv der Franckeschen Stiftungen, Halle*

   M2 B1:5; M2B1:5d; M2B1:6, Berichte aus Zoologie und Botanik

   M2 E27:18, Tagebuch von Christoph Samuel John, 12 December 1803—31 December 1804

6. *Franckesche Stiftungen, Halle*

   Kunst-und Naturalienkammer: R-Nr.0599

7. *Museum fur Naturkunde der Humboldt-Universitat zu Berlin*

   Uranoscopus lebeckii, Kolorierte Zeichung, 1787, Historische Bild- und Schriftgutsammlungen: GNF Christoph Samuel John

Anthias Johnii, Bl. Fischpraparat, 1792, Tranquebar, Ex.coll. Bloch, ZMB.336

Mesoprion Johnii, Bl. Fischpraparat, ZMB 8957

8. *Staatliche Museer zu Berlin*

Kupferistchkabinett

INDIA

9. *Historical Archives of Goa, Panaji*

Assentos do Conselho da Fazenda, codex 116

Moncoes do Reino, Livro 13B, 5-6/3-2

10. *Madurai Province Jesuit Archives, Shenbaganur*

Documents de la Mission du Carnatic, vol. III, no. 48

11. *Saraswati Mahal Library, Thanjavur*

Modi Bundles, 31C/ 44-1-11; 105C/45-1; 123C/17-9; 160C/9

12. *Tamilnadu State Archives, Chennai*

Commercial Department

Dispatches from England to the President and Council of Fort St. George, 10 May 1788

Letters to the Board of Revenue

Letter of Andrew Berry dated 26 August 1795 to Lord Hobart, the Governor and Council of Fort St. George

Madras Presidency: Board of Revenue Proceedings, vol. 251

Public Consultations, 187A/42

Extract from the minute dated 22 July 1789

Letter of James Anderson dated 6 January 1789 to Archibald Campbell

Surgeon General's Records, vol. 3

Tanjore District Records, vol. no. 3417, 3418, 3419, 3429, 3452, 3479, 3483, 3487A, 3492, 3503, 3535, 3539, 4353,4429B, 4432, 4436, 4438, 4455

Tirunelveli Collectorate Records, Vol. 3565, 3582, 4696, 4708

ITALY

13. *Archivum Romanum Societatis Iesu, Roma*

MSS Goa 54(a)

14. *Biblioteca Casanatense, Roma*

Codice Portugues

PORTUGAL

15. *Biblioteca da Ajuda, Lisboã*

Livro das Merces que fez Dom João de Castro, MSS Codice 51-8-46

16. *Bibliotheca Nacional de Lisboã*

Codice 11410

17. *Instituto Arquivo Nacionais/ Torre do Tombo, Lisboã*

Chancelaria de D.João III, Livro 21

Chancelaria de D. João III, Priveligios, Livro 1

Colecao Sao Vicente, MSS vol. X

Corpo Cronologico, IIa-114- 4; IIa-117-156

THE NETHERLANDS

18. *Nationaal Archief, Den Haag*

Overgekomen Brieven en Papieren, MSS VOC 154, VOC 856, VOC 857, VOC 861, VOC 1095, VOC 1123, VOC 1124, VOC 1130, VOC 1133, VOC 1269, VOC 1580, VOC 1596, VOC 1676, VOC 2505

UNITED KINGDOM

19. *Bodleian Library, University of Oxford*

John Johnson Collection, 1702-1714

20. *British Library, London*

Additional Manuscripts, 4448, 5266, OR.49

Lysons Collection, Mist's Journal, 1720 Microfilm: 20452

MSS Eur. E80-82, Eudelin de Jonville, Quelques notions sur l'Isle de Ceylan

Natural History Drawings of the India Office Collections

7/1001-25; 7/1029; 7/1031; 7/1032; 7/1033; 7/1034; 7/1036; 7/1039; 7/1087-94; 7/1094; 7/1095; 7/1096-97; 7/1100, 7/1101; 7/1102-03; 7/1104-1114; 7/1111; 7/1112; 7/1115, 7/1330

Oriental and India Office Collection

E/4/873, Madras Dispatches, Letter dated 21 July 1787

MSS Eur.85

P/174/13; P/339/123

The Board of Control, Board's Collection, 1796–1858, The East India Company Records, F/4/95, File 1933; F/4/154 File 2690; F/4/862, File 22786; F/4/946, File 26558

Western Manuscripts Collections, Sloane MS 2346, 3321, 3332, 3333, 3348, 3916, 4020, 4045, 4066

21. *British Museum, London*

Vier Zeichnungen auf Glimmer, 1913.2-8.0109-0112.

456. e. 11 (9)

22. *Natural History Museum, London*

Botany Library: DTC 5

Botany Library, MSS ROX

Zoology Library, MSS JOHN, Additional Observations on Snakes by the Reverend Dr. John

Patrick Russell, Indian Serpents, 1837, Accession no. 37.9.26.36, Colubridae 83C

Patrick Russell, 47 numbered 1–60, Water colour drawings of Reptiles: an important collection of water colour drawings of reptiles, some being original, Company School drawings for Patrick Russell's book on Indian snakes, etc. sold at Sotheby's, Catalogue of printed books, Tuesday, 22 November 1977, Lot 325, Accompanied by memo regarding the sale by P.J.P. Whitehead and A.F. Stimson, Zoology Department, Zoology, 96Ao TR; 96Ao Tr (drawings)

Z MSS IND (ii) no. 29, Venomous Serpents Received from the Asiatic Society of Bengal, undated

Z Mss IND (ii) no. 32, Serpents: Honourable Company's Collection: Thomas Cantor, 1838

Z Mss IND (ii) no. 55, Jars of snakes, lizards and a snake-lizard preserved in spirits, War collection from Tipu Sultan, Cir. 1800

Printed Documents, Contemporary Chronicles, Tracts and Accounts

DANISH

I. K. Daldorf, 'Uddrag af Hr. Daldorfs Dagbog Paaen Reise fra Kiobenhavn til Tranquebar fidst o Aaret 1790 og forst I Aaret 1791', *Skrivter af Naturhistorie Selskaber*, 2 (2), 1793, pp. 147-173.

DUTCH

Anthonisz, S., *Diary of Occurrences during the Tour of Gerrit de Herre, Governor of Ceylon from Colombo to Jaffna July 9, to September 3, 1697*, Colombo, 1914.

__________, *Memoir of Hendrick Becker Governor and Director of Ceylon for his Successor Issac Augustyn Rumpf 1716*, Colombo, 1914.

Arasaratnam, S., *Memoir of Julius Stein van Gollensee Governor of Ceylon 1743-1751 for his successor Gerrit Joan vreeland 28th February 1751*, Colombo, 1974.

Chijs, Van der, J.A., et al., *Dagregister Gehouden int Casteel Batavia vant Passerende daer te Plaatse als Over Geheel Nederlandts-India, 1628–1682*, 31 vols., The Hague- Batavia, 1887–1928.

Coolhas, W.Ph., ed., *Generale Missiven van de Gouverneurs-Generaal en Raden Aan Heren XVII der Verenigde Oostindische Compagnie*, 9 vols., 'S Gravenhage, 1960–84.

Pieters, Sophia., *Memoir of Ryckloff van Goens, Junior, Governor of Ceylon, 1675-1679 to his Successor Laurens Pyl Late Commandeur, Jaffnapatnam*, Colombo, 1910.

__________, *Memoir of Van Imhoff 1740*, Colombo, 1911.

Prakash, Om., *The Dutch Factories in India: A Collection of Dutch East India Company Documents Pertaining to India,* vol. I, Delhi, 1984; vol. II, Delhi, 2007.

Reimers, E., *Memoir of Joan Maetsuyker President and Commander-in-Chief Delivered to his Successor Jacob van Kittensteyn on the 27 February 1650*, Colombo, 1927.

__________, *Memoir of Joan Gideon Loten, Governor of Ceylon Delivered to his Successor Jan Schreuder on 28 February 1757*, Colombo, 1935.

ENGLISH

Anonymous, 'Memoir of the Life and Writings of Patrick Russell, M.D. F.R.S.,' in Patrick Russell, *A Continuation of an Account of Indian Serpent; Containing Descriptions and Figures, from Specimens and Drawings, Transmitted from Various Parts of India*, W. Bulmer & Co. Shakespeare Press, London, 1801.

Anonymous, 'Jerdon's Illustrations of Indian Ornithology', *Calcutta Journal of Natural History*, 1844, vol. IV (16), pp. 534-536.

A True and Perfect Description of the Strange and Wonderful Elephant Sent from the East Indies, London, 1675.

Blair, Patrick, 'The Anatomy and Osteology of an Elephant, being an exact Description of all the Bones of the Elephant which died near Dundee, April the 27th, 1706, with their several dimensions', *Philosophical Transactions*, vol. XXVII, 1710, pp. 53-54.

__________, *Osteographica Elephantina: Or a Full and Exact Account of the Bones of an Elephant which Died near Dundee*, London, 1713.

Boag, William, 'On the Poison of Serpents' in *Asiatic Researches Comprising History and Antiquities, the Arts, Sciences and literature of Asia*, 20 vols., 1788-1839, see vol. VI, 1809, pp. 103–126.

Boyle, Robert, 'General Heads for a Natural History of a Countrey, Great or Small', *Philosophical Transactions*, vol. 1, 1665, pp. 1-22.

Brunto, T. Lauder and J. Fayrer, 'On the Nature and Physiological Action of the Poison of Naja Tripudians and Other Indian Venomous Snakes–Part II', *Proceedings of the Royal Society of London*, 1873–74, vol. 22, pp. 68–133.

Campbell, Colonel Walter., *My Indian Journal*, Edinburgh, MDCCCLXIV.

Clive General and James Parsons, 'Some Account of the Animal Sent from the East Indies, by General Clive, to His Royal Highness the Duke of Cumberland, Which is now in the Tower of London: In a Letter from James Parsons, M. D. F. R. S. to the Rev. Thomas Birch, D. D. Secretary to the Royal Society', *Philosophical Transactions*, vol. 51 (1759-1760), pp. 648-652.

Corse John and Joseph Banks, 'Observations on the Different Species of Asiatic Elephants, and Their Mode of Dentition by John Corse, Esq. Communicated by the Right Hon. Sir Joseph Banks', *Philosophical Transactions of the Royal Society of London*, vol. 89 (1799), pp. 205-236.

Dance, S.P., 'Report on the Linnaean Shell Collection', *Proceedings of Linnaean Society London*, vol. 176 (1), 1967, pp. 1- 34.

Donovan, E., *An epitome of the natural history insects of islands in the Indian seas: Comprising upwards of two hundred and fifty figures and descriptions the most singular and beautiful species, selected chiefly from those recently discovered, and which have not appeared in the works of any preceding author. The figures are accurately drawn, engraved and coloured, from specimens of the insects; the descriptions are arranged according to the system of Linnaeus;*

with references to the writings of Fabricius, and other systematic authors by E. Donovan, Author of the natural history of the insects of China, London, 1800.

Elliot, Walter, 'Description of a New Species of Naga or Cobra Capello', *Madras Journal of Literature and Science*, 1840, pp. 39-41.

Foulkes, T., 'Biographical Memoir of Dr Rottler', *Madras Journal of Literature and Science*, New Series, 1861, pp. 1-17.

Hamilton, D., 'Description of the method adopted in the Coimbatore district for catching wild elephants by Captain D. Hamilton, Assistant Conservator of Forests', *Madras Journal of Literature and Science*, New Series, no.5, October – December 1857, pp. 58-60.

Hampe, 'An Account of a New Species of the Manis, or Scaly Lizard, extracted from the German Relations of the Danish Royal Missionaries in the East Indies, of the year 1765, published at Halle in Saxony, by Dr. Hampe, F. R. S', *Philosophical Transactions: Giving some account of the present undertakings, Studies, and Labours of the ingenious, in many considerable parts of the world*, vol. LX, 1771, pp. 36-38.

Jerdon, Thomas Caverhill, *Catalogue of the birds of the peninsula of India arranged according to the modern system of classification: with brief notes on their habits and geographical distribution, and descriptions of new, doubtful and imperfectly described species*, 1st ed. Madras, J.B. Pharaoh, 1839.

__________, 'Catalogue of the birds of the peninsula of India arranged according to the modern system of classification, with brief notes on their habits and geographical distribution, and descriptions of new, doubtful and imperfectly described species', *Madras Journal of Literature and Science*, 1839, vol. 10 (24), pp. 60-91.

__________, 'Catalogue of the birds of the peninsula of India arranged according to the modern system of classification, with brief notes on their habits and geographical distribution, and descriptions of new, doubtful and imperfectly described species' *Madras Journal of Literature and Science*, 1839, vol. 10 (25), pp. 234-269.

__________, 'Catalogue of the birds of the peninsula of India arranged according to the modern system of classification, with brief notes on their habits and geographical distribution, and descriptions of new, doubtful and imperfectly described species', *Madras Journal of Literature and Science*, 1840, vol. 11 (26), pp. 1-38.

__________, 'Catalogue of the birds of the peninsula of India arranged according to the modern system of classification, with brief notes on their habits and geographical distribution, and descriptions of new, doubtful and imperfectly described specie', *Madras Journal of Literature and Science*, 1840. vol. 11 (27), pp. 207-239.

__________, 'Catalogue of the birds of the peninsula of India arranged according to the modern system of classification, with brief notes on their habits and geographical distribution, and descriptions of new, doubtful and imperfectly described species', *Madras Journal of Literature and Science*, 1840, vol. 12 (28), pp. 1-15.

__________, 'Catalogue of the birds of the peninsula of India arranged according to the modern system of classification, with brief notes on their habits and geographical distribution, and descriptions of new, doubtful and imperfectly described species', *Madras Journal of Literature and Science*, 1840, vol. 12 (29), pp. 193-227.

__________, *Illustrations of Indian Ornithology*, 1st ed. Madras, J. B. Pharaoh, Vol. I of IV vols, 1843.

__________, 'Supplement to the catalogue of birds of the peninsula of Indi', *Madras Journal of Literature and Science*, 1844, vol. XIII (30), pp. 156–174.

__________, 'Second Supplement to the Catalogue of the birds of Southern India', *Madras Journal of Literature and Science*, 1845, vol. XIII (31), pp. 116-144.

__________, *Illustrations of Indian Ornithology* containing 50 figures of new, unfigured and interesting birds, chiefly from the South of India, Church Street, Vepery, India, R. W. Thorpe, Christian Knowledge Society's Press, Vol. II of IV vols, 1845.

__________, *Illustrations of Indian Ornithology*, Church Street, Vepery, India, Reuben Twigg, Christian Knowledge Society's Press, Vol. III of IV vols, 1846.

__________, *Illustrations of Indian Ornithology: Containing fifty figures of new, unfigured and interesting species of birds chiefly from the South of India*, printed by P.R. Hunt, American Mission Press, Madras, vol. IV of IV vols, 1847.

__________, 'On the Fresh Water Fishes of Southern India', *Madras Journal of Literature and Science*, vol. XV (1), 1848, pp. 139-149.

__________, 'On the Fresh Water Fishes of Southern India', *Madras Journal of Literature and Science*, vol. XV (2), 1848, pp. 302-346.

__________, 'Ichthyological Gleanings in Madras', *Madras Journal of Literature and Science*, vol. XVII, 1851, pp. 128-151.

__________, 'Catalogue of Reptiles Inhabiting Peninsular India', *Journal of the Asiatic Society of Bengal*, vol. XXII, 1853, pp. 462-479.

__________, 'Catalogue of Reptiles Inhabiting Peninsular India', *Journal of the Asiatic Society of Bengal*, vol. XXII, 1853, pp. 522-534.

__________, *The birds of India being a natural history of all the birds known to inhabit continental India: with descriptions of the species, genera, families, tribes, and orders, and a brief notice of such families as are not found in India, making it a manual of ornithology specially adapted for India*, 1st ed. Calcutta: Published by the author at the Military Orphan Press, 1862.

__________, *The Birds of India: Being a natural history of all the birds known to inhabit continental India: with descriptions of the species, genera, families, tribes, and orders, and a brief notice of such families as are not found in India, making it a manual of ornithology specially adapted for India*, 1st ed. Calcutta, Published by the author, Printed by the Military Orphan Press, 1863.

__________, *The Birds of India: Being a natural history of all the birds known to inhabit continental India; with descriptions of the species, genera, families, tribes, and orders, and a brief notice of such families as are not found in India, making it a manual of ornithology specially adapted for India*, 1st ed. vol. II-Part II of 2 vols, Published by the author, Printed by George Wyman and Co, Calcutta, 1864.

__________, 'On Pristolepis Marginatus', *Annual Magazine of Natural History*, (3) 16, 1865, p. 298.

__________, *The Mammals of India, Natural History of all the Animals Known to Inhabit Continental India*, London, MDCCCLXXIV.

Latham, John, *A General Synopsis of Birds*, London, MDCCLXXXI.

Leach, W.E., *The Zoological Miscellany, Being Descriptions of New or Interesting Animals*, London, MDCCCXVII.

Letang, Antoine de, *The practice of farriery calculated for the East Indies collected from the best authors and founded upon experiments made during a residence of ten years in this country, by Antoine de Letang, captain of cavalry Pondicherry, printed for the author*, 1795.

__________, *The Practice of Farriery Calculated for the East Indies*, Madras, 1839.

Linne, Sir Charles, *A General System of Nature: through the three kingdoms of animals, vegetables and minerals systematically divided into their several classes, orders genera, species and varieties*, Swansea, 1800.

__________, *A General System of Nature: through the three kingdoms of animals, vegetables and minerals systematically divided into their several classes, orders genera, species and varieties, vol. II, Animal Kingdom, Insects, Part I*, Swansea, 1806.

Lister, Martin, Part of a Letter from Fort St. George, in the East-Indies, Giving an Account of the Long Worm which is Troublesome to the Inhabitants of Those Parts, Communicated by Dr. Martin Lister, Fellow of College of Physicians and Royal Society, *Philosophical Transactions of the Royal Society of London*, 1683-1775, vol. 19 (1695-1697), pp. 417-8.

Mackenzie, William, 'An Account of Venomous Snakes on the Coast of Madras', in *Asiatic Researches Comprising History and Antiquities, the Arts, Sciences and literature of Asia*, vol. 13, 1820, pp. 329-336.

Moulin, Allan, *An Anatomical Account of the Elephant Accidentally Burnt in Dublin*, London, 1682.

Petiver, James, 'An Account of a Book: Musei Petiveriani Centuria Prima', *Philosophical Transactions*, vol. 19, 1697, p. 399.

__________, 'An Account of Mr Sam. Brown His Sixth Book of East India Plants, with Their Names, Vertues, Description, Etc. To These Are Added Some Animals, Etc.', *Philosophical Transactions*, 1702-1703, vol. 23, pp. 1055-65.

__________, 'Brief Directions for the Easie Making, and Preserving Collections of All Natural Curiosities', *Monthly Miscellany or Memoirs for the Curious*, no. 3, London, 1709.

Records of Fort St. George, *Diary and Consultation Book*, 1672-1746, 1749-1757, C.M. Schmidt, J.J. Cotton, A.V. Venakatarama Ayyar, B.S. Baliga et al, eds., 90 vols, Published by Madras Superintendent, Government Press, Madras, 1910-1953.

__________, *Public Consultations, 1672–1750*, 36 vols., Madras, 1910–38.

Roxburgh, William, 'An Account of the Pearl-Fishery in the Gulph of Manar, in March and April 1797—by Henry J. Le Beck, Esq.

communicated by Doctor Roxburgh', *Asiatick Researches*, Calcutta, vol. V, pp. 393-411.

Russell, Patrick, *An Account of Indian Serpents Collected on the Coast of Coromandel: Containing Descriptions and Drawings of Each Species; Together with Experiments and Remarks on their Several Poison*, London, W. Bulmer & Co., Shakespeare Press, 1796.

__________, *Descriptions and Figures of Two Hundred Fishes; Collected at Vizagapatam on the Coast of Coromandel, Presented to the Honourable the Court of Directors of the East India Company*, London, 2 vols., 1803.

Strickland, H.E., 'Bibliographical Notices: Illustrations of Indian Ornithology by T.C. Jerdon', *Annual Magazine of Natural History*, 1845, vol. (1) 15, pp. 274-275.

Stukeley, William, *Of the Spleen: To Which is Added Some Anatomical Observations in the Dissection of an Elephant*, London, 1723.

Woodward, John, *Brief Instructions for Making Observations in All Parts of the World as Also, for Collecting, Preserving, and Sending over Natural Things*, London, 1696.

FRENCH

Boddaert, Pieter, *Table des Planches Enlumineez d'Histoire Naturelle de M. D'Aubenton*, Utrecht, MDCCLXXXIII.

Choiseul, Claude du., *Nouvelle methode sure, courte et facile pour le traitement de personnes attaques par de la rage*, Paris, 1756.

Cuvier, Georges., *Le Regne animal ditribue d'après son organization pour servir de base a l'historie naturelle des animaux et introduction a l'anatomie compare*, 4 vols, Paris, 1817.

__________, & Achille Valenciennes, *Histoire Naturelle des Poissons*, 22 vols, Paris, 1828-1848.

__________, *The Animal Kingdom, Arranged after Its Organization, Forming a Natural History of Animals and an Introduction to Comparative Anatomy*, Williams S. Orr, London, 1840.

Flax, M. Legoux de, *Essai Historique Geographique et Politque sur l' Indoustan avec le Tableaux de Son Commerce*, Paris, 1807.

Le Comte, Louis, *Nouveau Mémoires Sur L'état Présent De La Chine*, Paris, tome II, 1696.

__________, *Memoirs and Observations: Topographical, physical, mathematical, mechanical, natural and ecclesiastical made in a late journey through the empire of China and published in several letters, by Louis Le Comte, Translated from the Paris edition and illustrated with figures*, London, 1697.

Martineau, Alfred, ed., *Memoires de François Martin: Fondateur de Pondichéry, 1665-1694*, 3 vols., Paris, 1932-4.

Perrault, Claude, *Memoires pour server a l'histoire animaux, Dresses par M. Perrault de l'Academie Royale des Sciences & Medecin de la Faculte de Paris*, Paris, MDCLXXVI

__________, 'The anatomical description of a great Indian tortoise' in *Memoirs for a natural history of animals containing the anatomical description of several creatures dissected by the Royal Academy of Sciences at Paris*, trs., Alexander Pitfield, London, 1688.

Varadarajan, Lotika, *India in the Seventeenth Century: Memoirs of François Martin*, Delhi, 1980.

GERMAN

Bloch, Marcus Elieser, *Allgemeine Naturgeschichte der Auslandischen Fische*, Den Konigl Akademischen Kunsthandlern J. Morino & Comp, Berlin, 1793.

__________, *Allgemeine Naturgeschichte der Auslandischen Fische*, Berlin, 1795.

Francke, Gotthilf August, ed., *Der Königl. Dänischen Missionarien aus Ost-Indien eingesandter ausführlichen Berichten, Von dem Werck ihrs Ams unter den Heyden, angerichteten Schulen und Gemeinen, ereigneten Hindernissen und schweren Umstanden; Beschaffenheit des Malabarischen Heydenthums, gepflogenen brieflicher Correspondentz und mundlchen Unterredungen mit selbigen heyden*, Teil 1–9, (Continuationen 1–108) Waiserihaus, Halle, 1710–1772.

Herbst, Johann Friedrich Wilhelm., *Versuch einer Naturgeschichte der Krabben und Krebse nebst einer systematischen Beschreibung ihrer verschiedenen Arten*, vol. 1 (1782-1790), vol. 2 (1791-1796), vol. 3 (1799-1804).

Jeyaraj Daniel and Richard Fox Young, *Hindu–Christian Epistolary Self–Discourses: 'Malabarian Correspondence' between German Pietist Missionaries and South Indian Hindus (1712–1714)*, Harrassowitz Verlag, Wiesbaden, 2013.

John, C.S., 'Einige Nachrichten von Trankenbar auf der Kuste Koromandel: Aus einem Briete von dem Missionarius Hrn John an Hrn Doktor Bloch in Berlin', *Berlinische Monatsschrift*, vol. 20, 1792, pp. 585-96.

__________, 'Beschreibung einiger Affen aus im nordlichen Bengalen, vom missionaries John zu Trankenbar', *Neue Scriften Gesellschaft Naturforschender Freunde zu Berlin*, 1: pp. 211-218.

__________, 'Beschreibung und Abbildung des Uranoscopus Lebeckii', Der *Gesellschaft Naturforschender Freunde zu Berlin Neue Schriften*, vol. III. 1801, pp. 283-287.

Knapp, Georg Christian et al., eds., *Neuere Geschichte der Evangelischen Missions-Anstalten zu Bekehrung der Heiden in Ostindien aus den eigenhändigen Aufsätzen und Briefen der Missionarien erausgegeben*, Waisenhaus, Teil 1–8 (Stück 1–95), Waiserihaus, Halle, 1770–8/95.

Lichtenstein, I.H.M., Die Gattung Leucosia: als Probe einer neuer Bearbeitung der Krabben und Krebse, *Magasin der Gesellschaft Naturforschender Freunde zu Berlin*, 7 (2), 1816, pp. 135-144;

Martini Friedrich & J. H. Chemnitz, *Neues Systematisches Concylie-Cabinet*, Nurenberg, 11 vols., 1769-1795.

Widemann, Vidua., *Ausser Europaischez Weiflugelige Insekten Zuseiter Theil Schulz*, Hamm, 1830.

ITALIAN

Borghesi, Giovanni, *Lettera Scritta da Pondischeri a 10 di febbraio 1704 dal dottore Giovanni Borghesi medico della missione sepedita alla China dalla santita di N.S. Papa Clemente XI nella quale si contengono, oltre a un pieno raconto del viaggio da Roma fino alle coste dell' Indie oriental, Anatomische, Botanische, naturali e d' altri generi e trasportata del Manuscritto Latin in Lingua Toscana di Gio Mario de' Crescembeni custode d'Arcadia, e Accademico Affrordita*, Roma, MDCCV.

LATIN

Aldrouando, Ulysse., *Ornithologiae hoc est de Avibus Historiae Libri XII*, Bologna, MDLIXCIX.

__________, *De Animalibus Insectis Libri Septem, cum Singulorum Iconibus as Vivum Expressis*, Bologna, MDCII.

Fabricii, Johann Christian, *Systema entomologiae, sistens insectorum classes, ordines, genera, species, adjectis, synonymis, locis, descriptionibus, observationibus*, Hafniae, MDCCLXXV.

__________, *Species Insectorum Exhibientes Erorum Differentias Specificas Synoynma Auctorum, Loca Natalia, Metamorphosin Adjectis Observationibus Descriptionibus*, MDCCLXXXI.

__________, *Entomologia Systematica emendate et aucta secundum classes, ordines, genera, species, adjectis, synonimis, locis, observationibus, descriptionibus*, Hafniae, MDCCXCIII.

__________, *Supplementum Entomologiae Systematicae*, Hafniae, MDCCXCVIII.

__________, *Systema Antilabrum Secundus Ordines Genere Species*, Brusvigae, MDCCCV.

Fischer, J.B., *Synopsis Mammalium Cotta*, Stuttgart, MDCCCXXIX.

Forskal, Petrus, *Descriptiones animalium, avium, amphihiorum. insectorum vermium quae in itenere orientali observavit*, Hafniae, MDCCLV.

Gmelin, Johann Friedrich, *Systema Naturae, per Regna Tria Naturae Secundum Classes, Ordines, Genera, Species, cum Characteribus, Differentiis, Synonymis, Locis*, 13th edition, Tome 1, Pars I, Lyon/ Leipzig, MDCCLXXXVIII

__________, *Systema Naturae, per Regna Tria Naturae Secundum Classes, Ordines, Genera, Species, cum Characteribus, Differentiis, Synonymis, Locis*, 13th edition, Tome 1, Pars II, Lyon/ Leipzig, MDCCLXXXIX.

Gronow, Laurence Theodor, 'Animalium Rariorum Fasciculus Pisces', *Acta Helvetica, Physico-Mathematico-Anatamico-Botanico-Medica*, Basile, MDCCLXXII, pp. 43-52.

Jonston, J., *Historiae naturalis,* Libri I – VII, Lesnae – Frankofurti, MDCL-MDCLIII.

Latham, John, *Index ornithologicus, sive systema ornithologiæ; complectens avium divisionem in classes, ordines, genera, species, ipsarumque varietates: adjectis synonymis, locis, descriptionibus & c. Studie et opera*, London, MDCCXC.

__________, *Supplementum Indicis ornithologici sive Systematis ornithologiae*, London, MDCCCII.

Linnaeus, Carl., *Systema Naturae per Regna Tria Naturae Secundum Classes, Ordines, Genera, Species cum characteribus, differentiis, synonymis, locis*, Tome 1, Stockholm, MDCCLXVI1.

Petiver, Jacobus, *Gazophylacii Naturae & Artis: Decas Prima*, Londini, MDCCII.

Raii, Joannis, *Synopsis Methodica Avium & Piscium, opus posthumum quod vivus recensuit & perfecit ipse insignissimus Author: in quo multas species in ipsius ornithologia & Ichthyologia desideratas adjecit: Methodumque suam Piscium Naturae magis convenientem reddidit cum appendice & Iconibus*, Londini, Impenis Gulielmi Innys, ad Insignia principis in coementerio D. Pauli, MDCCXIII. London.

Schneider, J.G., M. E. Blochii, *Systema Ichtyologiae iconibus CX illustratum*, Bibliopolio Sanderiano, Berolini, MDCCCI.

PORTUGUESE

Barros, João de, *Decada da Asia: dos Feitos, que os Portuguezes Fizeram no Descubrimento, ae Conquista dos Mares e Terras do Oriente*, Lisboã, 1973.

Bulhao Pato, Raymundo António, *Documentos Remetidos da India,* vols. I-V, Lisboa, 1880-1935.

__________, and António da Silva Rego, ed., *Cartas de Affonso de Albuquerque*, 7 vols, Lisboã, 1884–1935.

Correa, Gaspar, *The Three Voyages of Vasco da Gama and his Viceroyalty from the Lendas da India: Translated from the Portuguese with Notes and an Introduction by H. Stanley*, London, 1869.

__________, *Lendas da India*, 4 vols, rpt., Porto, 1975.

Cortesao Armando, and Luis de Albuquerque, *Obras Completas de Dom João de Castro*, Coimbra, 1976.

Dider, Hugues, *Correspondance 1535-1552: Lettres et Documents*, Paris, 1987.

Panduranga, Pissurlencar, *Assentos do Conselho do Estado,* vols. I-V, Goa, 1972.

Sanceau, Elaine, *Coleção de São Lourenço*, Lisboã, 1973-83.

Stephen, S. Jeyaseela, ed., *Letters of the Portuguese Jesuits from Tamil Countryside, 1666-1688*, Pondicherry, 2001.

Tikri Abeysinghe, *A study of Portuguese Regimentos on Sri Lanka at the Goa Archives,* Colombo, n.d.

SPANISH

Acosta, Cristoval, *Tractado de las drogas, y medicinais de las Indias Orientales, consus Plantas debuxadas albuio por Cristobal Acosta medico y cirurjana que las vio ocularmente*, Burgos, MDLXXVIII.

TAMIL

Aganaanuru, eds. N. M. Venkatasamy Nattar and R. Venkatachalam Pillai, 3rd edn., South India Saiva Siddhanta Pathippu Kazhagam, Madras, 1957.

Ayingurunuru, ed. U.V. Swaminatha Aiyar, 6th edn., Madras, 1980.

Gobalakitchenne, M., *Ananda Ranga Pillai Vrintha Naatkurippu, Srimukha Aandu, 1753-54*, Chennai, 2008.

Kurinchi paatu (of Kapilar), ed. M. S. Purnalingam Pillai, Madras reprint, 1994.

Kurunthogai, ed. U.V. Swaminatha Aiyar, 4th edn., South India Saiva Siddhanta Pathippu Kazhagam, Tirunelveli, 1978.

Maduraikanchi, ed. U.V. Swaminatha Aiyar, in *Pathupaatu*, Madras, 1974.

Malaipadukadaaam (of Perumkausiganar), in *Pathupaatu*, Tamil University, Thanjavur, 1985.

Nattrinai, ed. A. Narayana Samy Aiyar, South India Saiva Siddhanta Pathippu Kazhagam, Tirunelveli, 1976.

Nedunalvaadai, ed. U.V. Swaminatha Aiyar, in *Pathupaatu*, Madras, 1974.

Pathirtupathu, ed. Avvai Durai Samy Pillai, 2nd edn., South India Saiva Siddhanta Pathippu Kazhagam, Tirunelveli, 1955.

Pattinapaalai, ed., U. V. Swaminatha Aiyar, in *Pathupaatu*, Madras 1918.

Pratiyegamana Ananda Ranga Pillai Avargalin Sostha Ligitha Dinapadi Sethi Kurippu, vol. I, (1736-1746) Pondicherry, 1948; vol. II, (1746-1746) Pondicherry, 1949; vol. III, (1746-1747) Pondicherry, 1950; vol. IV, (1747-1748) Pondicherry, 1951; vol. V, (1748) Pondicherry, 1954; vol. VI, (1748-50) Pondicherry, 1956; vol. VII, (1751-52) Pondicherry, 1963, vol. VIII, pt I, (1751-52) Pondicherry, 1986; Pt II, (1752-53) Pondicherry, 1988.

Price, Frederick, H. Dodwell and V. Rangachari, (trs., eds.,) *The Private Diary of Ananda Ranga Pillai, Dubash to Joseph François Dupleix, Knight of the Order of St. Michael, and Governor of Pondicherry: A Record of Matters Political, Historical, Social, and Personal, from 1736 to 1761*, vol. I, 1904; vol. II, 1907; vol. III, 1914; vol. IV, 1916; vol. V, 1917; vol. VI, 1918; vol. VII, 1919; vol. VIII, 1922; vol. IX, 1924; vol. X, 1925; vol. XI, 1927; vol. XII, 1928, Madras, Delhi, rpt, 1980.

Puranaanuru, ed. U.V. Swaminatha Aiyar, Madras, 1971.

Thirukural (Parimelazhagar Urai), ed. M. Virasamy Pillai, Madras, 1849.

Epigraphical Sources

Aiyar, K.R. Srinivasa, *Inscriptions in the Pudukottai State,* Pudukottai, 1929.

Annual Report on Epigraphy (including Indian and South Indian Epigraphy from 1881 to 1922, 1923-1945, 1950 to 1990) New Delhi/ Madras, 1887–1955.

Epigraphia Indica, vol. I to XXXII, Calcutta/ Delhi, 1892-1978.

Krishnan, K.G., *Karandhai Tamil Sangam Plates of Rajendra Cola I*, New Delhi, 1984.

South Indian Inscriptions, Publications of the Archaeological Survey of India, vol. I to XXVI, New Delhi, 1890-1990.

Travancore Archaeological Series, IX vols, Trivandrum, 1910-41.

Travelogues

Barbosa, Duarte, *The Book of Duarte Barbosa: An Account of the Countries Bordering on the Indian Ocean and their Inhabitants, Translated from the Portuguese Text by M. L. Dames*, London, 1918-1921.

Bowrey, Thomas, *A Geographical Account of the Countries Around the Bay of Bengal, 1669–1679*, ed. Sir Richard Temple, Cambridge, 1905.

Carre, Abbe, *Voyages des Indes Orientales*, Paris, 1906.

Crooke, William, ed., *A New Account of East Indies and Persia, 1672-1681*, London, 1909, repr. Delhi, 1992.

Filliozat, Vasundhara, *The Vijayanagar Empire as Seen by Domingos Paes and Fernao Nuniz*, New Delhi, 1977.

Hakluyt, Richard., 'The voyage and travel of M. Caesar Fredericke, merchant of Venice into the East India, and beyond the Indies, 1563', in *The Principal Navigations, Voyages, Traffiques and Discoveries of the English Nation*, vol. V, Glasgow, 1907.

Hamilton, Alexander, *A New Account of the East Indies*, London, 1930.

Mandeville, Jean de, *Mandeville's Travels*, ed., C. M. Seymour, Oxford, Clarendon, 1967.

Pires, Tome, *The Suma Oriental of Tome Pires*, edited and translated by A. Cortesão, London, 1944.

Purchas, Samuel, *His Pilgrims,* 10 vols., Glasgow, 1905.

Sonnerat, Pierre, *Voyages aux Indes Orientales et a la Chine*, Paris, MDCCLXXXII.

__________, *A Voyage to the East Indies and China*, 2 vols., trs. Francis Magnus, Calcutta, 1788–89.

Tavernier, Jean-Baptiste, *Travels in India by Jean-Baptiste Tavernier*, ed., Ball, repr. Delhi, 2000.

Temple, R.C., ed., *The Life of Icelander Jon Olafsson Traveller to India*, London, 1931.

Varthema, Ludovico di, *The Itinerary of Ludovico di Varthema of Bologna from 1502 to 1508*, London, 1928.

Yule, ed., *The Travels of Marco Polo,* London, 1938.

Secondary Sources

Articles and Books

Ali, Salim, *Bird Study in India: Its History and its Importance*, Indian Council for Cultural Relations, New Delhi, 1979.

Almeida I.C, and R. A. Lino, *O Rinoceronte: Pegadas na Torre*, Lisboã, 1992.

Archer, Mildred, 'Indian Paintings for British Naturalists', *Geographical Magazine*, 28(5) 1955, pp. 220-30.

__________, and W. C. Archer, *Indian Paintings for the British, 1770-1880*, Oxford, 1955.

Archer, Mildred, 'India and Natural History: The Role of the East India Company, 1785-1858', *History Today*, 9 (2), 1959, pp. 736-743.

__________, *Natural History Drawings in the India Office Library*, London, 1962.

__________, 'Company Painting in South India: The Early Collections of Niccolao Manucci', in *Apollo*, 1970, pp. 104-113.

__________, *Company Drawings in the India Office Library*, London, 1972.

__________, *Company Paintings: Indian Paintings of the British Period*, Victoria and Albert Museum, London, 1992.

Barbosa, I.V., *Apontamentos para a Historia das Coleccoes de Zoologia em Portugal*, Lisbon, 1885.

Bartrum, Giulia, *German Renaissance Prints, 1490–1550*, London, 1995.

Bedini, Silvio A., *The Pope's Elephant*, Manchester, 1997.

Bentley, Jerry H., 'Sea and Ocean Basins as Frameworks of Historical Analysis', *The Geographical Review*, vol. 89, no. 2, 1999, p. 222.

Brigittee, Hoppe, 'Vonder Naturgeschchite zuden Naturwissenschaftern-die Danisch-Halleschen Missionare als Naturfurschen in Indien em 18 bis 19 Jahrhundert' in Heike Liebau, Andreas Nehring and Brigitte Klosterberg, eds. *Mission und Forschung: Translokale Wissenproduktion Zwischen Indien und Europe im 18,und.19 Jahrhundert*, Halle, 2010, pp. 141-166.

__________, 'Eine Fischsammelung aus Tranquebar die Berliner Gesellschaft Naturschender Freunde und deren Mitgliel Marcus Eliser Bloch', in Heike Liebau, Andreas Nehring and Brigitte Klosterberg, eds. *Mission und Forschung*: *Translokale Wissenproduktion Zwischen Indien und Europe im 18,und.19 Jahrhundert*, Halle, 2010, pp. 167-180.

Costa, A. F. da., *Les deambulations du rhinoceros de Modofar*, Lisbon, 1937.

Darwin, Charles, *The Origin of Species by Means of Natural Selection*, First edition, 1859, rep., Penguin, 1968.

Delbourgo James and Nicholas Dew, eds., *Science and Empire in the Atlantic World*, New York, 2008.

Desmond, Ray, *The European Discovery of the Indian Flora*, Oxford, 1992.

Dias, Pedro., *Historia da Arte Portuguesa no Mundo, 1415-1822: Espaco Indýco*, Lisboã, 1998.

Fenger, J. Ferd, *History of the Tranquebar Mission: Worked out from the Original Papers*, tr. Emil Francke, Tranquebar, 1863.

Garcia, J.M., *As Viagens dos Descobrimentos*, Lisboã, 1983.

Gois, D. de., *Cronia do Felicýssimo Rei D. Manuel, 1566-1567*, Coimbra, 1926.

Goldingham, John, 'Some Account of the Sculptures of Mahabaliporum Usually Called the Seven Pagodas, *Asiatick Researches*, vol. V, Calcutta, MDCCXCVIII, pp. 69-80.

Guerrini, Anita, *Courtiers' Anatomists: Animals and Humans in Louis XIV's Paris*, Chicago, 2015.

Guha, R., ed., *Nature's Spokesman: M. Krishnan and Indian Wildlife*, 1st edn., New Delhi, 2000.

Hall, Kenneth R., *Trade and Statecraft in the Age of the Colas*, Delhi, 1980.

Hirth F. and W. W. Rockhill, *Chau-ju-Kua: His Work on the Chinese and Arab Trade in the Twelfth and Thirteenth Centuries Entitled Chu-Fan-chi*, St. Petersburg, 1912.

Horsfield M. Thomas & Frederic Moore, *A Catalogue of the Birds in the Museum of the Honourable East-India Company,* WM. H. Allen & Co., London, 1854.

Inden, Ronald, *Imagining India*, Oxford, 1990.

Jones, P.M., 'Image, Word, and Medicine in the Middle Ages', in *Visualizing Medieval Medicine and Natural History, 1200-1550*, eds., J. A. Givens, K. M. Reeds and A. Touwaide, London, 2006, pp. 25-50.

Karashima, Noboru, *South Indian History and Society: Studies from Inscriptions, AD 850-1800*, Delhi, 1984.

Lach, Donald F., *Asia in the Making of Europe*, 2 vols., Chicago, 1970.

Lehmann, Arno, 'Hallesche Mediziner und Medizinen am Anfang Deutesch-Indischer Beziehungen' in *Mathematische–Naturwisssenchaftliche Reihe*, vol. 5 (2) 1955, pp. 11-32.

Louis, P.C.A., *Essay on Clinical Instruction*, Paris, 1834, tr. P. Martin, London; repr. 1910.

__________, *Researches on the Effects of Bloodletting*, Paris, 1836, tr. C.G. Putnam, Boston, 1918.

Luling, Wei, 'The Silk Road Linking Chennai and China', *Contributions of Tamils to the Composite Culture of Asia, Part II*, Chennai, 2014, pp. 173-198.

Macgregor, Arthur, 'European Enlightenment in India: An Episode of Anglo-German Collaboration in the Natural Sciences on the Coromandel Coast, Late 1700 and Early 1800s', in ed., Arthur Macgregor, *Naturalists in the Field: Collecting, Recording and Preserving the Natural World from the Fifteenth to the Twenty-First Century*, Leiden, 2018, pp. 365-392.

Macleod, N., *De Oost-Indische Compagnie als Zeemogenheid in Azie*, Rijswijk, 1927.

Marten, John, *A Treatment of the Venereal Disease*, London, 1711.

Martineau, Alfred., *Dupleix et L'Inde Française*, Paris, 1923–7.

Mathew, K.S., *Indo-Portuguese Trade and the Fuggers of Germany,* New Delhi, 1997.

Matos, L., *Imagens do Oriente no seculo XVI: Reproducao do Codice Portugues da Biblioteca Casatanense*, Lisboã, 1985.

Minakshi, C., *The Historical Sculptures of the Vaikuntha Perumal Temple Kanci*, Memoirs of the Archaeological Society of India, New Delhi, 1940.

Mohanavelu, C.S., *German Tamilology: German Contributions to Tamil Language, Literature and Culture during the Period 1706-1945*, Saiva Siddhanta Pathippu Kazhagam, Madras, 1993.

Muthusamy, A. Thirumalai, *Sanga Ilakkiyathil Vilangugazhlum Paravaigazhlum*, Chennai, 1959.

Nair, Savithri Preetha, *Raja Serfoji II: Science, Medicine and Enlightenment in Tanjore*, New Delhi, 2012.

Paepke, Hans-Joachim, *Bloch's Fish Collection in the Museum für Naturkunde der Humboldt Universität zu Berlin – An Illustrated Catalog and Historical Account*, Liechtenstein, A.R.G. Gantner Verlag KG, 1999.

Pennant, Thomas, *Indian Zoology*, Second edition, London, MDCCXC.

Perfetti, Stefano, *Aristotle's Zoology and its Renaissance Commentators, 1521-1601*, Leuven, Leuven University Press, 2000.

Pieters, F. F. J. M., 'The menagerie of 'the white elephant' in Amsterdam: With some notes on other 17th and 18th century menageries in The Netherlands' eds., H. V. Lothar Dittrich, D. V. Engelhardt & A. RiekeMüller, *Die Kulturgeschichte des Zoos*, Berlin, 2002, pp. 47-66.

Pinon, Laurent, 'Conrad Gessner and the Historical Depth of Renaissance Natural History', in *Historia: Empiricism and Erudition in Early Modern Europe*, eds., Gianna Pomata and Nancy Siraisi, Cambridge Massachusetts and London, 2005, pp. 241-67

Pratt, Marie-Louis, *Imperial Eyes: Studies in Travel Writing and Transculturation*, London, 1992.

Raj, Kapil, *Relocating Modern Science: Circulation and the Construction of Scientific Knowledge in South Asia and Europe, 17th-19th Centuries*, Delhi, 2006.

Raman, Anantanarayanan, 'Patrick Russell and Natural History of the Coromandel', *Journal of the Bombay Natural History Society*, 107 (2), 2010, pp. 116–121.

Raychaudhuri, Tapan, *Jan Company in Coromandel, 1605–1690: A Study in the Interrelations of European Commerce and Traditional Economies*, The Hague, 1962.

Ray, Haraprasad, *Trade and Diplomacy between India and China: A Study of Bengal during the 15th Century,* Delhi, 1993.

__________, *South India during the 15th Century: Studies in Sino-Indian Relations*, UGC Report, Jawaharlal Nehru University, 1996.

Reid, Anthony, 'Humans and Forests in Pre-Colonial Southeast Asia', *Environment and History*, vol. 1, no. 1, 1995, pp. 105-7.

Rockhill, W.W., 'Note on the Relation and Trade of China with the Eastern Archipelago and the Coast of the Indian Ocean During the Fourteenth Century', in *Toungpao*, vol. 16, 1914, pp. 419-47; vol. 17, 1915, pp. 61-159.

John,Rowlands, *The Age of Dürer and Holbein: German Drawings, 1400–1550*, London, 1988.

Salmon, William and Royal College of Physicians, *Pharmacopœia Londinensis: Or the New London Dispensatory*, London, Nicholson, 1702.

Samy, P.L., *Sanga Ilakkiyathil Vilangina Vizhlakkam*, Tirunelveli, 1970.

__________, *Sanga Noolgazhlil Sila Uyirinangal*, Chennai, 1993.

Saraswathi, A. Rangasvami, 'Political Maxims of the Emperor Poet Krishnadevaraya', *Journal of Indian History*, 6, 1925, pp. 60-72.

Sastri, K.A. Nilakanta, *Foreign Notices of South India*, Madras, 1939.

__________, *The Pandyan Kingdom*, Madras, 1972.

__________, *Colas*, Madras, 1984.

Sawyer, Roy, T., 'The Trade in Medicinal Leeches in the Southern Indian Ocean in the Nineteenth Century', *Medical History*, vol. 43 (2), 1999, pp. 241–5.

Schaffer Simon, et al., eds., *The Brokered World: Go-Betweens and Global Intelligence, 1770-1820*, Sagamore Beach, 2009.

Schurhammer, George, 'Iniqitembrane and Bete Perumal: Chera and Pandya kings in South India', *Journal of the Bombay Historical Society*, vol. III, 1930, pp. 1-40.

Secord, James, A., 'Knowledge in Transit', *Isis*, 95, 2004, pp. 654–672.

Sen, Amartya, 'Indian Traditions and the Western Imagination', *Daedalus*, vol. 126. no. 2, Spring 1997, pp. 1-26.

Sinha, Arvind, 'Implantation of Commercial Crops: Cochineal Culture and the Regional Ecology in the Eighteenth Century Coromandel', in *Coastal Histories: Society and Ecology in Pre-Modern India*, ed. Yogesh Sharma, Delhi, 2010, pp. 1–13.

Spencer, George W., 'Temple Money Lending and Livestock Redistribution in Early Tanjore', *Indian Economic and Social History Review*, vol. V, no. 3, 1968, pp. 277-293.

Stephen, S. Jeyaseela., 'Maritime Trade between the Tamil Coast in South India and Thailand', *Proceedings of the Sixth International Conference on Thai Studies*, vol. 7, Chinag Mai University, 1996, pp. 209–18.

__________, *The Coromandel Coast and its Hinterland: Economy, Society and Political System, 1500-1600*, Delhi, 1997.

__________, *Portuguese in the Tamil Coast: Historical Explorations in Commerce and Culture*, Pondicherry, 1998.

__________, 'The Nayaks of Tamil Country and the Portuguese trade in war Animals' in Pius Malekandathil and T. Jamal Mohammed, eds., *The Portuguese, the Indian Ocean and European Bridgeheads, 1500-1800*, Tellicherry, 2001, pp. 212-22.

__________, *Expanding Portuguese Empire and the Tamil Economy, Sixteenth-Eighteenth Centuries*, Delhi, 2009.

__________, *Oceanscapes: Tamil Textiles in the Early Modern World*, Delhi, 2014.

__________, 'Shipping and Trade in Elephants and Horses of Asia: The Commercial Topography of the Tamil Merchants and Rulers, 1626-1765 AD', G. John Samuel, ed. *Contributions of Tamils to the Composite Culture of Asia, Part II*, Chennai, 2014, pp. 199-231.

__________, 'Thanjavur: The Making of a Medieval Metropolis', in Yogesh Sharma and Pius Malekandathil, eds., *Cities in Medieval India*, Primus, 2014, pp. 209-239.

__________, *A Meeting of the Minds: European and Tamil Encounters in Modern Sciences, 1507-1857*, Delhi, 2016.

Stresemenn, E., 'On the Birds Collected by Pierre Poivre in Canton, Manila, India and Madagascar, 1751-56', *IBIS*, vol. 94, issue 3, pp. 499-523.

Subramanian, P., Venkataramaiyaa and Vivekananda Gopal, *Thanjai Maraattiyar Modi Aavana Thamizhaakamum Kurippuraiyum* (Modi Records of the Mahratta Rulers of Tanjore in Tamil Translation), 3 vols, Tamil University, Tanjore, 1989.

Tandon, A. Moquin, *Monographie de la Famille des Hirudirees*, Paris, 1846.

Trautmann, Thomas R., *Elephants and Kings: An Environmental History*, Ranikhet, 2015.

Vassalo e Silva, N., 'Preciosidades e Maravilhas entre Goa e Lisboa', in *Exotica: Os Descobrimentos e as Camaras de Maravilhas do*

Renascimento, eds., H. Trnnek and N. Vassallo Silva, Lisboã, 2001, pp. 27-37.

Venkataramaiyaa, K.M., *Thanjai Marattiya Mannarkaala Arasiyalum Samudhaaya Vaazhkaiyum* (Administration and Social Life under the Maratha Rulers of Tanjore), Tamil University, Thanjavur, 1984.

Welch, Stuart Cary, *Indian Drawings and Painted Sketches 16th through 19th Centuries*, The Asia Society, New York, 1976.

Willughby, Francis, *The Ornithology*, London, Printed by A.C. for John Martyn, 1678.

Yagti, China Rao., 'Medieval Telugu Literature and the Untouchables in Society', ed., S. Jeyaseela Stephen, *Literature, Caste and Society: The Masks and Veils*, Delhi, 2006, pp.103-118.

Index

F

G

H

I

Q

R

S

T